I Stood with

A Novel By

James Mace

Next to a battle lost, the saddest thing is a battle won.

- Sir Arthur Wellesley, 1st Duke of Wellington

Dedicated in memory of

Ronnie Edwin Chambless
1971 – 2012
A Brave Man and a True Friend

and

Sergeant James Martin Shepard, U.S. Army
1972 – 2011
I'll see you on the other side, my brother

The Works of James Mace

The Artorian Chronicles

Soldier of Rome: The Legionary (Book One)
Soldier of Rome: The Sacrovir Revolt (Book Two)
Soldier of Rome: Heir to Rebellion (Book Three)
Soldier of Rome: The Centurion (Book Four)

Other Works

I Stood With Wellington
Forlorn Hope: The Storming of Badajoz
Centurion Valens and the Empress of Death

Table of Contents

Preface

In February, 1815, after nine months in exile, Napoleon Bonaparte, the deposed Emperor of the French, escaped from the Isle of Elba. Seizing the initiative while the European powers bicker amongst themselves at the Congress of Vienna, Napoleon advances towards Belgium with an enormous army, where the combined forces of Prussia and England are cantoned. The French Emperor knows that if he can achieve a decisive capture in Brussels, it will shatter the already fragile European alliance.

Leading the allies is Sir Arthur Wellesley, Duke of Wellington; the venerable British field marshal who defeated Napoleon's best generals in Spain, yet who the emperor had never personally met in battle. Napoleon knows that if he can draw away Wellington's chief Prussian ally, Gebhard von Blucher, and destroy his army first, he can unleash his entire might against the British. A victory over the unbeaten Wellington will cripple the alliance even further, as it will then deprive them of both English soldiers and financing.

In Belgium, Captain James Henry Webster has finally returned to a line regiment after being terribly wounded at the Siege of Badajoz three years prior. He is given command of a line company within the 1st Regiment of Foot Guards, the elite of the British Infantry.

A series of indecisive clashes will lead to a collision between the two greatest military minds of the age and the bloodiest single day of the entire century, as Wellington and Napoleon lead their armies to either immortality or oblivion. For Captain Webster, he fights for both his nation and to protect his young daughter in Brussels. Along with the rest of the Guards Division, he finds himself at the apex of the battle, where the fate of the entire world will be decided; at a place called Waterloo.

Cast of Characters

The British:
Men of the 1st Company, 3rd Battalion of the 1st Regiment of Foot Guards

Captain James Henry Webster – Company Commander, promoted by Wellington after leading the Forlorn Hope at the Siege of Badajoz three years prior

Lieutenant Edward Grose – Subaltern under Webster, young, but extremely level-headed and pragmatic

Ensign William Barton – Another subaltern, purchased his commission just six months prior

Colour Sergeant Patrick Shanahan – Company's senior-ranking, non-commissioned officer (NCO) who saved Webster's life at Badajoz

Sergeant Thomas Billings – A Peninsular veteran from Webster's former company

Corporals Christopher Harvey, James Donaldson – Non-commissioned officers

Private David O'Connor – An Irish soldier from the same village as Shanahan

Privates Eric Adams, Douglas Farrow – Enlisted men

Senior Officers and other soldiers

Arthur Wellesley, Duke of Wellington – Commander of all allied forces in Europe, drove the French from Portugal and Spain during the Peninsular War

Lieutenant General Sir Rowland Hill – Commander of II Corps

Lieutenant General Henry Paget, Earl of Uxbridge – Commander of the British Cavalry

Lieutenant General Sir Thomas Picton – Commander of the 5th Division, which served as the British reserves

HRH Prince Willem of Orange – Prince of the Netherlands and Commander of I Corps

General Sir George Cooke – Commander of the 1st (Guards) Division, under Prince Willem

Major General Peregrine Maitland – Commander of the 1st Brigade, British Guards Regiments, under George Cooke

Ensign Lord James Hay – Aide to Maitland
Lieutenant Colonel the Honourable William Stewart –
Commander of the 3rd Battalion of the 1st Foot Guards under
Maitland
Major Henry D'Oyley – Stewart's deputy and Webster's
immediate superior
Captain Daniel Roberts – Commander of the Battalion's Light
Company and close friend of Webster
Sergeant William Lawrence – An NCO with the 52nd Oxfordshire
who fought beside Webster and Shanahan with the Forlorn Hope at
Badajoz
Corporal Martin Shepard – An NCO with the 95th Rifles, he is
the grandson of Webster's family butler

The French:
Napoleon Bonaparte – Emperor the French
Michael Ney – Marshal of France, commander of the left wing of
Napoleon's army
Nicolas Soult – Napoleon's chief-of-staff
Charles Reille – Corps Commander
Jean-Baptiste Drouet, Comte d'Erlon – Corps Commander
Jerome Bonaparte – Napoleon's brother, serves as a division
commander under Reille
Emmanuel de Grouchy – Marshal of France, commander of the
right wing of Napoleon's army

Chapter I: The Guns Have Stopped

Toulouse, France
10 April 1814

Nicolas Jean-de-Dieu Soult, Duke of Dalmatia

France is falling.

The French general gazed over the short rampart of the town and let out a resigned sigh. Nicolas Jean-de-Dieu Soult, Duke of Dalmatia, had served France his entire life, both under the Bourbon Monarchy, as well as the Empire of Napoleon. His military origins were humble, beginning in the ranks as a private and, thanks to his education, rising to sergeant in just a few short years before receiving his commission. Unlike their English adversaries, whose officers were almost exclusively wealthy gentlemen, many of France's best officers, like Soult, had come from the ranks. Though he was one of the Marshals of France, and thus often addressed as

13

Marshal Soult, this was an honorary title rather than an actual military rank.

He had celebrated his forty-fifth birthday less than two weeks prior, conducting the last of many tactical retreats to Toulouse. Ironically, he and Napoleon were just a few months apart in age, as was another of Soult's peers, Marshal Michel Ney. The year, 1769, had been the birth year of many of the greatest military minds of the age.

Soult turned to his left and apprised his men, who were busily positioning small artillery pieces and emplacing baskets full of rocks on top of the short wall, to be used for additional cover. Most were raw conscripts with little to no practical training. Years of continuous warfare had depleted the ranks of the imperial army; the loss of almost half a million during the disastrous Russian invasion two years before had all but broken France. Napoleon may have been able to recover from this catastrophe had his armies in Spain not been engaged in supressing, continuous rebellions while, at the same time, having to face the unexpectedly relentless British expeditionary force.

"All guns are in position, sir," a voice said behind him. Soult turned to see it was the sergeant major of the regiment assigned to defend this section of the city. He looked more like a young boy than a grown man, and Soult figured he was in his early twenties at most.

Most of the senior officers were either suffering in a camp hospital from injuries or various horrific diseases, a prisoner of the English, or a mutilated corpse somewhere between Toulouse and the Spanish border. The few officers who did remain were mostly young subalterns trying to command their individual companies. This left the sergeant major, who Soult guessed had been but a teenage conscript three or four years before, to coordinate the entire regiment.

"Well done," the marshal replied. "Hold this position, and I'll see to it the emperor commissions you, personally."

"Thank you, sir!" the sergeant major replied, saluting sharply and then returning to his post.

"If we still have an emperor when this is over," Soult said quietly to himself. He then shook his head. "How far we have fallen since Austerlitz?"

14

The battle he referred to had happened nine years before, was regarded as one of Napoleon's greatest triumphs, and was also the action that later earned Soult the title of *Duke of Dalmatia*. The combined armies of Russia and Austria had been annihilated, suffering ten times the number of casualties they were able to inflict upon the French. The Third Coalition had ended, and the Holy Roman Empire dissolved as a result. Napoleon seemed invincible at the time, yet now it was the French Empire that was on the verge of collapse.

Whilst Napoleon had been preoccupied with the wars against Prussia and Austria, as well as his attempt to seize Russia, a small British expeditionary force landed in Portugal in 1808 under the command of a general who'd made his name in India but had yet to be tested against the professional armies of Europe. That man was Sir Arthur Wellesley, now the Marquess of Wellington. He was also the same age as Napoleon, Ney, and Soult, and over the course of five years, his army clawed its way through the Peninsula, driving the French from Portugal and Spain. While the grand armies of the old European powers were being smashed by Napoleon with contemptuous ease, his best generals were suffering similar fates at the hand of Wellington. In fact, he had personally bested Marshal Soult on at least six occasions.

Soult looked once more at the hastily scrawled final orders that had been sent from the emperor. They directed him to hold Toulouse with his forty-two thousand men at all cost. Opposing him was a familiar nemesis, the venerable Wellington himself.

Just five months before, in December 1813, Soult had failed to break the British lines at the Battle of Nive and was forced to retreat. Then most recently, at the Battle of Orthez in February, Wellington's forces had completely routed the French yet again, inflicting more than twice as many casualties as they took with thousands more French soldiers being taken prisoner. What further incensed Soult was that these defeats had taken place on French soil. He was anxious, not just for revenge against the insufferable English general, but to drive the British troops from his homeland. Unable to defend both Toulouse and Bordeaux, he had elected to make his stand at Toulouse where supplies and rations would be easier to come by. Bordeaux fell to the British soon after with scarcely a shot fired.

What further embarrassed the French generals who faced Wellington in the Peninsula was, with only a couple exceptions, they almost always had the advantage in numbers, yet had been unable to inflict even a single decisive defeat on the British expeditionary force. Now Wellington had numerical superiority, which prevented Soult from even considering a counterattack. With Russia, Austria, and Prussia closing in on Paris, all Soult could do was try and hold Wellington off while praying that Napoleon achieved yet another miracle against overwhelming odds.

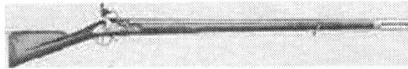

At the British camp, there was a feeling in the air amongst the soldiers that the war was, at last, coming to an end. Nearly every redcoat who cleaned and inspected his arms and equipment for the coming battle was brimming with confidence, though each man secretly prayed that he wouldn't fall now, with the war all but won.

It had been almost six years since the British expeditionary force under General Arthur Wellesley had landed in Portugal and decisively bested the French at Vimeiro. It was the first of many such victories. In fact, Wellesley, now known as the Marquess of Wellington, had never been defeated in a major battle. The combined powers of continental Europe had repeatedly fallen prey to the French Emperor, with Russia only being spared due to the harsh weather of their homeland rather than the tactical or strategic savvy of their generals. During the years in which Napoleon won his greatest victories against every army that dared face him, his best generals were humiliated time and again by this British upstart with fewer troops who were, at the time, far less experienced than their own.

It was only after the disastrous Russian winter had depleted and demoralized his army, that Napoleon finally looked west and took note of the ragtag army of redcoats who'd somehow won every major battle against his forces and had successfully driven the French completely out of Portugal and Spain. Wellington would later privately admit that he was glad to have never faced Napoleon directly in battle, and doubtless the French Emperor now wished that he'd abstained from invading Russia and had instead focused his efforts on personally crushing the British, once and for all. Sadly, for him the past could not be undone, and while his grip on the French throne slipped away, Wellington was building a reputation that exceeded that of any military leader of the age.

Amongst the near sixty-thousand men under his command was a young Irish soldier named Private David O'Connor. A member of the all-Irish 27th Inniskilling Regiment, he had only just arrived in camp two weeks prior.

Having taken the King's Shilling the previous summer, David thought he'd have just enough time to learn basic drill and marksmanship before being sent to Spain or southern France. Instead, recruit training lasted an arduous seven months. One luxury the British had, that neither their allies nor enemies were afforded, was the protected isolation of their island, which allowed them to take the time to ensure their recruits were trained properly before sending them into battle. Of course, for young David, the months of training had not felt like a luxury, particularly the hard lashings he took from a couple of brutal instructors who despised the Irish. Still he persevered and was glad when the day came that he turned in his white, soiled, recruit garb and was issued proper trousers, shako, and red tunic.

"Fall in and look lively about it!"

At the barking order from Colour Sergeant Shanahan, every soldier dropped whatever he was doing, grabbed his musket, and formed up into three ranks, muskets shouldered. There was noticeable tension in the air, but also a strange sense of relief that the wait before going into action was now over.

To David's left was an equally young soldier who had been with him in recruit training. To his right was a much older private, who he hazarded was old enough to be his father. They were in the front rank of the company, and David grudgingly reckoned they would be the first to fall. Like all line companies, they stood shoulder-to-shoulder, muskets loaded with bayonets fixed, and carried over the left shoulder. While it may have baffled the outside observer as to why the men stood so close together in formation, from a tactical standpoint it made perfect sense. Men in close order were easier to keep in line and coordinate as one unit.

Given the short range of the standard musket, after one or two volleys, most of the fighting was done with the bayonet, where one wanted friends on either side of him, all fighting as one.

"Company!" the captain shouted. *"Advance!"*

Orders and bugle calls echoed throughout, and the young Irish soldier could not make sense of any of it. He focused on as much of his commanding officer's voice as he could make out and was thankful that orders were echoed by everyone along the line, ensuring dissemination in even the loudest din of battle. Drummers beat a cadence, and the men of the Inniskilling began their march towards Toulouse.

The ground was damp, the long grass trodden down, sparse trees dotting the landscape as they advanced towards the fortified town. The Inniskilling had been kept in reserve and was now, at last, being committed to battle. As their footfalls made a unified thud into the earth, in time with the beating drums, the sights of the battle that had already happened greeted them. David swallowed hard as he saw his first dead human being. It was a young drummer; his head completely blown off by a cannon shot, a coagulated pool of blood running from his neck and mingling with the mud and grass. As they continued to march they came upon more dead, both British and French. The fatal wounds struck by musket ball and bayonet were horrific to behold. Bodies, and parts of bodies, littered the ground. David almost tripped over a severed arm that was still clutching a shattered musket.

Even more horrifying than the sights of the dead were the wounded, of which there were far greater in number. Even the strongest of men cried out piteously in anguish, as they clutched at the stumps where arms and legs had once been, or sobbed mournfully as they held their own guts in blood-soaked hands. In a tribute to their physical and mental fortitude, the British wounded made far less of a commotion than their enemies.

The fighting here had been particularly fierce, and the number of casualties on both sides was great. David saw one French soldier trying to crawl away, his right leg bloodied and dragging behind him. As he walked past, he heard the man give a fresh cry of pain as a redcoat bayoneted him in the small of the back. This brought a sharp rebuke from the man's corporal, as killing of the enemy wounded was viewed contemptuously. There was nothing brave about murdering one who was either stricken or attempting to surrender. It was generally accepted that wounded left behind following a battle would be cared for by the victorious army, as best as they were able, although, it was a given that atrocities still occurred on both sides.

The hour was growing late, and everything that could go wrong did. Wellington had misplaced his trust in his Spanish allies, giving them a strongpoint to attack, which they failed to break through. The venerable and highly aggressive Sir Thomas Picton had thought to take his diversionary attack and make it into a real one, like he had at Badajoz, only to be thrown back with terrible losses. David could hear a continuous crash of musket fire coming from his right, where Picton's division was reforming and pushing back against a French counterattack. Indeed, the French had fared little better, and Soult had to know that his position was precarious at best.

The slowly advancing Inniskilling regiment was, at last, at the outskirts of the town. An occasional tree, scoured by musket and cannon fire, lined the town. In front of the short slope was a small stream brought on by the recent heavy rains. Bodies from both sides littered the slope and lay grotesquely twisted amongst the rubble strewn about. A battered company of French fusiliers was scattered about the ruins, desperately making ready to take on this new wave of British redcoats. Cohesion was gone and there was no semblance of formation; they simply tried to reload their weapons as fast as possible and started shooting blindly. Were they fresh, they might have been able to make a decent showing of themselves. As it was, they'd been battered and bloodied all day, with many of their friends lying amongst the carnage.

The erratic shots mostly landed short or went over the formation, though the occasional musket ball slammed home, bringing shouts of surprise and pain from those hit. Even as men fell, the company advanced in step and in complete silence.

"Halt!" the captain shouted.

It was then that David realized just how close they'd come to the enemy. He fought to control his breathing and sweat started forming on his brow, despite the damp cold. He could see a tattered French soldier not fifty yards from him, just a few feet up the slope. The lad was probably his age, if not younger. His mop of hair was plastered to his head with sweat and grime, traces hanging in front of his eyes. His face was filthy, his uniform torn in many places. For a brief moment the two made direct eye contact, and the Frenchman started to furiously reload his musket.

"Front rank...make ready!"

David and the rest of the men in front lifted their weapons from their shoulders and held them straight up and down in front of their chests. He wanted to lower his weapon and shoot the young man, who was still glancing his way as he dropped the ball into his musket and furiously rammed it home.

"Present!"

The Irishman lowered his musket and looked down the barrel, past the bayonet, and right at the young French soldier who was simultaneously shouldering his weapon. David gritted his teeth and prepared to meet his fate.

"Fire!"

He squeezed the trigger of his flintlock before the captain had finished saying the order. A spark from the flint ignited the powder in the pan, with the subsequent flash firing the weapon. A volley of British muskets exploded and socked their front in with smoke.

"Front rank...kneel!"

David immediately dropped to a knee, glad that he was now a smaller target for the enemy. He pulled a paper cartridge from his ammunition pouch and made ready to reload, when he noticed that no one else on the line was doing so. He then realized why their commander had waited until they were so close to the enemy before engaging.

"Second rank...make ready...present...fire!"

The crash of the second volley of gunfire left his ears ringing. Subsequent commands and the second rank knelt behind them; the third rank firing their volley into the enemy that now none of them could see.

"Company up!"

The air was pungent with the smell of burned powder. It made David's mouth feel parched, leaving a foul taste. The men stood with their bayonets protruding forward. Cold steel would finish this battle.

"Charge!"

20

A loud cry echoed down the line, and the men made a mad dash towards the enemy's positions. As they sprinted up the slope, David thought he saw the body of the young French soldier who'd tried to take a shot at him. The lad's throat was ripped open, with a torrent of blood gushing forth. His eyes were wide open, and his tongue sticking out between his teeth, his entire body convulsing as death took him. There was no time to pause and get a good look at him as the company was rushing as fast as it could at the enemy lines. But when they got to the top of the slope, there were no Frenchmen left to face them. The soldiers stumbled to a halt and looked around, trying to see where their quarry had gone off to.

"Bloody hell," a soldier said. "They've all hoofed it."

"You don't suppose we got them all, do you?" the new recruit next to David said.

"Not likely with the way you lot shoot," Colour Sergeant Shanahan scoffed as he walked down the line.

They then noticed a series of outlying buildings that covered the area between the slope and the main wall of the city.

"Alright, lads," the captain called out. "Start clearing these buildings out. We're to hold this position until told to advance into the town."

A shot rang out, which caused the men to scatter and seek cover. Soldiers started reloading their muskets as more sporadic fire came from the far high wall. David and several of his companions rushed over to a small one-room shack and violently kicked the door in with a loud smash. Inside was a single table, two chairs, and a bed in the corner, yet it was devoid of any people. The sounds of musket balls slapping the walls caused them to drop to the floor.

"These damn plank walls are so thin they won't stop a bloody thing!" one of the soldiers grunted, as they crawled towards the single window that faced towards the city wall.

"At least it gives us some concealment," David muttered, as a shot smashed through the wall just a few feet above his head.

He removed his bayonet and knelt next to the window, which had already been smashed from previous clashes earlier in the day. He could make out the occasional flash and lots of smoke billowing from the ramparts. The French defenders were simply firing at random. They were at least a hundred yards from the wall, but the young Irishman decided to chance a shot. The blast of the musket echoed loudly in the hollow shack. As he lay back against the wall and began to reload, he quickly ducked to the side as the flash of a bayonet almost stabbed him in the eye.

"Damn it all, will you scabbard that fucking thing already!" he barked at his companion, slapping the weapon away. "Not like we're going to stick anyone lying here."

"Sorry, mate," the other soldier said with a trace of embarrassment. He detached his bayonet and then quickly fired a shot from the same window.

Two other soldiers who accompanied them were at the doorway which lay perpendicular to the city wall. One lay on his stomach, the other kneeling, as they, too, started firing shots at what they could see of their enemy. The remainder of their company, along with the rest of the regiment, were now either occupying the outlying buildings or finding cover amongst the trees and behind slopes of earth.

"Well, that's it then," David grunted. "A bloody stalemate this is."

"What should we do?" the nearest soldier asked him.

"Bugger it," David replied. He leaned his weapon in the corner, sat back against the wall, removed his shako, folded his arms across his chest, and closed his eyes.

"O'Connor, what the hell?" one of the soldiers from the doorway shouted back at him. "Get back up and start shooting already!"

"And what for?" David retorted, his eyes still shut, "They're bloody well out of range, and I don't feel like being out of cartridges when the frogs counterattack, now do I? Somebody wake me when they do."

The other soldier grumbled quietly, but said nothing more.

He didn't remember nodding off, though what startled him alert was the utter silence. It had since grown dark, and not a shot was heard. "What the devil?" he asked as he fumbled for his musket in the dark.

"Don't know," one of the soldiers said, who was now standing in the doorway. "The guns stopped a little while ago. Here, I see a rider over there." He pointed across the shack, off to the left where the glare of torches could now be seen.

"Alright, you bastards!" Colour Sergeant Shanahan shouted. *"Fall in and look lively about it!"*

"Always telling us to look lively," the soldier in the doorway grunted.

"Does this mean we won?" David asked with a grin, elbowing his companion, who he assumed was sleeping too. When the man did not budge, David shook him vigorously. "Come on, man, wake the hell up already!" It was then that he felt the dampness on the collar of his friend's tunic. He took a deep breath and in the darkness felt around his neck, which was torn away on the side and soaked in blood.

"Shit," he said quietly as he rose, grabbed his shako and musket, and headed for the door, which his companions had already left through. He briefly turned back and looked into the darkness where his friend now lay dead. "Rest easy, mate."

"Fall in at the double already!" Colour Sergeant Shanahan shouted as soldiers rushed towards him from various directions.

The captain and two subalterns were talking to the rider, who many of them recognized as Major Fitzroy Somerset, an officer from Wellingtons' staff.

As David morosely took his place on the line, the colour sergeant's voice was bellowing into his ear once more.

"Put on your bloody shako and do your tunic buttons up! Where the devil do you think you are?"

"Sorry, colour sergeant," the Irish private said quietly, eyes downcast as he put on his shako, hastily did up his top two buttons, and shouldered his weapon. Shanahan, who was getting accountability of the men, asked about his friend.

"He bought it," David said quietly.

The colour sergeant gave a sad nod and patted him on the shoulder. David thought he heard him quietly say 'I'm sorry'.

The captain quickly walked over and addressed the company. "The frogs have pulled out of the town," he said, eliciting a cheer from the men. "We will fall in with the rest of the regiment, push through, and set up pickets on the far side lest Soult manages to gather reinforcements and counterattack."

David chanced a glance over his shoulder towards the shack where his friend now lay dead. There were many who would scoff

23

that war was the worst place to form friendships, as they were often ended abruptly through death. And yet, for the average soldier, regardless of which side he fought on, it was precisely such a harrowing ordeal that brought them closer together.

It was utterly quiet as they marched through the town. Doors and windows were boarded up, and not a soul dared take to the streets once the redcoats came. Horrifying stories of what the British army had done to the citizens of the Spanish cities of Ciudad Rodrigo and Badajoz terrified the French populace. All was silent with the exception of the drum cadence and the matching footfalls of the advancing regiments; soldiers only talked, in hushed voices, as they reached the far side of the town and set up guard watch and pickets. David and several of his companions took up position in a ditch that ran parallel to the main road into town.

"This bloody grass is soaked," a soldier next to him grumbled. "Feels like me arse is in a puddle."

His mind numb, David sat down in the wet grass and leaned against his weapon, unable to ascertain how he should feel after what he'd been through. He thought about his friend who lay crumpled beneath the window of the shack. The two had carried each other through recruit training and had been elated when both were assigned to the Inniskilling and sent to southern France. David then wondered what would happen to his body. Would they be able to retrieve all of their fallen or would he only be found after the denizens of the shack returned to find the slain redcoat? This was far more likely, with the corpse being looted of anything of value and then tossed into the street for the dogs and vermin to devour. Whatever happened after this night, all David knew was his friend would never have to worry about a wet bottom ever again.

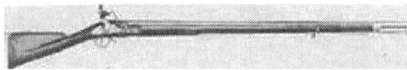

The next morning Wellington sat on a camp stool outside his tent. He had just woken and was still in his shirtsleeves, pulling on his boots. He was distressed over the previous day's battle, given the terrible, and he felt needless, losses they'd sustained. He paused and glanced up at his aide, Major Somerset. "For once that bastard Soult got the best of me," he lamented. "I've given him a damned good thrashing every time we've met in battle, and yet, in this place he finally manages to stop me in my tracks."

"Well, your grace," Somerset reckoned, "he did abandon the town, and so is it not our victory after all?"

"A very severe affair in which we defeated the enemy completely," the Duke replied, giving a nod. He could still claim Toulouse as a victory, even though Soult had voluntarily abandoned his positions in the night, rather than being driven from them.

It was then he noticed the horse riding at a fast gallop up the road. The rider was wearing a red officer's frock, and Wellington surmised that he must be a messenger from Bordeaux. The noose was tightening around Napoleon, with allied troops closing in on Paris. As the rider came up to his tent and slowed, the Duke recognized him as Lieutenant Colonel Fred Ponsonby. An officer of much distinction, he'd proven invaluable in a crisis on numerous occasions. Fred's brother, William, was nine years his senior and a major general, who had been in command of a 1,200-man cavalry brigade until handing command off in January and returning to his duties as a member of the House of Commons.

"Your grace!" Ponsonby said as he dismounted quickly, face full of excitement. "I bring extraordinary news."

"I thought you might," Wellington said, calmly pulling on his boots. "I knew it was only a matter of time before the allies made peace with Bonaparte."

"Not peace," Ponsonby replied, shaking his head. His face was red and the smile so broad that Wellington thought to chastise him for appearing unseemly. The officer's next words made those feelings evaporate. "Napoleon has *abdicated*. It happened five days ago."

"Abdicated?" Wellington echoed, quickly rising to his feet. Never one to show emotion, the feelings of joy and relief overwhelmed his usual stoicism. "By my honour, hurrah! Hurrah! Hurrah!"

Soldiers in the vicinity bore expressions of bewilderment. Their commander-in-chief, who almost never smiled and disdainfully referred to them as 'scum of the earth', was now dancing about and snapping his fingers over his head, singing boisterously as if he had just drunk an entire cask of ale and was frolicking with a dozen lasses in an Irish whorehouse. One of those men baffled by Wellington's conduct was Private David O'Connor, who had just come in from spending the night on picket duty.

"Well, fancy that," one of the soldiers said with a grin. "So the war's been over for five days now."

"Yeah," David replied, his face bore a scowl. "Pity then, that our lads died for nothing taking this damnable town." He spat on the ground in disgust, shouldered his musket, and quickly walked back to his company bivouac on the far side of town.

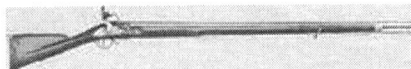

For Nicolas Soult, his feelings echoed those of the young Irish soldier as he sat atop his horse and watched his sad and defeated army march past. Their collective expressions showed sorrow, defeat, and yet even a sense of relief that the war was now over. There was also the frustration and anguish in the realization that their last battle had been an utterly pointless waste of lives. Any personal pleasure he may have felt at having finally given Wellington a proverbial bloody nose was lost upon seeing the futile sufferings of his men. Nearly one in ten of the defenders of Toulouse had fallen, and knowing that their deaths had come five days after the war ended turned the marshal's stomach. France was clearly tired of war, after so many years of fighting and countless lives lost or otherwise shattered.

For those who survived the war's shells, they would return to try and make sense of their fractured lives. Veterans who had fought for their nation would now be left to try and scrape up whatever they could for work. For those who'd been seriously injured or disabled, the prospects were even grimmer. This was universal, regardless of which nation's uniform a soldier wore. And for the armies of Napoleon, there was now the added stigma of enduring decades of relentless warfare only to be on the side that lost. Soldiers and generals alike would for the remainder of their lives attempt to make sense of what happened and what could have been done to prevent their ignominious defeat. While at one time being a member of Napoleon's imperial army was the most esteemed honour for a Frenchman, it was now an added mark of shame; the scorn of their nation's humiliating defeat falling upon them.

As for what would happen to Soult himself, he wasn't quite sure. The Bourbons had been out of power for more than two decades, and clearly if Louis XVIII was in fact being restored to the throne, he could not very well afford to sack all of his ablest generals. France would still require an army, even though it would be but a fraction of what it had been under the peak of the Empire. Louis would need men like Soult, as well as his peers, such as Michel Ney and Emmanuel de Grouchy. He would need the men in the ranks, as well, for there was certain to be much tumult with the deposal of Napoleon. A new world was dawning, and Soult knew not whether it boded good or ill for France.

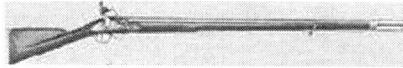

Where once had been silent terror, Toulouse suddenly became a city of celebration. The tricolour flags of Napoleon's French Republic were suddenly replaced by the white flags and cockade of the Bourbon Monarchy. People cheered and danced in the streets, welcoming the British redcoats as heroes and liberators.

"I bet they keep both flags in their trunks, depending on who's in charge that day," a soldier scoffed as a group of them walked down the street.

Colour Sergeant Shanahan was leaning against a column at the city hall and chuckled at the remark from the passing soldier. He looked up and saw a number of cheering townspeople battering away at the base of Napoleon's statue on top of the city hall. As the statue came crashing to the ground, eliciting cheers from hundreds of onlookers, the Irishman let out a sigh.

"So this is how it all ends," he muttered to himself. Having little luck finding work anywhere near his village of Sixmilebridge in County Clare, Ireland, Patrick Shanahan had been an easy target for the fancy-dressed recruiting sergeant, what felt like a lifetime ago. In actuality, it had only been seven years since he 'took the King's schilling', yet everything had changed. The past six years had all been spent on campaign in Portugal, Spain, and now

27

Southern France. His son and twin daughters would have grown so much by then and probably would not even recognize their father.

His wife, Anne, at first lamented that he had not tried to get her onto the company roles when the expeditionary force left for Portugal. All officers and up to six other ranks in each company could bring their spouses with them on campaign. Patrick had been adamant that he did not want his children raised in war, and so Anne had stayed with them in Ireland. Like many soldiers who had families back home, he had a stoppage taken from his pay to be sent to Ireland to provide for his family. Patrick had only kept enough coin to buy an occasional extra loaf of fresh bread, or new socks, and other essentials the army did not provide.

Though he missed his wife and children every day, he never regretted his decision; too many horrors had he faced and he was glad to spare his family. Families were by no means safe from the hazards of war either. He remembered one young private who had been so elated that his wife's name had been drawn by lottery to accompany him. They did not realize she was with child until after arriving in Portugal. The poor lass had a terrible time of it, with her husband trying to care for her in addition to all of his duties. The other wives within the company had been there for them and even helped deliver their son when the young soldier was on picket duty. Tragedy struck a week later; the private had just gone out of his wife's tent when a stray artillery round blew their living area to bits. There had been a dozen casualties, including his wife who, though alive, was missing a leg and part of a hand. Their new-born son was cut in half by the blast. The grievously injured woman was evacuated with the rest of the wounded to be sent back to England, but succumbed to infection less than a month later before even making it out of Portugal. The widowed soldier was a broken man, moving through life listlessly, speaking to no one, and keeping no company except his own. Many expected him to put a pistol to his head or charge headlong into an enemy barrage during the next engagement. Yet, six years later he still walked among the living, having faded into the background among the mass of redcoats, doing his duty in eternally silent mourning. Patrick had seen the young man earlier that evening, sitting alone in the corner of a porch on an abandoned house, drinking a bottle of looted gin. The colour sergeant asked the private if he was well, to which the young man replied, "I live only because God hates me."

Patrick wondered what would happen to the young soldier, as well as many of the others, now that the war was over. For that matter, he wasn't certain what would happen to himself. He reckoned some of the men would be sent across the ocean to fight in that utterly pointless war in America. He further guessed that the British government would try and burn Washington to the ground to teach the former colonists a harsh lesson.

As distasteful as he found the idea of fighting in America, his only other option seemed to be taking his discharge and going home. As with any war, once hostilities ended there was always a mass demobilization, seeing as how gigantic armies were expensive to maintain and no longer needed. There was the possibility of garnering other postings around the vast British Empire, though for most of the men their options would be to either go fight across the Atlantic or go home. If given the option, many would opt to leave the King's service, but Patrick Shanahan was a practical man. Tens-of-thousands of former soldiers would now be seeking work, and jobs were already hard to come by. This was particularly true in his native Ireland; hence the disproportionate number of Irishmen serving in the ranks. It was a bitter irony for many that despite the never-ending strife between Ireland and her English overlords, Irishmen made up a third of the entire British army, wearing red jackets and carrying muskets in the service of King George.

Patrick suddenly found himself in a dilemma. Meagre though the wages of a soldier were, despite Wellington's efforts to raise the pay of non-commissioned officers, it was still a steady source of income that provided for his family. Elated as he'd be to see Anne and his children again, he would be a poor excuse for a husband and father if he failed to find work after returning home. He doubted that the army would allow him to reenlist should jobs prove as scarce as he feared. On the other hand, leaving for America would mean being away from his family for even longer, to risk dying in a war that as best as he could tell neither side even understood why they were fighting in the first place. And once that war ended, then what?

"If only I knew where to find Captain Webster," he muttered to himself. The officer he referred to was a young man he'd only known for a couple days, yet the harrowing ordeals they endured had formed a bond between the two. They fought together during the hellish assault on the fortress of Badajoz, two years earlier. Patrick had been a corporal then, Webster a lieutenant. The two had been part of a group of volunteers known as the *Forlorn Hope*; the first men into the breach of an assault who were there simply to get into the enemy defences and die in place. Both men had miraculously managed to survive, though Webster was badly wounded leading the assault. Patrick had bound the officer's wounds and carried him all the way back to friendly lines. It was for this reason Wellington had personally promoted him to sergeant. Patrick figured he could call upon a favour from the officer whose life he'd saved. The problem was, last he knew Captain Webster had been sent home to England to recuperate from his injuries, which had proven far worse than initially thought, and was then made a recruiting officer.

Patrick had no way of knowing if Webster ever returned to the continent or stayed in England. Despite being a member of the upper class that often viewed the common rankers with disdain, the captain had been a decent fellow; openly acknowledging that Patrick had saved his life and even once calling him by his given name. No other officer had ever shown the Irishman what could almost be considered a sign of friendship. He then decided that if he were to save himself from the conundrum of having to decide between being discharged from the ranks or fighting in America, he had to find Captain James Henry Webster.

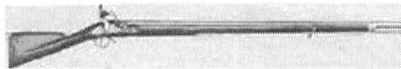

While the masses celebrated in the streets, an impromptu banquet was held with all of the senior British and Spanish officers. General Don Miguel de Alava was the ranking Spanish officer present. An interesting character to say the least, Alava had the unique distinction of having fought for both the French and English. Serving as a marine aboard his Uncle Admiral Ignacio Alava's flagship, he had served as part of the joint French and

Spanish force at the Battle of Trafalgar in 1805. The battle had proven to be one of the most one-sided naval engagements in history, and though it cost British Admiral Horatio Nelson his life, the French and Spanish fleets had been annihilated, with the British lone masters of the seas ever since. Alava's uncle had been seriously wounded, and his flagship captured. When Napoleon turned on his allies and invaded Spain, placing his brother, Joseph, on the Spanish throne, Alava changed his allegiance and would later find himself as an aide-de-camp of Wellington. The personal valour he had shown at both Ciudad Rodrigo and Badajoz had earned him the respect of both Spanish and British alike.

Despite their six years of service together, this evening was the first time Alava or any of his men had seen Wellington actually don the British uniform. Wellington always campaigned in plain civilian garb, preferring his blue overcoat to his red officer's uniform. But on this night he walked into the dining room sporting his best scarlet frock with its high black collar covered in elaborate gold embroidery. A fancy gold cord hung from his right collar and wrapped loosely around his arm, with tails hanging down. Running from his left shoulder, across the body down to his right hip, was the deep blue sash of the *Order of the Garter*, Britain's highest chivalric honour.

"Your grace," General Alava said with a deep bow as all officers in the room stood. The Spanish, who had all been drinking heavily beforehand, seemed jittery to the amusement of their English counterparts.

As few of the British spoke Spanish, and the Spanish officers at best only knew rudimentary English, cross-conversations proved impossible. About the only thing the British officers could do was try to keep up with the Spanish-level of drinking.

Uncertain what else to do, Wellington stood and held his glass high. "Gentlemen!" he said, "To Louis XVIII and the restoration of the Bourbon Monarchy!" As the assembled host echoed the toast, Wellington took a deep pull off his glass and sat down.

"I thought you hated the Bourbons," Somerset said quietly into his ear.

"A 'walking sore'," Ponsonby added, "Isn't that what you called Louis?"

"Have you ever seen the Bourbon king?" Wellington asked. "Dear God, the man's as big as a house and wracked by gout. His daddy lost them the throne to the guillotine over twenty years ago. The man cannot inspire a village idiot, let alone an entire nation. Still, he's our ally, and with him back on the throne we are at last rid of Boney and can all go home. I daresay, I'll have a portrait of that 'walking sore' hanging in my banquet hall!"

Though his voice dripped with sarcasm, both Somerset and Ponsonby surmised that Wellington was serious about hanging the French King's portrait in his dining hall.

"Gentlemen," Alava said with his deep accent, standing once more. "I must propose a toast. To his grace, the Duke of Douro, Marquess of Wellington, and 'El Liberador de Espana'!"

"El Liberador de Espana!" the Spanish officers all shouted before breaking into a series of whoops and shouts of celebration. Their drunken behaviour, which contrasted sharply with their smart uniforms, was undignified in Wellington's eyes.

Realizing that the dinner party was degrading into a drunken debauchery, he stood, finished his wine, bowed deeply, and quickly excused himself. Somerset and Ponsonby broke into laughter when they heard Wellington shouting down the hall, *"Coffee! Get me some damn coffee already!"*

Chapter II: Brave New World

Brussels, Belgium
July 1814

Field Marshal Sir Arthur Wellesley, Duke of Wellington

I arrived in Belgium a month ago, though I have yet to settle into proper quarters. I spent the week's end at the estate of the Duke of Richmond. Many of the other officers acting as Wellington's escorts were with me, though all of them have regiments to which they are assigned. Having just arrived from England, I know not whether I am to be given a permanent posting, or will I be sent back home to take up duty once more as a recruiting officer? I've sent my request forward to Wellington, who was made a Duke two months ago, asking for either a position on his staff or a company command. I was assured by his aide, Major Somerset, that the request was received and the Duke will address it in his own good time.

I've taken the liberty of bringing my daughter with me. I was so proud of my little Amy, as she handled the sea crossing better than most soldiers. I still wear the locket bearing her mother's image; until such time as Amy is old enough that I can give it to her. Though I still miss her mother and think of her often, I have finally stopped wearing my wedding ring. Father said it was unhealthy for me to continue pining for a ghost. Though his words struck deeply, I knew he was right.

With Napoleon deposed, the Bourbons restored, and the end of the war, I look to start a new chapter in my life, as well as my daughter's, in this Brave New World.

Captain James Henry Webster
15 July 1814

It was an unusually warm, sunny day when the carriage stopped in front of the barracks. Brussels was notoriously damp, even in the middle of summer, so the young officer was surprised by the glare of the sun as a footman opened the carriage door and he stepped onto the cobblestones.

His resplendent uniform was of a deep red with garter blue facings that denoted the venerable 1st Regiment of Foot Guards. His tunic bore a single epaulette upon his right shoulder, bearing the insignia of a captain. The epaulette had been given to him personally by Wellington, which meant far more to him that the actual rank it signified. Around his neck hung a crescent moon-shaped brass gorget, a symbol of an officer on duty. What stood out most on his uniform was the badge sewn into the blue sash that ran from his right shoulder down to his left hip. Dating back to 1643, during the English Civil War, it was one of the earliest known badges or medals awarded for valour; the *Forlorn Hope badge*, awarded to the brave souls who ventured first into the breach during a siege and somehow managed to survive.

Two years had passed since James had been to the continent. He'd never been to Belgium, his entire tenure spent in Portugal, with a brief foray into Spain. He hardly considered himself a veteran of the Spanish portion of the campaign, even though he had taken part in two of the most arduous sieges; Ciudad Rodrigo and Badajoz. For the young captain, he could not answer many questions about Spain itself, as the siege works of those two battles were really all he saw of the country.

Contrasting his military appearance was the sleepy-eyed little girl in a yellow dress that he lifted out of the carriage. She laid her head on her father's shoulder and slept quietly, oblivious to the activity going on around them. Her mother, also named Amy, succumbed due to complications soon after she was born two years before. James was left to raise his daughter alone. His sister and other family members had offered to look after her. However, this would have meant leaving her in England. While this would not be unheard of for a career-minded officer, for James, his daughter was the reason he wore the king's uniform.

"Captain Webster?" a voice said behind him.

James turned to see a rather striking woman, wearing a dress ironically similar to what his daughter wore. "You must be Emma," he replied, finding himself unable to stop staring. "Sarah said you were anxious for us to meet."

"Did she now?" the young woman asked with a coy smile. Lady Sarah Lennox was one of the daughters of the Duke and Duchess of Richmond and in several conversations with James had not-so-subtly mentioned her friend, Emma Capel, daughter of Lady Caroline Capel.

"My condolences on the loss of your fiancé," James noted.

Emma's betrothed, an officer on Wellington's staff, had been killed a year prior at Vitoria.

"Thank you," Emma replied, eyes downcast for a brief moment. "Did you know him?"

"No," the captain replied, shaking his head. "The army is rather vast, and Wellington's staff officers had little inclination to deal with subalterns in the line regiments. And besides, I missed the last two years of the war completely."

"Yes," Emma acknowledged. She then nodded towards the badge on his sash. "I heard you won your badge of honour at Badajoz."

"Won," James replied, unable to mask his disdain for the term. It was his turn to look downcast. While leading the Forlorn Hope into the breach had earned him both the rare badge, as well as his current rank, it was an event he rarely discussed with anyone.

Emma had heard tales of the horrors faced by those brave souls who were first into the breach of that brutal siege. Only a couple dozen of the hundred men James had led that night had walked away; the rest were left with traumatic injuries or as bloodied corpses on the slope. Of the survivors who had been able to still fight, most had gone completely mad and committed unimaginable atrocities upon the people of the city. As James' brow broke into a sweat, Emma immediately regretted mentioning Badajoz. There was one thing she still needed to ask him.

"I heard you were friends with my cousin, Benedict."

"I was," James was filled with conflicting emotions. Benedict Harvest had led the other Forlorn Hope at Badajoz; his men assaulting the Santa Maria bastion, while James and his men attacked the bastion known as Trinidad. "He was exceptionally brave; a true soldier and finer gentleman never lived."

"That he was a brave soldier, I have no doubt," Emma replied. "Whether he was a gentleman...well, let's just say I think my cousin had an eye for the ladies from about the time he was twelve."

"He certainly made the most of his remaining eight years," James chuckled. "I must say, though, that when it came to my wife, as well as those of the other officers and men, he always conducted himself with the utmost respect. I never did repay my debt to him."

"Your debt?"

"When we found Amy was with child," James explained, "I elected to garner her passage back to England. The army did not have resources to spare and hiring a private coach to take her all the way to Lisbon was frightfully expensive. There was the matter of chancing either finding quarters on an outbound military vessel or purchasing passage on a private ship headed to England. My personal funds would have been insufficient, and Benedict generously offered his assistance. I shouldn't say he offered, but rather he insisted on helping us. But sadly, he is gone now, as is my dear Amy." An awkward silence followed for a few moments before his daughter stirred and whimpered quietly.

"And this must be little Amy," Emma said with a big smile towards the little girl.

James' countenance quickly changed, and he matched Emma's smile, holding his daughter up, who was now awake and fussily wiping her eyes. "Can you say 'hello'?" James asked; only to have the girl grumble and lay her head down on his shoulder once more. "I'm sorry. I don't think she slept at all; and it was a rather long ride in the carriage."

"No worries at all," Emma said with a gentle laugh. "I think she's adorable."

"Yes," James noted. "Well, I was just trying to decide what to do with her. I have a meeting with the Duke in an hour and…"

"Why don't you leave her with me?" Emma interrupted.

"You wouldn't mind?" James asked. "I just arrived in Brussels and haven't had time to acquire a nanny…"

"It's fine," Emma persisted. She then placed a couple fingers under Amy's head and carefully lifted her up. "Do you want to stay with me for a while?"

The little girl gave a tired smile, which was enough for her father.

"Thank you so much!" James emphasized as he handed his daughter to the young woman. "I thought for a moment I was going to have to meet with Wellington with her sleeping over my shoulder. I'm not sure if that would have gotten a smile or a chunk ripped from my backside. With him one never knows."

"Always err on the side of caution with Wellington," Emma replied. "At least that's what Charles says."

Charles Lennox was the Duke of Richmond and former Lord Lieutenant of Ireland where Wellington, then known as Arthur Wellesley, had served as his secretary. Though made a duke eight years before Wellington and at one time his superior, Wellington's military promotion to field marshal in 1813 reversed the roles. To his credit, Richmond recognized Wellington's military genius and was, therefore, not resentful towards being subordinate to one younger than himself, who had only recently acquired his dukedom.

As James walked towards Wellington's temporary headquarters, he noticed there were a number of regiments encamped around the city, with many waiting for movement orders. He recognized the colours of the 27th Inniskilling Regiment and out of curiosity decided to take a stroll through their camp. He quickly looked from face-to-face at the men milling about, most of whom either quickly moved out of his way or gave a polite, 'sir', before going about their business. A freshly-commissioned subaltern noted the captain wearing the Foot Guards uniform and quickly made his way over, saluting before addressing him.

"Can I help you, sir?" the lieutenant asked.

"I'm looking for an old friend," James replied.

"Of course," the subaltern replied. "The officers' mess is the big tent at the end of the line. You should be able to find most of them there within the hour."

"It's not an officer I'm looking for," James responded.

"Beg your pardon, sir. It's not every day an officer, especially one from the Foot Guards, refers to a ranker as a *friend*."

There was the slightest trace of disdain in the subaltern's voice, typical of the prejudice that existed from gentry' officers towards the men in the ranks.

"One makes exceptions when that ranker saves your life," the captain said. "I'm hoping to find a Sergeant Patrick Shanahan; hopefully he still lives."

"Of course!" the lieutenant said, his face brightening. Whatever his inborn predisposition, the young officer apparently had a higher opinion of Patrick Shanahan. "We happen to be from the same company. He's *Colour* Sergeant Shanahan now; one of the first in the Inniskilling promoted to that rank when it was first authorized last year. He and a couple of the other lads elected to spend their own coin staying at a boarding house in town."

"Where can I find him?"

"Here, I'll get one of my men to write down the directions for you," the lieutenant answered.

As a scribe wrote the directions to where he could find Colour Sergeant Shanahan, James took a quill and wrote out a note himself. It read:

Patrick,

I have returned to Europe and am here in Brussels.
I have a meeting with Wellington presently that I
think will decide both our fates. I hope to have good
news when I see you next.

38

"Be a good man and have this delivered to Colour Sergeant Shanahan right away," he ordered the subaltern. "Tell him I will be there to see him after my audience with Wellington."

"Right away, sir," the lieutenant replied, handing the note to a messenger.

James' heart was full of mixed feelings as he continued on his way, thankful that the sun was out; for it would not do to be seen by Wellington in a sodden uniform! Like many, he felt a bit of uncertainty now that the war was over. For the past two years he had tried to make his way back to mainland Europe and re-join the fight. The only enemy he had fought during his tenure as a recruiting officer was insufferable boredom. He understood the need for officers to provide oversight, especially when accounting for the 'King's Shillings' used to entice new recruits. Since the sergeants and a small group of rankers did all the actual recruitment, there had been little for the captain to actually do. Every time there was a 'beating order' he would account for the shillings and verify that each issued out had a recruit bound to it.

Periodically, he would make an appearance when recruits were going through their medical exams to ensure fitness for duty, and a couple of times he even rode his horse at the head of a group being escorted to the training depot. These had been very rare, though. Doctors made him feel like he was in the way, and while the instructors at the training depot conferred respect to his rank, their demeanour made it clear they were anxious for him to be on his way. The first time he'd gone, he paid a visit to the colonel in command of the depot, who seemed both surprised and appalled to see him. James would later reckon that the only reason he had not been tossed out on his head was the sight of his Forlorn Hope badge, which the colonel, who had no actual combat experience, would not stop staring at. The colonel did state, however, that it was the captain's duty to supply the recruits and his to train them. While courteous enough in his manner, the chill in his voice made clear to the young captain that his presence within the training depot would not be required ever again.

As James had walked back towards the gate of the depot, feeling dejected and a little embarrassed, the sights within made him understand why the colonel did not like the idea of outside officers coming into his world. As an officer who had purchased his commission outright, James had never seen the brutal conditions new recruits were subjected to, long before they were allowed to wear the red coats. The training was brutal, and if a man managed to survive the seven months without being flogged, he was a fortunate soul indeed. Of course, the instructors who beat their charges when they stepped out of line during drill or failed to perform to standard, all while subjecting them to voracious verbal abuse, had all gone through the same ordeal when they'd enlisted into the ranks. The captain also had to remind himself of many of the men he'd served with; they were a hard people to begin with, and James had to reckon that the savagery of recruit training made them more ready for battle than many of the officers expected to lead them. The discipline in the British Army was severe, and if one were being brutally honest, part of the reason why the redcoats were so relentless in battle was because they feared the lash far more than death.

The recruit depots seemed a lifetime away as James took a deep breath and walked up the steps of the magistrate manor that was serving as the Duke's temporary headquarters. Wellington was only passing through on his way to Paris, so James understood how fortunate he was to have been given an audience.

The door at the top of the outside steps was partially open, allowing in the pleasant breeze. He wasn't exactly sure where he was supposed to go, so he was grateful when he saw, at the end of the corridor which opened into a foyer, a British major, going over paperwork behind a tall receptionist desk. James recognized the officer as Fitzroy James Somerset, Wellington's aide-de-camp; now slated to be his secretary when the Duke took over as Ambassador to Paris. Somerset was in his mid-thirties with a solid reputation for both organizational skill, as well as personal bravery in battle. Despite what on paper appeared to be a posh clerical job, he had performed heroically during the Peninsular War. Like all officers on Wellington's staff, he was expected to be a combat soldier first, and his valour and tactical prowess had earned the respect of the rankers, while gaining the personal trust of the Duke himself. Somerset had even taken part in the taking of the ramparts at Badajoz, personally closing and reinforcing the gate that prevented French soldiers in the castle from coming to the aid of those on the ramparts, while also leaving them to the mercy of Sir Thomas Picton's division which had successfully taken the castle.

"Captain Webster, here to see the Duke of Wellington, sir," James said with a sharp salute.

"At ease, captain," Somerset replied, returning the salute. He then pointed to a large, leather couch in the corner by a tall potted shrub. "Have a seat over there. His grace will see you presently."

James sat on the very edge of the couch, leaning forward slightly, turning his shako over in his hands as his palms started to sweat. Other soldiers came and went, though he did not see a single enlisted ranker amongst them. In fact, he was about the only company-grade officer there; the rest being majors or higher. He did see a lieutenant colonel sporting the familiar uniform of the Foot Guards, and he thought he heard someone address him as *Colonel Askew*.

The slamming of the outside door and the thunderous echo of stomping footsteps startled him. He glanced down the hall and saw an older gentleman wearing a resplendent general's uniform, briskly walking down the hall. His grey hair was mostly combed back, and he had a stern countenance about him. James thought for a moment that perhaps the man had never smiled once in his life. The older officer looked very familiar to him, though he could not quite place him.

"Is he in?" the general said, being deliberately louder than was necessary.

"He is, sir," Somerset replied calmly, stacking some papers on the desk. "However, he's not available at this moment..."

"Piss on that," the general interrupted. "He's always available for me." Before Somerset could protest, the general quickly turned and stormed towards what James assumed was Wellington's office. He gave a loud knock and then opened the door before even waiting for a reply. Even as loud voices echoed from the office, Somerset continued to work quietly, as if nothing had happened. He then glanced over and saw the captain's eyes wide and mouth agape.

"I take it you've never dealt with Lieutenant General Sir Thomas Picton before," the major surmised.

"So that's who that was," James said with a chuckle. "I suppose his demeanour and language should have given him away."

"His lack of gentlemanly behaviour does give the Duke fits," Somerset conceded. "However, he tolerates him because he's effective."

"Of that there's no doubt," James replied. "After all, he did take the castle at Badajoz."

"Indeed," Somerset said, looking back down at his papers. It was clear that, like Wellington, he only begrudgingly acknowledged Sir Thomas Picton's talents. The old general's conduct and language sounded more like that of a drunken ranker, rather than of one who'd been pursuing a peerage his entire life. His casual usage of extreme profanity in mixed company and during formal occasions had embarrassed Wellington more than once. That he could pull off the seemingly impossible, like when he broke the castle at Badajoz at a time when it seemed like all was lost, gained him a lot of leeway with his commander-in-chief. There was still plenty of tension between the two. Despite being formally thanked by the House of Commons seven times for exceptional service, Picton had been denied his much coveted peerage. James hazarded that that may have been what the general had wanted to see Wellington about, though there could have been a hundred reasons. Still, he had to stifle a chuckle as Picton stormed out of the office, and Somerset took the opportunity to harry him about this.

"Not recommended for a lordship yet, Sir Thomas?" he asked with an expression of false concern.

"Sod off, Somerset," Picton grunted, though James thought he could detect the slightest trace of a smile across his face.

Despite their extreme difference in rank, and the fact that Picton was old enough to be Somerset's father, there was a subtle amount of respect between the two men. Though they most certainly were not friends, each man knew too well about the exploits and bravery of the other, and that in their own ways both were heroes of England and Picton's native Wales.

Somerset had stepped into Wellington's office soon after Picton left, and James noted that the foyer was now mostly quiet. He was left to brood over his own thoughts once more, and he hoped that Sir Thomas Picton had not set off the Duke and left him in a foul temper.

"His grace will see you now," Somerset said as he came back down the hall. He then led James down the long corridor.

The captain took a deep breath and followed the man, clutching his shako under his left arm, the rattle of his sword scabbard bumping against his leg seeming to echo. Though the Duke had made it a point of requesting him come to Belgium as one of his honorary escorts, the two had never spoken in private. Now that he thought about it, the commander-in-chief had almost never spoken to him directly. The only exception was when Wellington promoted him to captain; but then James had been laid up on a hospital cot, delirious from his injuries. Here he was, about to have a personal meeting with the man who'd driven Bonaparte's best generals from Portugal and Spain!

Somerset stopped at the end of the hall and gave a sharp rap on the door.

"Come!" a voice boomed from within.

Somerset quickly opened and the door and waved for James to enter. "Captain Webster, your grace," the aide said.

James strode into the room and snapped off a sharp salute, though as Wellington was engrossed in some papers he was reading, he did not seem to notice, and James eventually let his arm drop.

"Webster," the Duke said at last as he looked up at him.

"Sir," the captain replied, unsure as to what else to say. Wellington allowed for a short pause and James swallowed hard. He hoped the Duke could not tell how nervous he was being in his presence alone.

"As you know," Wellington began, "I am a busy man with little time for pleasantries. I have your request, asking for either a place on my staff or a company command."

James had sent the document in a month prior and figured the Duke must be busy indeed if he was only now getting to it.

"Yes, sir," he replied.

"If there is one thing I despise, it is indecision," Wellington said sharply, taking James aback.

"Sir?" he asked, puzzled.

"You asked me for either a staff position *or* a command," Wellington continued. "Well, which is it? Don't waste my time with inane requests. If you want something, *ask* for it!"

"Sir…" James said slowly, lest he stumble upon his words. He then took a breath through his nose and spoke very quickly, "I request command of a line company."

"Anything else?" Wellington asked with a raised eyebrow.

"Yes, sir," James replied. "I wish command of a company within my former battalion, 3rd of the 1st Foot Guards."

"Done," Wellington answered, rapidly pulling out a parchment. "Lucky for you, the captaincy of the 1st Company within 3rd Battalion is now vacant. Both subaltern spots are filled, though they are new officers with no combat experience and scarcely old enough to require a shave. The company has no colour sergeant, so feel free to promote one of the NCOs or else bring your own over, if you've got one hanging about."

"Yes, sir," James said, smiling for the first time.

Wellington did not match it. "Your battalion commander is the Honourable Lieutenant Colonel William Stewart," he said. "Report to him at once. That is all." James snapped off a rapid salute and walked as rapidly as he could out of the Duke's office, forgetting to close the door behind him. Somerset quickly stepped over and did it for him, chancing a look inside the office. Wellington cocked half a smile and went back to his work.

"He knew, didn't he?" James asked, as Somerset escorted him down the hall. "He knew I would ask for a company command within my former battalion."

"Oh, come now," Somerset scoffed. "You really think his grace knows or concerns himself with the inner thoughts of every officer and man within his command?"

"Well, he's certainly intuitive then," James persisted.

"That he is," Somerset agreed with a chuckle.

"I mean, why else would he have my transfer orders already drawn up?"

"Like you said," Somerset replied, "He is very intuitive. Wellington saw your request and most likely had a clerk scribe the orders once he saw there was a vacancy in the Guards. I daresay he wanted to give you the opportunity to make the request directly and to see which posting you really wanted. Had you said wrong, and asked for a posting on his staff, he may have still offered you the command or he might have told you there were no positions on his staff available and shipped you back to England. With him, one never knows. You know the way out. Good day, Captain Webster."

"And to you, sir," James replied.

Somerset's words gave James much to ponder as he walked over to the barracks of the 1st Regiment of Foot Guards. The Guards were the elite of the British Infantry, with the 1st Regiment tracing its lineage back to 1656, when it formed part of Charles II's bodyguard. Guards' regiments were allowed to handpick their men, rather than being forced to simply take what was given to them from the recruit depots. Commanders also had the discretion to eject any soldier from the regiment who did not perform to standard, and as Guardsmen were paid a better wage and given higher priority on new arms and equipment, there was never a shortage of those seeking transfer into their ranks.

A recently renovated French barracks housed the 3/1st Foot Guards. They were among the few regiments living in permanent housing, rather than still sleeping in tents. James stepped into the outer office of the battalion headquarters and saw a major talking to a few enlisted aides.

"Captain Webster reporting to Lieutenant Colonel Stewart," James said, walking over to the men.

"Ah yes," the major replied, pulling out a set of documents, "The new commander of 1st Company."

James had to stifle his surprise that the battalion already knew he was coming.

"Colonel Stewart is out with Colonel Askew at the moment."

Lieutenant Colonel Henry Askew, who James saw in passing at the magistrate building, commanded the 2nd Battalion.

The major extended his hand. "Henry D'Oyley."

"James Webster," the captain replied, clasping the major's hand.

"You're the Forlorn Hoper I've heard about," Henry noted, nodding at James' badge.

"I suppose everyone knows who I am," James replied with a sigh.

The major chuckled and looked back through his papers. "Well, aside from you and William Mackie, there aren't many officers who've led a Forlorn Hope without getting blown to pieces."

"So I recall," James said with an unintended trace of venom in his voice.

Henry looked back at him and raised an eyebrow.

"Apologies, sir. It's just that a good friend of mine, Benedict Harvest, led the other Forlorn Hope at Badajoz. And, as you say, he was blown to pieces."

"There isn't anyone who's spent more than a day in this war who hasn't lost someone close to them," Henry replied coolly. "Those who volunteered for the Forlorn Hope knew the risks."

"That we did, sir," James said with a nod.

"Here," Henry said, handing him a list and smiling once more. "These are the other officers in the battalion. I'm sure you recognize some of the names. I doubt you know either of your subalterns, though. Lieutenant Grose has only been with us a year and doesn't have much experience; he's very pragmatic and level-headed, though. Ensign Barton purchased his commission barely six months ago. Poor fellow is still distraught that he missed out on all the fighting." The major chuckled at his last remark, which James matched.

He did recognize a few of the names, including an old friend named Captain Daniel Roberts, who was commanding the battalion's light company. Daniel had been James' company commander for three years in Portugal.

"I do have a colour sergeant I wish to bring over," he said after a moment.

"Bring whoever you wish," the major responded. "It's your company. However, you know that the common dregs and shirkers who infest ranks of the army are not welcome here. Like rotten apples, they spoil the entire bushel. Just be sure that anyone you raise onto our roles is of the highest calibre of soldier, worthy of the Guards."

"This one is, sir," James stated with conviction. "He saved my life at Badajoz."

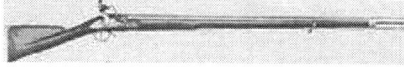

"You know I have been made ambassador to Paris," Wellington said with a grin, holding up a glass of claret. He was holding a dinner for a number of his senior officers before many of them parted ways. Among those leaving was the Duke's brother-in-law, Sir Edward Pakenham, who was being appointed as commander of British forces in North America. Edward, whose friends called him 'Ned', had a strange relationship with Wellington. Rather than being closer because his sister was the Duchess of Wellington, the Duke's extreme dislike for his wife occasionally strained their relationship. Still, Ned was a very able soldier, and that was enough for Wellington. If anything, his rapport with Ned actually helped his relationship with his wife.

"A fine posting," Ned asserted. "You, my brother, continue to do England proud."

"Here, here!" the host of men toasted their commander-in-chief. Though he joined in the toast, one man's expression betrayed his reservations.

"You do not approve of this posting, Sir Rowland?" Ned asked. The man he questioned was Lieutenant General Sir Rowland Hill.

Affectionately known as 'Daddy' by his men, he was one of the bravest and soundest tacticians in the service of King George. His abilities made him one of the only subordinate commanders who Wellington had any trust in. It was this trust that also allowed Sir Rowland a great deal of candour with his commander-in-chief, something even Wellington's brother-in-law did not have.

"If I may speak plain," Hill replied, turning his glass around in his hand for a moment before looking over at Ned, "I think it is a disaster waiting to happen."

This elicited an immediate round of protest from the assembled officers, though Wellington simply raised an eyebrow and took another sip off his claret.

"Do you mean to tell me you think my brother here is unfit to serve as ambassador, after having driven the frogs from Iberia?"

Ned asked, his mild inebriation causing him to sound haughtier than perhaps intended.

"If you would pull your face from the Duke's backside for a moment," Sir Rowland replied, causing the mass protests to turn to fits of laughter.

Ned sat red-faced, and even Wellington cracked a rare smile.

"It is because he defeated the French that this appointment is diplomatically dangerous. Napoleon may be gone, but many of his generals remain, to include those Wellington bested. Having the man who defeated them now serving as ambassador to the new government is a terrible insult."

"Then the frogs should not have lost," Ned scoffed, taking another drink while regaining his composure.

"Here, here!" another officer at the end of the table shouted in an attempt to end the conversation.

"All I'm saying," Hill persisted, "is I cannot help but wonder about the demeanour of men like Nicolas Soult or Michel Ney, having to work in close proximity to the very man who brought about their downfall." He then looked from Pakenham to Wellington. "Have you nothing to say, Arthur?"

Ned grimaced at hearing Wellington referred to by his given name. Sir Rowland was one of the only men the Duke allowed to address him as such publicly. Even Ned only rarely called him 'Arthur' in the company of his fellow officers.

"It will be curious," Wellington replied, "to see how the likes of Soult, Girard, Ney, and the others react when we finally meet in person."

"I suspect it will be either with contempt or else nauseating flattery," Sir Thomas Picton remarked, having been unusually quiet during this conversation.

"If given the choice, I'll take the contempt," Wellington remarked. "There's more honesty in it."

At the end of the evening, as each man took his leave of the Duke, Hill deliberately placed himself at the end of the line of men who were shaking hands with Wellington for what may have been the last time. At last, only the two men, along with the ever-present Somerset, remained.

"Apologies if I caused any offence, Arthur," Sir Rowland said as he took Wellington's hand.

"Not at all," the Duke replied. "Ned means well, though our relationship is awkward enough as is. I think a spell in America will do him good." That Wellington's marriage to Ned's sister, Catherine, was an unmitigated disaster was perhaps the worst kept secret in all of Europe. It caused no shortage of uncomfortable moments between the brothers-in-law.

"Quite," Rowland concurred. "Still, you do understand my concerns, I hope."

"One thing I've always liked about you, Rowland, is I always know where you're at; be it on the battlefield or in your speech." Wellington let his words sink in for a moment before answering directly. "Yes, I understand your concern. Though as brash as Ned's comments may be, he is right. The French will simply have to deal with my presence as ambassador. You know Castlereagh arranged for this after my brothers fell out of favour with Lord Liverpool."

"Your family is always falling out of favour with Liverpool," Rowland chuckled, referring to the British prime minister.

"Yes, well that makes it a bit difficult when one is trying to gain a position within the government," Wellington replied dryly. "I cannot very well vie for a cabinet post now; it would unnerve Liverpool, given my uncanny resemblance to Richard."

Though Wellington's face was serious, this brought a short laugh from Hill. Aside from the almost nine-year difference in age, and that Richard's hair had been grey for many years, there was a striking similarity in appearance between the two brothers. And as there was currently an extremely bitter rivalry between the Prime Minister and Richard Wellesley, it would cause much discomfort for Liverpool to daily deal with Wellesley's younger brother.

"Ambassador to Paris it is, then," Rowland said with a genuine smile as he extended his hand.

Wellington grasped it firmly. "I intend to keep you close," he said. "God only knows when I may have need of you again."

James pulled the note from his pocket and looked up at the name on the placard outside the boarding house. It was the right place, though he shook his head in disbelief. He stepped through the creaky swinging doors that were coming off the hinges and glanced around the dimly lit room. There was a bar on the left end of the foyer with a broken down table in the corner. A lone barman watched the captain intently as he polished a glass absently.

James noticed the two men in red coats sitting at the table. One was a private, who was resting his head on the table. The other, a colour sergeant, seemed to be consoling him.

"Hello, Patrick," James said as he walked over to the table.

"Bless me, if it isn't Captain Webster!" the colour sergeant said with a pronounced Irish accent. He quickly got to his feet and clasped James by the hand enthusiastically. He looked around, slightly embarrassed by the setting. "I'm sorry to have brought you here, sir, except I've got no other place to stay right now, unless I wish to return to the tent encampment outside the city."

"You do now," James replied, his grin growing wider. "You're done with living in tents and bawdy houses."

"By God, sir!" Patrick said enthusiastically. "This means you got your command, then?"

"A line company within 3rd Battalion of the 1st Foot Guards," James answered. "And I happen to be in need of a colour sergeant."

"I can't thank ye enough," Patrick started to say, then glancing over at his companion, whose head was still on the table, "Can we take the boy here with us?"

"Who is he?" the captain asked.

The young soldier started to quietly sing an old folk song.

"Hark, now the drums beat up again,
For all true soldier gentlemen,
Then let us enlist and march, I say,
Over the hills and far away."

"Young David here," Patrick explained, "also from Sixmilebridge, got to us just before Toulouse, and well…with the war now over and all, it's either he gets demobilized or prays they send him to America."

"I don't want to go to America," the drunken lad slurred. "I joined to fight the frogs, damn it all."

"There are no more frogs to fight," Patrick replied loudly and slowly into the man's ear. "But if you're courteous enough to the good captain here, maybe he'll find you a spot in the 1st Foot Guards."

"Bloody piss!" David said quickly, snapping upright. His glassy eyes then noticed James' officer's uniform, and he staggered to his feet, snapping an awkward salute. "Beg your pardon, sir."

"At ease, soldier," James said calmly, as Patrick helped the lad sit back down. He then pulled the colour sergeant off to the side and spoke to him quietly. "Patrick, you do know that the Foot Guards are an elite unit; the best marksmen, best drilled, and above all, best disciplined regiments in the entire army. Its members are hand-picked for their quality as soldiers; and with the added incentive pay, men will damn near cut each other's throats just to join. You, I know I can count on. But him? I don't know a thing about him, other than he's seen one battle, is from the same village in Ireland as you, and right now he is piss drunk and drooling on the table."

"I'll look after him, sir," the sergeant assured him.

"See to it that you do," James replied sternly. "Either he performs to the same standards as the rest of the Guards or he gets sent to America. Get over to the quartermaster first thing in the morning and exchange your uniforms. I want both of you looking smart by first formation tomorrow."

James started to leave, but as he got to the door, he glanced back over his shoulder. "And send word for your wife and family."

"Yes, sir!" Patrick replied with a smile as he went back to the table where David was now snoring loudly.

British Infantryman

The sun had gone behind the clouds and it felt much later than it was when James made his way to the quarters arranged for him. The Duke and Duchess of Richmond had been most kind in letting him stay in one of the many spare rooms at their grand house in Brussels. Not many captains or subalterns had such fancy living quarters. After seeing how the men in the ranks were housed, even those not living in tents, James was doubly grateful. Officers tended to be dismissive towards how the common soldiers lived. After all, class lines were extremely rigid within English society, and that the poor sods that made up the enlisted ranks would live in comparatively substandard conditions was accepted as a matter of course.

James privately admired a number of the enlisted men, at least those of real quality who were not simply loyal to gin, gambling, and whoring. He remembered fondly the sergeant who had acted as his second during the assault on Badajoz. The brave man had been diagnosed with a terminal illness, yet in spite of being offered the chance to go home and see his family once more, he instead chose a valiant death in battle. And of course there was Patrick Shanahan, the bravest of them all! Patrick possessed not only extreme personal bravery; he also had a matching intellect that often surprised those who mistook him for a simple poor Irish soldier.

As James removed his gorget and started to unbutton his coat, the locket that he still sometimes wore around his neck fell out. He'd forgotten it was there, and the sight of it in the mirror made him suddenly morose. He removed it from his neck and opened it. Inside was a miniature portrait of his deceased wife. He thought back once more to his father's words about pining for a ghost, which had compelled him to finally remove his wedding ring.

The locket was his most cherished possession, yet in many ways it enslaved him to the past. He now had a promising future ahead of him. He was finally free of the yoke of being a recruiting officer, in command of a company within the elite 1st Foot Guards, and if he could find a way to repay the Duke and Duchess of Richmond for their kind hospitality, then perhaps he could gain their patronage as well.

It was then that he resolved to not wear the locket anymore. He would keep it locked away safely, until such a time as Amy was old enough and it would pass on to her. The one unavoidable reminder of his past was his daughter. James was secretly both hopeful and fearful that she would come to resemble her mother as she grew older.

"Do you still love her?"

Emma's voice caused James to start. He'd been holding the locket in front of him, ready to place it in a small lockbox as he became lost in his thoughts. "Emma," he said with a smile, forgetting her question. "Where is Amy?"

"She's sleeping," Emma replied. "The moment you left she wouldn't stop talking. All she would talk about was her 'brave papa'. It was so cute."

James smiled and blushed slightly, quickly placing the locket in the box. It had pleased him greatly that Amy had learned to talk very early and had become articulate as soon as she learned how to speak. Though she would certainly have the best private tutors he could afford, he still looked forward to the time when she was old enough that he could teach her to read.

"I would like to have had a little daughter like her," Emma said with a sigh.

"You still can," James conjectured. At Emma's puzzled expression he quickly explained, "I mean you still have plenty of years with which to marry and start a family."

"Perhaps," Emma replied. Given that she was a couple years younger than James; he couldn't understand why she would think otherwise. "Thankfully though, Father and Mother have not pressed the issue of finding me another suitable husband. With the war now finally over, perhaps they might."

"There are plenty of suitable matches to be found in Brussels," James surmised.

"Yes," Emma concurred, "And all wear the red uniform. Did you know my fiancé's name was also James?"

"A good name to have," James said with a soft smile.

Emma responded with one in kind, though was briefly serious for a moment. "After he was killed, Mother told me she would rather I had been able to wear white *before* I wore black."

"Well, like you said," James replied, "The war is now over."

"And what will you do?" Emma asked, cocking her head to one side. "What do soldier gentlemen do when a war ends?"

"Wellington's given me command of a line company within the Foot Guards," he answered. "We're to remain in Belgium to keep an eye on the French northern border, so it looks like I'll be staying in Brussels for the time being. Outside of my duties, raising my daughter is most important to me. I've had to be both father and mother to her. And you?"

"Mother thinks it's good that I've stayed in the company of Sarah, as well as the Duke and Duchess," Emma said. "Besides, my being here gives her and Father a reason to come to Brussels. It seems to be the fashion these days that anyone of importance mingles with the society here. There is something exotic about being so close to the heart of Bonaparte's empire without actually having to set foot in Paris just yet."

"With Napoleon gone, the world is now gathering on his very doorstep," James surmised.

It felt strange to Patrick, wearing the uniform of the Guards. Always he had served in a purely Irish unit, and now he was among the minority, as there were maybe six or seven Irishmen in the company that numbered nearly a hundred. He was reminded that the Regiments of Foot Guards were the king's Household Division, the elite of the British Infantry. They were better equipped, housed, and even better paid than line infantry regiments.

Patrick noticed quickly the quality of the individual soldier was different within the Guards as well. Though all who wore the king's uniform had a standard to uphold, those selected for the Guards clearly took pride in their appearance and conduct. Discipline problems occurred, like they did in every regiment; however, the colour sergeant noted, in the company log books, that in the past year there had only been four floggings and six monetary fines for minor misconduct. Thankfully, there had been no serious infractions that would have resulted in hanging or the firing squad.

There was a knock on the door and before he could answer, in walked a sergeant and a pair of corporals. It was then that Patrick remembered he'd called for a short meeting with the other non-commissioned officers, or NCOs, of the company. For reasons he could not explain, the sergeant gave him an uneasy feeling. The man's demeanour was pleasant enough, though he did have a nasty scar across his forehead. He could not quite place it, but Patrick knew he'd met him before, and it had not been under pleasant circumstances.

"Is this all?" he asked. A company was authorized one colour sergeant, two sergeants, and three corporals, although since the Guards units were larger than their line counterparts, it was not unusual to see four or even five corporals in a company.

"We've been short NCOs for some time," one of the corporals explained. "You're the first colour sergeant we've had since they authorized the rank a year ago. The fat sod who holds the other sergeant's billet is back in England as a drill instructor."

"Can't figure out why we can't get our other corporal billets filled," the other junior NCO added. "Lieutenant Grose tried for a while, yet with peace now upon us, the paymaster keeps saying they won't pay for any more promotions, even though we're authorized the positions. And, of course, none of the lads will take the stripes and responsibility without the extra pay."

"Well, I can't say I blame them," Patrick said.

The financial noose had tightened considerably on those regiments spared from disbandment after the mass demobilization following the Peninsular War; even the King's Regiments of Foot Guards were not exempt.

"We make do with what we have," the sergeant replied.

The sound of his voice stabbed Patrick through the heart. He then remembered in stark detail where he'd seen the man before; in a place where the entire army had gone mad after battling through the 'caldron of hell', as they'd called it. Patrick's demeanour ran cold even as the NCO extended his hand. "Sergeant Thomas Billings."

"So you are," the colour sergeant replied, keeping his arms folded.

Sergeant Billings awkwardly retracted his hand, the insult not lost on either of the corporals. "This is Corporal James Donaldson and Corporal Christopher Harvey," the sergeant said quickly. "Is there anything else you need us for?"

"No," Patrick replied, shaking his head. "That will be all for now." As the men left the room, he knew he was wrong for not taking the sergeant's hand, but as the memories of the dark past overcame him, he could not bring himself to do so.

"What the bloody hell was that about?" he heard one of the corporals say once they were outside the door. "He calls a meeting that's no more than learning our names, and then doesn't even take your hand. Did you shag his wife or something?"

Patrick shook his head and pulled a handkerchief from his pocket, wiping it across his brow, when the door opened again. It was Captain Webster.

"Patrick, I see you got acquainted with the other non-comms," he said, then noticing the look of vexation on his colour sergeant's face. "Good God, man, are you alright?"

"Yes, I'll be fine," Patrick said quickly, putting his handkerchief away. "Tell me, sir, what do you know about the NCOs in the company?"

"The two corporals I've barely met," the captain replied. "I did hear something about Donaldson's father being a banker. I will have to see what skills he may have passed on to his son when it comes time to do the next payroll. Sergeant Billings I've known since I first joined the Guards, seven years ago."

Patrick swallowed hard and nodded. "A good soldier, was he?"

"As good as any," James shrugged. "He was just one private out of many, though I am glad to see he has since risen through the ranks. Last I saw of him was during the assault on Badajoz. You remember when we were pinned down in that hellish breach for so long. He and some of the other lads from my company ended up fighting alongside us. I do remember he got shot in the head at one point and knocked senseless. With as much blood as there was all over his face and head, I thought for certain he'd bought it. You were further off to the right from where we ended up. I do remember Billings seemed to come back from the dead soon after the frog guns had stopped, with Picton and the 3rd Division taking the castle. Until I saw him when I was posted here, I never knew what happened after we took the breach."

"I remember," Patrick whispered quietly to himself as haunting memories assailed him once again.

"What was that?" James asked, not hearing the colour sergeant.

"Nothing, sir," he replied quickly, shaking his head.

In the weeks that followed, the 1st Company of 3/1st Foot Guards settled into their routine of training and patrolling around Brussels. For both of the new Irish soldiers, there was much for them to live up to, particularly Patrick Shanahan as the company colour sergeant. Yet he handled the men like he had those in his former regiment, recommending both punishment and reward fairly and equitably. His rapport with Lieutenant Grose was one of mutual respect, though Ensign Barton was unsurprisingly aloof towards all of the enlisted men. As Grose directly involved himself with the company more, he noted the visible strain between Colour Sergeant Shanahan and Sergeant Billings. He kept his observations to himself, though, as there had been no breaches in discipline, and in fact, the men in the ranks made a showing of the respect they held for their colour sergeant. Though the regiment was overwhelmingly English, the soldiers expressed their admiration for Patrick by stating that they often forgot he was Irish; this despite the rather stark difference in his speech and accent.

For young David O'Connor, being a member of the Guards did far more to curtail any lapse in discipline than the threat of the lash ever did in his former regiment. Two soldiers in particular had befriended him. There was Private Douglas Farrow who, though close to the same age as David, had served two years in the Peninsular War and fought in seven major battles, and Private Eric Adams who was ten years older than David and became like an elder brother to him. Eric was the oldest of six and also married with children of his own. Perhaps that was why he so readily became like an older sibling to some of the younger men in the ranks.

And yet, for all the attempts by both officer and enlisted alike to find a sense of normalcy, there was no hiding the underlying strain that permeated all of Europe. There was an unspoken feeling that, though exiled, Napoleon was not really gone.

Chapter III: Adieu, Remember Me!
Isle of Elba, off the Coast of France
September 1814

Napoleon's farewell to the Imperial Guard

"I embrace you! Adieu, remember me!"

Those had been Napoleon's final words to his Old Guard, the brave souls who stood by him until the end, even as nearly one quarter of the rest of his army betrayed him. He loved every one of them like they were his sons. Many of the Old Guard were his age or even a little older, yet all looked to him like a father figure.

His farewell to his soldiers had been among the most emotionally distressing moments in Napoleon Bonaparte's life. He had been unashamed by the tears that streamed down his cheeks as he embraced the imperial standard, topped with its majestic eagle, for the last time.

Strangely enough, the only comfort he took was in the accompaniment of a British army officer who'd been offered as the emperor's personal assistant. The man's name was Colonel Neil Campbell. At their first meeting, Napoleon could not help but notice that Campbell had been recently wounded, as his head was bandaged and left arm in a sling. The French Emperor surmised that the Scottish colonel was a brave man, and a bond of mutual respect was soon formed.

Two months later, the former Emperor of the French, and one-time master of continental Europe, stood dejected on the balcony of his palace on Elba. His hands clasped behind his back, as they often were in moments of deep contemplation. He was alerted by the sound of footsteps crossing the room behind him, though he did not move.

"Salutations du Colonel Campbell," Napoleon said, his eyes still fixed on the city below.

"Et a vous, sire," Campbell replied. He had been appointed as Napoleon's attendant by Britain's Foreign Secretary, Lord Castlereagh. It was a fortunate thing that he was fluent in French, as the former French Emperor did not speak a word of English. Indeed, he often called Britain, and more specifically, England, 'a nation of shopkeepers'. He was further heard to lament, on occasion, that the only decent thing the English had given the world was Shakespeare, yet that by itself was not enough to compel him to learn their unsophisticated language.

It was no mere coincidence that the ever-shrewd Castlereagh had appointed the vociferous, yet astute Campbell as Napoleon's attendant. Though they had been at war with each other, Napoleon had never directly faced Wellington's army. Thus, Castlereagh was able to argue in favour of having a British officer assigned to the posting, rather than an Austrian, Prussian, Russian, or one from a score of other European nations. And though Campbell was an officer in King George's army, the appointment of a Scotsman, rather than an Englishman was twofold. Firstly, it was less likely to cause offense to the deposed emperor, which in turn, it was hoped, would perhaps bring Napoleon to allow Campbell into his confidence. Bonaparte was like a caged tiger; one that would require constant watching.

Another well-played move on Castlereagh's part was making Campbell's appointment contingent on whether or not the emperor wished to keep him on in the first place. The intent was not to use Campbell as Napoleon's gaoler, but rather to have the French emperor view him as an honoured guest, there to assist him.

"I trust you are well?" the Scottish colonel asked, still speaking in French.

"As well as you have seen me since the day I came here," Napoleon answered with a trace of dull irritation in his voice. He was actually fond of Campbell, though he made it clear when he felt his attendant was being patronizing. "I settled the mundane affairs of this island within my first month here. I modernized their agriculture, organized their mining industry, and even gave them a semblance of a navy. And while I am grateful that you persuaded your masters in London to allow me to keep the garrison armed to ward of Barbary pirates, it is an absurd question to ask one who once ruled most of Europe if they are now well."

"Apologies, sire," Campbell replied, stepping onto the balcony. "I had heard that you were having stomach pains again, and I was concerned over your health."

At this last remark, Napoleon at last turned and faced him, his brow creased as he assessed the Scotsman. "I like you Campbell, really I do," he said after a pause. "Were you not wearing that red uniform, I'd like to think of you as a friend. As it is, I cannot help but wonder whether your concern is strictly your own or rather that of your masters in England."

"I am a soldier, as you once were," Campbell said slowly, his face betraying a trace of hurt at the emperor's rebuke. Since arriving in Paris before the signing of the Treaty of Fontainebleau, where Napoleon abdicated and was voluntarily exiled to Elba, Campbell had grown surprisingly close to his former adversary. He came to understand the overwhelming force of the emperor's personality and was enamoured at the thought of being counted amongst Napoleon's friends. Yet when Bonaparte grew agitated, as he now was, Campbell had to choose his words carefully. "And I do serve a king, as you also once did," the colonel added. This calculated response brought a smile to Napoleon's face.

"It is I who should now apologize," he replied. "I did not mean to cause offense nor call into question your status as a soldier. I do appreciate you asking about my health. Of course you are aware of my embarrassing debacle when I tried to end my own life. I'd kept a poison capsule with me ever since the Russian campaign. I had thought to spare the world the ignominy of my exile, yet the effects had diminished, and all it did was make me violently ill. I daresay, it still causes me grief even now. I am better today, though, thank you." Napoleon paced back and forth across the balcony for a minute, his hands clasped behind his back. Campbell had been around the emperor enough that he could read in his demeanour that he had more to say. He respectfully maintained his silence.

"Despite my confinement to this tiny isle that my enemies have the audacity to call me emperor of," Napoleon continued, "they still fear me. That vile creature, Prince de Talleyrand, has his spies everywhere on Elba. They think I do not see them, but there are so many they are impossible to miss." The Prince de Talleyrand was a French diplomat who had served Napoleon up until 1807; after which he sided with the Bourbons in exile and worked fervently to restore Louis XVIII to the throne. "I only heard the other day that two of them ended up spying on each other by accident. Work of pathetic amateurs!"

"I take it then, that these spies are not the cause of your intestinal distress?" Campbell asked.

"Not at all," the emperor scoffed. "All it does is reaffirm my enemies' fear. They watch me like a hawk. I venture that they use you to watch me as well. Oh don't try and hide it, my dear colonel. You wear your king's uniform, and I know that in addition to seeing to my needs, you are also here as Castlereagh's agent."

Campbell pretended to ignore the remark. After all, what could he say? His duty to his king would, of course, override any sense of admiration or even friendship he felt for the deposed Bonaparte, and Napoleon could not fault him for it. And though Campbell's concern over the emperor's health was genuine, his interests this day revolved around Napoleon's brilliance as a soldier, which he'd displayed from the first day he donned the uniform. It was this subject that Campbell elected to steer their conversation towards. For all his shrewdness, Napoleon was still susceptible to flattery, and Campbell felt this was a good time to relay a message sent to him that morning from Castlereagh.

"His grace, the Duke of Wellington asks about your well-being," Campbell said.

Napoleon raised an eyebrow but did not respond right away.

Campbell continued, "I've been told that he admires you greatly."

"Does he now?" Napoleon asked with an expression of doubt. He then sighed and resumed his pacing. "I confess one mistake I made was never facing him personally. I thought my marshals in Portugal, as well as my own brother, could deal with that English upstart! But do tell me, how did Marshal Soult fair against him? I heard there was an unfortunate battle that took place several days after I elected to step down and spare the world further bloodshed."

"It happened at Toulouse," Campbell explained. "His grace is full of praise for Marshal Soult's handling of the defence, as he did hold our forces at bay for some time. However, once night fell he was forced to vacate the city."

The emperor glowered for a moment and then decided to dismiss Campbell. He continued to pace back and forth on his balcony, hands clasped behind his back, while traces of the ever-lingering stomach pains cast their shadow over his demeanour. He had received word from his own informers from the continent about Wellington's appointment as Ambassador to Paris, though he kept this knowledge from Campbell.

"And now that damned Sepoy General mocks me from my own capital," he growled quietly. His derogatory term for Wellington stemmed from the British general's time in India. To many, including the Duke's fellow English officers, his reputation had been built fighting poorly armed and ill-disciplined barbarians rather than professional armies. In truth, Napoleon's feelings towards Wellington were in a constant state of contradiction. At times he dismissed the Duke's military and civil accomplishments in the Indian subcontinent, yet there was no mistaking that he had defeated the emperor's best generals every time they faced each other in both Portugal and Spain. It baffled Napoleon that his and Wellington's names were inexplicably linked to the era, even though they had never faced in battle nor ever even met each other. While no doubt men like Soult and Grouchy were in Paris becoming acquainted with the man who'd humiliated them on the battlefield, Napoleon had never even laid eyes on him.

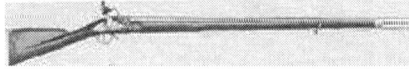

It was still an adjustment for Colour Sergeant Patrick Shanahan, being in a peacetime army. Still, he was grateful. It had taken his wife no time at all to pack up their meagre household belongings, though it was another month before she and his children arrived in Brussels. Emma Capel had arranged a job for Anne, working as an assistant to the groundskeeper at the Duke of Richmond's residence.

"I am sorry there were no vacancies within the interior household," Emma apologized as she walked the Shanahans to the gate which led towards the busy street, "but they just hired a new maidservant only last week, as well as a cook's assistant."

"I don't mind at all," Anne replied with a laugh.

"My wife is a tough Irishwoman," Patrick said with pride, placing an arm around her shoulder. "She does not mind working."

"Except work is impossible to come by back home," Anne observed. "I can't thank you enough for arranging this for me."

Out of the corner of his eye, Patrick saw the main door of the house open and a young officer step out. He kissed the hand of a young woman, who Patrick surmised was one of the Duke of Richmond's daughters. He paid it no mind, glad as he was that Emma had shown such kindness to him and his family. He'd never been to the Richmond's residence, and he was excited that his wife would be working at such a place. It truly was a move up in the world for them. Between her wages and his increase in pay for being a colour sergeant within the Foot Guards, they could afford a better place to live, as well as a proper education for their children.

"What's this then?" a voice barked. "No salute for an officer?"

Patrick looked over his left shoulder and saw Ensign Barton glaring at him. "Beg your pardon, Mister Barton," the colour sergeant replied, releasing his wife's shoulder and saluting.

"Your situational awareness is lacking, *paddy*," Barton snapped. "I'm shocked someone like you survived in the Peninsula. Best not let it happen again or I will have you flogged!" He then nodded to Emma. "Good day, Miss Capel."

"Who the bloody hell was that?" Anne whispered through gritted teeth as soon as Barton walked away. She then curtsied to Emma. "Beg your pardon, Miss Capel."

"He claims to be a proper gentleman, yet he lacks even the most basic human decency," Emma noted.

"Excuse me, ladies," Patrick said. His face was very calm, but Anne knew there was no mistaking the hard expression on his face.

"Oh dear," Anne groaned. She then turned to Emma. "Can I still have the job, even if Pat gets himself into a spot of trouble?"

"Mister Barton!" Patrick barked, causing the young subaltern to jump. "A word if you please, sir."

"What is it?" Barton retorted, walking very fast. "I'm very busy at the moment."

"Yes, I could tell." The thick sarcasm in Patrick's voice caused the ensign to turn and glower at him.

"You best watch your tone, *paddy!*" he snapped.

"Now there we have a problem," Patrick replied calmly. "See, I am expected to address you as *ensign, mister,* or *sir.* You are to address me as *colour sergeant,* not *paddy.* And while it may be your right to have enlisted men flogged, you may want to confer with the captain first. And one last thing, if you ever disrespect me in front of my wife again, I'll break both your legs. Are we clear?"

"How *dare* you speak to me in such a tone!" the ensign retorted. "By God, I'll have you..."

"Enough!" Lieutenant Grose was walking quickly towards the men.

"Lieutenant, sir," Patrick said, saluting.

"That will be all, colour sergeant," Grose replied, returning the courtesy.

"Sir!" Patrick snapped his heels and walked away, the smug grin never leaving his face.

Grose glared at Barton, though the ensign did not notice.

"You're just going to let him get away with..."

"Shut...up!" the lieutenant barked, finally catching Barton's attention. "What the devil is the matter with you? You threaten and disrespect our colour sergeant in front of his wife, and for what?"

"He failed to properly salute me!" Barton protested.

"You walked behind him," Grose retorted. "And he gave you proper respect as soon as you made your presence known. And rather than address him by his rank, you greeted him with a racial insult!"

"What? Got a soft spot for the paddies, do you?"

"You lack both intelligence as well as decorum," Grose replied, shaking his head. "Miss Capel was right. You, sir, are no gentleman."

"What do I care what she thinks?" Barton grunted as he turned and walked away.

Grose fell in beside him. "She's friends with the captain," he observed. "And she's very close with Lady Georgiana." This caused Barton to stumble. Georgiana was the younger sister of Sarah, both daughters of the Duke of Richmond. Barton then looked at Grose, eyes wide for a moment.

"I know you're trying to work your way in with Richmond's daughter," Grose continued. "Well, since you've drawn the ire of one of their closest friends, you can forget about getting any of them into your bed!"

"What? Are they friends with our paddy colour sergeant?" he sneered.

"Miss Capel is," Grose remarked. "I know you think you're untouchable because your father is a viscount, but do not forget who our captain is. You'd best hope that Miss Capel has forgotten the incident by the time she sees Captain Webster again."

That afternoon James called both subalterns into his office. Grose did his best to keep from laughing. Barton's face was red, and he was sweating profusely.

"Something the matter, William?" Grose chuckled as he knocked on the door.

"Come!" Captain Webster called from behind the door.

The two subalterns entered and saluted.

"Ah, gentlemen," James said, returning the salute. The captain was standing over the side of his desk, looking down at a pile of papers. Seated behind the desk was Corporal Donaldson, who looked unusual with his reading spectacles halfway down his nose. The NCO was the son of a London banker who'd served as an apprentice under his father before rallying to the King's colour

66

during the Peninsular War. Because of his knack with numbers, James had tasked him to help with the company payroll.

"That will be all for now, corporal," James said. "We'll finish up tomorrow."

"Very good, sir," Donaldson replied. He stood and saluted before leaving the office.

James then took the seat behind his desk. "Gentlemen," he said, "a couple of things. First off, I am leaving for Paris the day after tomorrow. I've been invited to several functions, plus I have a few errands to attend to. Given the time it takes to arrive in Paris, plus whatever other tasking the Duke may have for me, I surmise I'll be gone about a month. Edward, you will be in command during my absence."

"Yes, sir," Grose replied.

"Mister Barton," James said, interlocking his fingers as he laid his hands on the desk.

Barton swallowed hard. "Sir?"

"I received a rather stern complaint today, regarding a quarrel you had with one of our non-commissioned officers." James let the words sink in as Barton's face turned red.

"It was a minor misunderstanding, sir," Grose said quickly. "The matter has been addressed and resolved."

"Indeed," James replied. "Very well, then." He raised an eyebrow at his ensign. "Mister Barton, you do not look well. Are you alright, sir?"

"I'm fine, sir," Barton stammered quickly.

"You don't look fine," the captain remarked. "Whatever it is, I hope it is not contagious. Go have a lie-down for a bit, and for God's sake lay off the booze in the mess!"

"Yes, sir."

"Dismissed," James said, saluting before his ensign could.

Barton quickly stumbled into the door jam on his way out.

"Take it easy, man! You'll hurt yourself." He then shook his head and waited a moment before speaking again. "The man's a jackass."

"That he is, sir," Grose agreed. "Sadly, his kind infests the ranks of our officer class."

"I know what happened today," James said sternly. "I am grateful you happened to be there."

"I was just coming back from checking the post," Grose replied. "I happened upon Miss Capel and Anne Shanahan, who both told me in the strongest terms what our young lad of an ensign had done. I caught up to them just as the colour sergeant threatened to break his legs."

"A good thing you did," James asserted. "A jackass Mister Barton may be, but he still holds the King's commission. Had Colour Sergeant Shanahan felt compelled to follow through with his threat, well, we both know what would have happened then."

"We do, sir," Grose concurred.

Assaulting an officer, regardless of provocation, was a serious offence. In the very least, Patrick would have been stripped of his rank and brutally flogged. At worst, he could have been shot or hung.

"You know I was going to call Mister Barton onto the carpet for his actions," the captain continued. "I do not completely concur with you covering for him. However, I understand why you did."

"I do think the matter has been resolved, sir," Grose asserted. "The fact that he ruined any chance of getting into Georgiana Lennox's frock should wound his ego sufficiently."

"Well, serves the arrogant bastard right," James added for emphasis. "Just keep an eye on him while I'm gone. I called you both in because I want there to be no doubt that in my absence, you speak for me."

"Of course, sir," Grose nodded. He then grinned and asked, "So will you be seeing Miss Capel in Paris?"

"It's always a possibility," James chuckled. "Her parents are both gushing supporters of the Duke, and I suspect they will invite themselves to any formal functions he may throw in Paris. I wouldn't be surprised if Emma should accompany them at some point. Why? What are you suggesting?"

"Nothing at all," Grose said with a grin and shake of his head.

"Listen, Edward," James said, "Emma is a very dear friend to me, but there is nothing improper between us."

"Of course, sir," Grose acknowledged. He then added, "But if there was anything between the two of you, I doubt that one could ever call it 'improper'."

Chapter IV: Fear of the Dark
Paris, France
October 1814

Fitzroy James Henry Somerset

"A delightful ball!" Wellington exclaimed as he threw his cloak over his shoulder and raised his bicorn hat high. It was well after dark, and the oil street lamps burned softly in the still of night, only interrupted by the boisterousness of those departing the latest of many such balls that had taken place in Paris since the deposal of Napoleon. On this particular night, Wellington had elected to don his resplendent red uniform, rather than the more tactfully subdued civilian garb he usually wore. Since arriving in Paris in May, he had shunned the uniform; even riding into the city, inconspicuously enough, wearing a plain blue frock coat and top hat. He was there as the duly appointed representative of King George III, not as the conqueror who had vanquished France's best marshals. Yet, for reasons unknown to the other guests, on this particular night the Duke had elected to wear red.

It had, indeed, been a magnificent affair, put on by the Comtesse de Boigne. Wellington's two nieces, Mary and Emily, had accompanied him this evening. Emily had recently been married to Fitzroy Somerset, in a ceremony in which Wellington gave the bride away. Somerset was also there this evening.

"All eyes were on you this evening," Mary observed with a broad smile as she and her sister walked arm-in-arm with their uncle. Somerset walked behind the trio. He was smiling broadly.

"Paris has eyes on no one but our dear Uncle Arthur," Emily laughed as she released Wellington's arm and walked over to her husband, putting her arms around his neck. "Not even for you, my love." She then playfully kissed Somerset on the cheek.

"His grace is the only man in whose shadow it does not offend me to be," he replied with a laugh. That his wife was the daughter of Wellington's older brother, William, only drew Somerset even closer to the Duke.

"And how is our dear aunt, the Duchess?" Mary asked absently, causing Somerset to wince. "We never see her at these wondrous soirees; such a shame, really."

Wellington released her arm, though Mary did not notice the darkening of his countenance. Emily saw it and grimaced slightly. Her sister was one of the few who failed to openly comprehend the abysmal failure that was the marriage between the Duke and Duchess of Wellington. Even giving birth to two sons could not bring Sir Arthur to show any affection towards his wife. Emily was even under the impression that what little attention he did show to her cousins was done more out of a sense of duty, rather than any sort of fatherly affection.

"Your aunt is well enough," the Duke replied, trying to hide the irritation in his voice. The very idea of bringing Kitty to a ball put on by the Comtesse was beyond absurd, it was downright laughable.

"Such an affair would only bore her," Emily said quickly.

"Quite," Wellington replied.

"Dear, why don't you walk Mary home," Somerset added. "I need to speak with the Duke for a moment."

70

"You get to speak with him every day!" Mary protested. "We scarcely get to see our dear uncle as it is."

"Oh come, sister," Emily said, taking her by the arm and leading her away. "We cannot be selfish in this. You know how important a man Uncle Arthur is. You said so yourself."

"Well, that was awkward," Somerset said as he watched his wife lead her giggling sister towards their waiting carriage.

"I'm glad I married you off to Emily and not Mary," Wellington replied, his back to him, hands clasped behind his back. "At least she has some good sense about her."

"I did actually want to speak with you for a moment, sir," Somerset said.

Wellington turned to face him, eyebrows raised.

"As my wife said, all Paris has its eyes on you. You certainly drew glaring attention by wearing your uniform this evening."

"You mean the same one you are wearing?" Wellington observed with a raised eyebrow.

"Well, yes," Somerset agreed. "I am but a major in His Britannic Majesty's army, not his representative to the Parisian government. A number of high-ranking French officers were there this evening..."

"Yes, and I thought it fitting to meet with them soldier to soldier," Wellington interrupted. "Think I caused much offence?"

"If I may be direct," Somerset replied, "I think Sir Rowland Hill was correct when he said your very appointment would cause offence. That being said, I've watched many of our former adversaries and how they react to you. I overheard Marshal Ney quietly scoff that you never wore your uniform on campaign, yet you made it a point of donning English scarlet this evening. Still, General Massena seems agreeable enough."

"He is," the Duke concurred. "Do you know what he said to me? He said that I owe him a dinner because during the war I caused him to starve. I replied that he owed me one for depriving me of sleep. I actually went hunting with Ney the other day, though I found the experience to be a frightful bore. The French idea of hunting does not allow for much in the way of the chase. My time spent with him has been strange to say the least. Michel Ney is the bravest man to wear a French uniform, perhaps any uniform in history. And yet, I cannot find it within me to acknowledge my

71

admiration for his bravery. At the same time, I've heard he paid me quite the compliment, or at least as good as one could expect from him. He said that while Napoleon was the master strategist, I was the greatest tactician to have ever lived. That he said it in what he thought was a private conversation, and with much disdain in his voice, leads me to believe the authenticity of his words."

"And Soult?" Somerset asked. "He was there this evening as well. Did you notice him?"

"Of course I did," Wellington scoffed. "He kept to himself all night, though he would not stop staring at me; thought I didn't notice either. Suffice it to say, if a man could kill with his gaze, I would be a pile of smouldering ash." With the last remark, he donned his bicorn hat and strolled towards his carriage.

"And whose company will you be enjoying tonight?" Somerset asked. "Madame Grassini, perhaps?"

"You know me well, Somerset," Wellington replied as the footman opened the door to his coach, "Perhaps too well." The words would have been menacing, had not the Duke cracked a quick smile that Somerset just caught.

As Wellington placed his foot on the step of the coach, there was loud commotion off to his left, by the tall stone wall at the corner of the estate and the main road.

"Stop!" he heard a voice shout.

There was the struggle of two men seen in the shadows, and a flintlock pistol flew from one's grip and landed just beneath the corner lamppost. The hammer fell, causing a flash of sparks, yet the weapon failed to fire. Somerset rushed over as he saw a masked figure in a hooded cloak tackled to the ground by another man wearing a red Foot Guards uniform. The soldier was now on the man's chest, slamming his fist repeatedly into his face, as the masked assailant tried to scramble away. He rolled to his stomach, but was stopped from further movement when Somerset calmly placed the barrel of his pistol against his forehead.

"Merde," the man grumbled dejectedly. He then gave a startled shout when the soldier who tackled him stood up and kicked him hard in the crotch.

"Bâtard vile!" the soldier said.

Somerset recognized the man. "Captain Webster."

"Sir," James nodded, regaining his composure though his face was covered with sweat, and he was breathing hard. There was a tear in the right knee of his grey fall trousers.

"Webster," Wellington said calmly as he walked over to the men. He gave a casual glance to the man who'd attempted to murder him, for it had to have been the Duke who was his intended victim; there was no one else still on the street worth taking such a risk over. Yet judging from Wellington's demeanour, the man was little more than a piece of refuse on the street.

"I didn't even see you at the ball tonight," Somerset noted with a chuckle.

"He was my guest, though it would be difficult to spot him, what with all eyes on the Duke," a woman's voice said from the shadows. Emma then walked into the light and curtseyed before Wellington. "Your grace."

"Miss Capel," Wellington acknowledged. He then eyed James once more. "You've torn your trousers, Captain Webster. I'd advise getting them mended or, most likely, replaced. Can't be looking slovenly in front of the men when you return to Brussels."

"Of course, your grace," James replied.

"Somerset," Wellington said to his aide, "You and Captain Webster will be good enough to dispose of this compost heap. It's unsightly."

"Vous pisse dessus, Wellington!" the man on the ground barked. *"Vive l'empereur!"* His rant was cut short by a hard rap across the forehead from Somerset with the pistol.

As the Duke's carriage rode away, Emma shook her head as James and Somerset bound the hapless assailant.

"How ungrateful!" she snapped. "James just saved his life, and he doesn't even acknowledge it!"

"It's not his way," Somerset explained. "The Duke is simply not one for giving out praise. And if he did, it would give the appearance of him being indebted, and therefore one would expect him to dole out special favours. Trust me; he is grateful to Captain Webster."

"Well, he certainly has an odd way of showing it," Emma scoffed. "All he can tell him is to fix his trousers!"

"Well, they did get a bit torn," James laughed as he pulled the prisoner to his feet. "And in a way, I've helped repay my own debt to the Duke for saving my life."

The would-be assassin was seething in rage but had kept his tongue. Along with contempt was a certain amount of fear, as Somerset kept the pistol pointed at his head. Though the weapon had failed to fire, one never knew when it might accidentally go off.

"Something you should understand, Miss Capel," Somerset said in reply to her puzzled expression at James' last remark. "Before we landed in Portugal in 1808, no army had fared well against Bonaparte, not even us. Over the next four years, Wellington accomplished what no one else could, and that was victory. He may have berated the officers, while cursing and flogging the men, but at the end of the day he made certain they were well-fed, paid, and above all, *alive*. The men never loved him, but they respected him because he gave them the best chance of both victory and survival. In a sense , those of us who did survive the Peninsula owe him our lives."

"An unusual way of putting it," Emma replied, her brow furrowed in thought.

"It's becoming unsafe for the Duke," Somerset continued, his face serious. "There have been numerous attempts, or rumours thereof, on his life. This is the first time one was so brazen about it."

"I wonder then, if that is why he wore his uniform tonight," James conjectured, "To draw even more attention to himself?"

"As if that's possible," Emma scoffed before casting her eyes down in the face of Somerset's disapproving glare.

He turned to James. "Help me get this bastard to the authorities, and then you can escort Miss Capel home. We'll let the frogs keep him under lock, but I am going to post at least a partial British guard on him, lest some Bonapartist sympathizers let him go. I want you there when we interrogate him in the morning."

"Yes, sir." Somerset grabbed the man by one arm, while placing the pistol into the small of his back. James took the other, and they escorted him away. Emma walked a half-step behind them. As a matter of reassurance, she reached out and took James by the hand, yet he was so keyed up over the night's events, he scarcely noticed. At the gaol, a gendarme sergeant sat behind a desk, half asleep. He immediately sprang to his feet when he heard the door open with a loud creak.

"Cet homme juste essayé d'assassiner Wellington," Somerset said to the man in French.

The sergeant then stood with his face but inches from the prisoner's and started whispering sinisterly into his ear. At least James surmised they were sinister words, for the man wet his trousers and started shaking uncontrollably as the gendarme grabbed him hard by the ear. The sergeant then noticed Emma, and his face became calm, he released the man, and placing his hand over his stomach and bowing said, "Bonsoir, Madame." He grabbed the prisoner by the ear once more and gruffly dragged him down the hallway where a gendarme opened the thick, oak door. On the other side they could hear the sounds of cajoling as other prisoners greeted their new cellmate. Upon the sergeant's return, Somerset exchanged a few words with him before turning to James and nodding.

"I want you here after first formation," Somerset ordered as soon as they were outside. "I'll stop off at the barracks and get a couple of men posted here. We've still got the Duke's personal interrogator. A rather unpleasant fellow, but if we can get this man to confess, it'll save the beastly headache that will come from sending this to trial."

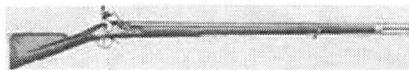

As Somerset and Webster took the would-be assassin to the nearest gendarme station, another carriage rode through the night, bearing a pair of the Duke's most hated enemies. Wellington was more right than he knew regarding Marshal Soult's animosity towards him. While the British ambassador to Paris sailed through the night in his carriage bound for his liaison with the Italian opera singer, who had also once been a mistress to Napoleon, Soult sat across from Marshal Ney in their own coach.

"A hateful predicament for our beloved France," Soult glowered as he gazed out the coach window into the Parisian night.

"In private you call it hateful, yet in public you call yourself a passionate royalist," Ney remarked.

"And what else can I do?" Soult retorted. "You know I hate the Bourbons as much as you, the difference is I can keep my feelings private. You, my friend, have treaded dangerously close to the abyss with your Bonapartist remarks of late."

"The king does not question my loyalty," Ney replied, "though his corpulent arse is too busy stuffing his bloated face to notice much of anything. I was at a dinner with him the other night. Upon receiving a dish of strawberries, he proceeded to dump them all onto his plate, without so much as offering but one to anyone else. There were twenty guests that night, including Wellington, and I swear Louis ate more than the rest of us combined. I don't know whether our English 'guest' was reviled or found it amusing."

"Probably both," Soult conjectured. "Wellington detests Louis almost as much as we do. Like us, he finds it unbecoming that a nation with so many starving and impoverished should have a morbidly fat monarch who stuffs his face from dawn till dusk and then complains about his gout."

"And doubtless, Wellington finds it amusing that we are saddled with such a disgrace for a ruler," Ney said bitterly. "But what can we do, Nicolas? What can we do to save France?"

"Right now, nothing," Soult replied. "But I will tell you this; as tired and war-weary as France was ten months ago, that fat bastard, Louis, has expended whatever goodwill may have come with his restoration. The main political factions that have dominated Paris since his return have been the royalists and republicans. However, the Bonapartists are stirring once more. I received a letter from General Foy, lamenting the state of our beloved nation."

"I thought Foy was in the pocket of the Bourbons," Ney conjectured.

"Like me, he is able to hide his true allegiances well," Soult replied with a smile. "He was wounded fourteen times in service to the emperor; if that is not a show of loyalty, what is?" Ney nodded in agreement as Soult continued. "His letter was simple enough, referring to how we so recently had been masters of Europe and were now reduced to servitude. Only God knows what our enemies will do with our lands at that farce they are calling a Congress in Vienna."

"Where are you, Napoleon?" Ney grunted as he beat his fist against the carriage door.

"Funny you should say that," Soult replied, "for those were General Foy's words as well. Do you remember the emperor's last words; the ones he spoke to the Imperial Guard?"

"*Adieu, remember me,*" Ney recalled.

"Remember, Michel," Soult said. "Remember."

Christmas was fast approaching when James returned to Brussels. He would not have long, it turned out. The British Prime Minister, Lord Liverpool, had determined that Paris was becoming too dangerous for the Duke, especially when working in a civilian capacity. At Castlereagh's request, Liverpool had decided to instead send Wellington to Vienna, to serve as a representative to the Congressional assembly.

"Does this mean you'll be leaving us again?" Emma asked as the two walked down the street through the gently falling snow.

"It does," James replied. "His grace seems determined to have me with him whenever he takes a new posting; at least for a while. I've yet to figure out exactly why. After all, I am not a member of his staff; I serve no official position within his higher organization. I'm simply a company commander within the 1st Regiment of Foot Guards, nothing more."

"Perhaps he just likes your company," Emma remarked sarcastically. She had never fully gotten over Wellington's reaction the night James saved his life from the would-be assassin.

"I might believe that, except he scarcely even says a word to me," James chuckled. "I've gotten to know some of his staff members fairly well, particularly Colonel DeLancey."

"Oh, yes," Emma said. "I know his fiancé, Magdalene, rather well. A delightful girl, she is! Well, I do hope he has more personality than his superior does."

"He is a good man," James concurred. "And so is the Duke. You may not see it in his daily appearance, but whatever his character flaws I firmly believe his grace to be a right-honourable man. No one else could have brought us victory the way he did in the Peninsula. That he came to see me in the hospital after Badajoz, and personally presented me with my captain's epaulette, says far more than any handshake or 'good day' ever will. I made a note in my journal when I came to Brussels, that if I ever have to draw my sword again, I hope that I will stand with Wellington."

"Well, I hope you never have to draw your sword again," Emma replied. She then added, "For both our sakes."

James did not seem to notice her words. "I remember my first Christmas in Portugal," he reminisced. "Daniel Roberts and I were both subalterns in the same company, and we'd just recently gotten acquainted with your cousin, Benedict. He was but a sixteen-year old ensign then."

"I was visiting my aunt and uncle during that time," Emma observed. "They were so excited when they received a letter from him, telling of his exploits since he'd arrived. I swear the letter was ten pages long! I should ask my aunt if she still has it, for as much as he talked about his friends, I would not be surprised if you're mentioned."

"Most likely," James smiled, "although I wonder just how much Benedict actually told his parents regarding his exploits in Portugal. As you alluded to, he was quite the dashing Casanova even then. We had managed to put ourselves up in a modest hotel, ran by some rather grateful locals who constantly begged us in their broken English not to leave them to the French again."

"And how exactly did my cousin celebrate the birth of our Lord?" Emma asked with a wry smile.

"All I will say is that he said given the circumstances, the Almighty would understand him finding a bit of cheer wherever he could manage," James replied evasively. "The next morning we were nearly jumped by a roving company of enemy skirmishers. It was Benedict who spotted them. Without even thinking twice, he led his men around them in a wide flanking manoeuvre, while my company was ordered to supress the enemy. He always acted quickly, but never impulsively. The irony was, his captain had elected not to lead the company that day on its patrol, instead deferring to Benedict. And though he was quick to praise the NCOs who aided him, it was your cousin who received a personal commendation from the colonel in the presence of his entire regiment. That evening we found ourselves back in the hotel for one last night, and he spent the evening reading *King John* to us from his copy of the Shakespeare folio that your aunt sent him."

"He always did like the Bard's more obscure works," Emma said with a smile. "I have his copy of the folio. It somehow made its way home, along with some of his other personal effects, after he was killed. My aunt gave it to me. She said I would appreciate it more, although I think it was because seeing it was too painful of a reminder for her."

"The lucky one," James remarked. "That is how we always thought of him. Whether it was clamouring for the ladies' affections, attempting to expand his purse with the occasional game of cards, or when battling the French, Benedict was always fearless; and he always came away unscathed. And for as young as he was, he was educated better than even the most high-born with the most expensive tutors."

"He was twenty years old," Emma stated, her voice suddenly dark. "All of his luck and education, and for what? To be blown apart attacking some ancient Moorish fortress in Spain."

James thought better than mentioning to Emma about the day before they assaulted Badajoz, when Benedict had come to him, predicting the ending of his luck and pending death. Though his wife had died soon after giving birth, that Benedict Harvest had helped secure her passage to England had perhaps saved hers and James' daughter. It was something that the captain was very much aware of, and he knew that for the rest of his days he would feel indebted to his deceased friend for Amy's life.

Chapter V: Enemies and Allies
Vienna, Austria
January 1815

Colonel Sir William Howe DeLancey

The journey east through the Austrian winter has proven insufferable, though I am now thankful that the Duke pressed us each day and only allowed us four hours rest each night. His grace finally conceded to the Prime Minister's request that he quit Paris and come to Austria to assist Castlereagh at the Congress of Vienna. It was either that or be sent to North America, to finish out a war that Wellington has made abundantly clear he does not support. The death of his brother-in-law, Sir Edward Pakenham, at the disastrous engagement in New Orleans has only darkened his grace's demeanour. That the battle took place after the war had officially ended, yet before Pakenham had received word of it, only adds to the tragedy. The Duke was quick to blame the lack of proper naval fire support, as well as Ned not being given sufficient intelligence assets. This was yet another tragic and utterly pointless loss of life.

Interestingly, one officer not with us is Fitzroy Somerset. He was tasked with remaining in Paris to continue work there; the Duchess of Wellington staying with him and his wife. It is no surprise that the Duchess remains in Paris, as the Duke finds her company utterly insufferable and does little to conceal this from anyone. That she hero-worships her husband only adds to his annoyance. Colonel Sir William Howe DeLancey is in command of our delegation of officers escorting his grace.

We arrived in Vienna late this afternoon. The rooms are very warm and a much-needed reprieve from the insufferable cold. Tomorrow the entourage of officers will accompany the Duke to his first meetings with his colleagues at the Congress. After which, I imagine we will only stay for a few formal ceremonies before returning to Brussels. I left Amy for obvious reasons, and she is staying with Miss Emma Capel, who has become as close a friend as one could hope for. I must get her a proper nanny soon, as it is rather awkward imposing on one of Emma's status to watch the daughter of a mere soldier.

I feel as if we are standing on the brink of history. Whatever the Congress of Vienna dictates will decide not just the fate of France, but of all Europe, and indeed the entire world.

Captain James Henry Webster
28 January 1815

There were at least a dozen officers accompanying the Duke to his first meeting of his colleagues, though most were lieutenant colonels and higher. James noted that he was the only company-level officer in the entire entourage. Wellington himself was in formal civilian dress, the resplendent display of redcoats the only thing adding a military flash to his presence. Greeting him was Prince Metternich, the Austrian representative to the Congress.

"Your grace," Metternich said with a short bow.

"Highness," Wellington replied, reciprocating the courtesy before bluntly asking the question that had troubled him since he first heard he was coming to Vienna. "Tell me, what has been done thus far to achieve a settlement in Europe?"

"Nothing," Metternich replied with unexpected candour, "absolutely nothing."

Upon hearing this response, James half expected Wellington to grumble or even spout off a few choice words of profanity. Instead, the Duke simply gave a curt nod and followed Metternich into one of the meeting rooms, where the door was promptly shut.

"So that's it then?" James asked as the group of officers started to disperse.

"For us it is," Colonel DeLancey answered.

Though the British system of purchasing officer commissions has infested its upper echelons with rich gentlemen of little to no military merit, Wellington had a knack for surrounding himself with as many high quality officers as possible. DeLancey was certainly one of these; having been 'mentioned in despatches' no less than four times during the Peninsular War for extreme valour and gallant conduct.

"Sir William," James said after recognizing him, "my apologies, sir. It has been a while since we last met."

"My apologies to you," DeLancey replied, "For I do not recall us having met before; though I do know who you are. Your *Forlorn Hope* badge gives you away."

"Perhaps 'met' is the wrong word," James explained. "You organized a group of us into a cohesive formation to repel a French counterattack at Ciudad Rodrigo."

"Yes, well, it was a touch smoky and confusing then," DeLancey replied with a smile. "I don't remember you, per se, but I do remember that action. I also recollect the discipline and courage shown by your men of the Foot Guards. You maintained your reputation as Britain's infantry elite that day."

"Thank you, sir," James replied. He then glanced around. "So what happens now?"

"Now," DeLancey said. "Now we go and find ourselves a spot of drink and entertainment for the time being. I fancy the Duke may call upon us once or twice more, but otherwise we should all be dismissed to go our ways in probably a week or so. At which time I hope to return to England to wed the lovely Magdalene. Are you married, Captain Webster?"

"I was," James answered, shaking his head. "I became widowed just before Badajoz."

"Pity that," the colonel replied as they walked together down the long, ornate corridor. "During war the greatest fear is that we will leave our wives widowed, rather than the opposite. I'm almost thirty-seven, and now that we finally have peace, marrying."

For the men of James' company in the Guards, drill and training continued even in their captain's absence. Lieutenant Grose, as acting commander, walked the snow-covered parade field over to where Colour Sergeant Shanahan was supervising bayonet drill. Twenty large canvas sacks, stuffed with straw, hung suspended from a short scaffold. Tied off about a foot from the top to form a rudimentary head and body shape, they looked almost like a macabre display of a gallows. The lieutenant stood off to the side, arms folded across his chest, breath forming in the air, as Shanahan paced in front of the assembled company, who were all huddling beneath their greatcoats.

"As all of you are veterans," the colour sergeant began, "there is no need for me to go through the rudimentary basics of bayonet fighting. The very fact that you are standing here in front of me says that you at least have some idea how to stick an enemy without getting yourself killed. So, a quick review." He then took his long pike and smacked the butt against the nearest straw-filled dummy. "When you stick an enemy, go for the stomach, throat, or groin. Avoid the chest, as your bayonet will often get stuck in the ribs. So I don't want to see any marks on the chest region of these targets. Are we clear?"

"Yes, colour sergeant!" the company sounded off as one.

"First twenty men, up!" Shanahan barked. "And off with those damn greatcoats! You won't be fighting with those on! Now...*bayonets ready!*"

"*Rah!*" the twenty men on line shouted, their muskets held at waist height, bayonets protruding forward.

83

"Attack!"

With shouts meant to inspire, as well as ward off the cold, the twenty infantrymen assailed the straw sacks with fury. Like they'd been drilled since first donning the uniform, they would stab their target, twist the bayonet hard, pull out, and the smash the head with the butt of their musket.

"Watch your strikes!" Shanahan shouted. "Not the damn chest, I said!" He then noticed Lieutenant Grose for the first time. "Corporal Donaldson, take over!"

"Yes, colour sergeant!" Donaldson replied. "Next twenty, up!"

Patrick made his way briskly over to his acting commander. "Lieutenant, sir," he said with a quick salute.

"A word, colour sergeant," Grose replied, signalling for Patrick to follow him. They walked until they were well out of earshot of the men training. Grose turned and faced him. "About your quarrel with Sergeant Billings..."

"With respect, sir," Patrick interrupted. "There is no quarrel between me and Sergeant Billings."

"Is that right then?" Grose replied. "Because the parts of your *discussion* that I heard last night carried across half the bloody camp!"

Patrick swallowed hard and kept his eyes straight ahead. There had been friction building between the two NCOs for months. Though they were the only sergeants in the company, the two never messed together; in fact, Patrick had made it a point of avoiding Thomas Billings. And that morning when the colour sergeant had found two men with buttons missing on their tunics, he'd pulled the sergeant off to the side and berated him to the point that the entire company could hear them.

"Is there anything I need to know?" the lieutenant asked.

That Patrick's disdain for Billings stemmed from an incident few cared to recall anymore did not dissuade his bitter feelings. Still, it was not for Lieutenant Grose to concern himself, as he would not understand the Irishman's feelings if he did make them known.

"No, sir," Patrick replied, looking the young officer in the eye.

"See to it that it stays that way, colour sergeant," Grose warned before turning and walking away. He then turned back briefly.

84

"The men look up to you, but they also look up to Sergeant Billings. Whatever your differences, resolve them!"

That evening, Patrick strolled past the line of barracks to where the non-commissioned officers of the battalion messed. If Lieutenant Grose had witnessed the contemptuous relationship that existed between the two senior NCOs, then who knew if the men in the ranks had as well?

"Sergeant Billings!" Patrick barked, causing a few heads to turn his way. As calmly as he could must, Billings set down his cup and stormed towards the door. "A word, if you please."

"I've been meaning to have a word with you for some time now, *colour sergeant*," Billings growled as the two men walked quickly down the street towards a nearby park.

The sun had already set, and the gas lamps of the city streets cast their glow, causing shadows to dance in the faint light. Tempers had been building for some time, and they were well past the gate of the park before Billings finally unleashed his pent up frustration.

"Damn it, colour sergeant, you have done nothing but ride my arse since the moment you arrived! I was the senior NCO of this company, and that position should have been mine. But since you happen to be friends with the captain..."

"You need not concern yourself with my rapport with Captain Webster," Patrick interrupted.

"Oh no?" Billings grunted. "And why not? You show up here from the damned Inniskilling regiments of all places, denying my promotion, and then you insist we've met before. Damn it all, I have no idea who the fuck you are! And as for your relationship with the captain; okay, so you were both in the Forlorn Hope. Well guess what? I was at Badajoz, too, you know! You were in the breach maybe five minutes before me."

"Badajoz is where we met," Patrick replied calmly. "As for my 'riding you', as you put it, we are short of NCOs in this company. You are the only sergeant we have, and we only have two corporals to assist. I expect you to step it up and be the standard's enforcer."

"And I have done that," Billings retorted. "I was enforcing the officers' will with the lash long before you turned up. It was after

85

Badajoz I made corporal, and after Vitoria they made me a sergeant. One does not pick up rank in the Guards without merit. So what is it then? What could I have possibly done to warrant this grudge you bear against me?"

Patrick paused for a moment and collected his thoughts. He knew he had to deal with what had been burning inside him ever since he came to the company and first put the name Thomas Billings behind that face.

"Perhaps some of my overt criticisms have been harsh and unfounded," he said slowly. "But as for what you've done to me; well, you haven't done anything. It wasn't me you harmed when we met at Badajoz. And perhaps you don't remember my face seeing as how we were both covered in soot and blood, and you were in a fit of drunken madness."

"The entire army went mad at Badajoz," Billings scoffed.

Patrick could see his face twitch slightly, perhaps at a memory. "Not everyone. If Captain Webster and I have any type of bond, it is because it was on my shoulders that he was carried from that cursed inferno."

"You?" Billings said, his eyes wide in realization. "You were the Irish corporal who saved his life."

"And it was you who chose to avenge him on the innocent."

"Now stop right there!" Billings snapped. "If you're referring to the girl, she was just some bloody frog's wife, that's all!"

"She was a human being," Patrick replied coolly. "And if it hadn't been a frog, then what? Would you have unleashed your animalistic fury on the Spanish women, like so many others?"

"Look," Billings pleaded, all trace of defiance gone from his voice, "you know what we went through in those god-awful breaches. Hell, I was beside most of what was left of the Forlorn Hope! Got shot in the head, too. I'm not using that, nor my indulgence in looted drink, as an excuse for my actions. But damn it all, I'd say half the men in this company were there, and their actions were just as deplorable as mine!"

"That may be," Patrick concurred. "But tell me this, when you saw me bearing Mister Webster across my back, who you claimed as your officer, what did you think to do?"

"You know what I did," Billings answered, turning away.

86

"I want to hear you say it," Patrick persisted. "Tell me what you did."

"I was enraged at the loss of my friends in that hellish breach," Billings explained, his voice cracking. "I'd taken a blow to the head; you can still see the scar. I had taken to drink, like so many of the others. And then I found her..."

"Who was she?"

"I don't know," Billings shrugged. "I didn't think to ask her name. She wasn't Spanish, that much I was certain; so she could only be a bloody frog. I assumed she was someone's wife, though for all I know she could have been some old officer's daughter. She didn't look a day over twenty. We were storming a small house, and I happened to be first into that tiny room in the back; a little room, no bigger than some closets."

"What was she doing?"

"Cowering in terror, I mean, what else was she expected to do? Here she was, a French woman, facing a maddened redcoat. I must have been a fearful sight to her; my eyes wild with rage, blood still streaming from that gash on my forehead." He then turned to face Patrick and in the faint light tears could be seen streaking his face. "I should have taken pity on her, poor thing. But you know what I did? I laughed. I laughed in the throes of madness as I grabbed her by the hair and pulled her from that room. I could have had me way with her right there, but I wanted to make a spectacle of it all. There was such a racket going in the front room that I dragged her outside. That's when I saw you and Mister Webster."

Billings put his hand to his forehead and fought back the tears, his breathing jagged. Patrick simply stood quietly and waited for him to continue.

"Please don't make me finish this," Billings pleaded. "I don't want to relive this anymore."

"I need you to finish," Patrick said firmly.

"And what for?" the sergeant snapped. "Are you going to give me absolution?"

"That's not up to me. Nor can I compel you to ask forgiveness of the Almighty."

"Ha!" Billings scoffed. "What use has God for me now, or any of us for that matter? God was nowhere to be found that night; not by us who suffered the fires of hell itself in the breaches, nor the frogs defending the city, who we cut down without mercy even as they tried to surrender. And most certainly, God abandoned those hapless souls we fell upon once the city was ours.

"You want to know what I did to that poor woman? Well, I'll tell you. I defiled her. I choked her, slamming the back of her head against the floor. I fucked her not with a shred of lust, only hatred. I hated her for what had happened to me friends. That she was French made her guilty. Oh, God, what did I do?" What remained of his composure left him, and Patrick allowed him a few moments.

"Did you kill her?" he asked at last.

"I did," Billings confirmed, nodding quickly and wiping his eyes. "It was my only act of compassion that damnable day. When I was done, all she would do is cry and beg me to kill her, to not let any of the others do what I had just done to her. So I did. For the briefest of moments, I took pity on the helpless wretch. I grabbed me weapon, and without thinking, put the barrel up to her head and pulled the trigger. I couldn't watch, though I was splattered with her blood and who knows what else. I never looked back at her, but quickly walked away. Some bloke from another regiment shoved me while calling me every name under the sun. It wasn't that I'd committed murder that upset him; it was that he'd wanted his turn with the woman, and I denied him his fun. I turned around and smashed him across the face with the butt of me musket. I had to flee then, because his fellows were out for my blood at that point."

"What did you do then?" Patrick asked.

"I hid behind a large hedgerow," Thomas shrugged. "Had me some looted gin still, so I got piss drunk and tried to forget the whole thing. I've prayed for death every day to atone for what I've done. But God mocks me, even now. I should have been proud when they made me a corporal after Badajoz, but all I wanted to do was vomit when Captain Roberts praised me for my 'conspicuous gallantry and impeccable conduct'. I'm too big a coward to put a pistol to my head, so every time we went into action, I would at least try and put myself in a position that gave the frogs the best opportunity to off me. As you can see, that didn't work. It was always the lads on either side of me that were cut down; and for everyone who fell and never rose again, so much more has my guilt compounded."

Though Billings' story reviled him as much as he feared it would, for some reason Patrick found he pitied the man to a certain degree. There was no doubt that he had committed a terrible atrocity; one that would have gotten him the hangman's noose had Wellington not lost control of the entire army in the madness that ensued after Badajoz fell. The irony that Thomas was instead promoted was not lost on either man.

"I thought for sure they'd get me at Vitoria," the sergeant continued. He was now voluntarily speaking, and Patrick recognized that he was releasing everything that had been pent up inside over the past two years. "But no, the Almighty mocks me still, and delays sending me to hell; for that is where I am bound. Instead, they transferred me within the battalion to this company. Both sergeants had been lost; well, to be fair, one only lost a leg. And since I had 'conducted myself with distinction' yet again, I was made *Sergeant* Thomas Billings of His Britannic Majesty's service. Men will spend twenty years in the ranks and never rise above private, and here I am, who should have been put to death as a criminal, am now a sergeant who doles out lashes and stops gin rations for those who commit the slightest infraction. Perhaps God delays sending me to hell because he knows I live it every day."

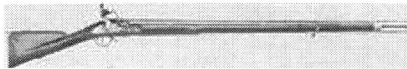

James was unaware of the strife between his two senior-ranking NCOs. He could only hope that Lieutenant Grose was conducting himself well in his absence and that any lapses in discipline amongst the ranks were handled by Colour Sergeant Shanahan. His main concern had been the behaviour of Ensign Barton, though ever since his run-in with Patrick, he'd done his best to at least publicly conduct himself appropriately.

With Europe now in the icy grip of winter, his immediate concern was hazards he would face on the roads if and when Wellington dispersed his entourage back to their respective units. The billets in Vienna were comfortable enough, although the rooms had been heated to excess, inadvertently giving Wellington, as well as numerous others of the delegation, nasty colds. James had counted himself fortunate to have avoided being infected and was quite glad to leave a ceremony in an enclosed hall, where it seemed like everyone present was coughing or sneezing.

"I was glad to be out of there!" he said, wrapping his greatcoat around him.

"I think you and I are the only two in Vienna not down with some form of illness," DeLancey concurred as he adjusted his hat and the two men walked through the snow towards their billets. Though ten years older, and markedly James' superior in both military rank and social class, the colonel had taken a liking to him.

"I swear they only keep us here for show," James noted as a gust of wind blew snow from the ground into their faces. "Anyplace we go, I hear a dozen voices talking *about* me, but no one actually talks *to* me."

"You make a good conversation piece," DeLancey said jokingly. "A man who has a Forlorn Hope badge, as well as all his limbs and as much of his sanity as one can reasonably expect, is a rare commodity. You're here to be admired, but that does not mean the delegates wish to hear anything you have to say. Personally, I'm quite content just being in the background, out of everyone's mind."

"Still, you'll be glad to have this done so you can return to England and marry."

"Yes, thank you for reminding me that I'm away from my Magdalene," DeLancey grunted. "The Duke has promised me leave soon enough. I can then wed my beloved and bring her back to Brussels with me. And what of you, any thoughts of remarrying?"

"I've not really given it much thought," the captain replied, wrapping his coat closer around him.

"Really?" DeLancey asked. "I hear that Miss Emma Capel has rather taken a liking to you."

"Respectfully, sir," James began, "between you and my subaltern, Edward Grose, one would assume she and I were betrothed. She has been a good friend to me, I admit."

"Friend," DeLancey echoed with a quiet laugh.

James wondered if his missing Emma was that obvious to those around him. He did not like admitting it, even to himself. It was an absurd feeling, yet he was stricken by the thought that his developing feelings for Emma Capel were somehow disrespectful to the memory of his wife, Amy Elaine Webster. Though he had not mentioned Emma in letters to his family, his sister, Angela, had told him repeatedly that nothing could ever diminish what had been between him and Amy. She further explained that it would be better for both him and his daughter if he were to find someone else to share his life with.

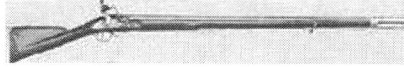

It was a dark day. Despite it being mid-afternoon, black clouds prevented the sun from casting so much as a glimmer upon the ground. Every soldier within ten miles of Brussels was gathered here, on orders from Wellington himself. The Duke may have been in Vienna, and he may not have even been in command of the army anymore, but his presence was still felt, and his orders were not to be ignored.

It was a day of punishment, and he felt the entire army needed to be reminded in the most brutal terms what it meant to commit a grievous offence within the British army. There was no lack of irony, given what Sergeant Billings had confessed to Patrick. Lieutenant Grose had briefed the NCOs regarding the offences of the men set to be punished this day. There were five, and Patrick was grateful that none were from the Guards regiments. Three were thieves, one a deserter. These were capital offences. However, with peace now at hand, the local British government had elected to show at least partial clemency. Two of the thieves had attempted to rob a coach and was each being given fifteen lashes. The other thief had been caught stealing from his fellow soldiers, and as such was sentenced to twenty lashes. The deserter was also condemned to twenty lashes. He would then be dishonourably discharged and struck from the roles of the army.

The first man was escorted to where a bundle of sergeants' pikes were lashed together and stood upright. This is what he would be bound to as the sentence was carried out. The hapless thief was stripped down to just his trousers, his hands then tied to the pikes. An adjutant unrolled a parchment and read the man's name, along with the charges.

"You were found guilty and hereby sentenced to fifteen lashes."

A corporal stood ready to dole out the punishment. In his hands was a fearsome instrument, a pole with numerous long knotted cords hanging loosely. Far more painful than a basic whip, it would bruise and tear into the flesh of its victims with such ferocity that anything past fifty lashes was paramount of a death sentence. A doctor was close at hand to ensure that the offender did not go into shock and die as a result.

Patrick had witnessed many floggings during his career, though they still turned his stomach to watch. He was one of the fortunate few to have avoided such punishments; the only time he'd faced the whip was during recruit training, and even that had only been five lashes. His face tightened up as he watched the hapless prisoner hang his head, trying to accept his fate. His arms were bound high above his head, stretching his back for the lash. He was breathing hard and sweat formed all over. The corporal slowly swung his arm back, and then brought the lash around in a hard swing. The loud slap of leather cords on flesh echoed throughout the parade field. The thief grimaced but managed to remain silent, despite the fearful scouring across his back from just the first lash. By the fifth crack, his back was covered in blood and he could stifle his screams no longer. Even the most stoic of men in the ranks cringed at the sights and sounds of the horrific punishment. The local Belgians were repulsed by such acts of barbarism, yet even Wellington staunchly defended the practice. After all, the men in this case had attempted to rob the local populace. It was for such acts that the Duke often labelled the men 'scum of the earth'. By the fifteenth lash, the poor man was losing consciousness and was quickly helped down by his companions. They helped carry him away, where they would bandage up his grievously stricken back. His sentence complete, he would convalesce for a couple days and then return to the ranks.

The remaining two thieves, as well as the deserter, were brought forward one at a time to receive their sentence. The deserter was not shown any pity once he took his final lash. Instead, he was unceremoniously dragged away and would be cast out onto the street. What happened to him afterwards, no one cared.

There was a lengthy pause following the last flogging. Every soldier's eye fell on the scaffold with the gallows erected. The fifth and final criminal would not be returning to his regiment. What was different about this case was that it involved an officer. A young subaltern had only recently come to Brussels and within two weeks was caught drunk and in the process of raping the daughter of a local magistrate. When she cried out, he'd drawn his pistol and shot her. Because the severity of this caused an incident with an allied government, only the most brutal of punishments would suffice. Despite the protestations of the man's father, he was stripped of his commission and afterwards sentenced to death by hanging.

Drums beat a slow cadence as the young man was led to the scaffold. He wore nothing but a linen shirt and trousers. There was no dignity left for him, given his horrific crime, and he wept openly. In fact, it caused such a scene that the adjutant read through the charges and sentence rather quickly and then signalled for the men tasked with carrying out the execution to do their duty. A burly sergeant placed the black hood over the young man's head, who wailed loudly.

"Can't even make a decent end of it," a soldier in the ranks muttered.

Patrick glanced out of the corner of his eye and saw that Sergeant Billings was sweating profusely. There was little doubt that he felt this should have been his fate after what happened at Badajoz.

The sergeant on the scaffold quickly secured the rope around the condemned man's neck, with the knot off to the side in order to snap it quickly. He then nodded to a corporal, who pulled the lever that released the trap door. The former officer gave one last scream as he fell through the hole, his neck breaking with a loud crack as his body twitched briefly before becoming still. The adjutant then nodded to the battalion commanders, each of whom stood stoically in front of his unit. Lieutenant Colonel Stewart pivoted in an about-face towards the men.

"Battalion!" he shouted. *"Dismissed!"*

"Bloody hell, I hope I never have to witness one of those ever again," David O'Connor said as the company marched away.

"Spend more than a day in the army, and you're bound to see this played out repeatedly," Corporal Donaldson noted. "There are those who simply cannot change what they are; brigands and thieves."

"Well, if they're looking to scare us out of ever stealing, they've done it!" David remarked, clearly unnerved by what he'd witnessed.

"Remind me to be sure to have the local whores' written consent before having my way with them," Douglas Farrow added with a trace of dark humour.

Chapter VI: A Caged Eagle
Isle of Elba
February 1815

Napoleonic Imperial Eagle

"I am emperor of my own prison," Napoleon lamented. He stood on the shore, glumly watching the waves lap at the sand. To the northeast, a mere five miles away was the shores of western Italy.

"They have caged an eagle," his mother said as she sat in a chair; a servant shading her with an umbrella. Maria Letizia Buonaparte had been but fourteen when she married Napoleon's father, Carlo Buonaparte. Napoleon was fifteen when his father died of stomach cancer, and he later changed the family's Corsican name to the French-sounding *Bonaparte*, with most of his siblings following suit. Only their mother maintained the original spelling.

"I feel like I'm suffocating," her son replied, turning to face her. His face was pale, and he'd gained a considerable amount of weight in the months of his exile. He held his palm up towards his mother, making a fist. "I once held all of Europe in my grasp. My very name echoes across time; the very age we live in bound to it. When Father died, you were left in near poverty. And then you became *Madame Mère de l'Empereur,* Madame Mother of the

95

Emperor. To have it end this way…" his voice trailed off, and he faced the sea once more.

"I don't think it has ended this way," his mother said sternly, "And neither do you." Maria stood as her son turned to face her once more. "I look at you and what this place is doing to you. You are not well, and while you grow sick, so does the rest of Europe. You, my son, saved Europe from the corruption of the monarchs and preserved the sanctity of our beloved Church."

Though a Catholic, Napoleon did not share his mother's fanatical devotion to the papacy. Like any ruler, he found religion but another weapon to be used to ensure obedience. Regrettably, this had not been enough to ensure submission from the Portuguese and Spanish, who'd instead allied themselves with Protestant Britain. Napoleon made mention of this to his mother.

"By defying you, they have defied God!" she spat in contempt. Maria's devotion to Catholicism only fuelled her hatred for the English. "It upsets me to know end that you tolerate the company of that English officer."

"Colonel Campbell is Scottish," Napoleon gently corrected.

His mother only spat once more, "A Scotsman who serves an English king. He is no more than the lapdog of mad King George and his idiot son, who now rules as regent."

"Whatever Sir Neil's country, he may still prove useful," the emperor explained. "I have taken him into my confidence, gaining his trust. In time, I will be forced to violate that trust if I am to fulfil my destiny."

As quickly as her temper had risen, Maria became serene once more. "We both know that you were not meant to die on this island."

"Explain," Napoleon said, raising an eyebrow.

His mother gave a deceitful grin. "Visit your sister," she replied. "She, too, is well-acquainted with your Scottish associate. She may have information that could prove useful to you; that is, if you ever intend for the eagle to soar amongst the heavens once more."

"What is this?" Corporal Donaldson asked as the company assembled in front of a horse-drawn cart. Colour Sergeant Shanahan grinned and threw back the tarp, revealing several wooden crates marked with ammunition cartridges, as well as additional blanks.

"Compliments of Captain Webster," he said triumphantly.

"Bloody hell," a private said. "You mean to tell us that the captain purchased us additional ammunition from his own pocket?"

"That's exactly what he's saying," Lieutenant Grose said as he walked over to the men, who immediately snapped to attention.

"Lieutenant, sir," Patrick said, snapping off a salute.

"At ease," Grose replied, returning the salute. He then addressed the men. "Captain Webster has procured a double issue of both live ammunition as well as blanks, for the company's weapons training. The Guards regiments are the elite of His Majesty's infantry, and the captain is determined that this company will be the elite of the Guards! I charge the NCOs to see to it that this ammunition is used well; for when Captain Webster returns, this company *will* be the fastest at loading, with the best marksmen in the regiment. Are we understood?"

"Sir!" the company sounded off as one.

Grose then nodded to Shanahan. "Carry on, colour sergeant."

"Yes, sir!" Patrick saluted again. He then turned to the men. *"Sergeant Billings! Corporal Donaldson! Corporal Harvey!* See to it that this ammunition is secured properly. Dry fire drills begin tomorrow."

The day was cloudy, and the ground saturated with melting snow. The only thing constant about the weather in Belgium was that it was inconstant. The day before, the skies had been sunny and it was almost warm enough to not need one's greatcoat. On this day, it was cold with a trace of wind, causing the melting snow to freeze once again. Despite this, the men of 1st Company were ecstatic at the thought of having double the ammunition with which to train. As soldiers quickly unloaded the boxes, with subsequent orders shouted by their NCOs, Grose walked over to where Ensign Barton stood with his arms folded across his chest.

"Tell me something," the young subaltern said as he fell in step with Grose, the remnants of snow and freshly-formed ice crunching under their feet. "Did the captain really purchase all that ammunition for the men?"

"Most of it," Grose replied. "I may have added a few shillings to bribe the quartermasters into offloading a box or two that no one will miss."

"A waste of your coin, if you ask me," Barton remarked, "now that the world has gone peace-crazy."

"Still upset you missed all the fighting," Grose sighed.

"That I am," Barton acknowledged. "My father is a viscount, yet as long as I have an older brother, the army is the only path for me. Promotions within a peacetime army are practically non-existent. It is only because Father purchased my commission into the Guards that I wasn't immediately put on half-pay."

"An officer should count himself lucky that he has the option of half-pay," Grose observed. "He still draws a wage from the king. When peace comes and regiments disband, the men in the ranks often leave with nothing but the clothes on their backs."

"Such is their lot in life," Barton grunted. He then noted Grose's rebuking glare. "Oh come off it, Edward! 'Beggars and scum' is how even Wellington refers to the rankers, and yet you and the captain seem overly fond of them. Giving them a haircut, a shave, and dressing them in fancy uniforms does not change the fact that most of them are but brigands and thieves."

"That they may be," Grose acknowledged. "But they are still ours; and they do not thieve from us or from each other. Regardless of where they came from, look at what they have accomplished. Wellington took the absolute dregs of mankind and turned them into the most powerful fighting force in the world."

"And now that the fighting's over?" Barton persisted. "Most will return to the dregs from which they came, once they can no longer wear the King's uniform."

"Dammit, William, what's your point?" Grose said, exasperated.

"Nothing at all," Barton said smugly, "Except that I find your rapport with the rankers a bit troubling. You speak to the colour sergeant almost like he's an equal. He's not only a ranker, he's a damned Irishman!"

"And for all that," Edward retorted, "I would say Colour Sergeant Shanahan is as well educated as you or I. He also conducts himself as more of a gentleman than you do."

"I take that as an insult, sir!"

"Then you are too easily insulted," Grose retorted. "Whatever bad feelings you may still have towards our colour sergeant are not my concern. He may not have been born into a place that allowed him to be raised as a gentleman, but Patrick Shanahan has used his time in the army wisely. I'll grant you that many in the ranks spend their free time gambling, drinking, and whoring, but not him. Oh, he may appreciate a good snort like any Irishman, but much of what free time he's had has been spent reading and educating himself. You may be surprised to find just how many of the men can read. Spend enough time with them and you will find that there are those who seek to better themselves so that they don't have to go back to the dregs from which they came. Our men in the Guards are the fortunate ones. They draw a slightly larger wage, and have little fear of ever being disbanded."

"I didn't exactly have a lot of time to spend before this blasted *peace* took us," Barton grumbled.

Grose let out a sigh. "How old are you, William? Twenty?"

"Seventeen," Barton corrected.

"Then I'd say you've got plenty of time," Grose remarked. "Peace is a fickle thing. Just don't think you need to be a colonel by the time you're twenty-five; most who do become overzealous wind up dead. Mankind has proven itself adept at trying to destroy itself at least once a generation. And when that time comes again, count yourself fortunate to have a captain who sees fit to provide the men with the resources necessary to improve their skills beyond that expected of even the Guards Regiments."

As they continued to walk in silence, Grose saw Barton's brow furrowed in contemplation and hoped that at least some of what he said sank in to the young man. He'd certainly made progress since the previous fall; at least now he was no longer openly berating the enlisted men or threatening NCOs with flogging without justification.

In truth, it was hard to overcome the prejudices the aristocratic officer corps felt towards the men in the ranks. It frustrated Edward when those prejudices and stereotypes played true. It pained him every time a soldier was flogged, or worse, hung for stealing, pillaging, or committing of other gross offences upon the people they were trying to liberate. Officers like he and Captain Webster would speak up for the men, only to have the prejudices of their peers prove well-founded on occasion.

The class difference alone was vast; far greater than that of any other modern army in the world. The French in particular were baffled by the deliberate separation between officers and enlisted in the British Army. Many of Napoleon's greatest generals had once been mere privates in the ranks, yet the very idea of a ranker even becoming an officer was a rare thing for the British. Years of continuous war, the raising of new regiments, and excessive casualties amongst the officers had made the occasional commissioning of NCOs a necessity. Yet even a pragmatist like Wellington abhorred the practice.

It was as the two men walked by a company from the 95th Rifles that they noted such an officer. The green-jacketed commander had traces of grey in his hair and looked to be at least forty.

"Captain, sir," Grose said, saluting as the riflemen marched past them.

"And there you have it," Barton grunted as soon as they were out of earshot, "one who is only a gentleman because he was given the King's commission."

Pauline Bonaparte, Princess Borghese

"Brother!" Pauline said excitedly, as Napoleon was ushered into the parlour. She rose quickly and kissed him on the cheek, bringing a brief smile to his beleaguered face. She then apprised him disapprovingly. "You are not looking well; you've grown fat, and your complexion looks like it never sees the sun! Clearly this place does not agree with you."

"Does it agree with you?" Napoleon asked, bringing a laugh from his sister.

Pauline Bonaparte, Princess Borghese, was perhaps the shrewdest of the emperor's numerous siblings. She had a way of assimilating into any environment or situation. That her husband was an imbecile and they were now estranged, with him living with a mistress, left her unfazed.

"You know me," she said with a wave. "I thrive anywhere I choose to. But you, dear brother, you need far more than emperorship of a tiny island with its twelve-thousand inhabitants. It was not long ago that you ruled an empire so vast that you were able to make your brothers kings!"

Napoleon scowled at this last observation. It was not that he'd ruled an enormous empire that bothered him; it was that the ineptitude of his brothers cost him so much of it.

"My brothers lost me my empire," he glowered. Jerome had been made King of Westphalia, only to lose it in an invasion by the Prussian and Russian armies. And Joseph's tenure as King of Spain was an unmitigated disaster. It was Joseph who bore the brunt of Napoleon's animosity, which he expressed to his sister.

"I can perhaps forgive Jerome for losing Westphalia," he said, "but Joseph was King of Spain, with an army of half a million men! He let the damned English expel him with an army one-tenth the size of his."

For all his genius, Napoleon was unable to comprehend that it had been his own policy of compelling his armies to forage off the populace that had turned his former allies in Catholic Spain against him. While most of Joseph Bonaparte's army was pinned down in an attempt to supress rebellions in every corner of Spain, the British expeditionary force under Wellington maintained a strong logistics line, going all the way back to England. They kept themselves supplied, with a vigorously-enforced policy that anything acquired from the locals was to be purchased, rather than simply taken. Such had driven the Spanish to forget the religious hostilities that existed between themselves and the protestant English.

"It is time for you to take back what is yours," Pauline said.

It inspired the former Emperor of France that in his lowest moments, his sister, who'd he'd been the least closest to, was the only one that was there for him. His other brothers and sisters, who all owed their titles and nobilities to him, were nowhere to be found when the powers of Europe converged to overthrow him.

"I have information that may or may not prove useful to you," she continued with a glint in her eye.

Her brother stood grim-faced and silent.

"Our beloved Scotsman, Colonel Campbell, has not been well lately."

"Yes, I know," Napoleon interrupted with a bored sigh. "He's got an ear infection or something of the sort. I told him to go see a doctor. What of it?"

"But not just any doctor," Pauline replied, her face twisting into a devious grin. "I happen to know that the dear colonel has a personal physician in Florence; not to mention a favourite mistress."

"I shudder to think how you find your information when my own sources have told me none of this."

Though his words had a trace of rebuke in them, the faintest hint of a smile gave Pauline all the reassurance she needed.

"Trust me on this, brother," she said soothingly before handing him a sealed envelope. "Here is the information about the physician. Once we compel Sir Neil to take a short convalescent holiday to Florence, you will be free to return to France."

"The English have become complacent," Napoleon noted. "There is not as much as a single warship patrolling the waters around Elba. If there were, I would have no chance of escape at all. I must speak with Drouot and begin planning my return."

Pauline smiled broadly as she saw a trace of her brother's former passion returning. Though troubled by his health, her hope was that a return to France and to glory would restore not just Napoleon, but all of Europe.

Chapter VII: The Eagle Escapes
Portoferraio, Isle of Elba
25 February 1815

The Bourbon King, Louis XVIII

Napoleon spent many hours walking the shoreline, especially when he needed to be certain that conversations with friends and associates were kept private. Though three generals had been permitted to accompany him to Elba, he usually only spoke to them one at a time, as private discussions with all four men would raise suspicion from even the most casual observer. Like Napoleon, Antoine Drouot was an artillery officer of great renown. He had even served as a commander of marines during the disastrous Battle of Trafalgar, nine years before. He'd been a soldier most of his life and had been in constant wartime service since 1793. So great was his devotion to his emperor, that upon Napoleon's exile, Drouot resigned his commission, renounced his French citizenship, and insisted on coming to Elba as a private citizen. It had only been with Napoleon's personal request that he'd agreed to take the position as governor. As such, their constant meetings drew little unwanted attention.

"If Campbell leaves for Florence," Napoleon said quietly, pacing along the beach with his hands clasped behind his back, "He will take with him the only British warship in the region."

"It is indeed baffling," Drouot said as he walked beside the emperor. "But a year ago all of Europe lived in terror of your name, and now they cannot spare even one additional warship to patrol these waters."

"And yet they will leave me with a small flotilla of ships of my own," Napoleon said with a dark chuckle.

"The *Inconstant* is the largest," Drouot observed. "Yet it is still but a small brigantine of sixteen guns."

"True, but then I do not intend to fight at sea."

That afternoon, Napoleon sought out the Scottish colonel. He found him sitting on the patio of his private quarters, a cup of tea in one hand, the other against the side of his head. Campbell was constantly popping his jaw, hoping to relieve the tension in his ear.

"My dear colonel," the emperor said, handing his hat to a servant, "it is my turn, it seems, to inquire as to the state of your health."

"I confess, I've been better, sire," Campbell replied. He took a drink from his steaming tea.

Napoleon took the pot from the table and sniffed it. "You may want something stronger than tea," he started to say before grinning. "Ah, I see you have more than just Indian leaves in this pot." "Indian leaves and Spanish rum," Campbell replied. "It is the only thing that seems to help. Or rather, it makes me not care about the incessant pain behind my eardrum. I swear, the doctors here are useless!"

"Then perhaps I can assist you," the emperor said. He sighed and handed the envelope his sister had given him to the colonel. "I was reluctant to share this, as one may think I have unstated motives, but please rest assured that my concern is for your health, as much as yours has been for mine."

"What's this then?" the Scotsman asked, opening the envelope.

105

"Information about a doctor," Napoleon explained, "one Federico Strozzi of Florence. I can personally vouch that he is able to cure any ear or sinus issues one can acquire."

"Hmm," Campbell thought aloud. "Of course it will mean having to leave the isle for a time."

"It's a day or two to reach Livorno," Napoleon observed, "another by fast coach to reach Florence. Why, you could be back in a week." The emperor ceased in his persistence, not wishing to seem overly anxious for Campbell to leave. If his sister was right, and Campbell did in fact have a favourite mistress in Florence, then he would make up his own mind soon enough.

"I thank you for your kindness, sire," Campbell replied. He swallowed before continuing. "I wasn't intending to share this with you, but I feel I must. There are those within the European delegations who are not satisfied with your removal to this island. They would rather see you relocated to someplace more…remote."

"How remote?" Napoleon asked with a raised eyebrow.

"There is an island within our domains called Saint Helena," Campbell explained. "It will not surprise me if you've never heard of it. It is but ten miles from end-to-end, located in the South Atlantic, halfway between Africa and South America. It is about as remote a place as one can imagine."

"And they wish to send me there?" the emperor asked. "Why? Am I still a threat to them?"

"I had not planned on sharing this information with you," Campbell said. "However, nothing in the dispatch from Castlereagh told me not to, and he is always very specific about what I should and should not say to you. By no means has this been decided, and the delegations may reckon that the logistical difficulties will make it too much bother. What is troubling, though, is that the Duke of Wellington has not dismissed the possibility. Whatever the continental powers may think of the English, and specifically the Prince Regent, they respect the Duke or perhaps they fear him. A pity the two of you have never met, for his force of personality is matched in this world only by yours and beyond this world by Almighty God alone. However, we should note that just because his grace has not completely dismissed this possible course of action does not mean that it is one he favours. I will let Castlereagh know my feelings about the subject, and if I can convince him that there is nothing to be gained by having you removed to Saint Helena, then I am certain he will convince Wellington of the same."

"You do me much kindness, dear colonel," Napoleon said after a brief pause. "I will draft my own letters as well, one to Lord Castlereagh, and the other to the Duke of Wellington. If you should decide to convalesce in Florence for a few days, I will have these prepared for your review by the time you return. And now, I have some other matters to attend to. Good day, colonel."

"He will go," Napoleon told Drouot that evening. The two men met in the emperor's private study after dinner. With Talleyrand's spies still roaming about, there was no sense in hiding the fact that the Governor of Elba was having dinner with the emperor. It was afterwards, when all the servants had left them alone, that the two men could speak candidly.

"Once he does, we will be pressed for time," Drouot pointed out. "If we anticipate he will be gone a week, then we must not allow ourselves one day more. The *Inconstant* is ready to sail just as soon as you give the word."

"I want her painted to look like an English vessel," the emperor directed as he took a drink of claret. The room was warm, with the soft glow of two candelabras. The study was small, with just enough room for two oversized chairs, a small table, with book shelves lining the walls. The candelabras cast their light from a pair of end tables, as all else was dark.

"A sound idea," Drouot concurred. "From a distance one will never suspect what she carries. I recommend we keep the flotilla as small as possible. All of our ships combined will not stand up to a single ship-of-the-line, and what we need is relative stealth and speed."

"Only enough ships to carry our baggage, as well as the thousand men from my Imperial Guard," the emperor added. "I long for that day when I can tell them that we are going home."

For Wellington, having to serve as the British representative to the Congress of Vienna was a tedious ordeal. Its intent was essentially to redraw the entire map of Europe, redistributing the lands conquered by the French Empire. Rather than having a central chamber for all the delegates, most of the negotiating was done behind closed doors in meetings with the main European powers; Britain, Austria, Russia, and to a lesser extent, Prussia. There were also French delegates, representing the restored Bourbon monarchy. Lord Talleyrand, who had at one time been one of Bonaparte's political supporters, only to betray him in favour of restoring the Bourbon monarchy, was appointed to head the French delegation by King Louis. There were at least a further dozen delegations, representing various nations with a stake in the outcome of the congress. However, they were relegated to little more than observers while the main powers determined their fate.

Though Castlereagh had served as the representative of the Prince Regent, he had since deferred to the Duke of Wellington and was returning to England. Richard Le Poer Trench, Earl of Clancarty, was acting as the Duke's second. What surprised many was that despite their recently conflict, to say nothing of Wellington's ill-concealed contempt for Talleyrand, the Duke was speaking very openly in favour of allowing France to maintain its status as a regional power.

Vienna was a beautiful city, and Captain James Webster was determined to see as much of it as he could. There was always ample time available. Each morning, he, DeLancey, and the other officers would accompany the Duke to congress. DeLancey kept a schedule of all official appointments they had to attend, though even at these there was very little for the soldiers to actually do. James found himself standing awkwardly in a corner most of the time. He spoke only passable French, a few words of German, and no Russian. He was there simply to act as a visual aid, to add to Wellington's already overwhelming aura. There were other soldiers from various nations in attendance, to include the French. Whether these were true royalists or simply Bonaparte's former soldiers who changed sides with the return of King Louis, one could never tell. Like their English counterparts, they were there simply for show, nothing more.

One thing James did appreciate was the Vienna theatre. He'd attended the opera twice, appreciating the music and pomp of the show, even though he could not understand a word that was sung. He'd even gone to see an Austrian rendition of Shakespeare's *Hamlet*. Although the words had been translated into Germanic, he was familiar enough with the story to enjoy the performance.

James was saddened the day Sir William Howe DeLancey announced he would be returning soon to England. The two had become friends, and DeLancey was also a very close confidant of Wellington. It was through him that James was kept abreast of the Duke's disposition. James stated as much one evening as the two officers messed with their companions.

"If it is of any consolation," DeLancey said, "you will be accompanying me as far as Brussels. There is little left for us to accomplish in Vienna, so it is time you returned to your regiment. I will be going on a long-awaited leave, where I will finally be wed to my darling Magdalene."

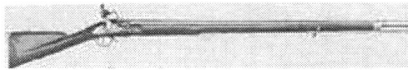

There was no turning back. As the salty sea sprayed him in the face, Napoleon took a deep breath and for a moment felt rejuvenated. His mother and sister had been right.

He was not meant to die on that cursed island! For the first time in many months, his soul was filled with hope. He would reclaim his place as Emperor of the French, restore the dignity of the republic, and damn all who would attempt to stop him from taking France to her rightful destiny! He would free her once more from the wretched clutches of that fat despot, Louis, and the Bourbons. He feared greatly for his people, and wondered just how badly they were faring under their new masters. To have foreign troops walking the streets of Paris, with a corpulent, feeble king on the throne was an insufferable outrage. In his heart, Napoleon knew it was his destiny to restore honour and dignity to France once more.

A stabbing pain in the abdomen caused him to double over against the rail. Several men rushed towards him, but the emperor quickly waved them off. He slumped to the deck, his back resting against the rail. Despite it being late February and the continuous spray of sea water against him, he suddenly felt hot and flushed. He removed his bicorn hat and tossed it across the desk, where a grenadier quickly snatched it up.

"Back to your duties!" Bertrand shouted to the assembled group of men. He then sat down next to the emperor, who looked over at him and swallowed.

"I curse my failing body," Napoleon said over the sound of the ship's prow surging through the waves. "My mind and my will are stronger than ever, yet they are trapped in this prison of a sickly mortal figure."

"It is your mind that won your greatest battles," Bertrand assured him, "And your will that led France to follow you to the ends of the earth. And she will again, I promise you."

"I am old," the emperor lamented. "I am not even forty-six years of age, yet my body is that of an old man. Once we drive the Bourbons out, I think my body and mind would be better suited to a type of constitutional monarchy; that amalgamation between a republic and a kingship. I know it would certainly be in the best interests of my son, when the time comes for him to take my place as Emperor of the French."

"Ship approaching!" a voice shouted, alerting Napoleon, as well as the *Inconstant's* captain, a man named Chautard.

"Do you recognize its sails?" Bertrand asked.

"Yes," Chautard said. "It's the *Zephyr*, under Captain Andrieux."

"I've met Andrieux," Napoleon said, "And I know *Zephyr* well enough. She's faster and has us significantly outgunned."

"We should still be ready to fight if needed," Chautard recommended as he joined the emperor and Bertrand.

Drouot was already alerting the members of the Imperial Guard who were on board.

Napoleon gave a nod of consent. "Have the men make ready, but I want all grenadiers to remove their bearskin hats and lie flat on the deck, under cover. As we cannot outrun them, we will not attempt to. Nor will we provoke them into a fight if we can avoid it."

"Sire, you, too, must seek cover," Bertrand said, standing and offering Napoleon his hand.

"I'm too tired to get up," the emperor confessed with a tired stare. "Hand me your frock coat."

Bertrand did as ordered, and Napoleon curled up on the deck beneath the railing. The truth was he wanted to hear what words may exchange between the two ships, if possible. Though he lay at the prow and Captain Chautard stood at the portside, Napoleon reckoned he'd still be able to hear any exchanges between the two captains. It was a maddening wait, and all the emperor could hear was the crashing of the ship through seas, which felt surprisingly rough, given how calm the winds were. At length the *Zephyr* mercifully closed with *Inconstant*. Napoleon had only met Captain Andrieux a pair of times, yet he recognized his voice over the splashing of the waves.

"How is the great man?" The voice was full of sympathy, rather than scorn. Andrieux had recognized *Inconstant*, despite their attempts to paint her to look like a British vessel. Andrieux knew the ship, and that it was the largest of Napoleon's small navy. There could be only one reason for it to be this far from Elba.

"Extraordinarily well!" Chautard replied.

"Where is your vessel bound?" Andrieux asked.

"Genoa," Chautard lied.

"Then fair seas to you!" Andrieux shouted, removing his hat and bowing at the waist.

Chautard returned the gesture and in just a few minutes the two ships passed beyond each other. Chautard was pale-faced when he walked over to the prow. Napoleon threw off Bertrand's frock coat and broke into a fit of laughter. "Well played, my dear fellow, well played!"

"I confess, sire, I was at my wits end when he asked about you," Chautard said, taking a handkerchief from his pocket and furiously wiping it across his brow. He then meandered off as Bertrand knelt next to the emperor.

"It would seem King Louis does not hold the absolute loyalty of all his captains," he surmised.

"I dare say not," Napoleon agreed. "Remind me when we get to Paris to make Andrieux an admiral."

Despite the glowing assurance that Napoleon was completely forgotten in Europe, Sir Neil Campbell could feel the tension in the air the moment he landed in Italy. There was also an endless barrage of self-criticism and doubt about his taking a leave of absence, no matter how brief. He did confess to himself that the doctor Napoleon had recommended in Florence proved to be as able as he'd stated he was. The Scotsman's ear infection had substantially subsided before he even returned to the sea. He was so full of anxiety that he only allowed himself a single night with his mistress, promising to return again once he was certain nothing had happened with his charge.

With all haste, he returned to port and had the ship make at once for Elba. The voyage was uneventful; the only thing of note had been a trio of ships spotted moving to the northwest. They had been spotted from a great distance, with the largest appearing to be an English brig. The crew surmised that she was escorting a pair of smaller vessels to protect them from roving pirates. As this was not uncommon practice, nothing else was said.

"Blast it all!" Campbell grumbled the next morning as he paced back and forth across the bow of his ship, *Partridge*. The seas were serenely calm and there was not a wind to be had. The Isle of Elba was in sight, but even with a steady wind they were still at least an hour away.

"We'll simply have to wait for the wind to return," the petty officer on the prow said to the impatient colonel.

"No," Campbell said, shaking his head. The thought of the three ships spotted moving northwest the day before grated on him, but he could not fathom why. "Something is not right. I can feel it." He slammed his palm on the railing. "That does it; get me a rowboat, at once!"

For Colonel Sir Neil Campbell, there was no sense of relief. He'd been personally invited by Napoleon to remain on Elba with him, even though he was acting as Castlereagh's agent. He shuddered to think what his superior would do if Campbell's worst fears proved true. He hoped against all hope that when he docked, he would find Napoleon Bonaparte still on the island, docile as ever. He would not rest easy until he saw the emperor's face once more.

"Come on, faster damn it!" he barked at the hapless rowers. It was approaching 7:00 in the evening, and night came quickly this time of year. The colonel stood as the boat approached the dock, and without waiting for it to be roped off, he leapt onto the gently surging boat ramp, practically sprinting up to the shore.

Sitting serenely on a chair in the grass was the emperor's mother. She was reading a book, her face creased in a soft smile.

"Where is he?" Campbell snapped, for a moment forgetting all manner of decorum.

Maria seemed to not notice. She was soon joined by her daughter, Pauline, who placed a hand reassuringly on her mother's shoulder. Campbell did not notice the envelope the woman held.

"My dear colonel," Maria replied without looking up from her book, "Did you really think an eagle could be contained on a tiny kingdom such as this? My son was not meant to die on this island. Surely you knew this, too."

"I will see him locked away on an even smaller island," Campbell growled.

Pauline then walked up to him and handed him the sealed envelope. "My brother asked me to give this to you," she explained. "Surely you'll understand." Campbell scowled, but took the time to tear open the envelope and read the enclosed letter:

My dear colonel,

It was time for me to leave the confines of this island and secure my destiny, as well as that of France. Please know that I do not wish for another war between our glorious nations. I want peace for both the French and the English. There is no reason why our nations cannot live together in harmony, and I will petition the Prince Regent personally regarding this.

I ask for your forgiveness in my deceiving you. It was necessary for me, in order that I may escape from the confines of my island prison. I further could not risk my enemies removing me to an even more hateful prison on Saint Helena. Please know that I will always cherish your friendship, and know that I will always remember you fondly and will miss your company.

I have the honour to be your humble servant, etc.

Napoleon Bonaparte

113

Campbell attempted to regain his gentlemanly composure, removed his hat, and bowed to the ladies. He then turned about and rushed back to the row boat, which had just been tied off.

"Cast off!"

"Is it really Napoleon's destiny to return as Emperor of the French?" Pauline asked as they watched the rowboat splashing in the water, its crew working their oars frantically.

"I cannot say, my child," Maria answered. "What I do know is that he was not meant to die on this island. What becomes of him now is in God's hands."

Genoa

ITALY

Cap Noli

Partridge

Antibes   Inconstant

Golfe Juan

Fleur de Lys   Livorno

Inconstant

Ligurian   Sea

Zephyr

Elba

Piombino

Portoferraio

Corsica

Sardinia

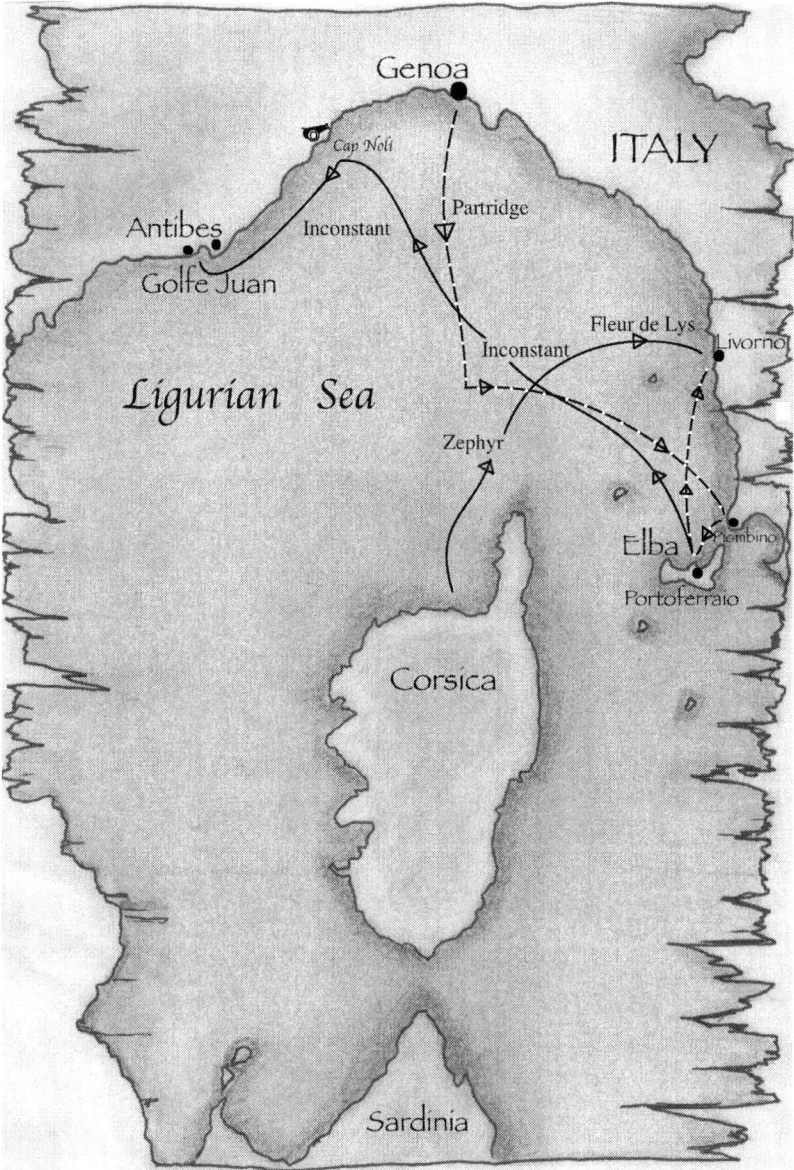

Napoleon's escape from Elba. *Inconstant* would narrowly avoid being recognized by *Partridge*.

Chapter VIII: The Emperor's Return
Antibes, France
1 March 1815

Napoleon's Return

Napoleon knew he had a substantial head start on any warships that would be sent to pursue him. Yet with *Partridge* being the only known hostile vessel, the emperor allowed himself to relax and feel confident once more. Chautard's bold-faced lie to Andrieux would only add to poor Colonel Campbell's confusion. The captain of *Zephyr* could, in good faith, tell *Partridge* where he'd been told their ship was headed without being accused of telling a falsehood. Of course Captain Andrieux had to know they were not, in fact, headed for Genoa, just as it could be surmised that he knew Napoleon Bonaparte had fled from Elba aboard *Inconstant*. There had been one more hazard as the flotilla passed Cape Noli. A British rocket battery was set to test fire over the water, yet they ceased in their drill and unwittingly allowed their archenemy to pass within their field of fire.

It was now the 1st of March and at last the small group of ships weighed anchor off the coast near the town of Antibes. There was much to accomplish before the emperor could even set foot on French soil once more. A pair of rowboats carrying a score of grenadiers made their way through the surf. Leading them was an army captain named Lamouret. He was a younger officer, unable to grow the customary bushy moustache seen on many of the Imperial Guard, yet his loyalty to the emperor was no less fierce than the most battle-hardened grenadier.

Yeomen leapt over the side and dragged the rowboats the remaining few meters until they washed up on the shore. Grenadiers jumped from the boat and formed up in a line facing the lone figure that stood to greet them. As the flotilla could be spotted miles out, the local magistrate had wasted no time in dispatching his customs agent to intercept the men. The man held a sheaf of forms and looked over the top of his glasses at the captain who made his way slowly towards him. The agent seemed to not even notice the armed soldiers accompanying the officer.

"Customs and health forms!" the agent said, shoving the forms into Lamouret's face. "No persons or cargo are permitted to come ashore until a thorough health inspection is made and proper permits issued."

"Damn it all, man," Lamouret retorted. "I'll have you know it's the emperor who's aboard that ship. Do you not recognize it?"

The agent held his spectacles up close to his eyes and squinted. "Almost looks like an English vessel."

"Look closer and you will recognize her as the *Inconstant*," the captain said with a twisted grin. "Your emperor has returned, and he can issue you the permits himself."

It was evening when Napoleon finally made his way to shore. He was rapt with anticipation but also feeling exhausted over the ordeal of the last few days. The sun was going down in the west, and he wrapped his great coat around him. As the boat rocked through the surf, he could see the carts of his paymaster and other logistics that had gone ashore before him being assembled for the march.

The emperor was disturbed by reports that reached him from the advance guard. A score of grenadiers had been welcomed into the fort at Antibes, only to have the gates slammed behind them and subsequently be taken prisoner. Captain Lamouret had escaped capture by leaping over the wall but suffered a broken leg as a consequence.

Though the sun was setting, there was still plenty of light to see by as the boat reached the shore. A dozen grenadiers, up to their waist in the rolling tide, held a plank for the emperor to walk down onto the beach. Napoleon was secretly afraid he might lose his balance and embarrass himself by falling into the surf, but he made it down the ramp in a few quick strides and then took a deep breath as he stood on the shores of France once more. He removed his hat and knelt down, closing his eyes and grabbing a handful of sand in his fist. He took a deep breath through his nose as traces of lapping waters rolled up just past where he knelt. He then raised the clenched fist-full of dirt to his lips and kissed it.

"Welcome home, sire," Drouot said, standing at the head of several dozen soldiers, who formed a cordon for the emperor to walk through.

"Vive l'empereur!" a Guards captain shouted, which was then echoed by the men.

"We've found a small cottage for you to use, sire," Bertrand said, joining Napoleon and Drouot as they walked up the beach to the dirt path that led towards Antibes. "It's not much, but it should do for the night."

"Good," Napoleon replied as a soldier helped him to his feet. "And tomorrow we will march on the fort!"

"Yes," Drouot concurred. "Twenty of our men were taken prisoner, but at least no shots were fired."

"Once they see their emperor has returned, that will beat some sense into the garrison," Napoleon emphasized.

A short ways up the path, they came to the abandoned cottage next to a grove of olive trees. A pair of grenadiers stood guard; one opened the door for the emperor.

Napoleon stepped inside and immediately turned up his nose. "This won't do at all," he grunted. "It is horribly smoky in there, and my lungs have been tormented enough as it is."

"What would you have us do, sire?" Drouot asked.

118

Napoleon pointed to the olive grove. "Have my bed and camp chair set up there. I'll sleep my first night back in France under the stars." His equilibrium was still unsettled after several days at sea, and Napoleon took a few minutes to just sit on his bed after removing his boots. He marvelled for a moment at the feel of the ground under his feet. He was in part elated to have escaped the hated confines of Elba, yet he was also overwhelmed at the astronomical task ahead of him. Reclaiming France would be easy, keeping the rest of Europe from attempting to depose him again would be the challenge. Above all, he felt exhausted, though he figured it was nothing a few hours' sleep couldn't rectify.

I'm tired of fighting, he thought to himself. He then said a rare prayer, *Dear God, let me fulfil my destiny to restore dignity to France. I crave peace and do not wish to fight the rest of the world any longer. Just do not let them take France from me again.*

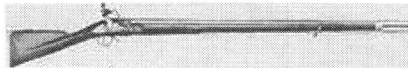

Riders reached Paris several days after Napoleon's landing at Antibes. At the royal palace, Marshal Ney was secretly ecstatic to hear the news, though he kept his demeanour stoic. He wore his most resplendent uniform when the king summoned him to the palace. One of the ministers escorted the marshal into the audience chamber, where Louis sat atop his throne, reading the despatch from Antibes.

Louis XVIII had lived in exile for two decades, and despite being internationally recognized as the rightful King of France, he had only just recently come to occupy the throne. Ney despised Louis immensely. The sight of an enfeebled, morbidly obese king did little to inspire a nation where starvation and poverty ran rampant after decades of war. The complete lack of inspirational leadership from their king was leading to the Bonapartist political faction rearing its head once more. Louis was very much aware of this, and so it was with little surprise that he summoned Marshal Ney to deal with the Napoleon situation for good.

"You know why I summoned you, Michel," Louis said, not looking up from his reading. Though it was perfectly within the king's right to address Ney by his given name, he despised Louis taking that liberty with him.

"Yes, sire," Ney replied. He stood rigid, eyes staring straight ahead, lest he have to look upon the monarch he detested so much.

"Please, stand easy, marshal," the king said, waving him to come forward. "I dispatched six thousand men to intercept Bonaparte before he causes further trouble. However, as you are a man the people love, and one who was at one time close to the usurper, I think it best that you personally bring him back to us."

"Of course, sire." Ney's stomach turned, but he kept his composure. Louis set the despatch down and looked up at the marshal.

"I know you love this man," he said, causing Ney to swallow hard. "No need to deny it, it's alright. You followed him for many years, so I understand. You love Bonaparte, but I know you love your country more."

"Yes, sire," the marshal replied. That at least was not a lie. Ney was fiercely devoted to Napoleon, but his first love was for France.

"Then you must do your duty," the king emphasized. "Do what is best for France, and bring the usurper to me."

"I will bring him in an iron cage!" Ney answered sharply.

"Well, there's no need for that," Louis replied with a bored sigh. "There should be little for you to do, as the men I've already sent should apprehend Bonaparte soon enough or kill him if he resists. Either case suits me just fine." The king was now reading a London newspaper and no longer paying any attention to Ney.

The marshal awkwardly bowed and quickly left the room; his boot heels echoing on the marble flooring.

"What will you do?" Nicolas Soult asked as he joined his fellow marshal. The two men would ride together as far as the edge of Paris. From there, Ney would join with a marching column that was heading south.

"These men, as well as those already on the move," Ney explained, "they go to join the emperor, not arrest him. That fat buffoon, Louis, has grossly underestimated the army's love for their emperor. He also expended whatever goodwill he may have had within the first month of his return. Gorging himself, providing no leadership to the people, while millions starve, that is not what

France abandoned Napoleon for. I tell you this, Nicolas, I turned my back on the emperor once, it will not happen again!"

Nine days had passed since Napoleon's escape from Elba, and on 7 March 1815, the 5th Regiment moved to intercept the emperor and his thousand men. Soldiers formed battle lines along the gentle slope on either side of the road. Several companies were deployed forward; their task to capture or kill Napoleon, should he resist.

"Only a matter of time before Louis got word of your return, sire," Drouot said as he rode next to Napoleon, who only chuckled quietly.

"I know these men," he said.

"I will have the Imperial Guard form a cordon to protect you, sire," Bertrand remarked.

"You will do no such thing," the emperor replied. "I will not risk French blood being spilled this day with the exception of my own. Wait here."

He then dismounted his horse and walked slowly towards the waiting line of soldiers. A young captain stood between the two centre companies. He looked terribly nervous, sweat dripping from his brow. The soldiers on either side all bore expressions of uncertainty as Napoleon continued his slow walk towards them, hands clasped behind his back, his expression one of serene resignation no matter what the fates decided this day. It was that resolve that unnerved the men who now stood in his way. The captain took a step back and drew his sword.

"Faire des prêts!" he shouted. Soldiers closed their eyes and grimaced as they un-shouldered their muskets. *"Présent!"*

Napoleon continued to advance unabated and without regard to the hundred or so weapons now pointed at his heart. When he was within a dozen paces, he stopped and opened his great coat.

"If you wish to kill your emperor," he said calmly, "here I am."

"Feu!" the captain shouted, ordering the men to fire. It was a word he would regret the rest of his life. No one on the line flinched, not a trigger was squeezed, and no flint hammers fell.

A deafening silence followed as no one dared even move. Finally, an older private shouldered his weapon and stepped forward, shouting, *"Vive l'empereur!"* This was followed by an immediate chorus of the same shout from the men, both on the line, as well as every soldier on the slope. Ovations erupted as the men swarmed around the emperor, tears of joy streaming down many faces.

One man did not share in the soldiers' celebrations. The captain who'd given the order for the men to fire stepped slowly away from the mob. His face was white, and the tears he now shed were of shame, rather than joy. No one noticed as he stared into his reflection in the blade of his sword, before throwing it into the dirt. He then removed and threw his shako before slumping onto a large rock, where he placed his head in his hands and wept.

It was after a few moments that the young officer sensed someone standing over him. He looked up, and through his tears saw it was the emperor himself. His face was stern, but he held the captain's sword and was presenting the hilt to him. The officer was in disbelief, but a reassuring nod from Napoleon and he immediately jumped to his feet, taking the weapon from him. The emperor gave him a reassuring pat on the shoulder, and the captain raised his weapon high, joining in with a shout of, *"Vive l'empereur!"*

While Napoleon slowly made his way north, deeper into France, word of his escape reached the Congress of Vienna. Captain Webster was saddling his horse, making ready for the return ride to Brussels. He hoped to pace himself better than they had during the arduous four days Wellington had made them ride en route there. His hopes of a quiet return were dashed as he looked up to the sound of galloping hooves. An officer, whose face was nearly as scarlet as his uniform, quickly dismounted and made his way towards the great hall where the delegates were assembled.

"Isn't that Sir Neil Campbell?" James asked, turning to DeLancey, who was also making ready to return to Brussels.

"By God, I think it is," he replied. "What the devil is he doing here?" He then called out, *"Colonel Campbell!"*

Campbell stopped in his tracks and quickly walked over to DeLancey.

"What is it, man?" DeLancey asked, taken aback by the Scotsman's flushed demeanour.

"The Monster's escaped," Campbell replied quickly. "Forgive me, but I must find Castlereagh at once." He then turned about and walked as rapidly as he could towards the hall.

"It looks like I won't be returning with the contingent after all," DeLancey said after a brief pause.

"Sir?" James asked. He was stunned by what he had just heard, though the very presence of Sir Neil Campbell in Vienna confirmed the worst.

"I'll have to speak with the Duke and find out how he wants to proceed," DeLancey explained. "I will most likely return to Brussels with him. The military contingent will leave as soon as I get a message from the Duke to give to Richmond. They must be warned at once. However, we do not want to cause a panic either. We must deal only with the facts at hand. It would seem that Napoleon has returned. He has not yet reclaimed the throne of France, and even if he does, that does not mean he will try and make war on the rest of Europe once again."

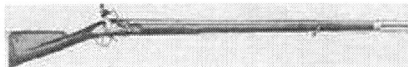

"Damn your eyes!" Castlereagh spat. "Were you not an officer, I would have you flogged to the brink of hell!"

Campbell knew he would be called on the carpet by the British Foreign Secretary and knew there was nothing for it. "I was there as his assistant, not his gaoler," the colonel said in an attempt to defend himself. In literal terms this was true, and perhaps the reason why Castlereagh could not push for a court martial.

All the same, he was not amused. "Gone to see a doctor, did you?" Castlereagh grunted. "Or was it your mistress? Don't play me the fool, I know all about the Florentine harlot you've been sharing your bed with!" "One man," Campbell retorted. "I am but one man; who was free to come and go as I pleased. Whatever may have been implied by my staying with the emperor on Elba, he could have dismissed me at any time. That our government chose to leave him there, without so much as a sloop or brig patrolling the waters, is not my responsibility!"

"Take heed in your tone with me!" Castlereagh snapped. "That Bonaparte was not officially a prisoner of war is the only thing that prevents his escape from bringing you to court martial. You will return to the army, and know that if war does come again, the blood of every British soldier who falls will be on your head. Now get out!"

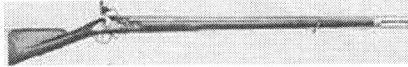

It was madness in the great hall of the Congress once word of Napoleon's escape was made public. Delegates, among whom were several heads-of-state, shouted derogatory epithets directed towards the French emperor, while still arguing amongst each other over the petty quarrels that had dominated the Congress of Vienna. The French delegation was at a complete loss, not knowing who they truly represented now.

In a far corner, at a solitary round table, Wellington sat with his chin in his hand, deep in thought. He had been given a despatch just as he was making ready to join in a morning fox hunt. He decided that he would not lower himself to the degrading spectacle that had taking hold of the delegation, and besides, it really was not his place to decide what, if anything, was to be done about Napoleon's return. A door behind him opened, and Colonel Campbell beat a hasty exit, having just been brought onto the carpet by Castlereagh. The Duke decided that the chaos in the chamber was beneath him, so he elected to go have a private word with his friend.

"We do not even know if Bonaparte has successfully taken Paris, and yet the collective heads of Europe have already gone mad," Castlereagh grunted as Wellington shut the door behind him.

"He will take Paris, if he hasn't already," Wellington surmised. "Bonaparte's support may be unstable, due to general fatigue from decades of war. However, I can personally vouch that on the whole, the people of France despise that bloated, enfeebled mass they were saddled with as a king. Given the option of restoring Boney, one can scarcely fault them."

"It is because Louis is such a feeble king that the rest of Europe will never allow Bonaparte to maintain power, even if he does want peace," Castlereagh reasoned. "They are terrified of him, and rightfully so. His legions fell upon them like a hammer on glass. Were it not for his army falling foul of the Russian winter two years ago, I daresay we'd still be grinding our way through Spain and southern France. His armies defeated every force sent against them, everyone except you, that is."

Wellington's face twitched into a near smile for a brief moment. "Such has brought us much resentment from those who would be our staunchest allies," he muttered. "They're quite happy to take English coin to fund their wars against the French, yet quietly they resent us. They take my victories against our common enemy as if they were an affront to themselves."

"And they're not always subtle in their contempt," Castlereagh concurred. "I've personally heard several make it plain that you never faced Napoleon directly. Well, I daresay you may get your chance."

"Of that I have no doubt," the Duke concurred. "The opposition back home will make a ruckus, but I know Liverpool and have no doubt that his cabinet will be resolved to overthrow Napoleon once and for all."

"I cannot help but wonder if Bonaparte somehow got word about Saint Helena," Castlereagh thought aloud. "It was just a proposal that was being discussed, though I do not know how seriously. It did puzzle me, though, that you did not come out in direct opposition to the idea."

"Were he on Saint Helena, Boney would never have made it to France," Wellington reasoned. "Any number of ships would have intercepted him. He is egomaniacal, and also a military genius; the most dangerous amalgamation of personality traits."

"As it is, we gave him the option of living out his days in relative ease; far better than what the people in France were left to face," Castlereagh continued. "I think we shall recommend to the delegation that once put down again, Napoleon Bonaparte be imprisoned on Saint Helena. It is desolate, thousands of miles from the nearest civilization, and one-fifth the size of Elba. Certain factions, the Prussians especially, will wish him dead. However, I see exile to Saint Helena as a far more fitting end."

"There is just that tiny matter of seeing to his fall," the Duke conjectured. "If Boney is able to rally his entire nation once more, he can rebuild his army and repel any invasion force the continental allies can muster. There is not one man in that hall with the military skill to defeat Bonaparte."

"There is one man who could do it," Castlereagh replied with a knowing grin. "It will take some diplomatic manoeuvring, but I daresay, Arthur, that before you leave Vienna you will be commander-in-chief of all allied forces in northern Europe."

Chapter IX: At War with Whom?
Brussels, Belgium
April 1815

Napoleon Bonaparte, Emperor of the French

Rumours had reached Brussels even before the official dispatch from Wellington. As James and the other soldiers from the escort rode towards the city, there was already a sense of fear in the air. Soldiers massed around the city, digging and improving fighting positions, while building barricades.

"These modest fortifications will not stop Bonaparte," an officer next to James noted.

"Agreed," he replied. "If Napoleon defeats us in the field, then God help Brussels and all of Europe."

"Here, it's Captain Webster!" a voice shouted off to the side.

James was surprised to see his entire company formed up behind one of the barricade sections. Then men gave a cheer, some waving their shakos, as their commander rode up to them. James quickly dismounted and walked over to Lieutenant Grose. "William, what's going on here?"

"Orders from the corps commander," his subaltern replied. "We're to make ready to defend the city once Boney unleashes upon us." There was a trace of sarcasm in the lieutenant's voice.

James simply shook his head. "There is no way Wellington will allow us to sit here on our backsides and wait for Bonaparte to come to us," he remarked. "He'll take the fight to the French as close to the frontier as possible. This is all a waste of time and effort, not to mention this is the work of militia, not Foot Guards!"

"I couldn't agree with you more," the voice of Lieutenant Colonel Stewart said from behind him.

James turned and saluted his battalion commander. "Colonel, sir."

"Stand easy, captain," Stewart replied. "As your subaltern has duly noted, our orders came all the way from His Highness, the Prince of Orange."

"Prince of Brat, more like," a private grunted from the ranks.

"Belay that talk!" Corporal Donaldson barked.

Colonel Stewart ignored the men. "The men are simply being kept busy," he explained as he signalled for James to walk with him. "It keeps their hands busy and mostly out of trouble. That and it might calm the populace to see soldiers active in providing for their safety."

"Sir, the men should be training and practicing drill, not digging trenches they will never fight from," James replied.

"I'm aware of that, captain," Stewart stated. "But until Wellington returns, hopefully as our commander-in-chief, then we must make happy the *Prince of Brat*, as your man so eloquently noted."

James kept silent, thinking there would be a rebuke from the colonel for his soldier's impudence, but thankfully there was none. Instead, he had some words of praise for the men.

"You will be happy to know that your company put to good use the additional ammunition you acquired to subsidize their training. With the possibility of renewed war on the horizon, it was a doubly-fortunate thing. During the most recent live fire and weapons drills, your company to a man had the fastest load times and superior accuracy of the entire brigade."

"That is good to hear, sir," James replied with a sigh of relief.

"It is not our Foot Guards that concern me," Stewart continued. "We are an elite regiment, and the men act like it. It is the rest of the army in Belgium that worries me. With both the Peninsular War, and that waste of a war in America brought to an end, there has naturally been a large drawdown within our armed forces."

"I read the Prime Minster stated that the nation had gone into a 'peace frenzy'," James added.

"Well, who could blame them?" the colonel sighed. "Decades of war takes it out of a nation. No doubt there will be a mad rush to recall those units still in America. The question remains if they can get here in time. Most of the army in Belgium is made up of Netherlands and Hanoverians, and many of them are untrained militia. Even what British soldiers do remain here are largely untried recruits, maybe one-in-three even served in the Peninsula! Should war come, I believe that Bonaparte will attack quickly, and he will come right to us."

"I agree," James added. "We are the closest foe he has to Paris, and defeating Wellington will not only give him a taste of revenge against those who drove his armies out of the Peninsula, but he also knows that defeating the Duke could shatter the coalition."

"My dear Captain Webster, you are indeed an astute one," Stewart replied. "Return to your company, and welcome back. We will speak again in the officers' mess later."

"Yes, sir."

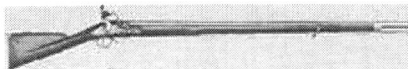

It was a royal meeting with both Emperor Alexander of Russia, as well as William, King of the Netherlands present. Numerous dignitaries and representatives of the various European nations were also in attendance. At the centre of the assembly was Wellington, this time in full military garb. Though he preferred to campaign in civilian clothes, on this day he wore his most resplendent scarlet frock, with all his decorations plainly visible.

"Until the threat of Napoleon is stamped out once and forever," Alexander began, "We cannot take any unnecessary risks. The armies of Russia and Austria will converge on the border of France as soon as we are able to muster sufficient numbers."

"In the meantime," William added, "You must return to Brussels at once. The Prussian army will remain under the command of Prince Blucher, while you will act as second under my son, the Prince of Orange."

"I will do no such thing," Wellington replied calmly, but sternly.

King William was taken aback by this rebuke, though Emperor Alexander simply smiled.

"You see, *subordinate* is not a term I understand."

"Grant you, he has served as an aide under your command," William said, trying to defuse the Duke. "However, as he is of the highest birth and already in command of the allied forces in Brussels…"

"He is twenty-two years old, inexperienced, and you want to send him against the most formidable military leader since Genghis Khan," Wellington interrupted again. He then shook his head. "No, your majesty, I will not be subordinate to him. I do not believe in seconds-of-command; they are a useless position. You may want military glory for your son, and I grant you he is of the highest birth. I, however, wish to defeat Bonaparte. The Prince of Orange is eager and a willing student, but he is still a tactical novice. Napoleon is a master of warfare, and he will thrash the prince like a disobedient schoolboy, and my British soldiers will pay the price in blood. Your highnesses must know that there is only one man in this room who can defeat Bonaparte."

"You speak very highly of yourself," a delegate from Austria spoke up, scarcely hiding the trace of a sneer. "And yet you have never faced Bonaparte in battle."

A quick glance to Castlereagh confirmed to Wellington that this man was among his detractors. "That is correct," Wellington replied calmly. "You, however, have faced him and lost. Repeatedly, I might add. Gentlemen, I will speak plain. You know I come to you with the authority of the His Royal Highness, the Prince Regent of Great Britain. And by his authority I tell you this; unless I am commander-in-chief of all allied forces in Brussels, I will not take part in your little venture nor will any British soldiers on the Continent. My men will not be sacrificed in this folly. We can simply head for home and leave you to deal with Bonaparte, if you think you are able."

There was a murmuring amongst the delegates, and Wellington chanced a glance over to Castlereagh, who gave a quick nod of approval. Though he'd overplayed his hand, not to mention exceeded his authority by threatening to remove British troops from the Continent, both men conjectured that the European powers would not be willing to take that chance. William looked over to Alexander, who nodded in approval.

"Very well," the Netherlands king consented. "You will be commander-in-chief of all allied forces in Brussels. You will work in conjunction with Marshal Blucher and are charged with defending Belgium from any attacks made by the Monster."

"If it pleases your highness," Wellington added, "the prince will be left as commander of the First Corps."

"Very well," King William nodded, looking slightly consoled.

The delegation soon broke up, and Wellington made to leave. He was stopped short when his name was called by one of the Russian delegates. He turned to see the man who'd shouted to him escorting the emperor.

"Your grace," Tsar Alexander said, extending his hand, "It is time for you to save Europe once more."

It was a fitting compliment from the Tsar, and one that Wellington took to heart. Even though Alexander had seen Napoleon's army driven from Russia by the severe winter and had been part of the force that converged on Paris before the abdication, he still understood the significance of the British army's role in the Peninsula. And if nothing else, he was willing to acknowledge that, on an even playing field, Wellington was likely the only man capable of defeating Napoleon.

Fred Ponsonby stood in the hallway, his hat in hand, waiting for the Duke. He handed Wellington his hat and the two men made a quick exit. Outside, they were met by DeLancey, Somerset, and others from the Duke's staff. Somerset had ridden from Brussels as soon as he received word about Napoleon's return, anxious as he was to do his duty by the Duke's side once more.

"That went well enough," Ponsonby surmised. "I daresay that if you had been given a subordinate role, they still would have thrown all responsibility for anything that went wrong upon you, without ever giving you the authority to enforce your wishes in the first place."

"As you heard him say, *subordinate* is not a term the Duke understands," Somerset added.

Wellington gave a short nod of approval and then addressed his men. "We make for Brussels at once," he ordered. "From there we will see just what kind of army we have to face Boney with."

"You're not going to like it, your grace," Somerset replied, shaking his head. "It's mostly continental militias, with our Foot Guards battalions being the only decent troops available."

"The Guards alone will not be enough to stop Bonaparte," Wellington said, shaking his head. "I need my veterans back! Castlereagh is sending word to London, and God willing Lord Liverpool will start recalling my men from America. Boney will have his own issues to deal with in restoring both confidences to the French people, as well as rebuilding his army."

"Something else to keep in mind," Castlereagh said as he joined the men, "is we're not exactly at war with France. It is Napoleon who is our enemy, not the people of France. That little detail makes the situation more delicate."

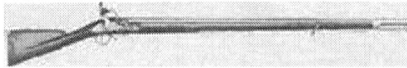

It was a more sombre evening in the usually boisterous officers' mess. James enjoyed the evenings spent here, as it was often the only time he could see some of his closest friends. Indeed, he and Daniel Roberts had had scarcely any time at all to catch up since his return. The mess was shared by both battalions of the Guards' Brigade. It was often presided over by General Maitland, who had recently been given command of the brigade. However, on this evening he was assumed to be dining with the Prince of Orange, as were a number of the other most senior officers.

The mess was a social gathering, and like such groups, it was prone to cliques. It was also usually populated with mostly bachelors, as those with wives tended to dine at home. However, ever since the news of Napoleon's return, even the married men were known to frequent the officers' mess more often. It was one of the only times they could meet with their peers to glean information and rumours from each other.

There were two large oaken tables, each long enough to accommodate a battalion's worth of officers. They were placed end-to-end, with the colonels often seated at each end. The silver and furniture was all very ornate and, in fact, belonged to the officers. This was driven home when James noted the deductions made to his pay for the purchase and upkeep of the regimental silver.

The two battalion commanders naturally dined together when not at home with their wives; the battalion majors doing the same. Company-grade officers mostly dined with their friends, or at least with those who they viewed as their social peers. Young ensigns like Edward Barton would flock around those who they felt best able to provide their route to patronage, and they would shun those who, in their opinion, came from insufficient birth, or worse had been commissioned from the ranks. Remarkably, there were no former enlisted men in the Guards officers' mess.

On this night, James sat with Daniel Roberts. Though recently married, Daniel was anxious to hear of James' time in Vienna, as well as any more substantiated news than the flock of contradicting rumours that flooded into Brussels.

"I hear such a plethora of differing reports that may or may not have even come out of France, that I don't know what to believe," Daniel grunted before taking a drink of his dinner wine.

The food and drink supplied to the officers' mess certainly far outpaced anything the enlisted men received, although the uniformed gentlemen were quick to point out the substantial sum they had to pay for each lavish meal. Officers were often a contradiction who gave the appearance of wealth and prestige, yet many of whom were broke or in debt due to the expense of maintaining the lifestyle expected of proper gentlemen.

"We can only go with the facts as we have them," James noted. "And the only thing we know for certain is that Napoleon has returned, and the Bourbons have fled once more."

"I say good riddance to them," Daniel replied. "That bloody dynasty has been nothing but a source of embarrassment."

"That may be," James concurred, "but we both know that the rest of Europe will never sleep easy with Bonaparte lording over the French. Even if he renounces his claims to the rest of Europe, there will still be that driving fear of what he could unleash. His empire exceeded even that of Rome; who's to say he would not wish to reconquer it once more? No, the world prefers a harmless, enfeebled glutton on the throne of France."

Even in France there were those who preferred the bloated Bourbon king to the restored emperor. Whether it was out of genuine royalist loyalty or simply fatigue brought on by all the years of Napoleon's constant wars, one could not say for certain. The emperor was deeply troubled by the unrest and as such had dispatched numerous regiments of his reconstituted army to put down any royalist uprisings.

"I want to make it clear," he told Marshal Emmanuel Grouchy, who he was sending south to Valence. "I want no French blood spilled! Arrest whomever you must from the ringleaders, but let the people see that I will not tolerate Frenchmen killing each other. Now is the time for unity, as we will soon have most of Europe breathing down our necks."

"The sight of my men and the tricolour flags will be enough to dissuade any further uprisings," Grouchy assured him. He then saluted and left.

Napoleon was then left with only two other men in the hall; his brothers, Jerome and Lucien.

"The dignity of France is made whole once more," Lucien asserted.

"More so because I made you a Prince of France?" Napoleon asked with a wry smile. He then sought to reassure his younger sibling, who was looking at the floor, slightly embarrassed. "Know that I am grateful for your loyalty, brother. If and when I must take to the field with my armies again, I trust you to maintain order and belief of our people."

"I will make certain France follows you to the heavens and back again," Lucien asserted.

Napoleon then turned to his other brother.

"And what will you have of me?" Jerome asked. "I ask that you take me with you as a corps commander, to serve you and the armies of France."

"You will follow me," Napoleon acknowledged, drawing a look of relief from his brother. He was immediately crestfallen by the emperor's next statement. "But not as a corps commander. You have my love, brother, but not my trust to the degree necessary to give you an entire corps. Not to worry, you will still hold sufficient command. I'm placing you as General of Division under Reille's II Corps. Serve him well, and you will be serving me."

Charles Reille was one of Napoleon's most battle-tested generals. After the emperor's fall, King Louis had named him inspector-general of two divisions, though Reille had been among the first to rally back to the emperor after his return. He was a fitting mentor for Jerome to serve under, and he appeared satisfied with his new posting.

"A pity our father never saw what we became," Lucien noted.

Napoleon had been just fourteen when Carlo Buonaparte succumbed to stomach cancer; Lucien, ten; and Jerome, not even a year old.

The mention of their father made Napoleon uneasy, especially given the nature of how Carlo had died, just prior to his thirty-ninth birthday. Though doctors always assured the emperor that the pains in his stomach were brought on by stress and hard campaigns, there was always the lingering fear that he would be struck down by the very abomination that had taken his father. Jerome and Lucien were unaware of their brother's ailments and were quick to blame his pale complexion and unfit physique on his time in exile. Napoleon had assured them that given a few months his health would be restored to its prime.

Napoleon went to bed early this particular evening, despite the volume of work still requiring his attention. He was reminded of the conversation he'd had with Bertrand aboard *Inconstant*. He was, indeed, quickly growing old, far before he should have. As he stared up at the ceiling, discomfort in his stomach prohibiting sleep, he thought about other men his age and their state of health. Both Nicolas Soult and Michel Ney were his age, as was Wellington. On a more personal level, Napoleon had grown to hate that English aristocrat. According to Ney, the Duke had the appearance and stamina of one still in his twenties. A deeper humiliation came from that damnable Mademoiselle Georges, the emperor's one-time lover. She publicly claimed to have shared her bed with the Duke of Wellington, which he never denied. She further expounded that the Duke was a far more vigorous lover than the French Emperor had been.

"I will emasculate Wellington on the battlefield," Napoleon swore to himself as sleep finally took him.

Lucien Bonaparte, Prince of Canino

"Hanoverian militia, Brunswickers, Dutch, and Belgian boys with little training and no combat experience," Wellington muttered. "To top it all, many of our Belgians once wore Napoleon's uniform. We have no way of knowing whether they will flee at the sight of their former emperor, or worse, will they turn their guns on us?"

Having taken a thorough assessment of the forces available under his command, the Duke was understandably disgruntled. Wellington had made as expedient a return to Brussels as he had leaving for Vienna and lost no time inspecting his army. The Prince of Orange was dejected at the loss of overall command, though like his father, his pride was soothed with the knowledge that he would still control the I Corps.

The Duke had called upon many of his senior officers, as well as select members of his staff, to join him for dinner this evening. There would be many more gatherings to follow, as the nerve-wracking and painfully slow process of mobilizing what troops were available went on, to say nothing of waiting to see what Napoleon's next move would be. Indigenous spies were unreliable, and those employed by allied governments had a habit of disappearing and never turning up again. It was as if France was covered in a shroud, leaving Napoleon's enemies blind as to his intentions.

"We have 15,000 men, currently," DeLancey further lamented. "And even our British troops are largely inexperienced."

"There will be more, I promise," the Prince of Orange spoke up. "I have word that the 2nd and 3rd Netherlands Divisions are already on the march."

"More than half my men were discharged after the Peninsular War ended," Wellington added. "Others were sent to America and still more to quell the riots of those damned Irishmen."

"Troops are on their way back from America," Somerset replied. "And three battalions that were en route there have been turned around at sea. Since all their baggage and logistics stores are aboard the ships, they will be able to head straight here. We estimate they will arrive within the next couple weeks. As for the other units, we cannot say for certain."

"And Boney has blinded us as to what his disposition is," Wellington grumbled. "I know not whether he is still putting down royalist uprisings or if all of France has rallied to his cause. We must expect the worst, and that he will reconstitute his armies at full capacity. If that is the case, then they can be ready to strike within two to three months."

Men returning from America had yet to receive word of Bonaparte's return. Sergeant William Lawrence had served in Wellington's army since it landed in Portugal in 1808 all the way to Toulouse. He had still been a private when he joined then-Lieutenant James Webster's *Forlorn Hope* during the assault on Badajoz, where he'd taken a full volley of French musket fire, shot in both legs, and only saved from certain death when a musket ball to his side was deflected off his canteen. It was not just officers who could make a name for themselves by surviving as part of the Forlorn Hope; enlisted men who performed valiantly could expect to be rewarded as well. Lawrence managed to avoid the amputee saws, despite the severity of the wounds to his legs, and after making a full recovery quickly rose through the ranks. That he had been approached by Wellington himself and been tended to by his personal physician had not gone unnoticed.

The sergeant now stood on deck of the ship bearing them to Portsmouth. He'd been given a brief period of leave at home in Dorset before shipping to America. At first he hoped to marry a former sweetheart who'd been enraptured by her 'soldier gentleman', though while in America he discovered she had run off with someone else.

Soldiers crowded onto the deck, anxious for the long voyage across the Atlantic to finally be over. There was also much apprehension, as with the war over, many would now be facing discharge as the king no longer had need of their services. Seeing as how most had joined the army because they had no other career prospects, the thought was particularly unnerving.

"They never know what to do with us once the shooting is over," Sergeant William Wheeler said as he joined his friend on the rail.

"It's true," Lawrence agreed. "Many of us were born into war, raised in war, and sent off to fight in war once we were old enough to take the King's schilling. Now that it's over, only God knows what will happen to most of us. Look at most of the lads, they have no other skills but soldiering. They can clean a musket, march twenty miles in a day, follow basic drill commands, and stick a Frenchman with a bayonet, yet none of these things matters in 'normal' society."

"I hope to stay in the ranks," Wheeler added. "I love England, but sadly there is nothing for me here. Like most of the men, I have no other skills. I don't care if I have to go back to Canada, India, Ireland, or Belgium to do so."

"I was born in Boston the year the colonies won their independence," Lawrence mused. "A pity that was. My father served in Cornwallis' army and was captured at Yorktown; though he was soon paroled once it became clear the fighting was over. Up till then, the war had been a bloody stalemate. Interestingly, Father never hated the Americans. In fact, he never ceased viewing them as his fellow countrymen, and it pained him to watch them die as much as when his fellow soldiers were killed. He quietly cursed King George for not giving the colonists parliamentary representation, as that could have very well prevented the war in the first place. And once hostilities did break out, he loathed that the government was slow to commit resources to fight it. Our army won most of the major battles, yet they did not have the manpower or logistics to stamp out the rebellion."

"My father was an NCO in Tarleton's British Legion," Wheeler remarked. "He was invalided out of the army after he was wounded at Camden."

As the ship closed on the docks, they saw a man in a naval uniform standing at the end of the pier, signalling madly with a set of flags. The crowd that had gathered to welcome the soldiers home was kept at bay in order for the ship to clearly see the man. Orders were shouted amongst the officers and crew of the vessel and with a series of reefing of the sails, the ship lurched to the right, taking them away from the dock.

"What's happening?" a soldier on the deck asked.

"It looks like they're waving us off," Lawrence replied.

"Clear the way, damn you!" the voice of their colonel shouted as he came down from the upper deck. Lawrence looked over his shoulder and saw all of the battalion's officers in a conference with their commander. The colonel then climbed up the steps and waved his hat, calling his men's attention. *"Men! Napoleon has returned to France. We are being diverted to Brussels!"*

Homesick though the men were, the news actually brought about a raucous cheer from the ranks.

"Well," Lawrence said with a chuckle, "it looks like we'll be able to wear the King's uniform for a little while longer."

The tension was still noticeable in Brussels, though Wellington had done much to defuse it, mostly by his own example. The city had become an amalgamation of numerous nationalities, to include many British citizens, since the first abdication of Napoleon, and the Duke was now responsible for all of their safety.

It was a fortunate façade that many of the allied soldiers wore red coats similar to those worn by the British. The majority of citizens had no way of discerning between the varying insignia, coloured facings, and shako plates of the various units. Whether a unit marching past was of untrained Brunswick militia, elite British Foot Guards, questionable Belgians, or the venerable King's German Legion, many were men in red jackets; and it was men dressed as such who, under Wellington, had driven the French from the Peninsula. The British soldiers in Brussels all knew better, and the wait was maddening as they hoped for the arrival of their mates from America and England.

James had heard some encouraging news regarding these events and went to tell his friend, Daniel Roberts. When he was not to be found, a subaltern from the light company told James where to find him, out for a walk beyond the city. When he found Daniel, his fellow captain was walking along a secluded path in the trees. He was slightly staggering, and a bottle hung limply from his hand.

"Daniel!" James hailed him. His friend turned towards him with a glazed expression.

"Oh, hey," he replied, taking a drink off the bottle. "And what do we owe the pleasure on this day?"

James was befuddled by this response and quickly walked over to his friend. "Good God, sir. It's 4:00 in the afternoon. Are you drunk?"

"I am, sir," Daniel replied with a sheepish grin and lazy nodding of the head.

James took the wine bottle and read the label. "Here, this is from the regimental mess!"

Daniel indignantly took the bottle back from him. "Don't be daft, I didn't steal it," he retorted. "You can ask the quartermaster if you wish. Bastard charged me more than the damn thing is worth."

"Easy, Daniel," James replied, "I'm not accusing you of anything. I just know you are not one to abuse the bottle, especially during the middle of the day."

"I'm not on duty, thank God," Daniel said with a grin, taking another drink of what James knew to be a waste of very expensive table wine. Still, if Daniel had purchased it from the mess, he could do with it as he pleased. Knowing his friend well enough to understand there was something amiss, he simply waited quietly until his fellow captain spoke up again. "I'm to be a father."

"Well, damn it all, that's wonderful news!" James said with a friendly smack on the shoulder.

"Normally, yes," Daniel conceded, "but not when a hundred-thousand frogs are soon to be coming this way with the intent of using my head for target practice."

"Daniel, we don't know what Boney has planned," James remarked. "Besides, I've never known you to quell in the face of the enemy."

"Yes, well back then I wasn't married, and deliberately so. If I died in battle then, my family could take solace in that I served honourably and that would be enough. I waited until I knew for certain the fighting was over before I even started looking for a suitable wife. I won't lie to you, James, it was a marriage of convenience, but damn it all, I do love her. And I want to see my son or daughter…whatever."

"Well, if you need a bit of confidence," James said, "the 95th Rifles just landed, and the King's German Legion is expected within the next few days."

The Legion, though made up of German troops, was in actuality part of the British army. Their tactics, training, and uniforms were the same, and many of their officers and NCOs were Englishmen. Iron-disciplined and utterly fearless, they were among the few units that Wellington spoke of with near universal praise. The 95th were elite skirmishers, who wore green instead of

141

red and were often handpicked for their superior marksmanship and ability to operate independently. French officers were terrified of them, as they would target them specifically, often with unnerving accuracy. It was even rumoured that an officer would try and dress like a private if he knew that the infamous Rifles were lurking on the battlefield.

"Well, there's a spot of luck!" Daniel laughed, then realizing his bottle was empty, tossed it into the bushes. "My light company are excellent skirmishers and the best shots in the Guards; sorry James, but I still rate them as better than even your men."

James grinned, but said nothing.

Daniel continued, "I just wish I could get my hands on some of those Baker rifles carried by the 95th. I know they take longer to load and you have to swab the fouling out of the rifling every few shots, but damn they are accurate! I went and asked, no I *begged* Colonel Stewart to let me get some Bakers for my men. He asked me if my men wear green jackets and reiterated that only the green jackets get rifles. I told him we needed to issue my company green jackets, then!"

"And what did he say to that?" James asked, matching his friend's laughter at his absurd story.

"I can't remember," Daniel said after a pause of recollection. "All I know is there was a lot of shouting involved. Clearly our dear colonel was not amused." Daniel then absently smacked his shako off his head with a laugh. He then folded his arms and leaned back against a tree. "And what about you, James?"

"What about me?" the question puzzled him.

"When are you going to quit being such a damn fool and try for Miss Capel?"

"She has been a good friend to me," James remarked, drawing a biting rebuke from Daniel.

"Idiot!" Daniel snapped in a far more venomous tone than he intended. His expression was unapologetic, though. "James, she adores you! And she cares for your daughter; you leave them together often enough."

"I don't know," James started to say.

"Well, I do," Daniel interrupted. He then closed his eyes and took a deep breath before continuing. "I'm drunk, so I'll speak more plainly than I normally would. And if I offend you, well the hangover I'm sure to have tomorrow will doubtless hurt worse than any beating you may give me." He then beat his fist against the tree behind him, finding the resolve to say what James could now hazard he'd wanted to tell him for some time. Daniel's voice was surprising calm and lucid.

"James, Amy died three years ago. We all loved her, and I know she meant everything to you. Hell, you damn near got yourself killed leading the Forlorn Hope at Badajoz so you could be with her again. And God bless her soul, we know she rests with the angels. But do you really think she would want you to be in mourning for the rest of your life? Admit it, you've never let her go."

"You're right," James said quietly. "It's not like I haven't tried, though."

"Oh, bugger it," Daniel replied, shaking his head. "You've taken to the occasional brothel so you can unleash the fire in your loins like a good fellow, but you've never allowed yourself to open up to anyone. I know how Emma feels about you. I daresay she'd marry you tomorrow if given the chance."

"You can't possibly know," James tried to retort, though his voice lacked conviction.

"I have friends," Daniel noted, "and so does my wife. They talk. And now, old boy, if you'd be so kind as to help me find my way home without causing a scene."

James nodded and smiled, then picked up his friend's shako and jammed it cockeyed onto his head. Daniel did not seem to notice.

It was rather tedious getting Captain Roberts home. Soldiers still patrolled the streets as a means of keeping the populace confident in their protection, and every time James and Daniel passed one, the NCO in charge of the small group would very loudly call his men to attention and salute the officers. James could tell that each shout made Daniel's head wince. He recalled that the light company was scheduled for live fire drills on the morrow and chuckled quietly at how much Daniel's head would hurt by then.

At length they found their way to the modest house, more of a cottage. Though the owners of such properties enjoyed the protection of the British army, it was well-known that they still charged a ridiculous amount in rent. Daniel had his arm around

James' shoulder at this point, and as they got to the front door, it was quickly opened by not a servant, but Daniel's wife, Carolyn.

"Off celebrating, was he?" she asked James with a half-smile.

"You could say that," he replied, aware that he wasn't exactly telling the truth. But then, what issues Daniel needed to address with his wife were his own business.

"Don't forget what I told you about Miss Capel," Daniel said as he put an arm around his wife's shoulder.

"Oh, you're going to go see Emma then?" Carolyn excitedly asked James.

"Yes," he said with a nervous nod, unsure of what else to say.

"She is such a darling," Carolyn observed. "I daresay all of Brussels is in love with her, and you'd be a fool if you aren't."

"I'll see you in the morning, Daniel," James said, deflecting the remark.

"Evil be to he who evil thinks," Daniel replied, quoting the regimental motto, though certainly referring to his pending hangover as the source of said evil.

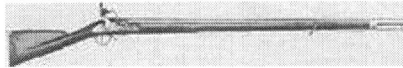

The emperor's cabinet met in the imperial palace, anxious to hear his grand plan for ending the strife in Europe. Much of the enthusiasm at his return had buckled with the loyalist rebellions that had been bloodily put down, despite Napoleon's directive not to spill French blood. The mass mobilization of European armies from those states that had declared him an outlaw and usurper had caused the people to begin to doubt the permanency of the emperor's return.

"How go the conscription and mobilization efforts?" Napoleon asked.

"Not all that well, sire," Marshal Soult confessed, shaking his head while looking over a pile of documents. "While the Imperial Guard has been resurrected from its veterans, the raising of new troops in the numbers we need has proven difficult. In some areas where every man of military age has been ordered to muster, only 10% have turned out."

"The country needs a reason to mobilize again," Ney asserted. "They love you, sire, but they need to know that France will be spared needless bloodshed and destruction. They need a reason to hope."

"A victory," Napoleon replied after a moment's pause in thought. "That is what France needs. And not just any victory; we need one of such decisiveness that it will drive the coalition to its knees." He then pointed with emphasis to a place on his map. "And here in Brussels we will find him."

"You speak of Wellington," Soult grumbled. The months of peace and having to endure Sir Arthur Wellesley as Ambassador to Paris had only fuelled Soult's loathing for the man.

"Wellington is the key to everything," Napoleon emphasized. "I can defeat the Russians and Austrians and it will mean nothing in the strategic picture. But if I defeat the pride of England, it will not only rally our people, it will break the alliance. It's not just British troops that have been used against us, but British coin. They have a five million pound annuity to fund the Austrian and Russian war machine. We stop that, and they will not be able to buy any more weapons, or pay their troops. Without the wealth of England, the alliance will collapse."

"And you think defeating Wellington will bring that about," Soult remarked.

"Of course I do," Napoleon said. "The Prince Regent returned my letter, which asked for peace, without so much as opening it. If we smash his army and humiliate his best general, then he will not be able to ignore me any longer. I will be magnanimous with our brother, England, granting them safe passage. The removal of what remains of the Anglo Army from continental Europe, and the ceasing of payments to the alliance, is all I will ask. Popular sentiment amongst the English people will force the Prince Regent's hand."

"It's settled then," Ney observed. "We must go on the attack."

"You are correct, Ney," Napoleon concurred. "All of Europe has ignored our calls for peace. Therefore, we must make them realize the depths of their folly. We may not have the manpower to face the entire alliance at once, but after Wellington is sent back to England in disgrace, the people will rally to the eagles once more.

And we do have more than enough men to smash him and the Prussians into oblivion."

Major Henry D'Oyley handed James a sheaf of papers as he walked into the battalion headquarters. This weekly meeting, called by Lieutenant Colonel Stewart, was of particular significance.

"Division assignments," Henry explained while James scanned through the documents as he took his seat at the long table.

"As we all know," Colonel Stewart began, once the remaining officers arrived and were seated, "we've recalled as many of our veteran units as possible. It now seems that the force we have is what we will be going into battle with, if and when Napoleon should go on the offensive. Though British troops make up the largest contingent of this amalgamation, we are still overall but one third of the total Anglo-Allied army. Knowing that most of our allies are inexperienced and of questionable reliability, Wellington has arranged so that most of the divisions are a mix of both British and allied brigades. We seem to be the exception. If you look at those organizational charts, you'll see that our division is strictly made up of not just British units, but the elite of His Britannic Majesty's Guards regiments."

James looked at the top paper, which read:

1st (Guards) Division – General George Cooke

1st Brigade – Major General Peregrine Maitland
    2 / 1st Foot Guards – Lieutenant Colonel Henry Askew
    3 / 1st Foot Guards – Lieutenant Colonel the Honourable William Stewart
2nd Brigade – Major General John Byng
    2 / Coldstream Guards – Lieutenant Colonel James MacDonnell
    2 / 3rd Foot Guards – Lieutenant Colonel Francis Hepburn
Artillery
    Sandham's Battery, Brigade Royal Artillery – Captain Frederik Sandham

Kuhlmann's Battery, King's German Legion – Captain
Heinrich Kuhlmann

James glanced through the other divisions and noted that all
consisted of British, King's German Legion, Hanoverian, and
Netherlands brigades. There were also two divisions consisting
entirely of Netherlands troops.

"As we are the only pure British division in the entire I Corps,
doubtless Wellington will rely on us to take the brunt of the
fighting," Stewart continued. "The Regiments of Foot Guards are
the best damned infantry in the entire world, and it is time we
proved it once more."

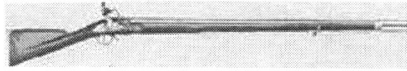

While the men of the Guards regiments felt a sense of relief
that they'd be fighting beside their brother elite regiments,
Wellington himself was only marginally satisfied with the overall
structure of his army, which with the arrival of units from America,
Netherlands divisions, and other allied troops now numbered
around 70,000 men. In a letter to the Secretary of War, Lord
Bathurst, he lamented that he had an entire army made up of men
he'd never seen, who were of questionable loyalty and ability. He
stated as much to Sir Rowland Hill, with whom he was sharing a
private meeting with in his study.

"You've done the best you can," 'Daddy' Hill surmised.
"You've managed to keep cohesion at the brigade level, while
allowing for divisions to place allied units in close proximity to
ours. Hanoverian militia are less likely to run, even from
Napoleon, when they know our men will stand."

"If only I could have gotten back more of my veterans,"
Wellington said as he turned a glass of claret around in his hand.
"Aside from the opposition, who would have us negotiate with
Boney, the whole of Liverpool's government want us to smash the
French and crush them once and for all. Yet for all their bluster,
they hamstring my ability to fight with my best men."

"You refer to the national militia," Hill observed.

147

"Many of our men joined so they could remain in uniform, even on a part-time basis. The problem now is that there has been no declaration of war against France. Instead, Napoleon has been called an outlaw and usurper, so war has only been decreed against him personally."

"And with no declaration of war, the national militia cannot be mobilized," Hill noted.

"Exactly," Wellington emphasized, taking a drink off his claret, "A damn technicality that deprives me of the vast majority of my best men. Only 7,000 of our men served in the Peninsula, meaning the other 90% are minimally trained with no real experience. I tell you, Rowland, I feel like I'm in command of an army of teenage schoolboys."

"You're not far off the mark, Arthur," Hill replied. "I've spent the last week inspecting my corps, and I swear that even the sergeants look too young to require a shave."

As Wellington glanced out the window, watching the sun finish setting while flames from the fireplace danced in a reflection on the glass, the door behind him was roughly swung open.

"I see you made it, Sir Thomas," he said dryly without looking over his shoulder.

Sir Thomas Picton was the only man who would be so brazen as to barge in on the Duke without so much as knocking.

"I'm here, Arthur," Picton replied gruffly, slamming the door behind him. "I should tell you that my health has not been the best, and I cannot help but wonder why you sent for me."

"And I cannot help but wonder why you made me damn near beg you to come," Wellington retorted, his gaze still out the window. "If it was anyone else, I would have left them to rot on half pay."

"Oh, yes," Picton snorted, "I can tell just how much you really need me."

"Still smarting over being denied a peerage?" Hill said, knowing it would strike a nerve in Sir Thomas. "You know, if you wanted to be thought of as a peer and gentleman you should probably act like one."

"Piss on you, Rowland," Picton retorted. "My men may not have loved me like they did you, but I still won just as many victories!"

"Take it easy," Hill said, showing his hand towards an empty chair. "We're all friends here, Thomas. Since you're here, you may as well join us."

"Thank you, I think I shall," Picton replied. His tone had softened, though his voice still dripped with sarcasm. He poured himself a glass of claret and sat in the chair with his back to the fire, tossing his hat casually onto a side table.

"Good God, man, what is that?" Wellington asked, finally taking notice of Picton. "You wear a top hat with your uniform?"

Though Sir Thomas often preferred civilian clothes to army red, he was this evening wearing one of his better dress frocks, which contrasted with the black top hat he had tossed onto the table. "I prefer my round hat, but this one suffices," he replied.

"I hear you once went into battle with a red nightcap on," Hill noted with a laugh.

"So what if I did?" Picton retorted, though he was actually smiling, at least as much as he ever allowed himself. "My head got cold, and I was damned if I could find another hat to wear."

"You are nothing if not eccentric, Sir Thomas," Wellington noted. "However, you are effective, and that is why I called you back. I'm giving you the 5th Division which will serve as our reserve. A number of your regiments are Scottish, including the Gordon Highlanders, the Royal Scots, Cameron Highlanders, as well as the Black Watch."

"Their fighting disposition should suit you well," Hill observed.

"Just tell me where the enemy is, and my boys will kill them," Picton remarked.

"Good to have you back, Sir Thomas," Wellington replied.

Chapter X: The Most Famous Ball Ever
Brussels, Belgium
11 June 1815

The Duchess of Richmond's Ball

Emma paced nervously along the path that led through the hedgerows and gardens. The sky was dark, but at least the rain had stopped for the time being. Despite it being June, it was a cool day, and she wrapped her shawl around herself. She had not seen James since the I Corps was now cantoned at Braine-le-Comte. It was only about fifteen miles to the southwest, but it may as well have been on the other side of the world. Indeed, Brussels was mostly devoid of soldiers now. With an enormous French army massing on the Frontier, Wellington had divided his forces to cover any possible avenues of approach Bonaparte might take. Braine-le-Comte stood between Brussels and Mons, where Wellington surmised was Napoleon's most likely approach. It terrified Emma to think that James and his men would be the only ones that stood in the way of the French juggernaut, once unleashed.

What had particularly wounded Emma was that James had acquired a paid nanny to take care of his daughter. He insisted that he simply did not wish to burden Emma any further, as it was beneath her position. While she understood his intent, Emma found herself missing the little girl deeply. They had spent so much time together, and as Amy grew and started to walk and speak more, the two had formed an inseparable bond. And at least when she was watching Amy it gave her something to take her mind off the coming storm. She grimaced and thought that the dark clouds were rather appropriate, given the mood of the city. She was about to turn around when she heard voices from just around the nearest hedge.

"My dear Duke," she heard the Duchess of Richmond say. Smiling, Emma quickly walked around the corner to see Charlotte speaking with Wellington. "I wish to give a ball. It has been in the planning ever since Napoleon abdicated. However, I feel it prudent to ask for your grace's permission before sending my invitations. I do not wish to pry into your secrets or garner any information which does not concern me. At one word from you, I will cancel my ball and ask no reasons as to why."

"My dear Duchess," Wellington said, taking both her hands. "You may give your ball without fear of interruption or for your safety." He then kissed her hand and made ready to leave when Emma spoke up.

"Please, tell me you will invite Captain Webster!"

"Miss Capel," Wellington acknowledged, "I will deliver Captain Webster's invite personally." The Duke then left the two women alone.

Emma's face betrayed her excitement at the thought of seeing James again.

"My dear," Charlotte said with a smile, "you are quite taken by the captain. He would be a suitable match for you."

"Thank you," Emma replied. "Ever since they left for Braine-le-Comte, I have lived in fear that I would never see him again. I confess James has become very dear to me."

"Wellington had asked us to provide him a place to stay when he came to Brussels," Charlotte remarked. She then noted Emma's puzzled stare. "I don't expect Captain Webster would have told you, as he doesn't know nor is he to know. One of Arthur's unfortunate habits is that he will rarely speak well of someone and never to that person directly. He has, however, made mention of Captain Webster's quality as an officer and gentleman to me and Charles on more than one occasion. "

"It will be a splendid ball!" Emma emphasized. "Mum and Dad have spoken of nothing else since they arrived." Her parents had arrived in Brussels two months before, despite the growing threat from Bonaparte and the French.

"Your mother is a delight," Charlotte smiled. "She has insisted that Charles and I come stay with them when we visit England."

"I hate to say this," Emma remarked, "but I think Mum is wilfully oblivious to the terror that lurks not forty miles from here." She then noted the strain on the duchess' face and knew that she, too, feared the worst, should Bonaparte invade Belgium.

"Perhaps," she replied, "just for this one night, we might all allow ourselves be wilfully oblivious."

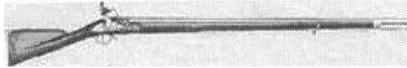

The *Armée du Nord*, nearly 130,000 strong, stood massed on the Belgium border, just south of the River Sambre. While their enemies were indecisive and uncertain of both where the French would attack, as well as their ability to stop them, the soldiers of Emperor Napoleon were poised to strike the decisive victory for France.

"We've blinded our enemies," Napoleon asserted. "We've fed plenty of false information to Wellington's spies, our armies mass on the northern frontier, and still the English and Prussians have no idea from exactly where we will strike!"

Once Napoleon had left Paris, it was impossible to hide that the war was imminent, and that it would come via Belgium. However, with so many ways for the French to invade, Napoleon still held the decisive advantage. That and he knew his enemies would wait for him to make the first move, thereby handing him the initiative.

"Their reconnaissance is an embarrassment," Marshal Ney remarked. "No proper force of cavalry scouts has crossed the Sambre, only renegades and mounted militia who either go back with poor intelligence or none at all, when they get too careless and fall into our hands."

"We've also allowed him to think we'll come via Mons," the emperor noted. "The roads there are paved and easiest to move mass numbers of men and equipment. He'll have his largest concentration of troops there. But for all that, Wellington cannot protect all of Belgium at once."

"The Prussians have mostly concentrated in the vicinity of Ligny and Namur," Soult said, pointing to a spot on the emperor's map to the northeast. He then motioned towards the west. "Wellington, on the other hand, has scattered his forces to the west, trying to cover every possible avenue we may approach from."

"The Prussians are massing, hoping to engage us in one decisive battle," Ney conjectured. "The English are trying their damnedest to protect Brussels. Clearly Blucher and Wellington have differing strategies on how to stand against us."

"And by doing so, they have completely undermined their ability to coordinate and fight together," Napoleon stated with elation. "Wellington is right to protect Brussels, as its fall would break his alliance with the Belgians and Netherlands. Yet his prudence has led Blucher to the slaughter. He has four major routes to protect, spread out over sixty miles. Blucher only has one. Well, if the Prussians want a decisive battle, we will give it to them!"

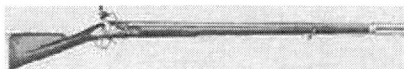

James finished walking the line of his company. The inspection had taken more than an hour, and he was pleased that he had once again found minimal deficiencies amongst his men and none involving the serviceability of their weapons or equipment. A missing tunic button or scuffed shako plate he could deal with. Dirty weapons, unserviceable flints, dull and rusted bayonets, or soiled ammunition cartridges he could not. There was one soldier who stepped in front of the formation, along with Corporal Donaldson.

"What have we here then?" the captain asked.

"Only the best shot in the company, sir," Donaldson answered. "We wished to do a demonstration for you to show that the ammunition you purchased for the company was put to good use."

"Indeed," James replied. He then apprised the soldier. "Private Adams, is it?"

"Sir!" the soldier said confidently.

"Eric here is also the fastest loader in the company," Colour Sergeant Shanahan further explained. "Most soldiers can take twenty-five to thirty seconds to load his weapon. The company average is twenty seconds. As for Private Adams, well sir, I think he should show you."

"Agreed," James replied with a grin. He then pulled out his pocket watch. "Are you ready, soldier?"

"Yes, sir," the private replied.

"Then...load!" James watched as Private Adams went through the sequence in a very fluid motion; withdrawing a paper cartridge, tearing it open, priming the pan, pouring the powder down the barrel, dropping the ball in, withdrawing the ramrod, ramming the ball home, ramrod stowed, weapon at the ready. "Seventeen seconds, not bad. There is a target out there about eighty yards."

"Yes, sir."

"Kill it!" James ordered as he stepped to the side. The soldier quickly shouldered his musket and fired. His motion was so quick that the captain wondered if he'd even tried sighting on his target. James nodded to Corporal Donaldson, who jogged over to the target. After a quick assessment, he looked back and nodded.

"Centre mass, sir!" A murmur of approval came from the men in the company, still in formation.

"Well done," James acknowledged as Donaldson re-joined them. He then grinned and shouted, "Reload!" The order caught most of the men off-guard, yet Private Adams instinctively reached into his cartridge pouch and proceeded to reload his musket. James gave a nod of approval when the soldier replaced his ramrod and shouldered his weapon once more. "Sixteen seconds."

"That a way, Eric!" a soldier from the ranks shouted.

James directed the soldier to discharge his weapon once more. Once complete, he spoke to him once more.

"How old are you, lad?"

"Twenty-eight, sir," the soldier replied.

154

James then felt foolish, calling him *lad*, as the private was a year older than him. But then, such terms came from social position and rank as much as age.

"You're married," James noted the ring on the soldier's finger. "Any children?"

"Yes, sir," Adams replied. "Me wife was on the company roles during the Peninsula, and both my son and daughter were born in Spain."

James then reached into his pocket and pulled out a shilling, which he handed to the private.

"Then get them something special for their supper tonight," he directed, "with my compliments for their father's skill."

"Thank you, sir!"

"Dismissed, private."

Adams shouldered his musket and saluted before returning to his mates in the ranks.

James then stood in front of the formation. "Dismiss the company, colour sergeant," he said to Patrick, the two men exchanging salutes.

"Sir!" Patrick said before pivoting to face his men. *"Company...dismissed!"*

James removed his hat and ran his fingers through his hair as he walked towards the tent that was serving as the officers' mess. Outside he saw Major Henry D'Oyley speaking with Captain Stables, who commanded one of the other line companies.

"Ah, Captain Webster," Henry said. "I take it your inspection went well?"

"Their weapons are clean and functional," he replied. "Their kit serviceable. I daresay they will kill a lot of frogs and look smart doing it. You probably heard the shooting demonstration from one of my lads. I would put his speed and accuracy against any in the entire army."

"You have a solid company, James, no doubt," Stables said, extending his hand.

"Yes, well I just wish there were more of them," James replied, clasping his fellow captain's hand. "I swear every unit in this damn army is understrength. We should have twelve-hundred men in this battalion, and as it is we have less than a thousand."

"Our quality is second-to-none," Stables remarked. "Even Boney's Imperial Guard won't stand against us."

"I'm getting ready to announce to the mess that Captain Stables is being appointed as acting-major," Henry interrupted. "I've been the only major in this battalion for God knows how long. Though the actual billet is held by some sod that purchased it in England while convalescing, reality is, we still need someone to control the left wing of the battalion. Captain Stables has seniority and will take this posting, even if it is temporary."

"Well, perhaps after we thrash Boney it can be made permanent," James said, taking Stables' hand again.

"Much obliged, James," Stables replied as a soldier-servant held open the tent flap and the men made to enter the mess.

"Captain Webster!" the voice was unmistakable, and it froze James in his tracks. He immediately turned about to see Wellington, along with several members of his entourage, walking briskly towards him.

"We'll catch you later," Henry said, giving James a friendly slap on the shoulder as he and Stables quickly made their way into the mess tent.

"Your grace," James said, saluting.

"Compliments of Miss Capel," Wellington replied dryly, handing him an envelope. James recognized the seal as belonging to the Duke of Richmond. He quickly opened the letter, and his face was beaming at what he read.

To Captain James Henry Webster,
Your presence is requested by the Duchess of Richmond to attend a most resplendent ball at Rue de la Blanchisserie on 15 June. The finest of Brussels society will be in attendance…

There was more, but James' thoughts were interrupted.

"You can thank Miss Capel when you see her," Wellington said sternly, his arms folded across his chest. "And I trust you will thank her *properly*."

"Yes, sir," James replied, though the Duke did not wait to hear it and immediately started to walk back the way he'd come.

Colonel DeLancey remained for a minute. The two men had not seen each other since Vienna, However, James held him in the highest regard and still viewed him as a friend. DeLancey had taken a well-deserved leave in England, with his young wife, Magdalene, accompanying him back to Belgium.

"You would do well to follow the Duke's *suggestions*," DeLancey said with a grin. "It's not every day that he can be compelled to personally deliver an invitation to perhaps the grandest ball seen in a century to a company-level officer."

"I take it you are going too, sir?" James asked.

DeLancey sadly shook his head. "Unfortunately, no," he replied. "My wife has only just arrived. Between my duties, plus getting her settled, it will be impossible for us to attend. No doubt Magdalene will be devastated, being that she is friends with the Duke and Duchess of Richmond's daughters, no doubt she has already been acquainted with Miss Emma Capel."

"Understood, sir," James said, matching DeLancey's grin.

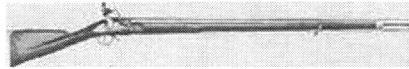

The next morning, Colour Sergeant Shanahan walked the line of makeshift targets and viewed the handiwork of his men; his NCOs following close behind. The smoke was finally dissipating as the men had expended the last of the extra training ammunition Captain Webster and Lieutenant Grose had purchased for them. With Bonaparte back on the French throne and hostilities imminent, he was thankful that his officers had had the foresight to acquire extra ammunition. Marksmanship was a perishable skill, so the timing of this last training event could not have been better.

"The British soldier is best shot in the entire world," he noted as they walked to the end of the target line. He then turned to face Sergeant Billings and his two corporals. "I would place the marksmanship of our men against those of any in the entire British army, even the 95th Rifles."

"Whatever they see, they hit," Sergeant Billings asserted.

Patrick nodded and then reached into his haversack and pulled out a small pouch with some coins in it, which he tossed to Billings. "Take this and get the men an extra ration of gin and a cask of ale," he directed. "We'll give them the afternoon and evening off, *after* they've cleaned their muskets and passed inspection. They've earned it."

"Right you are, colour sergeant," Thomas replied with a grin.

Whatever issues may have existed between the two NCOs had abated. Captain Webster had never been made aware of the spat between the two, but then he did not need to know. Thomas Billings had confessed his dark past to Patrick, and though he could not give him absolution, he understood the cloud of guilt the sergeant lived under, and there was no need to exacerbate things further. The sins of his past could only be atoned before God.

"But then we all have much to atone for," he said quietly after his NCOs left.

There was a loud cheer from the men when Sergeant Billings announced the refreshments being purchased, courtesy of their colour sergeant.

"Well done, colour sergeant," Lieutenant Grose said as he walked over to where Patrick leaned against one of the target posts.

"Sir," Patrick replied, standing erect and saluting.

"Captain Webster's compliments," the lieutenant continued. "He regrets he could not be here today, but with a personal invite from the Duke to return to Brussels for the Duchess of Richmond's ball, one can hardly fault him."

"No, we cannot," Patrick agreed. "I hope you don't mind my indulging the men a bit, sir. With war now inevitable, I figured it may be the last chance to do so."

"No harm done," Grose replied. "One cask of ale and an extra quarter-ration of gin will hardly do the lads in."

As the two men were talking, Ensign Barton was walking quickly towards them, his face flushed. "Lieutenant Grose!" he said, catching his breath.

"What is it, Mister Barton?"

"Boney's crossed the River Sambre," Barton replied. "I just got word of it. The Prussians at Charleroi are engaging the frogs even as we speak."

"Does Wellington know?" Grose asked, his arms folded across his chest and brow furrowed in consternation.

"Yes, of course," the ensign answered. "Oddly enough, he's still going to the Duchess' ball with Colonel Stewart and Captain Webster. He must not be that concerned."

"That and we cannot know if the attack on Charleroi is nothing more than a feint," Patrick spoke up.

Under previous circumstances, Ensign Barton would have berated any enlisted soldier for taking part in a conversation between two officers. Thankfully, due in no small part to Grose's constant oversight and Captain Webster's veiled warnings, Barton's demeanour towards the men in the ranks had calmed considerably. He may have still harboured a private grudge towards Colour Sergeant Shanahan, but he, at least, quietly acknowledged that Captain Webster's purchasing of extra training ammunition was not a waste of coin.

"What were the orders?" Grose asked Barton.

"To be ready, but nothing more," the ensign replied.

"Bonaparte is a master strategist, and it would be like him to draw all our forces into what would amount to a false move," Patrick asserted.

"And we all know Bonaparte is the last person one wants to make a false move against," Lieutenant Grose observed. "Charleroi is at least a full day's march from here, probably more with how much the blasted weather has ruined the roads. It's mid-afternoon already, and the issue there will be long decided before we can arrive. And if we move now and the attack does prove to be a feint..." He shook his head and let his thoughts trail off.

"It's like playing a game of chess," Patrick thought aloud. "Only difference is we don't get to see our opponent's pieces until they are halfway across the board. Shall I belay the order of extra gin and ale for the men, sir?"

"No," Edward replied, shaking his head. "As I said, a cask of ale divided up amongst a hundred men will hardly impair their judgment. Allow the men this night to indulge themselves a bit, but do not let them go far. All soldiers will be confined to camp tonight. I daresay, the order to move will come sooner rather than later."

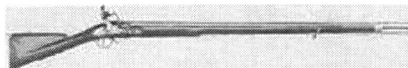

Upon arriving back in Brussels, James first went to see his daughter who was staying with her nanny while he was away. It

159

was a very small apartment flat in the middle of the city, but James did not feel it would be right to impose upon Emma or the Duke of Richmond any further. He walked up the steps and gave a quick knock before letting himself in.

"Papa!" Amy shouted excitedly, running into his arms. The little girl was now three and growing faster than James could keep up with buying clothes for her.

He picked his daughter up and held her close, remembering once more what he was fighting for. Each time he left her, he feared he would never see her again, yet he also knew that he would willingly give his life to protect hers.

"Captain Webster!" the surprised nanny said as she came out of the small kitchen. She was a young Englishwoman named Jenny and the wife of a private in the Guards. "I had not expected to see you back so soon."

"I'm only here for a short while," James explained. "I've been invited to a ball hosted by the Duchess of Richmond."

"Even those of us in the working class have heard all about it," Jenny replied. "The Duchess has been planning this affair ever since the fall of Bonaparte. Of course, with his return it was uncertain if she'd be able to have it at all."

"I believe Wellington allowed it to proceed in order to maintain a sense of normalcy within the city," James explained. "Though as you can guess, things are anything but normal anymore."

"I hope it goes well with my husband," Jenny said with a sigh. "We survived the Peninsula, and it would be awful to lose him now."

"Well, let's hope saner heads prevail then," James said with as much reassurance as he could must.

"Will you at least join us for supper?" Jenny asked. "It's not much, just some soup I've made."

James looked from her to Amy, who smiled at him with pleading eyes. "I would love to," he said.

He refrained from mentioning anything he'd heard earlier in the day regarding the French attack on Charleroi. Wellington was rightly trying to keep mass panic from spreading needlessly, and there was no need to let the word out until they knew all the facts. He hoped it was nothing but a feint or that perhaps, by some miracle, the Prussians were able to hold the bridges that led across

160

the Sambre. For now, all he wanted was one last peaceful moment with his beloved daughter.

While James supped with his daughter and her nanny before readying himself for the Duchess of Richmond's ball, the thunder of cannon echoed across the plain of the River Sambre, as French soldiers stormed across the bridges leading towards Charleroi. The Prussian defenders had made a stalwart, albeit hopeless, stand. Napoleon had, indeed, unleashed his entire army on Charleroi, knowing that the road through Mons was where Wellington had the largest concentration of men. Here he could get his entire army across and drive a wedge between the British and Prussians. Though the dirt roads through Charleroi were muddy bogs that slowed his army's movement to a crawl, he knew his enemies would face the same difficulties when they finally realized his attack was not a mere feint.

The emperor sat on his camp chair alongside the road that ran past an inn called La Bell Vue. Though the sky was grey with sputtering of rain, the morale of the *Armée du Nord* soared as they crossed from French soil into Belgium. Legions of infantry and cavalry marched past, all with loud ovations and shouts of *"Vive l'empereur!"* Napoleon sat alone for some time, his staff officers keeping a respectful distance while he had his moment alone with his men as they marched towards their destiny. There was still a lot of fighting to be done within Charleroi, but with the bridge now his and his army pouring across in overwhelming numbers, Napoleon was unconcerned. An hour passed before the emperor signalled for his officers to join him. As Marshal Ney, Marshal Soult, Marshal Grouchy, and Generals Reille, d'Erlon, Foy, Jerome, and a host of others joined him, Napoleon pointed to the carts and stretcher bearers, bringing back the wounded.

"And so it begins," he said with a trace of a scowl. "This is not what I wanted, but by God, if my enemies are determined to come for my blood, then I shall spill much of theirs."

"All of France is with you, sire," Ney said with certainty.

"Ney," the emperor said, "once we have finished with our business here, I am placing you in command of the left wing."

"Thank you, sire!" the marshal clicked his heels together.

Soult shook his head, thinking his enthusiasm a bit overplayed. Napoleon pretended not to notice, but instead turned to another of his marshals.

"Grouchy," he said, "you will be in command of the right wing."

"Yes, sire." The reluctance in his voice contrasted sharply with Ney's excitement.

"You will head to Ligny and together we will destroy the Prussians," the emperor further ordered. "Ney, you will advance on Quatre Bras. Wellington has been rightly cautious about massing his entire army, unlike the Prussians. However, his caution will also be his undoing. You will take Quatre Bras and thereby cut all lines of communication between the Prussians and the English. You will also smash into the ground anything that Wellington throws at you."

"Very good," Ney acknowledged.

Napoleon stared at him hard for a moment, emphasizing his next point. "Whatever you do, do *not* allow Wellington to come to Blucher's aid! I will personally handle the Prussians, and when I do, we will converge on the English and annihilate them. Wellington will finally taste the ignominy of defeat that all of you failed to deliver in Portugal and Spain." The rebuke was far more biting than Napoleon intended, but then, he felt he had to reemphasize to his generals who the master strategist was. He would succeed where they had failed and humiliate the previously unbeaten Wellington in one fell swoop. In the emperor's mind it was coming all-too-easy. He felt the flashes of his former brilliance on the battlefield resurfacing. If only his health was not deteriorating so badly! He had hoped that a return to France would revive his health, but the pains in his stomach were as bad as ever. Though he was only forty-six years of age, he often felt much older. He inwardly harboured much resentment towards his English adversary, who though the same age as Napoleon, was again said to possess the health and vitality of a man in his twenties. That his generals kept repeating this assessment irritated the emperor immensely. After dictating a handful of subsequent orders, he dismissed all except Marshal Soult, who as his chief-of-staff was ever by his side.

"I mean to achieve the impossible again, Nicolas," Napoleon said. His eyes were closed, and his arms folded across his chest. He was taking slow, deep breaths, trying to quell the pain that was shooting through his stomach once more. "The entire war will be decided within the next few days. Blucher, I can stamp out in my sleep, but Wellington is still an unknown to me. I know you faced him many times, and of all my generals, you came the closest to beating him at Toulouse."

"If only I had faced him on even terms," Soult lamented. "I stopped him at the gates, but with the condition of my men, we could not have held much longer. His army had me outnumbered with troops that were fresh and far more experienced."

"Yes, well now we have the advantage," the emperor observed. He chose not to mention the times that Soult had had Wellington outnumbered with equally experienced men and still been soundly defeated. "I know the disposition of Wellington's army as well as he does. Indeed, some of them used to fight for me."

"You refer to the Belgians, sire," Soult noted with a contemptuous snort.

"I do," Napoleon nodded. His eyes were now open, and he was thankful that the pain in his guts had subsided considerably. "They're unreliable, and Wellington knows it. How can he trust men who likely still wear the same uniforms I gave them? The Hanoverians, Brunswickers, and Netherlanders have little training and almost no experience. Even his English army has few decent men in its ranks. The question now is how will he deploy such an inadequate force against me? I do not fear his army, but I know that Wellington is unbeaten for a reason. But I promise you, Soult, I will *break* him. And when I do, the war will be over."

Soult stood in silence as he and the emperor watched the seemingly endless columns of soldiers march past. He knew Napoleon's plan well enough, for they had discussed it on numerous occasions. It was extremely bold and risky, but also the only real plan that had any chance of achieving final victory. If they could defeat both Blucher and Wellington while capturing Brussels, the alliance would crumble.

"God willing, we can dry our boots off in Brussels," Soult remarked.

"God?" the emperor asked. "God has nothing to do with it. The Almighty was not there for France when we were occupied and humiliated by a foreign power, and I will not ask for His help now."

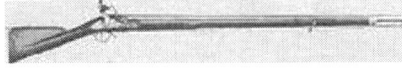

James stood with a number of fellow officers outside the great hall that had been elaborately decorated for the duchess' ball. They awaited the arrival of their wives and ladies, who were being brought in a series of coaches procured by the duchess for this occasion. He had a new uniform jacket which he was wearing for the first time. The uniform he'd worn up from Braine-le-Comte rolled up in his pack, which he'd left with a groom, along with his borrowed horse. He'd also elected to leave his sword and scabbard. The last thing he wanted was to trip over the blasted thing, embarrassing himself in front of the finest of Brussels society. He'd purchased a new officer's sash, though his *Forlorn Hope* badge that was sewn to it was rather worn in contrast. All of his brass was highly polished, as was the plate on his shako, which was tucked under his left arm. His palms were sweaty, and he held his breath in anticipation as each coach arrived, disappointed each time when it was the wife of another officer. As gentlemen escorted their ladies into the great hall, James soon found he was the only one left waiting. He glanced at the pair of footmen who were watching the doors, and though their faces remained stoic, he wondered if they were laughing inside.

He let out a sigh and was about to resign himself to entering the ball alone when the tell-tale sound of horses hooves on cobblestones caught his attention. It had to be Emma. The only other possibility was Wellington himself, who had yet to arrive. It would be quite the embarrassment to be caught standing alone on the steps by the Duke. Sweat formed on his brow as the door to the coach was opened, and his face broke into a broad smile as Emma Capel stepped out. A clap of thunder caught them both by surprise,

164

and Emma quickly walked to the door as the first sprinkles of the coming storm started to fall.

"Looks to be a beastly night," she observed.

James took her by the arm and kissed her gently on the cheek. "Not for us it isn't," he replied, his smile still glowing.

In that moment, the coming war, Napoleon's attack on Charleroi, even the beginning thunderstorm was forgotten.

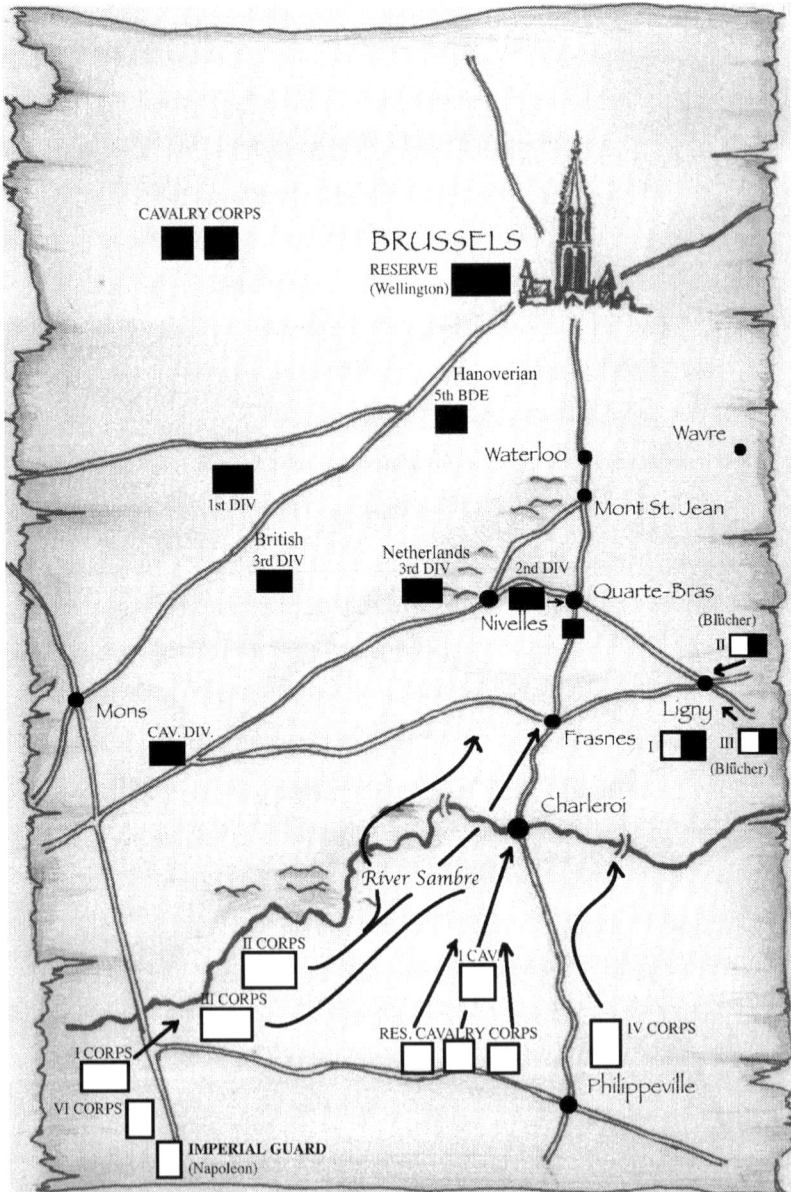

Situation the night of 15 June 1815. Instead of taking the paved roads to the west via Mons, Napoleon advanced up the unimproved roads in the centre, concentrating his forces at Charleroi. The Prussian Army is assembled at Ligny, with Wellington's Anglo-Allied troops still scattered, lest Napoleon's advance prove to be a feint.

Chapter XI: I've Been Humbugged!
Brussels, Belgium
15 June 1815

French Infantry

"Charleroi is ours," Marshal Ney asserted. "Our scouts have confirmed what we expected. The Prussians are massing on Ligny, and Wellington hasn't even moved! There's but a smattering of Dutch troops covering Quatre Bras."

Napoleon sat astride his horse, oblivious to the downpour of rain. Ney's words sounded almost too good to be true. It was completely dark, and with most of his army now across the Sambre and bivouacking for the night, there was nothing left for the emperor to do this night. He rode the short distance to where a house had been procured for his usage. A groomsman met him and helped him down from his horse. A pair of grenadiers from the Imperial Guard stood on either side of the door, which they opened for him. Grouchy and Soult stood up from a small table in the front room, Ney soon joined them. A servant removed the emperor's great coat and hat.

"Everything is proceeding according to plan," Napoleon said as he took a seat. His face was pale, and he was exhausted, but at least the stomach pains had left him alone for the day. "Grouchy, tomorrow we will advance with right wing and crush Blucher's army at Ligny."

"Very good, sire," Grouchy replied.

"If there's one mistake I made in my life, it's not burning Berlin to the ground," Napoleon grumbled.

"The Prussians are persistent," Soult remarked, "but they die just like other men."

"That they do," the emperor agreed. "Still, the sooner we get them out of the way, the better." He then looked over to Marshal Ney, who was still standing by the door. "Ney, you will proceed to Quatre Bras as planned. We have not yet cut all communication between Wellington and Blucher, so there is no doubt the English now know that this is the main effort and not a feint. Luckily for us, they are spread so thin that they cannot possibly mass all their numbers against us within the next few days. However, I suspect that come morning, you will have more than just Dutch militia to face."

"I will smash whatever Wellington throws against me," Ney replied, no small trace of venom in his voice.

"Do that," Napoleon agreed with a tired nod, "and as I told you before, no matter what happens, do not let Wellington send so much as an infantry company to Blucher's aid. I do not want to see a single redcoat at Ligny."

"The only way they will leave Quatre Bras is with their tails between their legs, running back to Brussels," Ney emphasized.

Hours had passed since Napoleon had crossed the Sambre, and yet aside from the downpour of rain, all was calm in Brussels. Wellington had made his entrance into the Duchess of Richmond's Ball at just past midnight with, of course, all eyes on him. James and Emma had scarcely ceased in the dancing. Emma could not stop laughing in delight, and James was unable to remember the last time he felt this much joy. As the latest musical score ended, James took her by the arm and led her to a secluded place off the ballroom floor. Emma laid her head on his shoulder for a moment, and he placed his other arm around her.

"Oh, Emma, I am so sorry," he sighed.

She stood upright and faced him, her face puzzled. "Sorry for what?"

"That I was too blind to see you for what you've been to me," he stammered. It was still awkward for him, but he knew there was no going back now. He placed both hands on her hips, their faces but a few inches apart.

"Please tell me it didn't take the Duke to make you realize how I feel about you," Emma said playfully.

James' face turned red. "Well, now that you mention it..." his voice trailed off and he was suddenly wide-eyed and looking past Emma.

"What is it?" she asked, startled by his sudden change in demeanour.

"That's my cousin," he said, nodding towards the young subaltern in the soaked frock coat who was talking quickly to Wellington while handing him a despatch.

The Duke read it quickly and then nodded to the man, who made to leave. He clearly did not wish to make a scene. However, his very presence caused the band to cease playing and now the assembled guests were talking quickly amongst themselves.

"This is not good," James said, shaking his head, his hands gripping Emma's hips hard. "He should not even be here. Please, give me a moment, that's all I ask."

"Of course," Emma replied as he dashed away. She took a deep breath and wiped her hand across her eye quickly. She cursed herself quietly and swore she would not cry, though she knew the news had to be bad.

"Anthony!" James shouted, starting the young lieutenant, who turned to him, eyes bloodshot and face dishevelled.

169

"Oh, hello, James," he said. "Fancy seeing you here." He followed this with a nervous laugh. His great coat was splattered with mud, as was his shako.

"Damn it all, man, what is going on?" James snapped. "You did not just ride all the way here in the pouring rain on a whim."

"Well, now that you mention it, you, sir, have a keen grasp of the obvious," Anthony replied with sarcasm. Were James not his cousin, and with them both now out of earshot of anyone who might care, he never would have dared to speak to a captain in such a manner. His face was serious, "Napoleon's crossed the Sambre."

"So we gathered," James replied. "Where at? We heard he attacked Charleroi, but were uncertain if it was a feint. If he's come via Mons, he'll run right into our I Corps."

Anthony shook his head in resignation. "No. Napoleon has completely outmanoeuvred us. He unleashed his entire force on Charleroi. I do not think he knew the disposition of our forces any better than we knew his, However, with Mons being the easiest approach to Brussels, he had to know we would concentrate there. It was too obvious. Instead, he's made the more difficult crossing to the east and fallen upon the defenders of Charleroi like a hammer on glass, as he's done so many times before. The Prussian garrison never had a chance. They made a valiant stand, but were completely outmatched." "God, save us," James breathed quietly.

"God?" Anthony scoffed. "You think God gives a damn? He'll let us and the French annihilate each other and then deal with whoever's left. I'm sorry, James, but I have to go. Promise me, if we're both still alive when this is over, that we can get falling down drunk together and try and forget this nightmare."

"I promise," James replied, grabbing his cousin by the shoulder reassuringly.

As soon as he received the despatch from Lieutenant Webster, Wellington quietly asked the Duke of Richmond if he had a map available. When Richmond replied that he did, Wellington discretely made his way into a side study, a number of his senior officers quickly following. Though he loathed the thought of a panic ruining the Duchess' ball, he knew there would be no hiding what was quickly turning into a disaster.

"Damn it all," Wellington grumbled, "it would seem Boney has humbugged me!"

Richmond laid out his map on a table, and all the assembled officers gathered around. In addition to the two dukes were Sir Thomas Picton, General Maitland, the Duke of Brunswick, Prince of Orange, General Clinton, the Earl of Uxbridge, Sir Rowland Hill, and Sir William Ponsonby.

"Let's see what we know," Wellington said. "Boney has attacked Charleroi and driven the Prussians back."

"If that's the case, he's bound to make for Quatre Bras," Brunswick noted, pointing to the town with the major strategic crossroads, just a few miles north of Charleroi. "There's a small town called Frasnes in between. I suspect that is where the French will bivouac, moving on Quatre Bras in the morning."

"Yes, but just how much of their army?" Wellington asked. "The Charleroi garrison was not very large. It would have taken minimal effort to dislodge them. We still do not know Bonaparte's total dispositions. If I send every man we have towards Charleroi, and this is nothing but a feint, he could still easily manoeuvre his main army up the road to Mons and then behind us. If he does that, he will have cut us off from both Brussels as well as Marshal Blucher's army."

"What are your orders then, your grace?" Hill asked.

"Place your men on alert, but do not move en mass until we know for certain where Bonaparte has concentrated his main army," Wellington directed.

"I still have troops in Quatre Bras," the Prince of Orange spoke up. "I know your grace directed them to abandon the position. However, once they saw French reconnaissance troops in their vicinity, they knew the situation had changed and that by holding in place they'd still meet your overall intent."

"Very good," Wellington acknowledged. "We will reinforce them once we know Bonaparte's intentions. Have Alten's and Cooke's divisions ready to advance at a moment's notice."

"Yes, your grace," the Prince replied.

"We'll be ready to move just as soon as you give the word," Cooke spoke up. His division, which included Maitland's Guards brigade, were among the best troops in the entire Anglo-Allied

Army, and Wellington knew he needed to deploy them wherever the enemy massed the majority of their numbers.

"Blucher has massed his army here, at Ligny," Wellington noted, pointing to a position on the map just a few miles southeast of Quatre Bras. "That is where he will concentrate. Boney has a couple of options. He will either still try to outflank us via Mons, or if he's feeling particularly brazen, he'll attempt to drive us and the Prussians apart, thereby picking us off one by one."

"Divide and conquer," Cooke noted, folding his arms across his chest.

"Indeed," Wellington agreed. He then ran his thumb up the map, north along the road that ran from Quatre Bras towards Brussels. He tapped his thumb on the area where two small towns were located, Mont St Jean and Waterloo. "I know this area well. If Bonaparte unleashes his entire army on Quatre Bras and Ligny, I doubt the Prussians will be able to stand. And if they don't, and we cannot hold Quatre Bras, then this is where I'll stop him!"

"Looks like you'll get to see your first action sooner than you thought," Maitland said to his aide, Ensign Lord James Hay, as the two men exited the study.

"It can't come soon enough," Hay said excitedly. "I promised both the duchess and her daughter, Sarah, to bring them each back the helmet of a cuirassier."

"Lady Sarah Lennox is quite the striking young woman," Maitland observed.

"I think she spent an equal amount of time dancing with both of us," Hay noted. "Beg your pardon, sir, if I, in any way, was interfering."

"Not at all," Maitland chuckled. "She appreciates dashing and military ardour, and you, young sir, have plenty of it."

"I hope to prove myself worthy of her," the ensign said with determination. "Granted, she's a few years older than me, and the daughter of a duke. My father is an earl, and if, perhaps, I do something on the field to prove my worth, both Sarah and her father will take notice."

"You'll get your chance to prove your mettle soon enough," Maitland reasoned. "Her mother, the duchess, spoke highly of your dashing. I would not be too anxious, though. And trust me, you do not want to face a cuirassier in hand-to-hand combat. Oh, I don't doubt your courage or tenacity, but if you are unfortunate to run across those armoured giants, you will find out what I mean in a very painful way. Face a cuirassier, and you'll be lucky if he doesn't gut you like a fish and then cut your head off to take home as a trophy."

Emotions ran high in the ballroom as the assembled officers made ready to depart. The crash of thunder and torrential downpour of rain beat down mercilessly outside. There were feelings of both pride, as well as fear, from amongst the guests. There was little doubt that not everyone who came to what would later be known as *the most famous ball ever* would return.

James had a borrowed horse waiting for him, and he would ride back with Colonel Stewart to their battalion. The colonel had conferred with General Maitland and received instructions for his men. They made their way slowly towards the door, his hand clasping Emma's, though he found he was afraid to look at her. There was a final clap of thunder, and then the rain seemed to drizzle out. Many of the officers made a great showing of their departure. James watched as young Lord Hay made a few grand gestures, accompanied by flowering words he could not hear. The young man then leaned down and kissed the hands of both the Duchess of Richmond, as well as her daughter, Sarah.

As they at last approached the door of the great hall, James squeezed Emma's hand hard and then finally turned to face her, though his eyes inadvertently fell to the floor. "Emma," he said, "I am sorry that we must be parted now. It's not what I wanted." He then looked her in the eye and was relieved that, though sad, she wasn't crying. "We knew this would come, I just wish I'd taken the time to tell you…" His voice trailed off and he turned to leave. Emma's words stopped him.

"I love you," she said quietly.

James' heart soared, and without another thought, he turned and kissed her passionately, his hands on either side of her face. Emma's hands hand been folded in front of her chest, but she now reached under his arms and grabbed onto his coat. As they continued to kiss, James could hear approving remarks from both the men and women surrounding them.

"That's our boy," Colonel Stewart said to his wife, giving her a more formal kiss before making his exit.

James finally pulled his lips from Emma's, took a deep breath, and kissed her one more time, very gently, before parting. He smiled and winked at her before turning away. As he stepped towards the door, he felt a hand on his shoulder. He was surprised to see it was Wellington, who waiting by the door until the last of his men left before making his exit.

"When I tell one of my officers to do right by a young lady," he said sternly, "I do not expect them to wait until the very last minute to do so." Though his words sounded reproachful, James noted that the corner of the Duke's mouth was turned up ever so slightly, in what could pass as a smile for him.

"I don't think my exit was quite as flamboyant as young Lord Hay's," James observed.

"He is both eager and full of ardour," Wellington noted. "I do hope that neither gets him killed. It would break poor Sarah's heart."

As James donned his shako and wrapped his cloak around him, he wondered just how many hearts would be broken within the next few days.

Chapter XII: Quatre Bras
Quatre Bras, Belgium
16 June 1815
10:00 am

Michel Ney, duc d'Elchingen, Marshal of France

Wellington had ridden as fast as he could to Quatre Bras, which at the moment was held by a force of 8,000 Dutch-Belgian troops. DeLancey and Somerset were ever by his side, as was General Karl von Muffling, his Prussian liaison.

"Your grace," the Dutch commander, General Perponcher, said as he rode up to Wellington. "My men are dug in in the Bossu Wood. We can hold for a while, but not if Napoleon makes a serious push against us."

"I have three divisions coming to reinforce you," the Duke replied, "Picton and the Duke of Brunswick from the north, Alten from the west. They are about five hours' march from here, and I have more men coming behind them."

"Five hours, we can hold," Perponcher replied. "The enemy has not made a move against us yet, but they are not far. My skirmishers report thousands of men concentrating along the road from Charleroi to Ligny."

"That means Bonaparte is massing most of his army against mine," Muffling noted. "Your grace, Marshal Blucher will need reinforcements."

Wellington did not answer, but instead turned his horse east towards Ligny and rode off at a canter. At approximately five miles, it was a quick enough trek with a horse. As they approached a picket line just west of the town, General Muffling rode forward and spoke to the men.

"This way, your grace," Muffling said. "Marshal Blucher's headquarters is just up this road."

The road took them along a two-mile ridge, where they passed through numerous squadrons of cavalry, as well as gun emplacements, all facing to the south. The village of Ligny itself was across the open valley with another high ridge just beyond. The Ligny Brook divided the town. The Duke noted that while men, horses, and cannon flooded the valley, the ridge south was completely empty of Prussian soldiers.

They found Marshal Blucher seated on his horse, just south of a short hilltop. He had placed himself left of centre of his forces, with one more corps under General Thielmann on his left.

"Guten Tag, Feldmarschall," Blucher said, removing his hat as the men approached.

"Guten Tag," Wellington replied. Though he spoke no German, he understood this basic greeting.

Most educated Europeans also spoke French or English as second languages; the Duke himself being fluent in French since he was a young boy. Surprisingly, Blucher spoke neither. His chief-of-staff, Lieutenant General von Gneisenau, rode up beside Blucher. Gneisenau's facial expression betrayed his lack of trust in Wellington and the Anglo Army. It was no secret that he cared little for the Duke or the English, and that were he in command, he would face Napoleon alone, never trusting in his allies. As it was, he was also staunchly loyal to Blucher and would follow his orders wherever they took the Prussian army.

"Tell him he's chosen a good position with which to face the French," Wellington said to Muffling, who quickly translated.

Blucher grinned and nodded in approval. He pulled out a flask and took a long drink, before offering it to Wellington. Though he cared not for the harsh, stomach-turning liquors of the Germanic peoples, the Duke felt the least he could do was demonstrate appreciation for Blucher's courtesy. He put the flask to his lips and made a great show of taking a drink, though he only let the smallest trace pass his lips. It was a savage schnapps with an aroma of pure alcohol. That Marshal Blucher could consume mass quantities of it on a regular basis and still function exceedingly well, made Wellington wonder if his stomach and liver were made of concrete.

"Ich hoffe, Sie können meine rechte Flanke zu verstärken," Blucher said as Wellington handed him the flask.

"Marshal Blucher says that he trusts you'll be able to reinforce our right flank," Muffling translated.

"If at all possible, I will be here," Wellington asserted. "Be sure to let him know that it also depends on if I am decisively engaged or not. If Napoleon sends his left wing against me, then that is where I will be doing my reinforcing."

Muffling nodded and spoke to Blucher in German. The Prussian field marshal scrunched his eyebrows in contemplation.

"Also," Wellington continued, "tell him that while he has chosen a strong strategic placing for his army, I fear that too many of his troops are exposed in the open."

Muffling frowned, but knew his place was to translate directly between the two men, and not judge what he should and should not tell Marshal Blucher. There was a trace of reluctance in his voice as he spoke.

Gneisenau snorted, a smirk of defiance crossing his face.

"Ich bevorzuge es, meine Männer zu haben, wo ich sie sehen kann," Blucher said slowly.

"He says, 'I prefer to have my men where I can see them'," Muffling stated. He had served with Blucher for too long not to know that the proud Prussian hussar, though he held an immense

177

amount of respect for the Duke of Wellington, disliked being questioned on his strategy and tactics.

"If he can see them, so can Bonaparte," Wellington said, shaking his head. "The emperor is a master of artillery, and he will chop them to pieces."

"We know what it means to face Bonaparte," Gneisenau interrupted.

Though his accent was thick, it irritated Wellington to discover after all this time that Blucher's chief-of-staff spoke English. The Duke glared at him, his next words cold as ice. "General von Gneisenau," he said, "when I address you directly, you may speak to me. Do not interrupt me again." The Prussian general glowered at him and took a deep breath through his nose, but remained silent.

"Do you wish me to translate your last concern?" Muffling asked.

"No," Wellington replied, shaking his head.

As the Prussians operated as a separate allied army, he knew he could not order Blucher to reposition his men. He also suspected that despite the field marshal's extreme personal bravery and the inborn Prussian tenacity, they were setting themselves up to take a severe beating at the hands of the war master himself.

"I do not trust the English," Gneisenau said as soon as Wellington and Muffling rode away and were out of earshot. "They are opportunistic and only come to assist their allies once they know victory is eminent. Wellington also has the audacity to question your placement of our army, as if he were the expert on fighting Bonaparte!"

"That may be," Blucher said. "However, whatever our differences in tactical doctrine and whether or not you trust them, we cannot win this war without Wellington and the English. I am seventy-two years old and am tired of fighting. I would ally with the devil himself if it meant defeating Bonaparte."

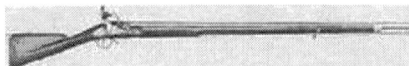

"I mean no disrespect to Marshal Blucher or the courage of the Prussian army," Wellington said to Muffling as they rode back towards Quatre Bras. "But he should know that tenacity and bravery alone will not be enough to defeat Bonaparte."

"Respectfully, your grace," Muffling replied, "General von Gneisenau is correct; the Prussians have experience facing Napoleon."

"Whereas I do not," the Duke interrupted. "Yes, the good general's insult was not so veiled. But tell me this, Karl, how many times have the Prussians defeated Napoleon in open battle?" That Wellington used Muffling's first name showed the general that the Duke's remark was a mere observation, rather than a blatant rebuke, for Wellington was not one to use given names when lashing out.

"What is your plan, your grace?" Muffling asked after a few moments of riding in silence.

"To rally my men to Quatre Bras," the Duke answered. "And to pray I am wrong in my assessment about the disposition of the Prussian army. If I am correct, then Marshal Blucher has set himself up to take a sound thrashing."

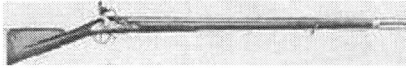

Shouts and volleys of musket fire echoed to Marshal Ney's front, just up the road towards Quatre Bras. Drums beat a steady cadence as regiments advanced towards the fray.

Napoleon had been right, there were now far more than just a few Dutch militia confronting Ney and the French left wing. Initially, a division of Netherlands Infantry had arrived to support the single brigade that was holding in place. Despite being outnumbered four-to-one, they were well entrenched and holding resolutely. Within just thirty minutes of the initial French attack, a British division had been spotted off to their left front, rushing to link up with the Dutch. Cavalry scouts had also just reported to Ney that another British division was coming down from the north and would be arriving on the field any minute.

"Damn it all," the Marshal of France spat.

Though unimaginative and lacking as a tactician, Michel Ney was regarded as arguably the bravest man in the entire imperial army. As such, he always placed himself with the lead units of whatever sized force he led.

"Forward, damn you!" he shouted as he rode his horse down the line just behind the advance brigades. "They are but a handful of Dutch militia, and you men are France!"

This led to renewed battle cries as the columns surged forward. The fire from the Dutch soldiers was less concentrated as the thunder of French cannon smashed into their ranks and crude defensive positions. Ney gave a sinister grin as a solid shot smashed into the hastily thrown up earthworks to his, smashing apart the militiamen seeking its cover. Gouts of dirt mingled with blood and body parts were thrown into the air. A reinforcing group of Dutchmen were caught out in the open, another cannon ball slamming into the earth not ten feet from them, bouncing off the earth, and smashing into their ranks. Men screamed as their bodies were shattered; the survivors dropping their weapons and fleeing in terror.

Ney spurred his horse forward, his sword held high as he shouted encouragement to his men. At less than a hundred yards they unleashed a controlled volley of musket fire before giving a loud battle cry and charging head on towards what remained of the Dutch defences.

The sounds of bagpipes and highland drums gave a distinctly Scottish overtone to the 5th Division as they marched south towards Quatre Bras. Indeed, of the twelve regiments under Lieutenant General Sir Thomas Picton's command, four were Scottish. Thieves, brigands, and bastards he may have called them, but Picton knew he had some of the hardest fighting men in the entire Anglo Army. He was also fortunate enough to have the 1/95th Rifles with him. The fleet-footed men in green jackets were screening the front of his division. The sound of cannon and musket was growing closer, and Picton knew it would not be long before they were in action. The men in the ranks sensed it as well, as the music of the highland bagpipes grew more fevered in pitch, the blood rising amongst the kilted men who knew no fear. Per

Wellington's instructions, he'd placed his brigade of Hanoverian soldiers in between his two Anglo brigades. Neither the Duke nor Picton knew the quality of the Germanic soldiers, though both understood that they would certainly not balk with battle-maddened Scotsmen on either side of them.

A bit of amusement for the men was the speculation around what their eccentric general would don on the day of battle. Like Wellington, Picton always fought in civilian clothes, though what exactly they would consist of depended on his mood. On this day, as he led over 7,000 redcoats towards Quatre Bras, he was wearing a simple black tailcoat and round hat. Indeed, he looked more like a distinguished gentleman on his way to meet his lady at the park, rather than a highly experienced army division commander about to go into battle.

"Rider approaching from the 95th, sir," noted Major General Sir James Kempt, whose brigade was at the lead of Picton's division.

The old Welsh general rode forward and met the rider, who was a major from the Rifles.

"Colonel Barnard's compliments, sir," the major said. "The Dutch-Belgians have been pushed back, out of Bossu Wood. Boney has thrown an entire wing of his army against us in an attempt to keep us from reinforcing the Prussians at Ligny, just up the road."

"Damn it all," Picton swore. He then looked at his pocket watch and surmised how long it had been since he first heard the thunder of cannon. "They've only been engaged for about the last thirty minutes, and they're running already!"

"Yes, sir," the Rifle officer concurred. "However, they were so badly outnumbered, there was no possibility of them holding for long."

"Any idea on the French bastards' total strength?" Picton asked.

"We think at least twenty-thousand," the major replied. "Marshal Ney was spotted by the Dutch, and we believe he is the one leading the attack."

"That means Bonaparte is going after the Prussians personally," Picton noted. "It will be a hard day for them." He shook his head and then looked at the major. "Give my compliments to Colonel Barnard. Tell him the 95th is to deploy to the extreme left and prevent the frogs from flanking us."

"Sir," the major acknowledged, riding off.

Picton then turned to his leading brigade commander. "General Kempt, the rest of your brigade will fall in alongside the 95th. The Hanoverians will be on your right, General Pack on theirs."

"Yes, sir!" Kempt replied, excitement building in his voice.

The order to quickstep was sounded on bugles, with the pipes and drums increasing their cadence to match the order. Picton looked through his telescope and saw dozens of green jackets to his left front, following their major's shouted orders. He then scanned to their right and could just make out the first echelons of French fusiliers emerging from the woods. They were forming up in standard columns and starting to advance slowly, having spotted the approaching Anglo-Allied division. The Welshman grinned sinisterly and collapsed his telescope.

"On! On, you bastards!" Picton shouted as his regiments stepped quickly past him. Where he sat on his horse marked the position the division would deploy from marching columns to battle lines. He then pointed with his telescope towards the approaching French columns. "See! Those sodden frogs are coming at us in the same old style. Well, let's knock them down in the same old style!"

A cheer erupted from the men forming into lines of three ranks. The Scottish regiments, in particular, were seething for a brawl. Sir Thomas Picton was practically hated by his men the vast majority of the time; his language and severe treatment winning him no friends amongst the division. And for all that, as he sat atop his horse, personally leading them into hellfire, they were inspired to know that he would willingly die beside them.

The 42nd Royal Highland Regiment, known as the *Black Watch*, was forming up just in front of Picton. Their colonel, Sir Robert Macara, had elected to dismount his horse and lead his men on foot. He stood in front of his regiment, basket-hilt claymore held high.

"Look to your arms, Black Watch!" he shouted at the top of his lungs.

The highlanders roared with rage, their blood boiling as they anxiously waited for the order to advance. As the last of the

Hanoverians deployed on their right, Sir Thomas gave the signal, and his entire division stepped off towards their hated foe.

Off to his right, Picton spotted a familiar figure riding down the line, shouting orders to the battalion commanders in turn. Sir Thomas calmly rode towards him as the snap of rifle fire came from the 95th. With their far superior range, they had started engaging well before the line regiments.

Picton tipped his hat as Wellington rode up to him. "Nice of you to join us, Arthur."

"Damn your eyes; do not get impudent with me!" Wellington snapped. The crash of musket fire from the 42nd Black Watch reverberated as each of its three lines unleashed in turn. "Anyway, good to have you here. The Dutch-Belgians did not hold for long, and I'm trying to get them reformed. Alten is at least another hour's march, perhaps more, but he will be coming in from your right. Cooke's Guards Division is a couple hours behind him. They may or may not get here before this battle is decided. How far are the Brunswickers behind you?"

"Not far," Picton answered. "They should be on the field within the hour as well."

Rolling volleys of musket fire interrupted their speech as Picton's division mercilessly hammered the advancing French fusiliers. The front ranks of their enemy were returning fire, but as they attacked in column, they could not bring nearly as many weapons to bear at the same time. Still, their fire was effective enough that the screams of pain from men struck down added to the wall of unholy sound.

"The frogs are pulling back, sir!" General Pack said, riding up excitedly. He then noticed Wellington for the first time and quickly saluted. "Your grace."

"They'll be back," the Duke said. "Keep knocking them down, but don't get overzealous. Marshal Ney has us badly outnumbered, and we have yet to see his cavalry engage. We have no way of knowing their strength, but they're out there. Boney is too smart to send an entire wing of his infantry against us without strong cavalry support." Wellington then looked around and shook his head. "I hate this blasted terrain. It's all flat! For the first time in my life, I've had to go into battle outnumbered and without the advantage of choosing my ground."

183

The loud smash of cannonballs slamming into the ground alerted them. One smashed into the ranks of the Black Watch, smashing apart the bodies of close-ranked highlanders.

"Damn it, where the hell is my artillery?" Picton snapped.

"They're coming up the road now, sir," Kempt said, pointing over his shoulder.

To their front, his brigade was advancing up a short hill that the road crossed.

"Have your batteries form on either side of that small hill," Wellington ordered. "Pour some counterbattery fire onto those guns. Hold this position on the road. I'll reform Perponcher and the Dutch, and have the Brunswickers fall in beside them. Hold this position and do *not* let the enemy take the Quatre Bras crossroads!"

A ricocheting cannonball flew past Wellington as a volley of musket fire from the reforming French fusiliers was directed towards them. Picton winced hard and Wellington thought he saw a round impact the general's side.

"Sir Thomas, are you hit?" the Duke asked.

"Fine...I'm fine!" Picton said quickly. "Just a scratch is all. I'm alright, Arthur, though I'd best get back to my men."

Wellington did not say another word, but rode off quickly towards the 95th. Enemy troops had formed up to attempt a flanking maneuverer near where the road crossed the stream, and the Duke needed to make certain that the Rifles could hold them.

"Damn it all," Picton said, his face sweating as he clutched his side.

"Are you sure you're alright, sir?" General Kempt asked.

Steel cannonballs continued to slam into the earth around them, occasionally striking home against the hapless mass of Anglo soldiers.

"Yes, I'm *fine,* damn it!" Picton snapped. "Get your bloody guns deployed forward and start hammering those frog batteries before they chop our whole division to shreds!" As soon as he was alone, Sir Thomas pulled back his black coat and sighed in dismay. A pool of blood was saturating his shirt underneath, where a hole was clearly visible in the side.

One thing about the silk shirts worn by officers, as well as the few enlisted men who could afford them, is that they served both a fashionable and practical purpose. Unlike cotton or wool, which would disintegrate upon impact of a musket ball, silk held together. It therefore made the extraction of an enemy musket ball much easier, when one simply had to find two ends of the torn fabric within the hole and use those to extract the ball. Sir Thomas did just this, reaching painfully into the bleeding hole in his side and immediately finding two edges of torn fabric. He quietly hoped the musket ball was held between them, as he gritted his teeth and pulled. He gasped in both pain and relief as the lead ball spurted out of his side. The wound was deep and extremely painful; far worse than any injury he'd suffered in the past, even when he'd been hit in the groin at Badajoz. Still, he was lucid, and the bleeding was but a trickle. He took a deep breath and spurred his horse towards his right, where a battery was emplacing in front of Pack's division, while the Brunswickers double-timed down the road, following Wellington to where they would make their stand.

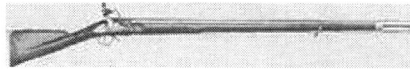

"The English have deployed an entire division to the east of Quatre Bras," General Foy said as he rode up to Ney. The marshal was still with Jerome's division which had, after several brutal assaults, driven the Dutch-Belgians from the Bossu Wood.

"Our advancing columns were beaten back," Foy continued. "We've turned our artillery against them, though they do have batteries of their own returning fire against ours."

"Our artillery is more numerous and better concentrated than theirs," Ney noted. "Even if you cannot break their lines, we are still preventing the English from reinforcing Blucher. The Dutch have reformed, and they look to have been joined by the Brunswickers. Still, the terrain favours us, and our cannon will give them a damn good hiding."

Ney then turned his horse about and rode towards the rear of their lines. Pire's cavalry stood in massed columns, awaiting the order to attack. The Marshal of France then produced his telescope and scanned up the road to the south.

"Damn it all," he grumbled. "Where is d'Erlon's corps?"

185

What Ney did not realize at that moment was that Marshal Soult, still thinking that Ney had just a few Dutch militias facing him at Quatre Bras, had sent word to the Comte d'Erlon, diverting his corps of nearly 20,000 men to Ligny to envelope the Prussians who were holding stubbornly. This was only revealed to Ney a while later, when an aide brought a message from d'Erlon, informing him that he was being diverted to Ligny.

"Damn it all!" he swore as he slapped the parchment with the back of his hand. "The emperor has more than enough men and resources to thrash Blucher! If I had d'Erlon's corps, I could hit Wellington from multiple directions at once and break him here. Instead, I am forced into a bloody grind! Every moment we delay, more of Wellington's army arrives." He then snapped his fingers, summoning his adjutant. He dictated a pair of messages; one to d'Erlon, telling him to turn back around and head for Quatre Bras with all haste. The other was sent to the emperor himself, informing him of the gravity of his situation, and why he needed d'Erlon and the I Corps.

"A victory over the Prussians does us little good if I cannot finish Wellington here," he muttered.

"I hear you were a first-class cricketer, sir," Ensign Lord Hay said as he rode up beside General Maitland.

The thunder of cannon from Quatre Bras boomed in the distance. Though they could hear the sounds of battle, it would still be at least a couple hours longer before the Guards Division reached it. It was a maddening wait for the young ensign, anxious to see his first action.

"Feels like a long time ago," the general remarked. Though he had a number of officers on his staff, with Hay being the most junior, he'd taken a liking to the young man, and the two often rode together when the army was on the march. "I competed for ten years, although it's been seven since my last match. The Peninsular War impeded my ability to continue. I never did get a chance to return to it during our short interlude of peace. I still had many duties to perform, plus I wished to get to know my son, who had not seen me in four years."

"Beg your pardon, sir," Hay replied. "I did not know you were married."

"Widowed ten years ago," Maitland stated. "My son is now eleven. Remarkably, he shares the same birthday as Wellington." There was a trace of pride in Maitland's expression at this last remark.

"Think we'll get there before the battle is decided?" Hay asked, his consternation getting the best of him.

"No idea," the general replied. "We march expediently, though the men still need the strength for a long fight once we arrive. Still thinking about getting a cuirassier's helmet for Lady Sarah?" He chuckled at his last observation.

"I confess I was, sir," Hay admitted. "It's a silly thing to think about; trying to impress a lady when we're getting ready to march into battle."

"Time and place for everything, Mister Hay," Maitland observed. "Enjoy your thoughts of Lady Sarah now, while you can. Once the brigade forms into battle lines, let her go. You will be my eyes and ears forward on the right, where Colonel Stewart will advance."

"Yes, sir," Hay asserted, serious once more.

"Survive this and perhaps you can do more than just think about Lady Sarah," Maitland said with a smile.

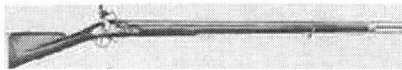

It was no less maddening of a wait for Captain James Webster and his men. They marched directly behind the Grenadier Company, and once the order to deploy was given, would form up on their left. James remembered that this was not only his first action since Badajoz, but it was also his first time actually leading the company into battle. Yet despite the normal nervous tension that preceded any engagement, he was not particularly worried. He knew the skill of his men and, in a standoff, they would break any French unit they encountered with their fast-loading and superior marksmanship. He also had complete trust in his officers and

NCOs. Lieutenant Grose was solid and dependable. Even Ensign Barton was slowly coming into his own. James hazarded that this battle would make or break the young man as an officer. Though he had been perpetually short on NCOs, the ones he had were second to none. All were experienced, and he felt that as long as Colour Sergeant Patrick Shanahan stood, the company could not be broken.

"It still amazes me that Boney massed his forces here," Grose said as he walked up beside his captain.

"The road to Mons is paved," James noted. "So I understand why Wellington felt he would come up that way, even until the very last. Bonaparte is known for being a master of strategic manoeuvre, and using those roads that guaranteed the fastest movement made the most sense; especially since he could have used them to get in behind us."

"That's the trouble, sir," Grose stated. "Boney knew this, and that we would know it, too. It was too obvious for him to use the Mons road in any capacity. So, he makes use of the crossing at Charleroi, using these dirt roads that are absolute shit, and catches us essentially with our pants down."

"Well, then it's time we pulled them up," James chuckled.

A short ways down the column, David O'Connor marched with his gaze fixed on the boots of the soldier in front of him. There was nothing else for him to see, as he was in the middle of the column. To his right, he could just make out the expression of deep worry on Private Adams' face.

"Eric, what the devil's the matter?" he asked. "You look as if you're about to pass out. Not winded already, are you?"

"No worse than you," Eric remarked, though his expression was one of pain. "I don't know what it is. I'm not ill, just have a terrible feeling is all."

"You're the best shot in the entire regiment," David reasoned. "So if you fall this day, well, the rest of us are pretty well fucked anyway."

His remark drew a few nervous laughs from the men around them, though Eric Adams still looked as haggard as ever, his expression unchanging. His demeanour unnerved David, and so he focused back on staring at the marching boots in front of him, while the cadence of the drummers beat rhythmically in his ears. The sound of cannon fire was slowly growing louder.

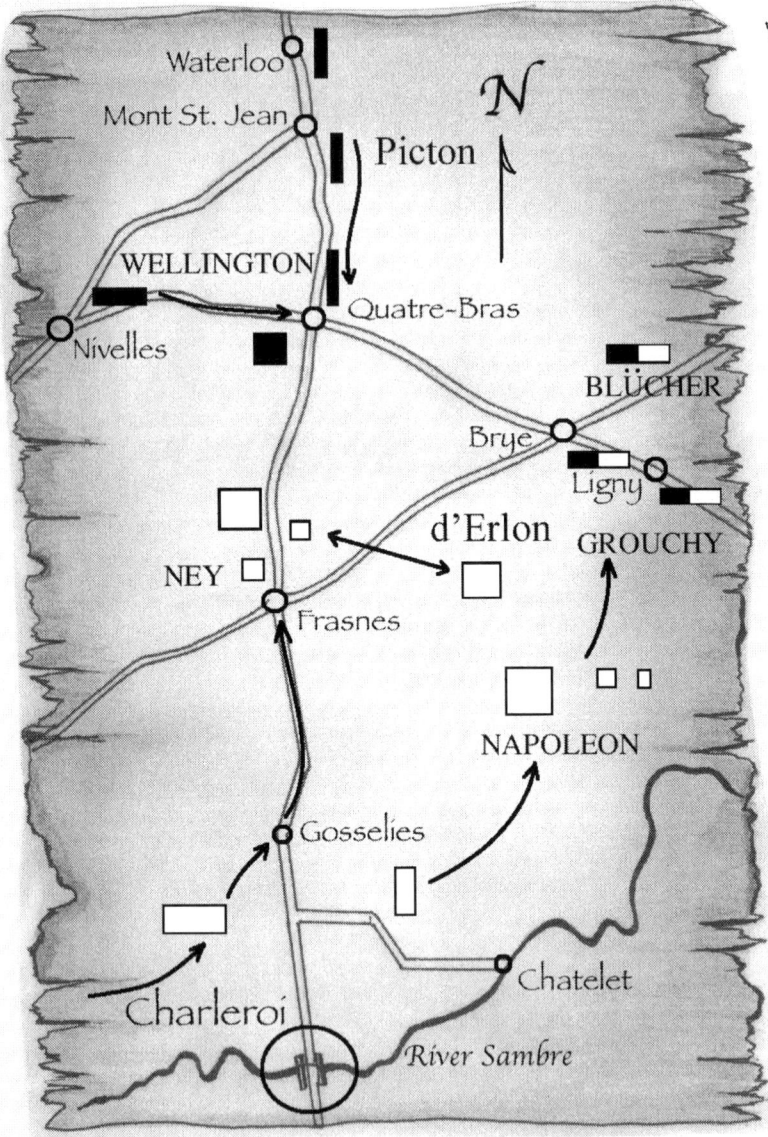

Quatre Bras and Ligny. Ney advances to take Quatre Bras, while Napoleon and Grouchy attack Blucher at Ligny. D'Erlon is diverted to Ligny, only to have the orders countermanded by Ney. Due to the confusion, his corps takes part in neither action. Wellington moves quickly to reinforce the Dutch at Quatre Bras, with Picton advancing from the north. The Guards Division, with Captain Webster, approaches from the west.

Chapter XIII: A Bloody Grind
Quatre Bras
16 June 1815

Charge of French Cuirassiers

The trumpets sounded, alerting the men of the Guards Regiments who'd been in a daze since they started the long march from Braine-le-Comte. Though they had been able to hear the sound of the guns coming from Quatre Bras for some time, they had still marched a number of miles further. A large wood loomed a couple miles distant, and off to their extreme left they could see the smoke billowing from their artillery.

"Battle formation!" Colonel Stewart shouted from atop his horse, Major D'Oyley and Captain Stables echoing the command.

As his company quickly formed into two ranks, James placed himself in the centre, Lieutenant Grose and Ensign Barton took their positions on each end, NCOs dispersed throughout. Though it was customary for sergeants to carry long pikes, many of those in 3rd Battalion had elected to carry muskets instead. As Colour Sergeant Shanahan had put it; since the British army relied on firepower to break the enemy, it made no sense to deprive each battalion of up to thirty weapons.

To their immediate right, the grenadier company fell into an identical formation, the 2nd Company on their left. Daniel Roberts' light company was on the extreme left of the formation, meaning that this day they would fight on the battle line, rather than as skirmishers. Major D'Oyley, coordinating the right wing, rode about fifty paces behind the formation. With the battalion in only two ranks, so as to maximize the number of firearms they could bring to bear, their frontage was very large, and he had to stay back far enough to keep eyes on all of his men. With Captain Stables taking control of the left wing, Lieutenant Colonel Stewart had only to worry about controlling two men, while keeping in line with Colonel Askew's battalion.

Muskets were still kept shouldered as the bugle call sounded the advance. While the men in the ranks had only to focus on their immediate front, James kept a few paces in front, often turning about to see what was going on behind them. It was crucial to maintain situational awareness, especially since once they were in small arms range. It would be difficult to hear commands.

"Our brigade is to take the Bossu Woods," Major D'Oyley ordered, riding up on his horse.

"Yes, sir!" James replied before turning back to his front. That was it, then.

The battle had been raging for a couple hours at this point. The sun was out and it beat down upon them. It had been cold and wet the entire time on the march, yet now when they needed to exert themselves, the sun was being unmerciful.

The ground seemed to explode in front of them as cannon balls burrowed into the earth, kicking up gouts of mud and detritus. Were the ground dry, every shot would have bounced straight into the advancing Guards. One solid shot did bounce, slamming into poor Ensign Barton, who fell screaming to the ground, clutching his mutilated leg.

"Damn it, where the hell did that come from?" a soldier shouted.

"That was no frog cannon, sir," Shanahan said from behind James.

"Bastards!" James said through gritted teeth. He looked off to his left and in the far distance could see the tell-tale smoke coming from artillery guns.

"Those are our own bloody guns!" David O'Connor shouted.

James pushed his way past his men as even more cannon shot slammed into the earth to their front. He waved to Henry D'Oyley, though the major had already seen where the shots were coming from. James then looked over to see Ensign Barton, lying on the ground, gritting his teeth, his face twisted in utter agony. His left leg was smashed above the knee, bone fragments jutting through the skin, his lower leg barely hanging on. He then watched Major D'Oyley ride over to Colonel Stewart and closed his eyes at what he saw next.

"Sir, those bastards are shelling our own men!" Henry shouted to Colonel Stewart.

Before the colonel could answer, and as if to emphasize the major's warning, a shell of carcass shot exploded in the air, directly behind Stewart. The blast blew him from his horse, face first into the torn up earth. As he jumped from his horse, Henry saw Ensign Hay riding quickly up to him.

"Mister Hay!" he shouted. "Tell General Maitland that the artillery from Pack's division is firing on our troops. They need to shift fire now!"

"Sir!" Hay replied, saluting quickly and then riding off as fast his horse could go.

A groan of pain told Henry that the colonel was still alive. He knelt down and saw where Stewart's jacket and trousers were torn in at least a dozen places. The stench of seared flesh assailed his nostrils as smouldering shards of carcass shot continued to burn into the colonel.

"Hang on, sir, I've got you," Henry said, drawing his knife. Though he was wearing gloves, they were very thin, and his fingers were burned repeatedly as he cut the scorching metal from his battalion commander. Stewart rolled to his side and grabbed him by the arm.

"Damn it, man, don't worry about me!" he said, panting hard, his face red and covered in sweat. "Take command of the battalion and win this battle!"

"Yes, sir," Henry said quietly. He then looked over to see the colonel's horse, though shaken and appearing to have been grazed in a few places, was mostly unhurt.

"Leave me," Stewart said through gritted teeth, losing his patience. "You can come back for me when you've whipped the frogs. Go!"

General Maitland had also seen the shelling of his 3rd Battalion, even before Ensign Hay rode up, and he flew into a rage.

"Keep the brigade advancing!" he yelled to Hay as he wheeled his horse about and rode at a sprint towards the artillery. Hay turned his own mount about and rode back towards the battle.

It took ten minutes of hard riding for the general to reach the artillery batteries, and as each cannon and mortar thundered, he wondered how many more shots were going to fall upon his men.

"Cease fire, God damn you! Cease fire!"

The battery commander, who Maitland recognized as Captain Frederik Sandham, quickly echoed his command, and the guns immediately stopped.

"General, sir," the captain said, saluting.

Maitland did not return it. His face was beat red, and he flew into a rage.

"Are you fucking blind?" he screamed, causing the men on the guns to take a few steps back.

Sandham had no choice but to remain where he was. "Sir?" he asked, the general's choice of profanity taking him aback.

"Those are damn redcoats you're firing on!" Maitland retorted, his temper boiling over. "Don't tell me you can't see them!"

"Sir, our guns were pre-sighted in and around the woods," the captain explained. "And with all the smoke, we can't see a blasted thing." He waved with his hand towards the woods for emphasis.

When Maitland looked back over his shoulder he immediately understood. The issue with black powder was that it socked in the area with smoke, and unless one had a decent breeze blowing through, it was impossible to see much beyond one's immediate front. Even from atop his horse, the general could not even see the

194

Bossu Wood, let alone his brigade that was advancing on it. The captain's face was full of horror at the realization of what had happened.

"Sir," Sandham said quickly, "no one even told us there were more British troops coming. For all we knew, the Guards were still at Braine-le-Comte. I...I'm sorry." That British soldiers had been killed or maimed by his guns would haunt Frederik Sandham for the rest of his life.

Maitland felt for him, but he also knew that he had to get Sandham's guns back in the fight. "Are your weapons sighted for the other side of the woods?" he asked in a softer tone.

"Yes, sir, of course!" Sandham said with emphasis.

"Shift your fire," Maitland ordered, "Keep the French from reinforcing the woods, and you just might save the lives of my men."

"Sir!" Sandham said with renewed resolve. *"Battery...action left!"*

Maitland rode at a slower canter as he returned to his brigade, while Captain Sandham barked out subsequent orders, and soon his six cannons and single mortar were firing upon the far side of the woods. It upset him greatly that word of his brigade's arrival had not been passed along. In battle, particularly large-scale ones, miscommunications were common. However, it was a pretty serious omission to not let an artillery battery know that the area they were shelling would soon be occupied by their own troops.

James exhaled in relief as he noted that the barrage had stopped as they made their way closer to the wood line. The entire battalion had unconsciously increased its pace, and they were within about 300 yards of the trees.

"No sign of the bloody frogs yet," he heard a private mumble.

As ferocious as the battle had been, and given the cover and concealment offered by the woods, there was little doubt that they were crawling with French soldiers.

"They're in there," O'Connor replied, sweat forming on his brow. "Just wait till we're within range. They'll say 'adieu' soon enough."

They then saw a mounted figure riding at the gallop around them, sword held high as he rode back and forth in front of them.

"Why it's young Lord Hay!" Corporal Donaldson said, amused. "What the devil is he doing?"

"Providing a bit of added motivation for us," Patrick replied with a grin. "Full of military dashing and ardour, that one. He needs to get out of the way soon, though."

"He'll move," James said calmly. "Once he sees us lower our weapons to fire."

It was, indeed, rather dashing to watch the young man ride in front of them, showing that he was unafraid. When a young officer lacked training or experience, he had to rely upon personal valour to inspire the ranks. Rather than think him foolish, most of the men quietly admired his fanatical bravery.

"Keep up the advance, men!" he shouted. "Remember your families! Remember your homes! *For England!*"

His last cry elicited a loud battle cry from the battalion, and their pace increased to a fast walk. As Hay rode in front of James' men, an entire company of French skirmishers, who'd up to this point been hiding in the undergrowth, opened fire. Dozens of weapons erupted, and the young lord was torn to pieces. Musket balls slammed into his hip, thigh, torso, chest, and even knocked his hat from his head. One ghastly shot tore through his neck in a spray of deep crimson. His sword arm fell as the blade was shattered in two, and the gallant young man tumbled unceremoniously from his horse, which was now sprinting away in terror. Hay's body twitched violently as his eyes glazed over and gouts of blood gushed from his mouth.

"Poor Sarah, that'll break her heart," James said quietly to himself. He then shouted to his men, "We're within two-hundred yards! Advance quickly before the frogs can reload!"

Ensign Hay's sacrifice may have saved a number of lives in James' company, as a complete lack of discipline had led the French skirmishers to all fire at once. In a sign that Major D'Oyley had the same thought, the bugle calls to double-time were heard. The companies on either side of James' men immediately broke into a jog. His own gaze was fixed on at least a dozen Frenchmen who may have been inconspicuous before, but now seemed to stand out starkly against the tree line. Knowing the superior marksmanship skills of his men, and also not wishing to give the enemy skirmishers a chance to finish reloading, he gave his next command at a much greater range than one would expect.

"Make ready!" he shouted, halting and raising his sword high.

His men immediately stopped and lowered their weapons as James brought his sword down.

"Fire!"

A concentrated volley of musket fire exploded on either side of him. A thick cloud of smoke blinded them, and James knew there was nothing to do but run through it.

"Charge!"

A battle cry erupted from his company, and to a man, they sprinted the remaining hundred yards to the trees. Rolling volleys of gunfire came from the other companies as they, too, then executed their charge. Shots rang out from the trees, followed by the occasional shouts of pain as men were hit. A number of the French skirmishers lay dead or dying as the company stormed into the woods. James saw one man who'd been shot through the stomach, lying on his side, guts splayed across the ground. He was on his side, trying to reach for his weapon. The captain ran forward and viciously kicked him in the head, snapping his neck. His men overwhelmed the few remaining skirmishers with blows from their musket butt-stocks and thrusts of the bayonet. As the enemy light troops who survived the onslaught fled into the woods, James knew the fight had just begun.

Enemy fire was now concentrating more on them, as the French units in the woods comprehended the size of the force now attacking them from the flank. A soldier next to James took a musket ball to the face and fell screaming to the ground, as he clutched his shattered cheekbone.

"Reload!" Lieutenant Grose shouted from the end of the line.

Given the density of the woods, James knew that he could not hope to coordinate his entire company. It would be up to his NCOs to execute his intent.

"Bound by sections!" he ordered. "Fire and advance!"

As he clawed his way through the thicket to his front, groups of his men would fire a volley, then advance quickly about a dozen yards before taking cover to reload; sections on either side then executing the same. This type of manoeuvring kept a sustained rate of fire on the enemy, while allowing the men to advance relatively

197

quickly. It also required much coordination at the platoon-level, and the captain was glad to have some of the best drilled men in the entire army.

Periodically, they would encounter pockets of French soldiers and a hand-to-hand brawl would ensue. James fired his pistol into one such melee and then knelt behind a bramble bush to reload. He then noted his drummer, who was hiding behind a nearby tree and shaking uncontrollably.

"You alright, son?" James asked as he rammed the ball down the short barrel of his pistol, his sword tucked under his arm.

The lad he spoke to was probably no older than fourteen, and since drummers did not normally fight, he seemed uncertain as what to do next.

"I don't know what to do, sir," the lad said. "The entire battalion charged, and I didn't know what else to do but charge as well. This is my first battle, sir, and with no more drumming to do…" His voice trailed off as a musket ball slammed into the tree he sat behind.

"Well," James said calmly as he tucked his pistol into his belt, "There's a dead frog a couple feet from you. If you're feeling ambitious, take his weapon and ammunition pouch and join the fight. You do know how to use a flintlock?"

"Oh yes, sir!" the lad said excitedly. He then loosened the straps on his drum and set it off to the side. He saw the dead Frenchman his captain referred to and removed his ammunition pouch.

"Just be sure you come back for your drum kit later," James ordered as he rose and started making his way back into the fray.

In the thick woods he could only make out small groups of his men, but at least he could tell they were advancing. Off to his right, he saw Lieutenant Grose leading about two dozen men towards a pocket of French soldiers. His men unleashed a volley and then scampered through the woods. As they stopped to load once more, Grose looked back at them while pointing his sword towards another group of enemy soldiers. Before he could issue any further orders, a single shot rang out and his sword arm fell to his side. His jaw twitched and blood streamed from the corners of his mouth. He collapsed face-first to the ground, a gaping gunshot wound at the base of his neck.

"No!" James shouted, running towards his subaltern. Lieutenant Edward Grose had been more than just his subordinate officer. James had also thought of him as a friend.

Of their own volition, the soldiers who he'd led rose up together and let their muskets unleash another volley. As they charged, one of them fell doubled over as he was shot through the stomach. Another's head snapped back, and he fell lifeless to the ground. They soon fell upon their hated foe with men screaming curses, stabbing, and trying to bash each other's brains in.

James knelt down next to Grose and placed a hand on the man's lifeless shoulder.

"I'm sorry, Edward," he said quietly. He looked up to see his men overwhelming the Frenchmen who were starting to flee.

Off to his left other groups of soldiers were further back and taking a lot of fire from concentrated enemy positions. He quickly got to his feet and ran over to the men Grose had been leading, who now seemed uncertain as what to do next. James was further shocked to see there was not a single NCO amongst them.

"What now, sir?" he recognized the voice of Private David O'Connor, who'd taken the lead as much as he was able. "We think the grenadier company is almost to the far tree line, but it's hard to see a damn thing in this!"

"The rest of the company is pinned down over there," James answered, pointing with his sword. They could just make out the occasional glint of steel and red tunic. "Whatever they're up against, we'll now hit in the flank."

"Alright, lads!" David shouted. "Reload and make ready to advance!"

Discipline and drill taking over, the men, who now numbered perhaps twenty, formed into a single line facing towards where they knew the flank of the enemy had to be. In the past, officers would manually call out the sequence for loading, but now each man performed the task on his own. Paper cartridge from the ammunition pouch, tear it open with the teeth, prime the pan, pour the rest of the powder down the barrel, drop or spit in the ball, remove ramrod, hammer the ball home, replace ramrod. Every man finished and stood around the same time. James surmised it had taken less than twenty seconds for these men to reload. He was now considering the money he'd used to purchase extra training ammunition the previous winter well-spent.

"Advance!" he ordered as he placed himself in the centre and a couple paces in front of the men.

They moved as quickly as they could through the dense undergrowth, jumping and climbing over fallen logs, and making every effort to move both safely and expediently. It was still a maddeningly slow pace; with their long muskets and bayonets catching on every tree branch, men slipping on patches of flattened grass and slick fallen trees, as well as sinking in the mud. Wafts of smoke and the crack of musket shot alerted them to the enemy. James' eyes were wide, trying to spot the tell-tale blue and white of the French uniforms.

"There they are, sir!" Private O'Connor shouted, pointing with the bayonet of his musket.

It was then that James saw numerous French soldiers gathered behind a short berm. They were clustered together, as there was not much else for cover available. It may have protected them from the redcoats to their front, but for Captain Webster and his men, they were completely exposed.

"Ready!" James shouted, raising his sword, *"Fire!"* He gave his orders loud enough so that his men pinned down by the French would know it was English soldiers firing and not more enemy troops.

There was no need for a subsequent order; a scramble of hands digging into twenty ammunition pouches, and his men were rapidly loading their weapons once more. The haze of smoke made it even more difficult to see, and James hoped that the Frenchmen who'd been mauled by his soldiers' fire would not be able to orient on where it came from.

He gave a slow count to twenty in his head before giving his next order. *"Ready...fire!"*

Another crash of gunfire and James' ears were numb. He wondered how many soldiers who survived to old age were completely deaf. He was able to make out the voice of one of his NCOs off to his left-front.

"Hey, it's Captain Webster!" This elicited a renewed shout of determination from the company.

James then called out to the man. *"Corporal Donaldson!"*

200

"Sir?"

"We'll give them one more volley, then advance the company. We will hold our fire then."

"Yes, sir!"

James quietly hoped that Colour Sergeant Shanahan was still alive, though at that moment he was glad to find anyone in a leadership position still in the fight. His company had been short a sergeant and two corporals as it was going into battle. He then noted quickly that he was grateful to Private O'Connor, who had stepped forward after Lieutenant Grose was killed.

"Ready...fire!"

One final burst and James hoped the French were now broken. He cursed himself for allowing his men to get scattered like they did, but reckoned the rest of the battalion was going through the same difficulties, as likely was Colonel Askew and his men.

"Let's go!" he heard Corporal Donaldson shout.

There was a loud roar from his men as they crashed through the thickets. There were many curses, snaps of branches, and tumbles of men who tripped and fell, but there was no enemy fire heard.

"They've all hoofed it!" James heard an English voice say from the vicinity of the berm.

"Move out," he ordered the men with him. The smoke was dissipating and he was shocked at just how close they'd been to the French soldiers they fired upon. He surmised they hadn't been more than twenty yards away.

Between the trees and dense undergrowth, the entire fight had taken place at an unnervingly close range. Behind the berm were at least a dozen dead French soldiers with about twice as many badly wounded. Men cried piteously, clutching shattered arms and legs. Others had been struck in the chest, hip, or stomach, and their faces told of the abject pain they were suffering. The ground was slick with blood and chunks of flesh ripped away by the smashing musket shots.

"Hey, shall I stick this one?" a private said, waving his bayonet menacingly over a badly injured Frenchman. The poor soldier's eyes were wide in terror as the blade flashed in front of his face.

Corporal Harvey shoved the private hard, away from the wounded man. "Knock that shit off!"

201

"We don't kill the enemy wounded!" James emphasized. "For now, leave them be. If we win this battle, then we will care for them like we would our own. You would expect the same from them. Now form up!"

The soldier's behaviour had angered James. He especially found it unbecoming of the Guards. He chose not to dwell on it, as they still had to work their way through the rest of the woods, find the remainder of the battalion, and see how the rest of the battle was proceeding. He had no way of knowing whether it was going good or ill for the British army. His small company was but a microcosm of a much larger effort.

"We're ready to move, sir," the voice of Patrick Shanahan came as an immense relief. James then walked down the line of his men. A number were missing, but it appeared the majority were still in the fight.

"Where's Sergeant Billings?" James asked, noting that his only NCOs present were Shanahan and Corporals Donaldson and Harvey.

"A bunch of frogs got the jump on us, sir," a private said, who could only shake his head in further explanation.

James nodded and then waved them forward with his sword. "Advance!" His company may have just been in a brawl, but there was still much fighting left to do. His soldiers had been cognisant enough during the lull to gather up ammunition from the dead, as well as any from the French casualties that may have been useable. The French muskets were of a slightly smaller calibre, however, in an emergency, their cartridges could still be fired from a British, albeit with a loss of muzzle velocity.

James was thankful that as they approached the far end of the woods, the undergrowth thinned considerably, and the mass of trees was not nearly so thick. He was further relieved when he saw off to his right the grenadier company reforming at the edge of the tree line. He could not see any other companies off to his left, but he could hear the sounds of orders being shouted in English and noted that the sounds of gunfire had mostly tapered off. He grimaced as they reached the end of the trees. The main battle was far from decided, the thunder of cannon and musket fire a continuous roar. He heard the sound of a horse galloping to his left and saw Major D'Oyley riding towards him.

202

"Captain Webster!" he hailed. "I am glad to see you still with us, sir."

"And you, sir," James replied, saluting his commander with his sabre. "Do we know how the rest of the battle goes?"

"No idea," Henry replied with a nervous laugh and a shrug. "It's been a bloody grind, that's for damn sure. At least we cleared the frogs from these woods. That will give the rest of the army some breathing space. The battalion should be on line within the next twenty minutes or so, and I'm meeting with all company commanders by the 4th Company."

"Yes, sir," James replied as Henry rode off to meet with the commander of the grenadier company. He then turned to Patrick. "Form up a defensive position with the grenadiers, the rest of the battalion will fall in on you. Hold in place until I return."

"We'll be here, sir," Patrick acknowledged. He then looked around for a moment. "What about Lieutenant Grose?" He bit the inside of his cheek when he saw his captain shake his head.

James sheathed his sword and walked down the line towards where he guessed the 4th Company would be. He was soon joined by the commanders of the 2nd and 3rd Companies and saw other officers making their way from the extreme left of the battalion line. He was particularly glad to see Daniel Roberts coming from the vicinity of the light company.

"Still among the living?" James asked, taking his friend's hand.

"For the time being," Daniel replied with a trace of dark humour.

James noted a handful of subalterns present and could only guess that their captains were either dead or wounded. Captain Stables soon joined them, as did Major D'Oyley.

"I feel I must apologize to you men on the right wing," the major said as he dismounted. "The colonel's been hit, and I had to take command of the entire battalion. In the heat of battle, I neglected to have one of you replace me."

"We're still here, sir," the grenadier captain said.

Henry nodded. "We only have a few moments. As you can see, the issue of this battle is far from decided. I've sent word to General Maitland to see if we can get a better grasp of the overall situation." He then looked at James. "Captain Webster, you will take control of the right wing."

203

"Very good, sir," James replied. He paused and noted, "I lost both of my subalterns. I have no officers to command my company."

"Well, there's a spot of bad luck," Henry said darkly. "We don't exactly have excess officers just hanging about. Ah, there's the man who can help us." He nodded towards General Maitland who rode up to them.

"Henry," he said, "it would seem Marshal Ney is leading the French attack, with Bonaparte himself battling with the Prussians at Ligny. We've ascertained Boney's generals Jerome and Foy are to our front, and General Cooke has ordered the entire division to launch an assault on their flank."

"Understood," Henry replied. He then stopped the general from riding off. "One moment, sir. We've been depleted of officers..."

"Yes, the entire brigade has," Maitland noted with a trace of irritation. It was only when the brigade had assaulted the woods that he had come across young Hay, whose mutilated body lay in a deep puddle of his own blood and bodily fluids.

"I'm placing Captain Webster in control of my right wing," Henry quickly explained. "He lost both subalterns..."

"There's a spot of bad luck," the general said in an echo of Major D'Oyley's earlier statement.

"Our only option is to commission a man from the ranks," Henry said quickly. "I do not have the authority, but you do."

Maitland's face twitched at the prospect. Like Wellington, he abhorred the practice of creating officers from the enlisted men. Yet he was also pragmatic enough to know when it was crucial to cast personal bias aside. "Alright, where is he?" he said impatiently.

James did not hesitate. *"Colour Sergeant Shanahan!"* The call was quickly echoed down the line of companies, within just a couple minutes they saw Patrick running towards them. He was breathing hard, stopped, and saluted before removing his shako and wiping his forehead.

"Colour Sergeant," Maitland said to him.

"General, sir," Patrick replied, just now noticing his brigade commander.

"You are now *Lieutenant* Shanahan," the general emphasized. "I'll have a temporary order drawn up once this battle is decided and I can find one of my A.D.C.s who isn't bleeding to death."

"Sir!" Patrick said, saluting once more. He turned to head back to the company when James grabbed him by the tunic.

"You're company commander now," he whispered. "Don't go anywhere yet."

Patrick's face turned red in embarrassment for a brief moment as General Maitland rode off in the direction of Colonel Askew's battalion. Major D'Oyley then addressed the battalion once more.

"Alright, return to your units and make ready to advance. Captain Stables, Captain Webster, keep close eye on your companies. James, I'm sorry we don't have a horse for you. I'm certain we'll be able to get you one once this is over."

"Yes, sir," James replied.

The officers then all saluted the major, who was back on his horse.

James leaned over to Patrick, "Now you can leave."

There was a look of deep consternation on Patrick Shanahan's face as he returned to the 1st Company. He took up the commander's position in the centre and took a deep breath.

"Where's Captain Webster?" Corporal Donaldson asked.

"He's now coordinating the right wing," Patrick answered.

"So who's in command of the company, colour sergeant?"

"I am," Patrick replied after a brief pause. "And I'm not a colour sergeant anymore. I'll be buggered, but General Maitland just made me a lieutenant!"

"Bollocks!" a private said with sarcasm.

"Belay that!" Corporal Harvey shouted, cuffing the man across the ear.

"Alright, lads!" Patrick called out, immediately taking control. "Line formation! We're going to advance out of the woods and put an end to this brawl!" He leaned over, and with a trace of humour in his voice, said quietly to Donaldson, "Don't tell anyone, but I have no idea what I'm supposed to do."

"Just point in the right direction and tell us who to kill," the corporal said with a matching grin, "and I'm sure you'll do just fine...*sir*."

205

Lieutenant Patrick Shanahan was not the only one uncertain as to what he was doing. James placed himself a few paces back, centred behind the 2nd Company. With the battalion still occupying the woods, he'd have to wait until they were in the open before he could get a proper spacing. It was baffling to him that he now had four line companies, plus the grenadiers that he had to coordinate. Captain Stables would maintain the remaining four line units, plus the light company.

"At least he has a horse," James muttered. He figured there was nothing for it but to try and be light on his feet, if and when he needed to direct each company under his control. A bugle sounded and James opened his mouth as if to give the command to advance, then cursed himself in the realization it was no longer his position. Company commanders gave the order to advance and the drummers, who'd reformed with Major D'Oyley, were now beating the cadence of march. James then remembered the 1st Company's drummer and hoped he was with them.

Any hopes of the Guards Division being able to decisively decide the battle evaporated as they emerged from the woods. The French soldiers who'd fled had re-joined with Jerome and Foy's divisions, who were now fully aware of the threat on their flank and had reacted accordingly. Deep ranks of enemy soldiers occupied the rolling hills to their front, and they started firing on the Guards as soon as they cleared the woods. Drummers quickened their cadence; though James' face twitched as he saw men fall. Individual companies halted and returned fire. As the British preferred using firepower to the bayonet, it now turned into a shooting match between them and their foe. British Foot Guards were superior marksmen and quicker at reloading than their French counterparts, and James surmised that his men got off three volleys to the enemy's two. The French still had the superior ground, which they were not going to give up easily.

Volley after volley was fired with a murderous crash, men falling on both sides. The volume of fire from the British Guards was certainly taking its toll, and it had to be reckoned that the French of Jerome's division had been in battle much longer than they had. There was little for James to do, and he found it maddening to just stand there and watch the battle play out. He inadvertently kept looking over at the 1st Company, and it tore him up inside each time he saw one of them fall. He saw movement off to his right front, around the nearby hill.

"Cuirassiers!" he shouted as loud as he could.

An entire regiment of Napoleon's highly-feared armoured cavalrymen were galloping around the hill and making straight for them. But it was not just the cuirassiers, there were also squadrons of lancers advancing on their flank.

Major D'Oyley heard the warning and the bugler started frantically calling for the battalion to form into a square. There was too little time, and James swallowed hard as he watched the terrifying elite of Bonaparte's cavalry bearing down on his men.

"Oh bloody fuck!" a soldier shouted as the 1st Company caught sight of the wall of fast-approaching horsemen.

"What the hell do we do?" another cried out, his voice near panic.

"We give them a volley, and then meet them with the bayonet," Patrick said calmly, though inside he was absolutely terrified. Despite his many battles during the Peninsular War, he'd never actually seen a cuirassier up close, but he knew their fearsome reputation. In an age where the average soldier on either side stood maybe 5'6", Napoleon had required these men to be at least 6' tall. Patrick had always dismissed such stories as French myths meant to scare their enemies, but when he saw the armoured horsemen racing towards him, screaming in fury, he reckoned they were not men at all, but giants.

"Giants can still be killed," he said quietly to himself. He then steeled his resolve and brought his musket up while issuing his next command. *"Ready...fire!"*

He fired his weapon along with the rest of his men, bringing a wave of men and horses crashing to the earth with horrific screams of pain. Their companions were not slowed and immediately smashed into the ranks of British Infantry. Though the chest plates worn by the cuirassiers gave them much protection against the bayonet, the infantrymen still had greater reach than they had with their sabres. For the French Cavalry, speed and manoeuver was their advantage.

The wall of lancers that bore down upon the grenadier company did enjoy the advantage of reach. The grenadiers also fired a volley into their ranks, and then braced themselves as men, horses, and lances smashed into them. The men of the grenadiers started to waver as their companions were impaled by lances. Soon groups of men started to break and run, and James quickly rushed over before it turned into a complete rout.

"Stand fast!" he shouted. "You can't outrun their horses, damn you! If you're going to die, then stand and die as men!" He then raised his pistol, causing one of the men to panic, thinking it was pointed at him. The captain fired, and a lancer behind the soldier fell screaming from his horse, holding his face, where torrents of blood gushed between his fingers. "Now reform the line!"

The soldier nodded, his eyes still wide, but he turned about, and many of his fellows did the same. James then noted the 1st Company, where Lieutenant Shanahan was using a rarely used drill to extract his men. His third rank sprinted back ten yards, turned about, and quickly reloaded their muskets. The second rank soon withdrew ten yards behind them, the first rank following suit. As soon as the first rank passed what had been the third, these men fired a singled volley into the cuirassiers before withdrawing again. It was a fighting withdrawal, with the French Cavalry being met with a near-continuous volley of gunfire, impeding their chances of affecting a pursuit.

"Follow the 1st Company's lead!" James shouted to the distraught commander of the grenadiers, who was desperately trying to restore order. "Fall back by ranks; keep up a steady fire in the faces of these bastards!"

"Yes, sir," the fellow captain answered.

James could not wait to see what else happened, as he still had three more companies to coordinate their withdrawal. He cursed once again that he did not have a horse to use. His blood was pumping, his heart pounding in his chest as he rushed over to the 2nd Company, which was also heavily engaged with the cuirassiers. The 3rd and 4th Companies were still mostly battling the French Infantry, who had regained their composure after the arrival of their cavalry. With half his wing now tied down by Ney's armoured horsemen, the remaining two companies were drastically outgunned by the French, who despite their terrible losses had held their ground.

Hope was then renewed as off to the right a full regiment of British Infantry emerged, firing concentrated volleys into the cuirassiers and lancers. This fresh onslaught was too much for the French Cavalry, and they quickly wheeled about and rode away from the battle. The bugles sounded recall, and the cadence of drums helped companies maintain order as they slowly backed towards the wood line once more. James noticed that the French Infantry were pulling back as well in a simultaneous, and unspoken acknowledgment that the battle was over. It was late in the day, and neither side had the strength or will to continue the fight.

Upon reaching the woods, men leaned against trees or dropped to a knee, exhaustion and strain overtaking them. James saw a mounted officer riding towards him from his right. He walked over to the man and saluted.

"Lieutenant Colonel Harris, 73rd Regiment," the officer said, returning the salute.

"Captain Webster, 1st Foot Guards," James replied. "Thank God your men got here!"

"We've been here all day," the colonel remarked darkly. "Had a run in with those same bastards you did. That insufferable arse, the Prince of Orange, ordered our entire brigade to come out of our squares and maintain line formation, even though we knew there were regiments of French horse in the area!" Major D'Oyley rode up and joined the men, the colonel addressing them both now. "The 69th got routed and even lost the King's Colour. That will leave a black eye on the army and give Boney something to cheer about. If not for these woods, we would have been annihilated. I'm grateful you cleared them out for us."

"Any word on the rest of the battle, sir?" Henry asked. "We arrived late in the day and have heard nothing."

The sky was red in the west, and night would be upon them soon.

"Best I can tell, we ground the frogs to a halt," Colonel Harris replied. "I know Old Nosey was hoping to reinforce the Prussians at Ligny, just up the road, but with the French hitting us so hard here, we had to hold until the rest of the army arrived. At least we kept the frogs from taking Quatre Bras and cutting all lines of communication. Still, we have yet to hear how the fight goes at Ligny. If the Prussians can hold like we did, then we'll be in a good position for tomorrow. If not…" He shook his head as his voice trailed off.

As soon as Colonel Harris had ridden back to his regiment, Henry addressed both James and Captain Stables, who'd just joined them. "We'll send men out under a flag of truce to retrieve our dead and wounded," he said. "I'm certain the frogs will do the same. We need to get a full count of our losses, as well as how much ammunition we have left. The quartermaster wagons are somewhere between here and Braine-le-Comte, so until they arrive, scavenge what ammunition you can."

Napoleon walked the field just north of the Ligny Brook, his hands clasped behind his back. Bodies littered the landscape; the cries of wounded and spine-cringing screams of maimed horses made his skin crawl. Years of constant warfare and countless battles with similar aftermaths had done nothing to desensitize the French emperor. His name was synonymous with war, yet it was something he now abhorred.

"What the Prussians lacked in tactical savvy, they certainly made up for in their fanatical bravery," Marshal Soult observed as he joined the emperor, who gave a short nod.

"True," he said, "but the brave man is just as dead when shot as is the coward." He continued his walk to where a number of Prussian cannon had been abandoned. Bodies of French soldiers, ripped to pieces by close-range canister shot, lay scattered in front of the fearsome weapons. Though they had made a valiant stand, which cost Napoleon far more than he'd hoped, once he committed the Imperial Guard, the defeat of the Prussians turned into a complete rout. The bodies of the dead and wounded beyond the cannon were overwhelmingly Prussian, and with such a sight of destruction the emperor could not help but think that they were completely broken.

"Sire!" Marshal Grouchy greeted as he rode up on his horse, saluted, and then quickly dismounted. "The entire Prussian army is on the run. Thousands have thrown down their arms and either surrendered or fled. It is a glorious day!"

"If the Prussians truly are broken," Soult remarked, "then we can unleash everything we have against Wellington. I doubt that Marshal Ney had the strength to beat Wellington, but if he can at least hold him in place, we can envelope and destroy the English!"

"Wellington won't stay once he learns the Prussians were routed," the emperor observed. "He knows how to utilize terrain, and that around Quatre Bras makes for a lousy defence. No, I think he will withdraw and attempt to face us from ground of his own choosing."

"What are your orders for now, sire?" Soult asked.

"The hour grows late," Napoleon noted, his face showing extreme fatigue. "For now, we solidify our gains and care for the wounded; ours as well as the Prussians. A little charity towards our fallen enemies, and perhaps they will be more amicable when I press them for terms of peace. And we paved the road to peace with the bodies of 16,000 Prussian casualties."

Unbeknownst to Napoleon and the rest of the French army, Marshal Blucher himself was amongst those still stranded on the battlefield. The 72-year old Prussian commander lay unconscious beneath his slain horse. Cavalrymen stampeded on either side of him as General Gneisenau led a last-ditch counterattack. Men and horses were spent from the day's hard fighting, and against the onslaught of cuirassiers and Polish lancers, any attempts at driving the French back were quickly proving futile.

"Sound the retreat!" Gneisenau ordered the nearest bugler. He then turned to one of the staff officers, Colonel Clausewitz. "Organize a rear guard. Keep the enemy from enveloping us as we extract what's left of the army."

"Yes, sir," the colonel replied. He then turned his horse, signalling for a major named von Nostitz to follow him with a squadron of dragoons, armed with carbines. It was Nostitz who first spotted the fallen field marshal.

"Sir, it's Marshal Blucher!" he shouted excitedly, leaping from his horse. He reached down and checked the old man for signs of life. "He's still alive!"

"Help him," Clausewitz ordered a group of cavalrymen. They lifted the dead horse off him as Nostitz drug his unconscious body from beneath.

"He doesn't seem to be hurt badly," the major said after a quick check. "Just a crack on the head is all."

"Put him on your horse," the colonel directed. "We must get him clear of this place at once."

Chasseur a Cheval Captain

While pickets maintained a watch at the tree line and working parties went forward to retrieve casualties from the open field, other groups of men went back through the woods to try and find anyone else still missing. Patrick happened upon Sergeant Billings, who lay with his back against a tree, covered in blood, eyes wide open.

Patrick knelt and placed a hand on his shoulder. "I hope you found peace in the next life," he said quietly. He looked over his shoulder and saw Corporal Donaldson standing behind him. "You're senior corporal. Take his rank."

Donaldson nodded and stooped down to cut the insignia from Billings' sleeve. "I hate being promoted this way."

"Don't we all," Patrick said quietly. As he started to continue his search, he heard Captain Webster call to him.

"Patrick!"

"Sir?" he asked, turning around. He saw his captain carrying a tunic under his arm, which he tossed to him.

"I think we're about the same size, and I always carry a spare. I don't have a spare officer's shako or any of the extra accessories, but at least we can get you wearing the proper rank."

Patrick held the officer's tunic and stared at the single epaulet that he ran his thumb over. He then looked up at James. "Sir, you really don't think Old Nosey will let me keep this, do you? Even if I can acquire a free vacancy, I'll lose it as soon as some aristocrat's son shows up with enough pounds to buy it out from under me. Besides, you know the Duke hates the thought of officers coming from the ranks."

"The Duke has a lot better things to worry about than one colour sergeant being commissioned," James retorted. "If we have to deal with the issue of purchase when this is over, so be it. But for now, you're out of uniform, *lieutenant*."

"We certainly took a beating," Major D'Oyley said to his assembled officers that evening. They all met in a hastily erected tent that served as the battalion's temporary headquarters. "However, it could have been much worse, when you look at the scrap we got in at the end. And besides, I daresay we gave the French a better licking than we took." He then nodded to his adjutant, who read from a notebook he'd just finished writing in.

"Final count," he said, "barring any who die from their injuries, is twenty-two dead, two hundred and sixty wounded."

"Damn," Daniel Roberts said, shaking his head. "That's 25%, and we weren't even in the fight as long as most of the army."

"That may be," Henry D'Oyley replied, "but we still had one of the hardest tasks in clearing those woods, and we did so effectively and with resounding discipline and valour. Your men should be commended for what they did today. The bad news is, the Prussians did *not* fare as well as we did."

"How bad?" James asked. "Did they at least hold Ligny?"

"No," the major replied. "They were stalwart and pressed the French hard, but in the end, Boney was just too damn effective against them. He's thrashed the Prussians so many times, he's got it down to an art."

"So what happens now?" Captain Stables asked. "If Boney kicked the Prussians in the arse, we cannot possibly hold here."

"That is true," Henry agreed. "If the Prussians are, indeed, out of the fight, then the frogs have us substantially outnumbered and can turn their entire force against us. But it's not hopeless, gentlemen. We can trust Old Nosey, and I'm certain he's prepared for a situation such as this. Remember, he was not always able to rely on his Portuguese and Spanish allies in the Peninsula, so I doubt he's put all his trust in the Prussians. But for now, our priority is holding our position, refitting, getting the men a hot meal if possible, and above all, evacuating the wounded."

"Speaking of wounded," Daniel Roberts asked, "how is the colonel?"

"He's tore up pretty bad," Henry conceded, "but as long as his wounds don't get infected, I think he'll live. Captain Webster, I've acquired the colonel's horse for you, with his compliments."

"Thank you, sir," James said. After all the running he'd done that afternoon, trying to coordinate between five companies, he'd wondered if his boots or his lungs would give out first.

"If that is all…" the battalion commander started to say.

"One thing, sir," Patrick spoke up.

"Yes?"

"There is a soldier from my company I would like to mention in the despatches; Private Eric Adams. I've confirmed that he killed five frogs with head shots today and bayoneted two more. He even managed to get a cuirassier beneath the arm and right through the heart as we were pulling back."

"Duly noted," Major D'Oyley replied, nodding to his adjutant, who was writing the details down. The major then dismissed the men, who stood and saluted and started to leave.

"Lieutenant Shanahan," Henry said as Patrick stopped at the tent flap.

"Sir?" he asked.

"That uniform looks smart on you. See to it that you can keep it."

Today was a bloody one. While the Prussians took a severe thrashing and are now on the run, we've managed to fight the French to a grinding standstill. I am now in control of the right wing our battalion. Normally this would be a major's posting, but since our only major is now battalion commander, this has fallen upon me. Patrick Shanahan was commissioned by General Maitland and now commands my former company. What will happen to us when this is over, I cannot say. Should we survive, I think he will make a fine officer, and anything I can do to help him keep his commission, I will.

With night upon us, and nothing more that duty can ask of me, I am now haunted by thoughts of those I love. If we fail, and the worst should happen to me, I hope Emma is able to take Amy and escape to England. I now know what my daughter means to her, and I curse myself for ever parting them. If I die, I want Emma to take care of Amy. Regrettably, I never put anything in writing, so she would have no legal claim, and like a fool, I never let anyone at home know our feelings for each other. My family does not even know she exists! Perhaps if someone finds this journal, it will suffice. I know Father and Mother would welcome Emma into their granddaughter's life, if they knew it was my wish. However, if the worst happens to me, then this work will probably fall into the hands of an enemy soldier, who will perhaps read it for his own amusement.

Thoughts of my daughter, and of Emma, deprive me of sleep, despite my complete exhaustion. But then, I suppose it's the same for all of us, on both sides. After all, every French soldier who fell by our hand today left behind someone who loved him. How many of their survivors are writing similar journals or letters to wives and family? How many will ask God to protect those they love should they fall in battle?

I guess we're not so different after all. Time to stop contemplating the thoughts of my enemy, tomorrow will be a time for duty once more. For now, it is time for sleep.

Captain James Henry Webster
16 June 1815

Chapter XIV: Why Are We on the Run?
Quatre Bras
17 June 1815

British cavalry officer and French infantry

"Pass, friend," the voice of the picket alerted Patrick. The predawn made it easy to see by, though it would still be another hour or so before the sun was fully up. He saw a group of men wearing green jackets passing through one of his picket lines. They were from the 95th Rifles and had been scouting the French positions to try and ascertain Marshal Ney's, and therefore Napoleon's, next move. A major from the 95th was waiting for the men, and he spoke with the corporal in command of the small group. The NCO said they had been relieved by a group from the 60th Rifles, but that they had made no contact with enemy skirmishers.

"It's the damnedest thing," the corporal said, removing his shako and shaking his head as he wiped a rag across his forehead.

"It's as if the enemy isn't even trying to see what our next move will be. They're just sitting there. Probably start making their breakfast here in a while."

The two men exchanged a few more words before the major dismissed the man. He then saw Patrick for the first time, and though he undoubtedly had other matters to attend to, he instead decided to engage the lieutenant.

"Never an easy thing, coming up from the ranks," the major said.

Patrick gave a tired chuckle in reply. "Is it really that obvious?"

"Many officers with a single epaulette look like they could still be schoolboys," the major shrugged. "You appear to have already seen your share of battles in the service of King George."

"Well, I wasn't exactly a schoolboy when I joined the ranks," Patrick confessed. "Eight years I've worn His Britannic Majesty's uniform when they elected just yesterday to commission me."

"You men of the Guards had a hard go of it," the Rifles officer noted. "After a bloody grind like that is usually when you'll see an officer or two rise up from the ranks."

"Well, I have neither sufficient funds nor patronage," Patrick replied. "I suspect I'll be returned to a colour sergeant by the time this is over. So much the better anyway; bloody rankers never make proper officers."

"Now that's just foolish talk!" the major retorted. He then nodded to Patrick's left hand. "I see you are married. Any children?"

"Yes, sir," the Irishman replied, "three, to be exact."

"Then you'd be a damned fool to lose your commission," the major said bluntly. "Make no mistake, being an officer who comes up from the ranks is a difficult position. Your peers will shun you for some time, and even the men in the ranks will resent you. The lowliest scum that wears the red uniform knows exactly what he is, and he will find it distasteful to see a fellow such as himself trying to be a proper officer and gentleman. But if you've already been a colour sergeant, then you know how to lead the men. Just continue to do so like you always have. Only now make certain the men call you *sir*. I assume you joined the ranks to make a better life for your family. So if you want to do best by them, then find a way to keep

218

your commission." The major then nodded and turned to walk away.

Patrick was still surprised that this officer, who he'd never even seen, had suddenly taken such an interest in his commission.

"Sir," he said. "If I may ask, what is your concern with whether or not I become a proper officer?"

"Personally," the major replied, "it means nothing. However, I feel that we prior-rankers need to watch out for each other." The major cocked a half smile, and it was only then that Patrick noticed that he looked to be at least forty.

"How many years?" he asked.

"Twelve," the major replied. "Twelve years I served in the ranks, and I've held my commission for just as long. After twenty-four years, I may retire from His Majesty's service, provided I'm still alive a week from now. Good day to you, lieutenant."

"And to you, sir"

Patrick took a deep breath and let what the major said sink in a bit. He felt like he'd served in the ranks for a long time, yet the Rifles officer had worn the uniform three times longer than he had. It was still overwhelming for him, not to mention rather surreal. By the same token, as the company colour sergeant, he was used to leading men into battle; nothing had changed there. It was when the fighting was over and he had to figure out the administrative tasks that it would get complicated. He remembered Sergeant Donaldson aiding Captain Webster with much of the paperwork, especially payroll.

"Donaldson had better survive this," he said with dark humour.

"Well, if I have it my way, I'll still be alive when this is over."

The sergeant's voice startled Patrick and he quickly turned to face the man, who then saluted. "Beg your pardon, sir."

That was something else Patrick knew he'd have to get used to; being saluted and called 'sir'. Sergeant Donaldson was very adamant about addressing him as such, especially in front of the men. The bloody business with Napoleon was far from being decided, and the last thing they needed was the men scoffing about whether or not their former colour sergeant was a proper officer.

"I need you right now, James," Patrick said, addressing the sergeant by his given name. "We took a pounding yesterday, but the majority of the lads are still with us. What we're short on are men to lead them. We have no subalterns, and you and Harvey are the only non-comms left."

"There's that other Irish lad, O'Connor," Donaldson noted.

"I know David O'Connor well enough," Patrick remarked. "He isn't as rash as some of the younger men, and he does usually have a good head about him when not sopped up on gin, but he's just a kid who's only seen two engagements. I don't know if he's even eighteen yet."

"He may be a kid," Donaldson concurred, "but he's very level-headed, and he kept the lads from balking when Lieutenant Grose bought it yesterday. He might make a good corporal. Just something to think about, sir. Oh, and the reason I came to see you, sir, is about our subalterns. Ensign Barton has asked to see you."

"Barton's still alive?" Patrick asked.

A cannonball had bounced straight into his left thigh, and for all he knew, the young lad had bled to death. After the battle, a couple of men had evacuated him to where the hastily-erected hospital was set up, but that was the last he'd heard.

"He's not looking too good," Donaldson confessed. "The docs removed what was left of his leg as soon as the lads got him there. They said he was pretty stoic about it, didn't make a sound. The captain went and saw him; let him know about what happened after we hit the woods. He's now specifically asked to see you."

"Very well," Patrick nodded.

The sergeant saluted and returned to his duties.

Patrick walked down the long path that led through the woods, his hands clasped behind his back in thought. The trees were scarred and burned from the previous day's brawl. Gouges from musket and cannon shot, the scorching of trunk and bough disfigured what would otherwise have been a pristine scene. And, of course, there were the French bodies. Under a flag of truce, the thousands of French wounded were paroled to their mates. The British had buried as many of their slain as possible, but since they would be withdrawing, they would let Boney handle his own dead. The bodies had been stripped of weapons, ammunition, and anything of use, before being tossed unceremoniously into the bushes and off the main paths.

Just beyond the woods, the lieutenant could smell the stench of the hospital before he ever saw it. Scorched flesh, amputated limbs now crawling with flies, vomit, excrement, and a host of other nauseating smells assailed the senses of any who walked within a mile of the site. Patrols of soldiers passing by would often have handkerchiefs over their mouths, though Patrick appeared unaffected. The breaking of his heart at seeing so many broken men made him supress the pungent stench.

The nasty business of amputation had been done all throughout the night. Any whose severely maimed limbs prevented them from being saved underwent the saw, lest gangrene or a host of other terrible infections take them. There were a host of other hideous injuries to behold as well; men with jaw and cheekbones shattered by musket fire, shrapnel to the guts, various burns, and painful stabs from the bayonet. It was beyond comprehension for the Irish lieutenant that in thousands of years of civilization, men could still inflict such horror upon each other.

"But we'll never learn, will we?" he said quietly to himself.

"Lieutenant Shanahan!" the voice was that of Private Farrow, one of the men who'd carried poor Ensign Barton to the hospital. Patrick turned and the man saluted him. "Sir, I'm glad you came. Mister Barton has been asking about you. They're loading him onto a wagon over there."

He pointed off to his right, where scores of badly wounded men were lying on stretchers, waiting for transportation back to Brussels. Though they'd been hard pressed to get to Quatre Bras in the first place, Wellington was, thankfully, a master of logistics, and had procured every wagon and draught animal within a hundred miles. Though each side would more often than not care for each other's wounded as best as they were able, the Duke was not about to leave his broken men as enemy prisoners.

The private took Patrick down the long line of men on stretchers, until just before the one of the wagons they found him. The young man's face was so pale. Patrick was surprised he hadn't bled to death. He still wore his tunic, though from the waist down he was covered in a dirty sheet that was soiled in blood from the stump that had once been his left leg. His eyes were closed, and his breathing jagged.

"Lieutenant Shanahan here to see you, sir," the private said, leaning over the ensign so as to be heard.

Barton's eyes opened wide for a moment and then he squinted up to see Patrick standing over him. He instinctively licked his parched lips before speaking. "I heard what happened yesterday after I fell," he said. "A pity about poor Edward. He always tried to keep me in line, like a big brother, and he's the one who gets a musket shot in the neck." He shook his head while looking off to the side for a moment, remembering the man who'd been as close to a friend as he'd had in the company.

"I owe you an apology," Barton said, looking up at Patrick, who remained silent. "To think that it took this to make me see my folly." He lazily waved his hand towards his missing leg in emphasis. "I heard about how you led the men in taking those woods, while giving the frogs a damn good thrashing. The captain also told me about how you saved the company from being slaughtered when the cuirassiers caught us in the open. I always deplored the thought of an officer coming from the ranks, but General Maitland was right to commission you. You may have been denied by birth, but you always were the proper gentleman that I should have been. Please accept my humblest apology, *sir*." With what little strength he had, Barton extended his hand, which Patrick took. There was a sense of relief in the ensign's face as he collapsed back once more. "There's one more thing," he said. "My sword, Private Farrow."

"I have it here, sir," Farrow said, handing it to Barton, who turned it over in his hands and shook his head.

"Don't think I'll be needing this now," he lamented. "It was my great-grandfather's, who served with Marlborough at the Siege of Bouchain. I'd like you to have it. An officer needs a proper sword." He held the weapon up in both hands, and Patrick reached down and took it from him. It was a plain infantry officer's sword. Though both the weapon and scabbard were well-maintained, the wear on the scabbard leather, as well as the pommel of the sword, told that they were very old.

"An honour," Patrick said with a nod.

"It is you who honours me, sir," Barton said, grimacing in pain as he saluted as best as he was able to from his back.

Patrick stood to attention, drew the sword, and returned the salute.

"Time to go now, sir," an orderly said as four men grabbed the stretcher and quickly lifted the young officer onto the wagon, along with several other badly wounded men. There was no time for further goodbyes. It was approximately forty miles to Brussels, and by wagon it would take at minimum a day or two for the wounded to reach the city.

"He's right, sir," Private Farrow said as the two men watched the last of the wounded being loaded onto the wagon before it departed. "An officer does need a proper sword."

"I cannot believe Marshal Ney is just sitting there," General Cooke said with a trace of exasperation. "What is he playing at?"

"If he wants to be a fool, let him," Wellington replied. "We ground him to a halt yesterday, and he thinks we'll attempt to do the same while he waits for Bonaparte to arrive and smash our left flank in."

"We are in a precarious position, your grace," General Alten added. "The Prussians took a serious pounding and for all we know, could be out of the fight completely."

"I warned Blucher about the positioning of his army," the Duke grunted. "There was plenty of defensible terrain where he could have placed his men, and instead he leaves them in the open, where Boney could use his masterful skill at artillery. Still, they are a tenacious lot, and if we can re-establish communications with Marshal Blucher, then perhaps we can support each other after all."

"What are your orders then?" Cooke asked. "We've established a good frontage should Ney try and attack us again, but if the Prussians are on the run, then we cannot possibly hold if Bonaparte brings up the rest of his army."

"Agreed," Wellington acknowledged. "That is why I sent word to Sir Rowland to have his corps head for Mont St Jean." He then turned to his chief-of-staff. "DeLancey, you remember that piece of ground we discussed, with the woods behind and the good reverse slopes?"

"Of course, your grace," DeLancey replied. "Near Waterloo, the woods give the appearance that we'd be sitting with our backs

223

against a wall, but there is no undergrowth. We can manoeuvre at will through them, if need be."

"I need you to take an advance party there at once," Wellington ordered, pointing to a position on the map. "Stake out the positions for the entire army. If we are to have any chance of holding, with or without the Prussians, then that is where we will make our stand."

"It will be slow moving," Alten added. "I don't think we could get much further before the frogs caught up with us, especially as we are still evacuating our wounded."

"Damn good ploy, paroling the French wounded," DeLancey remarked. "Evacuating our own is a logistical nightmare in itself, to say nothing of the added depletion of medical supplies."

"And by giving Boney back his injured, we slow him further," Wellington stated. "That and it adds to the false notion that we intend to stay. He will think that we would not bother, were we withdrawing, as they would simply be able to recover their men once they advance. The weather promises to be dreadful, so we must make ready to move at once. Cavalry and horse artillery will conduct a robust rear-guard action. The rest of the army will head for Waterloo."

The rain had started even before the men had finished breakfast. After the bloody business of the previous day, there was many a grumble when word passed down that the ground they had fought and bled for would now be given up to the French without a fight. The dark skies, gusts of wind, and relentless rainfall only added to the black mood of most of the army. To make matters worse, before the campaign, most of the men had been directed to turn in their greatcoats to be shipped back to their home barracks, as it was thought they would not be needed in the summer months. As an officer, James had had to purchase his own greatcoat, and therefore had kept it with him. However, he elected that if his men were being soaked by the torrential downpour, then so would he. Granted, his men may have thought him foolish, allowing himself to be drenched while his greatcoat was rolled up in his saddle pack.

As the army made its long, slow trek north, James rode with Major D'Oyley and Captain Stables. Occasionally each man would ride down the column to check that their men were maintaining good marching order, and to let the ranks know they were still with them. James could not help but spend extra time checking on his former company. They'd been his men for almost a year, and in the span of less than a day it felt as if they'd been taken from him. Yes, they still fell under his leadership, but so did four other companies. He owed all of them his attention. Many of the men walked with heads and shoulders stooped, the neck flaps on their shakos unfolded to give them some protection. They leaned forward so as to allow their packs to deflect as much of the rain off them as possible. A gust of wind would then drive the rain directly into their faces, adding to their suffering. Though many walked in silence, others bantered incessantly.

"Bloody pneumonia will kill us before the frogs get a chance," one soldier grumbled as he shrugged his shoulders hard to adjust his pack and clutched his musket close.

"And if it was the Prussians who got kicked in the teeth, then why are we on the run?" another spat.

Such talk would normally be met with a sharp reprimand, but with officers and NCOs in an equal state of misery as the men, it was mostly ignored.

All were still in a state of shock over the previous day's brawl, and it embittered them that, in their minds at least, they had fought for nothing. James could not get over how badly depleted they already were, especially among leadership positions. His company had already been short to begin with, but where there should have been three officers and at least six NCOs, now only Lieutenant Shanahan, the newly-promoted Sergeant Donaldson, and Corporal Harvey remained. Though it was only roughly eight miles from Quatre Bras to Waterloo, the unpaved road was turning into a quagmire, slowing the men's pace considerably. A distance that normally would take no more than two to three hours would now be an insufferable march through mud and rain that would last most of the day.

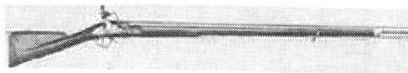

It was dark, the rain continuing to downpour, as Wellington rode to where he'd told DeLancey to stage the army. Oddly enough, his colonel was nowhere to be found.

"Over there, your grace," Somerset said, pointing to where DeLancey sat astride his horse at the top of a ridge.

The Duke and his staff rode up to him.

"I hope you'll pardon my presumptuousness," DeLancey said. "But when I arrived at the position you told me to, I realized it will not do at all. I placed the unit designations further up, behind the slope. That still puts us within range of the building complexes, while protecting the army from Boney's artillery."

"And he'll think with the woods at our back that we've trapped ourselves," Wellington observed. "Well done, DeLancey. The first regiments will arrive from Quatre Bras within the hour."

"We're ready for them," DeLancey said. "I have guides designated for every regiment, as well as the logistics trains and field hospital. It pains me to say it, your grace, but as hard pressed as we were at Quatre Bras, tomorrow will be much worse."

"I agree," the Duke replied. "Bonaparte needs a decisive victory, and he needs it now. If he defeats us, the Prussians will flounder, especially after the damned beating they took at Ligny."

"And with us and the Prussians out of the way, Brussels will fall," DeLancey added, "which will fracture the alliance with the Netherlands. It will effectively end the war."

"Bonaparte has already attempted to sue for peace with the Prince Regent," Wellington continued. "If I am beaten tomorrow, the Prince has to know the people will not support continued war with Napoleon. Russia and Austria may have gigantic armies, but without English coin, they cannot afford to keep them. The fate of Europe hangs on whether or not we can hold this ridge. Believe me, DeLancey, when I tell you that it *ends* tomorrow!"

Insufficient rations had been brought on the march. Between the trek from Braine-le-Comte to Quatre Bras, fighting an intense battle for a couple hours, then the eight miles in torrential rain, the men had expended an extreme amount of energy. Their stomachs turned in knots, not having eaten since breakfast. The hunger only added to their exhaustion and misery, which was further

226

exacerbated by the continuous downpour and the knowledge that there were no tents or other cover for them to try and shield themselves from the insufferable weather. Once positioned where DeLancey's advance party had placed them, all the men could do was sit or lie down in the drenched earth. Sleep would be impossible to come by.

"I'm going to check that farmhouse we passed just up the road," Private O'Connor said as he and his mates tried to settle down for the night.

"You can't just take from the locals," Private Farrow protested, despite the pangs of hunger that tormented him as well. "You get caught, they'll hang you!"

"The bloody place is deserted," David retorted. "Besides, with the Prussians now on the run and Boney sending everything he's got against us, we're all dead anyway, and I intend to die on a full stomach!"

"Lieutenant Shanahan has assured us that rations are coming," Farrow persisted. "I cannot imagine Old Nosey letting us die hungry. It's not his way."

"Look at this damn weather," David emphasized, looking up and letting the rain beat down on his face for a moment. "You saw how bad the roads were where we came from. Who's to say the mess wagons will even get here before Boney decides to send us to the Almighty. And don't worry, I'll bring you lot back something, too."

The constant torment of rainfall, combined with the complete lack of any ambient light made the short walk down the slope to the abandoned farmhouse a rather treacherous one. David just hoped he could trace his steps back and avoid running into other regiments, or worse, one of the senior officers. He lost his footing several times on the slick grass, and once had his feet come completely out from under him before he made it to the sodden road that ran past the building.

"Right you are," he said quietly as he pulled himself to his feet, "nothing broken but me pride."

As he quickly bounded across the road, the sound of the side gate clattering startled him for a second. Given the positioning of his regiment in relation to the farmhouse, he was surprised that it wasn't already occupied with soldiers. But then, much of the army was still on the march, and David guessed that it would be well-manned before long.

"At least those sods will get to stay somewhat dry," he grunted. He then saw movement out of the corner of his eye, and the startled squeal of a pig brought a grin to his face. "Well, fancy that."

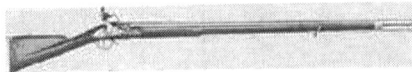

A number of officers accompanied Wellington as he inspected the area around the farmhouse, known as Hougomont. Since it was in General Cooke's sector of the Guards Division, he would be assigning men to defend it. Cooke's brigade commanders, Maitland and Byng were with them, as were the officers from the closest battalion; Major D'Oyley, along with Captains Stables and Webster. DeLancey and Somerset carried torches for the Duke to see by, though in the rain they scarcely held their light and hissed as the downpour tortured what was left of their flames.

"This is a good position," Wellington noted. "It gives us something for Boney to become fixated on, which we will be able to provide support and reinforcements for. General Cooke, you will have a battery provide over-watch for the defenders."

"Yes, your grace," Cooke replied.

As the men continued to walk around the back side of the building, Wellington himself almost ran straight into a Guards soldier who was carrying a pig under his arm.

"Oh, bugger," the soldier said under his breath, then with as much nonchalance as he could manage, "Lovely evening, your grace." As he tried to walk past the men, the Duke grabbed him by the shoulder strap on his pack.

"What have you got there, sir?" Wellington asked.

"Oh, this?" the soldier said, looking quickly down at the pig. "'Tis nothing of importance, sir."

"I would say it is, sir," the Duke replied, his expression unchanged. "You do know the penalty for looting."

The soldier swallowed hard and then on a glance noticed Captain Webster, whose face was white. "No gin before the battle tomorrow, sir?"

"Like hell, the penalty is death!" Wellington retorted, his face hard.

"It would be, t'were I stealing from the locals," David confessed. "But see, sir, this building is deserted, and this poor creature is left all by itself. I doubt the owners of the house will be back, and well, I thought maybe I could help this little pig find its way home."

"He is right, your grace," DeLancey spoke up, "Hougomont has been deserted for some time."

"You do know how to hold an indefensible position, sir," Wellington said to the private.

"He helped rally his section in Bossu Wood, after Lieutenant Grose was killed," James spoke up quickly. "He took charge, and in the absence of orders, helped direct a flanking attack that dislodged a sizeable enemy force."

"Indeed," Wellington said with a nod. He then leaned in close to the soldier. "If you were charged with defending a section of this house, you'd stand in the face of an entire French corps, wouldn't you? Better that than the hangman's noose."

"Of course, your grace," David asserted. "Just let me die with a full stomach, sir."

"That I shall," Wellington replied. "And if Hougomont should fall, I do not expect to find you amongst the living."

"I'd rather stare down Boney's entire army, than stand against you for much longer, your grace," David said with a burst of candour.

While the officers were uncertain how to take the young soldier's remark, Wellington actually burst into a brief fit of laughter. "I believe this man means what he says," the Duke said, serious once more. He then looked back at Webster and D'Oyley. "Advance him to corporal."

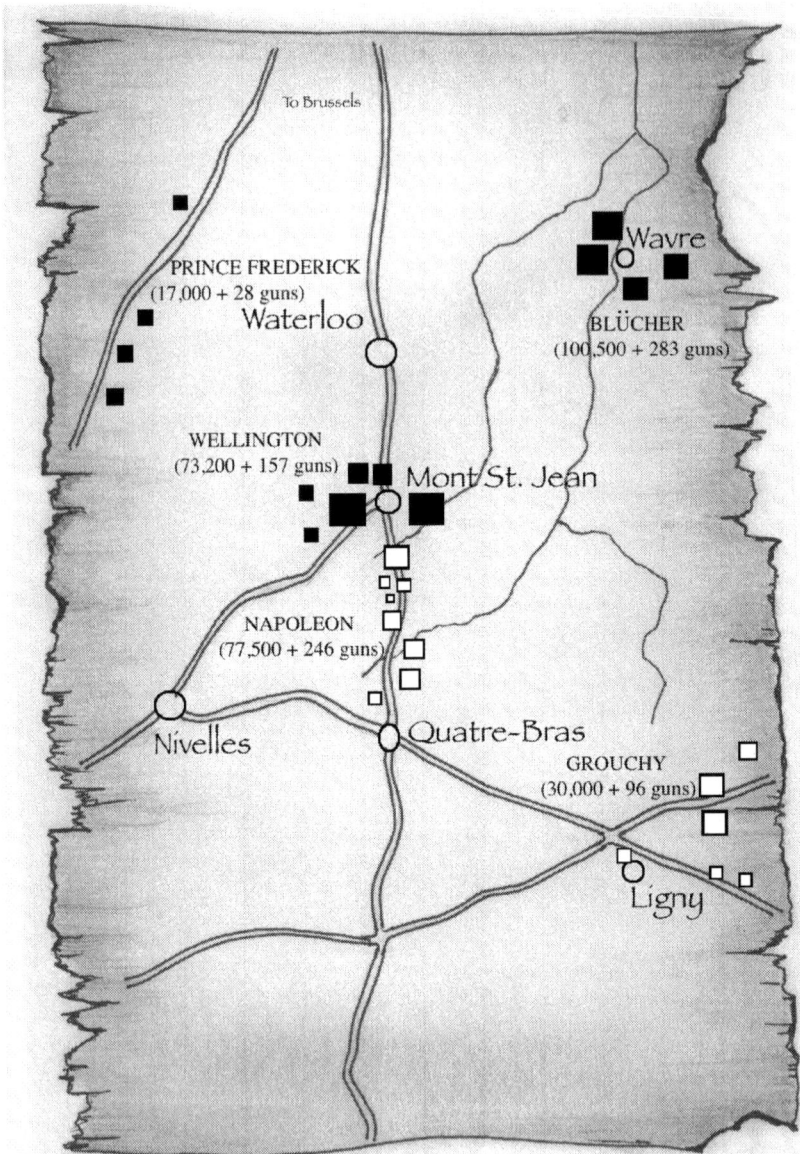

Situation, the night of 17 June. Grouchy is sent to pursue Blucher; however, he does not know where they have gone, or that the surviving Prussians have rallied at Wavre. As Wellington digs in on the ridge south of Waterloo, Napoleon is convinced of an easy victory and readies to attack the next day. The two greatest military minds of the age will finally face each other in battle.

Chapter XV: A Tortuous Night
Field of Waterloo
17 June 1815
Midnight

Prince William of Orange

Sleep seemed impossible to come by for the tormented Anglo-Allied Army that now occupied the long ridge just south of Mont St. Jean, along with the three small groups of farmhouses at Hougomont, La Hay Sainte, and La Haie. Men were soaked and filthy to the core. That they had been ordered to send off their greatcoats before the campaign only added to their misery. A few had been able to pilfer greatcoats off the French dead and wounded at Quatre Bras, but these were few and far between. They had been soaked during the night time march to Quatre Bras; the heat of the following day contrasted to the shivering cold of the night, and they had sweated through the exertion of forced march and the bloody grind of battle. There had been little time to rest and wash away the filth and grime before they'd been marched, in the rain once more, up the road to the field of Waterloo. Now they froze once again, despite it being mid-June. The rain was unrelenting, and many of the men feared that even if they survived the battle on the morrow, that various sickness would take them.

At the western edge of the 3/1st Foot Guards, not far from Hougomont, the glow of a fire shown in the hellish night. Hovering over it, with a scrounged cooking pot, was Corporal David O'Connor. How he managed to even start a fire, much less keep it lit in the relentless downpour, was anyone's guess. Between the time of his terrifying encounter with Wellington, after which he'd had to go immediately relieve his bowels, he had managed to find the pot, get some wood for the fire started, butcher his prized pig, and was now sewing his newly-authorized stripes onto his coat. After giving him a hard blow to the stomach for getting caught taking the pig, Sergeant Donaldson had given David his corporal's chevrons that he'd kept in his pack.

"How the devil did you get a fire started?" Private Farrow asked as he slumped down beside him.

"How the devil do I do any of the things I manage?" David answered with his own rhetorical question. "I should be swinging from a tree right now, but instead Old Nosey makes me a bloody corporal!"

"I heard you had to take quite the shit after," Farrow laughed as he huddled as close to the feeble flames that still danced in spite of the rain.

"And wouldn't you?" David retorted. "I consider myself lucky I didn't crap me trousers right in front of his grace. It's all so damn surreal to me, especially this!" He held up the sleeve of his tunic, where he'd just finished sewing his stripes on.

"Yeah, there's something you don't see every day," Farrow observed.

"I think it's because Wellington expects me to die tomorrow," David thought aloud. "That and he knows he needs every weapon he can muster against Boney. I made him laugh for a brief moment, so he spared me life, made me a corporal, and expects me to die in place tomorrow, for King and Country."

"A lot of us are going to die tomorrow," Farrow observed, placing his hands on the pot for warmth as the flames sputtered in their losing battle against the endless rain.

"Well, if I do make it through tomorrow, I'm going to have to learn how to be a damned corporal," David grunted. "Thank God I can read!"

"That is important," Farrow concurred.

The two men were bantering endlessly, like so many of their companions, as it was the only way to pass the time and at least attempt to take their minds off the miserable conditions. In the faint flicker of light given by the tortured flames, David saw a shadow against a rock. Curious, he threw on his tunic, got up to investigate, and saw that it was Private Adams, leaning against a rock by himself. His musket was cradled in his lap, hand over the pan and flint. The corporal could not make out his face very well, but from what he could tell, it looked like the soldier's expression was completely vacant.

"Here, Eric!" David said over the sound of pouring rain.

"Evening, corporal," Eric said in a distant monotone.

David held out a chunk of cooked pork. "Pig?"

Eric shook his head. "No."

"Look, Farrow and I can't eat this entire damned thing by ourselves, so you may as well come and join us," the corporal persisted.

"I'm tired of killing, David," Eric finally said.

David's expression grew serious and he sat next to the troubled soldier. "You know you were mentioned in despatches. Quite an honour for a mere ranker like us. I thought you were going to bonk out on us during the march, but after what you managed in Bossu Wood, I would not be surprised to see your name posted in *The Times* back home."

"Mentioned in despatches," Eric said, his voice heavy with regret. "I should have left the army as soon as we finished in the Peninsula. Yet all I know how to do is kill. Me dad taught me how to shoot at a young age, so I could be an effective hunter, and now I use this skill to commit murder."

"Is it really murder?" David asked. "After all, it's us or the frogs."

"Well, what else would you call it?" Eric snapped. "Everyone talks like I'm a damned hero for shooting those bastards the way I did yesterday. And it was only dumb luck that I was able to stick that cuirassier where he was unarmoured. I don't want to do it anymore; not for Old Nosey, not for King George, not even for God Himself."

"If it makes you feel better, I don't think the Almighty gives a pile of shit over what us and the frogs do to each other," David mused.

"How can we keep doing this?" Eric's voice was close to breaking, and David wondered just how many men on both sides were close to madness, knowing the worst was still to come. "How can we keep killing one another? How can we?"

There was nothing else he could say, so David patted his friend on the shoulder and staggered back towards his dying fire, which by now was little more than a soft glow with a lot of smoke. He ceased in his banter with Douglas Farrow and simply sat eating chunks of pig in silence.

Corporal, 1st Regiment of Foot Guards

Just a handful of yards away, Captain James Webster stumbled along the soaked ground, trying not to step on soldiers who were huddled together in vain attempts to keep warm in the freezing rain. Like them, he was cold and miserable. The dawn could not come soon enough, and however horrific the coming battle would be, he just hoped the damned rain would stop before they and the French sent each other to oblivion.

"Under here, sir!" a voice said from near his feet. James could scarcely see at all; the flicker of light from Corporal O'Connor's pitiful fire hindering his night vision more than it helped. James did not even realize he was right next to a supply wagon.

Numerous soldiers were clustered underneath; the fortunate few who'd gotten there first as the entire army futilely sought shelter of any kind. James knelt down, though he could not make out the faces of the men in the shadow of the wagon and the constant downpour.

"Captain Webster, is it?" the soldier asked.

"It is," James replied. "Who are you men with?"

"Various companies," the soldier replied. "But most of us are with 3rd Company, 3/1st Guards."

"Ah, so you're one of mine then," the captain noted.

"That we are, sir," the man answered. "And since you're our officer, we can make enough space for you to squeeze in, that is if you don't mind playing sardines with a bunch of rankers like us."

"On a night like this, I'd take shelter with Bonaparte himself!" James stated as he removed his shako and crawled beneath the wagon.

"Here, sir," the soldier said. "There's a spot right by the wagon wheel. We all have to kind of sit upright as best we can, but at least here you can lay your head against the spokes. Not much, but it's better than lying out in that mess."

"Indeed it is," James agreed over the sounds of rain hammering down on the wagon. "I'm much obliged to you."

Napoleon passed the night in very similar fashion as Wellington, not entirely certain as to his enemies' dispositions, wondering where Grouchy's wing of the army was and if they would make for Waterloo once they heard the sound of the guns. As the emperor felt that the Prussians were indeed out of the fight completely, he lamented even sending his marshal with 30,000 men in pursuit. But like his rival, he too knew what the incessant rain was doing to the ground. It troubled him as to how much it would impede the movement of cannon, as well as slow the advancing of his infantry and cavalry. Still, he was not as concerned as one might expect.

"My army is superior to his," he said quietly to Marshal Ney, who sat once more on a chair across the room. The emperor himself sat with his feet up on a windowsill, arms folded across his chest, eyes half shut. He was so tired, yet as sleep was not ready to come, he'd joined his marshal in the foyer.

"How is your stomach, sire?" Ney asked. Most of his officers were not brave enough to ask what they all wondered, but Ney's candour had brought him Napoleon's admiration at a very early age.

"It will be fine in the morning," the emperor replied unconvincingly. "You still have command of my left wing. I expect you to use it to break the English tomorrow."

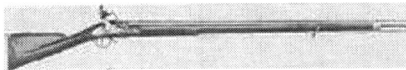

This night feels like it will never end. The rain soaks us to the core, as if the Almighty were enjoying our plight. But then, perhaps the rain may prove a means for our salvation. Surely the enemy is being tormented just as much as we, and since I have no doubt that it will take days for the ground to dry, the weather will negate Bonaparte's most decisive weapon, his artillery.

I count myself fortunate to have found the underside of this cart, occupied by men from one of my companies. They still count me as one of their own, and should the worst happen tomorrow, I am honoured to die as one of them. There is a universal feeling, undoubtedly on both sides, that the entire war will be decided tomorrow. Wellington and Napoleon will finally face each other; the consummate tactician meeting the master strategist.

If we fail, no power in the world will be able to stop Bonaparte. England will remove herself from the war, and the rest of Europe will fall, one-by-one, in his unstoppable onslaught. And should we triumph, I predict it will finally be the end of the Napoleonic Era, and the French Emperor will never rise again. I would say that it is in God's hands now, yet I think my cousin, Anthony, was correct. The Divine will allow us and the French to destroy each other, perhaps granting grace to whomever wins, or at least is left standing when it is done. So, it is in our hands now, and may God have mercy on the fallen.

Captain James Henry Webster
17 June 1815

Chapter XVI: You May Fight Your Battle
Field of Waterloo
17 June 1815
Midnight

General Friedrich Karl Ferdinand Freiherr von Muffling

It was a maddening wait for the Duke. A small oil lamp burned upon the table in the tiny room. He paced back and forth in front of the window, as the rain beat mercilessly outside. He was joined by a few of his senior officers and staff; at least those who'd found their way to the tiny farmhouse despite the inclement weather and utter blackness of night.

"I have never felt so blind on the eve of battle," Wellington said at length. He turned to face the men, who were clustered around the Duke's sodden map on the table. Somerset had been scribbling notes in pencil, along with the placements of units.

There were a number of large arrows from the south, pointing up to where they thought the French may advance on them.

"Your grace, you've chosen the best ground possible," Somerset asserted. "Even if Boney has us badly outnumbered, he has to cross large areas of open ground, while advancing uphill, in order to get at us."

"Not only that," General Cooke of the Guards Division added, "but we hold all the structures that will allow us to pour enfilade fire upon his columns as they advance between them."

"Still, it does come down to the Prussians," DeLancey said, when the Duke added nothing to Cooke's remark. The colonel knew his superior all-too-well, and he guessed that Wellington held the same thoughts as he. "Are they out of the fight or are they not?"

"And that is why I need Muffling back here as soon as possible," Wellington finally said. "Blucher took a sound whipping, and there have been rumours of Boney sending Grouchy with a sizeable force in pursuit. What I must know is how many men does Grouchy have, and are they between us and Blucher? Even if it is a sizeable force, Bonaparte still has us outnumbered, outgunned, with troops far more experienced than mine."

"We cannot afford to put all of our trust in the Prussians," Uxbridge noted. "We can only trust in each other." The army's second-in-command then pointed to the farmhouses of Hougomont and La Haye Sainte. "Hougomont makes a nice diversion for us. It is well ahead of our main line, yet easier to defend with its high walls."

"And if it should fall, it matters little," Wellington interrupted. He then pointed to La Haye Sainte. "This is the crucial point. La Haye Sainte overlooks both our centre, as well as the main crossroads. If Boney should take it, then our centre will break, and it will be just a matter of counting the dead." He then looked to Uxbridge. "We'll keep your cavalry in reserve and use them to counter any threats to this position."

"Very good, sir," Uxbridge replied.

The door was then thrown open and General Muffling staggered in. The Prussian's hat and greatcoat were completely soaked, his face drenched and filthy, eyes bloodshot and face red from cold and exertion. Clearly the man had not slept since

Wellington dispatched him to ascertain the capabilities of the Prussians following Ligny.

"Herr Field Marshal," he said while catching his breath, "you may fight your battle tomorrow."

"Where is Marshal Blucher?" Wellington asked. "Are the Prussians still in this game, and can they send even a single corps to Waterloo?"

"We are not done with Napoleon yet," Muffling replied. "We left many dead at Ligny, and our army is anxious to avenge them. Marshal Blucher was injured, but has recovered enough to lead us to victory tomorrow."

"How much of your army is approaching?" Cooke asked.

"All of it," the Prussian general replied, "minus a detachment we left at Wavre to deal with Grouchy. Marshal Blucher says to tell your grace that he will be at Waterloo with all possible speed, though with the roads I would guess they will not be here until mid-afternoon at the earliest."

"Wavre is about fifteen miles from here," DeLancey noted, "a day's march at least. And will the Prussians have the strength left in them to fight?"

"We will be here, and we will fight," Muffling said sternly.

"Then it comes down to when Boney launches his attack tomorrow," Cooke remarked.

"Gentlemen, I think that is where this awful weather will prove our advantage," Wellington said with a rare grin. "It may torture both armies tonight, but in the morning, Bonaparte will not be able to move his guns to advantageous firing positions; nor will the solid shot of his cannons bounce when they strike the ground that has turned into a virtual swamp. If we can hold, or even turn back his attack, by the time Blucher arrives, he should only need to mop up what's left. And if we fail, then the Prussians will be caught in the open while on the march. In which case, God help us all. Whether all goes good or ill, I daresay that tomorrow the war ends."

"We've positioned the army as best we can," DeLancey noted on the map. "The units from Sir Rowland Hill's II Corps that have arrived are forming up on our right, I Corps in the centre. We've placed Sir Thomas Picton's division in reserve, though I imagine they will see plenty of action before the day is done."

Exhausted from lack of sleep, and realizing there was little left to do but wait for the coming dawn, Wellington dismissed the officers and sought to catch a few hours' sleep. Out in the hall, DeLancey caught up to General Picton, who was leaning against the door jam.

"Everything well, Sir Thomas?"

"Everything is, indeed, well," the old general replied. His face was clammy and DeLancey noted he was clutching his side. Despite his best efforts to hide his affliction, the stain of blood on his undershirt showed through the opening in his jacket.

"Hang on, there," DeLancey said. He pulled the general's hand away, who was too weak to resist. "By God, sir, you've been hit!"

With the strength of anger, Sir Thomas grabbed him by the collar. "Not a word to Wellington!" he growled.

"But, Sir Thomas, you must see the surgeon!" DeLancey protested.

"Damn it all, I already extracted the shot," Picton retorted. "There's nothing the blasted surgeon can do, except dump me onto a waiting cart and wait for infection or blood loss to take me. If I am destined to die here, then I will die leading my men."

"You're in no shape to lead your division..." the colonel's words were cut short when Picton, with surprising strength, slammed him against the wall.

"I have enough strength of character to lead my men to glory once more. When the time is right, they will follow me, and when I am no longer needed, then the Almighty may take me." Picton stared hard into DeLancey's eyes and reiterated once more, "Not a word to Wellington!"

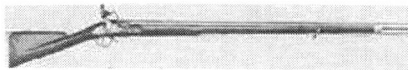

Napoleon would have gladly traded places with any one of his men who were trying to sleep in the downpour, if only it meant being spared from the incessant pain in his stomach. There were no blankets on the bed he laid down on, and the ceiling leaked, but he did not care. He simply wrapped his great coat around him like a blanket and used a saddlebag as a pillow. He had watched the British army as it emplaced itself, until darkness, rainfall, and the

241

crippling abdominal pain forced him inside. He had abruptly dismissed his staff officers and now lay curled up, hiding in the darkness that engulfed him. Only Marshal Ney remained.

"I will need you tomorrow, Michel," the emperor said through the darkness. "I need you more than I ever have."

"I am here, sire," the marshal replied. Secretly, he was still bitter about having d'Erlon's corps diverted from Quatre Bras. By the time word had reached the Comte to turn his force back around, he'd been too late to engage in either battle at all. Granted, this meant his troops were fresh for the coming battle, though Ney surmised that had d'Erlon been at Quatre Bras, there may not have been a coming battle in the first place. Unsure what else to say, Ney left the room and quietly stepped down the very short hall to the foyer where Marshal Soult sat behind a table, a small oil lamp giving off a faint glow. Outside, the rain continued to beat down.

"He begins to doubt himself," Ney remarked quietly.

"That is why he will be so dependent upon you tomorrow," Soult observed. "The emperor has no doubt that he can beat Wellington, but with his health, he knows he must be able to trust you, as you will be leading the brunt of our forces tomorrow."

"I tell you, Nicolas," Ney said as he paced slowly, his hands clasped behind his back. "Had he not taken d'Erlon's corps from me, we would not even be looking at a battle tomorrow. And now he's sent Grouchy with over 30,000 men in some wild pursuit of the Prussians. Who knows what that will lead to? Despite their losses, we do not know if they are still in this war or not."

"If Marshal Blucher still lives, then they are still in the fight," Soult asserted. "The emperor knows this, which is why he sent Grouchy in pursuit."

"Yes, but he does not know which way the Prussians have gone," Ney persisted. "There are numerous routes they could have taken, all as plausible as the next. And if Grouchy guessed wrong, and his forces are not between the English and the Prussians, then they can still come to Wellington's aid."

"You make a number of assumptions, Michel," Soult remarked. "And even if you are correct, do you really think the Prussians can rally sufficient forces and get to Waterloo in a single day? Let's just suppose they can; I personally think that they will arrive too late. We will decide the issue long before they can come assist

Wellington. Remember, we have a slight advantage in numbers against the English, even with Grouchy not directly available to us. And Wellington's army is nothing like what he had in the Peninsula. I stopped him at Toulouse, and you ground him to a halt yesterday with but a fraction of our army. Wellington *can* be beaten, and with our help the emperor will be the one to do it."

What Soult did not tell Ney was his own reservations about the battle. The chief-of-staff had looked through the overview of the emperor's plan for the morrow, and it troubled him deeply. The plan was not particularly imaginative, and hardly of the tactical scope that Napoleon showed in previous campaigns. In reality, it amounted to little more than unleashing a standard artillery barrage, and then conducting a massed frontal assault against Wellington's line. Soult was worried that the emperor was understating the consequence the unending rains were having on the field. Cannon would be nearly impossible to move, as half the guns were sunk up to their axles in the mud. The effects of their solid shot would also be greatly reduced. And then there was the issue of the infantry and cavalry. Manoeuvre would be hindered, and the horses would scarcely be able to canter, let alone charge at a full gallop. Perhaps then, that was why Napoleon was conducting a direct attack, as he knew that complex tactical movements would prove impossible given the boggy terrain.

Sometime after midnight, Marshal Soult finally drifted off to sleep his dreams tormented by thoughts of what would happen to France, should they be unable to break Wellington.

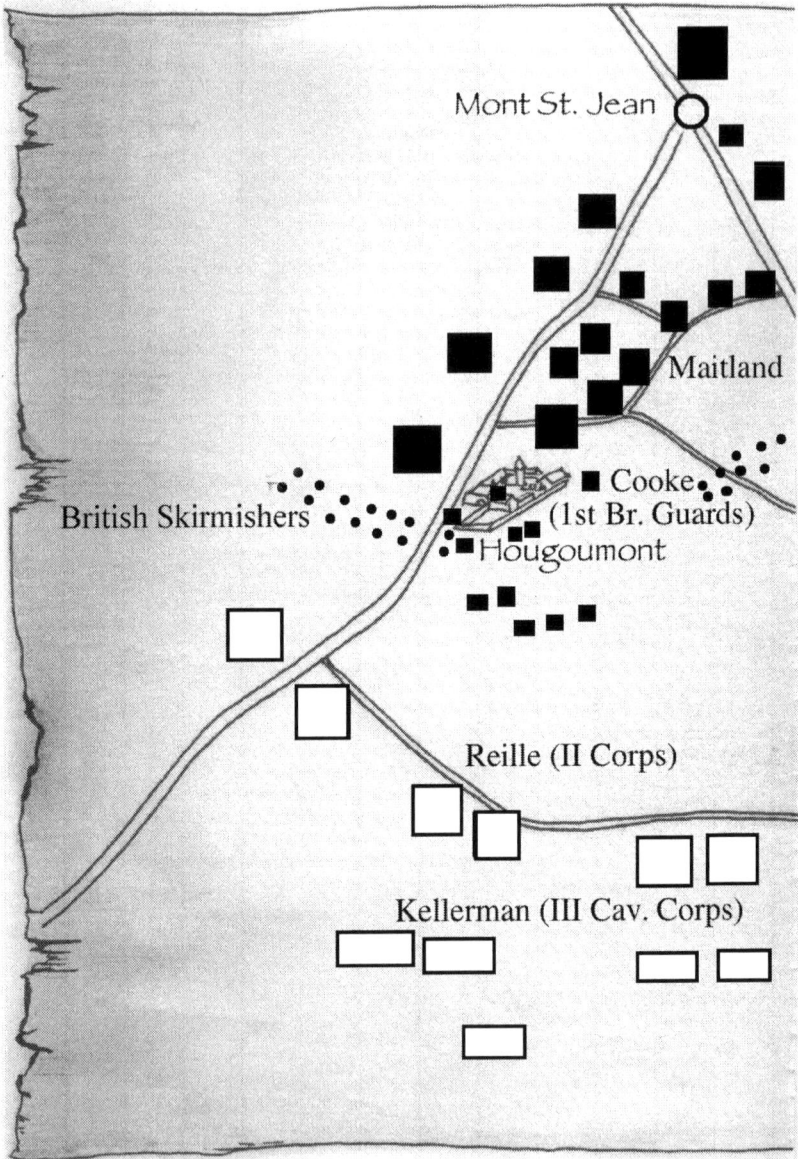

The extreme right of Wellington's Army (Napoleon's left), note the farmhouse of Hougomont to the south. It would be Reille's II Corps that would conduct the brunt of the assault on Hougomont. Webster and the rest of 3/1st Foot Guards are just to the north.

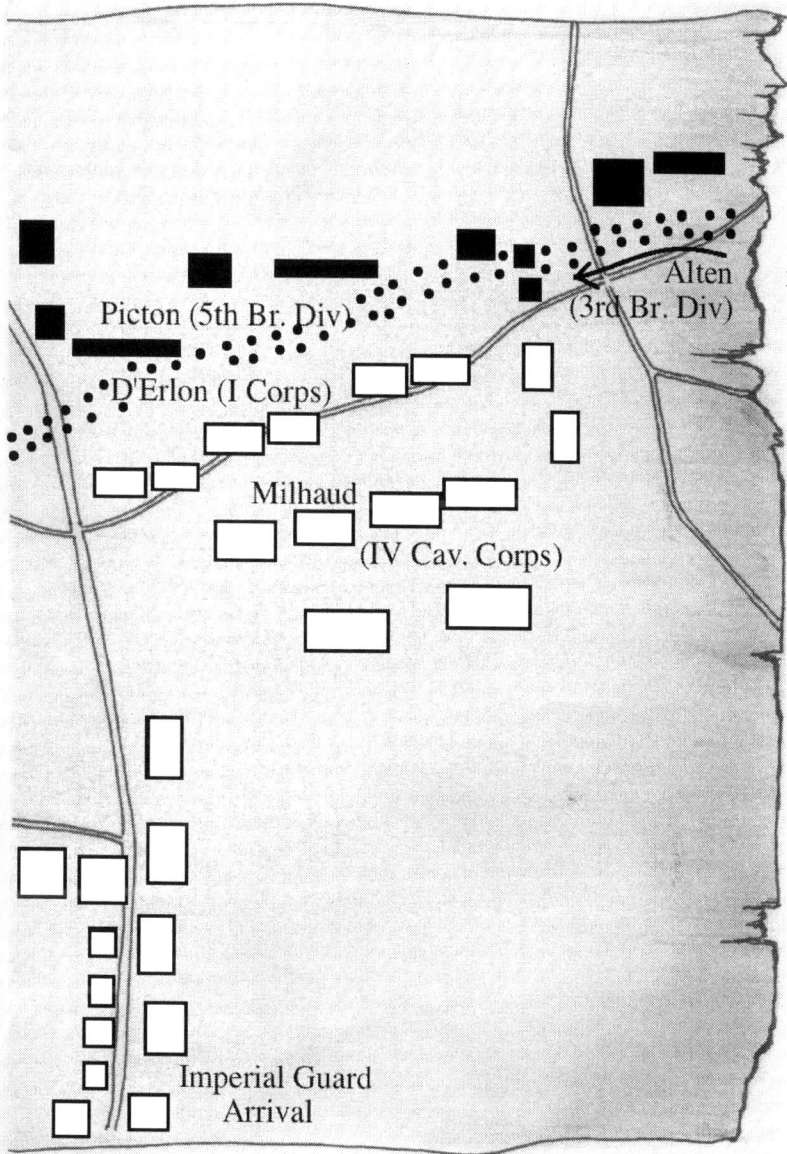

Picton (5th Br. Div)

Alten (3rd Br. Div)

D'Erlon (I Corps)

Milhaud

(IV Cav. Corps)

Imperial Guard Arrival

Wellington's left (Napoleon's right). With d'Erlon's corps fresh, they will lead the assault on La Haye Sainte and the British left. The Imperial Guard is held in reserve to the south.

Chapter XVII: Dawn is Breaking
Field of Waterloo
18 June 1815
Sunrise

Wellington at Waterloo

Two hours before the sun broke through the clouds and over the eastern horizon, the hellish rains finally ceased. It was during this interlude that the armies, who would soon do battle, finally fell collectively into a deep slumber. It was not to last.

James instinctively woke about an hour before sunrise, as the false glow of the predawn made his surroundings visible. He crawled his way out from underneath the wagon, thankful that he had at least managed to avoid the constant pummelling from the rain for a few hours. He was still completely soaked, and he longed to feel the early morning rays of the sun. The ground sloshed beneath his feet as he walked to the edge of the ridgeline and got his bearings.

Down the slope, off to his right, was the farmhouse of Hougomont. Men from the Coldstream Guards manned the ramparts of the wall, as well the rooftops. The King's Colour flew from one of the roofs, goading the French into trying to take the stronghold from them. To his left, the rest of the army formed a long line, mostly behind the reverse slope. Only cannon and a handful of advance units showed the enemy that they held the high ground. Behind the Guards, Sir Henry Clinton's division formed a reserve, well behind the main line. A handful of Dutch battalions were also substantially behind the main line, off to the right, in order to prevent the army from being flanked. These elements aside, James realized that for all intents and purposes, the Guards formed the extreme right of Wellington's army.

"Captain Webster!" a voice shouted.

James turned and saw it was Captain Stables walking his way. First thing James noticed was how haggard his fellow officer looked. His usually immaculate uniform was filthy and soaked, his shako plate smudged and streaked with mud. The man's eyes were bloodshot and he had yet to shave. James wondered if he was as wretched of a sight.

"A fine morning," was all James could find to say.

"And it will be a fine day, should we give Boney the thrashing he deserves and still be standing when it's over," Stables replied. "Major D'Oyley's compliments; he is assembling all company commanders over by the quartermaster wagon."

"Very good," he acknowledged.

Thankfully, the five companies under his control were all bivouacked very close to each other, and finding their commanders proved easy. James instinctively walked beside Lieutenant Shanahan, though scarcely a word was spoken as they joined the other officers of the battalion.

A pair of wagons was just off the side of the rutted and muddy road. One carried the battalion's extra ammunition, the other much-needed rations. Major D'Oyley leaned up against the rations wagon. He was every bit as haggard as Captain Stables, the only difference was he'd managed to just finish up shaving and was wringing out a rain-soaked towel before wiping his face.

"God bless the quartermasters!" he said as James and the other officers approached. "They arrived well past midnight, but at least they are here. I don't know if there is even a scrap of dry firewood within a hundred miles, so the men may have to eat their breakfast cold."

"Still better than dying with an empty stomach," Captains Stables reasoned.

Men from each company were lining up on the far side of the wagon, while the quartermaster and regimental sergeant major distributed the day's rations to each company.

"I had the wagons placed close for security during the night," Major D'Oyley explained. "Once we get the rations offloaded, they will be placed well behind the main line. God forbid our ammunition wagon takes a shot from Bonaparte's cannon. That, gentlemen, would not do at all."

"What are the orders, sir?" Captain Daniel Roberts asked. "What is Wellington's plan?"

"His grace's plan," Henry shrugged, "is to beat the French."

This elicited a quiet chuckle from the assembled leaders of 3/1st Foot Guards. In truth, each man was privately nervous about how the day would go. None had ever been in battle against Napoleon, Quatre Bras notwithstanding. And even that was really a battle against Marshal Ney, as the emperor had been a few miles away, thrashing the Prussians at Ligny.

"Sir, my men have formed a skirmish line and linked up with 2nd Battalion's light company," Daniel explained. "We had to place ourselves well forward of the main line, but at least we have a good defensive position and can provide covering, as well as flanking fire for the defenders of Hougomont."

"Very good," the battalion commander nodded. He then turned to James. "Captain Webster, have two companies ready to shift towards Hougomont, should it become untenable."

"Yes, sir," James replied. "I'll have the grenadier and 1st Companies ready to move at a moment's notice and will lead any reinforcing actions, personally."

"The terrain has become a boggy mess," Captain Stables noted. "Manoeuvre will be a nightmare, whether on foot or horse. Lucky for us, Boney will have to do most of the manoeuvring today."

"Indeed," Major D'Oyley agreed. He then asked Captain Roberts, "Any movement from the enemy?"

"No, sir," Daniel replied. "I think they had just as hellish of a night as we did."

Henry nodded and then took out his pocket watch. "Gentlemen, it is now 5:10. Boney will want to give his men a meal and as much rest as possible before they attack. We have time for the men to square their weapons and kit away as soon as they've eaten. And I want everyone shaved this morning, too. We can't do much about everyone's sodded uniforms, but we will make every effort to look the part of true soldier gentlemen on this historic day."

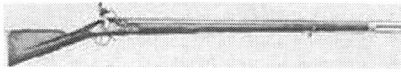

Newly-promoted Corporal David O'Connor was already performing kit inspections on the men while they ate their cold breakfast. He made corrections as needed, and to any man whose kit looked above standard, he offered a piece of cooked pig from his haversack.

"Your ammunition pouch is torn," he told one soldier. "Lay out your cartridges; make sure they aren't torn nor have water in the powder." As he inspected another soldier, he directed the man to show him his bayonet. "What in the bleeding hell happened to this? The point is completely blunted!"

"Sorry, corporal," the soldier said. "I was trying to stick a cuirassier when we were pulling back to Bossu Wood. Damned tip broke off against his armour."

"Get this re-sharpened," David ordered. "And next time, don't try and stick a cuirassier in the bloody armour."

"Those stripes have gone right to his sodden head," the soldier grumbled as soon as David walked away. "He should be swinging from a gallows right now, and yet somehow Old Nosey makes his teenage arse a damned non-comm!"

"Belay that shit!" Private Farrow retorted. "It was a deserted farmhouse, and he was getting food for the men. And don't forget, he helped turn the enemy flank in Bossu Wood after Lieutenant Grose bought it."

249

"Besides," another soldier chimed in, "he's right. You won't do nothing with that blunted bayonet except maybe tickle a frog to death."

This last remark drew a laugh from the disgruntled soldier, who could only shake his head.

"You have a knack for leadership," Sergeant Donaldson said approvingly as David joined him. The company's only remaining sergeant was squinting in front of a mirror as he attempted to shave.

David counted himself fortunate that he could not grow facial hair even if he wanted to.

"It's still baffling how you got those stripes to begin with."

"Well, they're your old stripes," the corporal observed. "And how I got them is bloody stupid. That disgruntled sod with the blunted bayonet thought I could not hear his rebuke. Thing is, he's right. Still, I figure if by some miracle I survive this day, then I'd better learn how to act like an NCO."

"Many spend a lifetime in the ranks without so much as earning a chosen man's single chevron," Donaldson said as he winced from where he nicked himself. "To think, a year ago you were a rookie recruit in the Inniskilling, straight from the turnip patch, and now you're a corporal of the Guards. If you make it through today without a scratch, then I'd say you must be blessed by the Almighty."

"And for that, I cannot for the life of me think why," David grunted. "I've not stepped into a church nor spoken a single word of reverence to God since I was about seven."

"Perhaps after today you should make it a point to find out why," Donaldson said as he wiped his face off and then checked the cut on his neck. "Damn it all, this nick is going to bleed all day."

"Let's hope it's all the bleeding you do," David thought aloud.

They were soon joined by Corporal Harvey, who was constantly wiping his hand over his face and eyes.

"Bugger it all," he grumbled. "I didn't sleep a wink. My eyes and face feel like they've been beaten with a hammer." He then broke into a coughing fit and fell to his right knee.

"Good God, Christopher," David said. "Don't die on us before the frogs can take a crack at you."

"Damn it all," Harvey grunted as he staggered to his feet. "I survived the entire Peninsula War without so much as catching a cold, and now I've got a blasted cough and the shakes like an epileptic whore!"

"I think everyone is going to come down with something after this," Sergeant Donaldson conjectured. "That is, if there is anyone left when this day is done."

"It's going to be bad, isn't it?" David asked, knowing full-well the answer.

"Neither Boney nor Nosey is going to budge today," the sergeant replied. "What happened at Quatre Bras is but a taste of what will come today. Only thing I can say is I am thankful we have the terrain advantage."

David left his fellow NCOs and decided to see how the rest of the men were managing. Douglas Farrow was running a rag over his musket and checking the firing mechanism to make sure it functioned properly. Farrow did not excel as a soldier, but neither did he ever cause any trouble either. He was steady and reliable, and that was all anyone could ask of him that day.

"Morning, corporal," he said, grinning to his friend. His face bore the same fatigue as every other soldier on the field. An endless night of torrential rain, accompanied with little to no sleep, and it was all any of them could do to function properly. Farrow went through the motions of checking his weapons, ammunition, and kit as much to maintain any semblance of alertness, as it was to ensure everything functioned correctly when it was time to engage the French once more.

David then found Private Eric Adams, who was going through a similar inspection of his weapon. While he went through the same drill, there was no sense of purpose like there was with Private Farrow. Eric, who'd always been an exceptional soldier, was completely listless, and not just from fatigue and lack of sleep. His words from the night before rang in the corporal's ears.

"Still with us, Eric?" David asked as he knelt in front of his friend, who was seated with his back against a small rock outcropping. When the private did not reply, David grabbed him by the shoulder. "Eric!"

"Corporal," Adams replied, seeming to notice him for the first time.

"Knock that shit off," David grumbled. "It's still me. Don't act like we haven't been friends for the past year, especially since there's a good chance we could both be dead before the day is done. But since I am your corporal, it is my duty to check on your welfare, so that neither you nor anyone on the line next to you dies needlessly. I ask you again, are you still with us?"

Eric appeared to ignore him as he looked off to the side and squeezed the trigger of his musket. The hammer snapped, causing a spark from the flint, startling David. The private then seemed satisfied with his weapon's serviceability, and he set it down next to him. When he spoke next, he was still looking off in the distance, as if in a trance.

"I...I cannot see the face of my wife," he stammered, "or my children. How many years have we been together, yet try as I might, I cannot envision her. A terrible omen, if there is such a thing." Tears were now streaming down his face.

"Damn it, Eric, snap out of it!" David said with exasperation. He was not used to being a leader, and yet here was one of his soldiers, one who was ten years older with infinitely more experience, having a sort of breakdown long before the battle was set to commence. Unsure what else to do, he grabbed the private by both shoulders and shook him hard against the rocks.

Eric shook his head and was suddenly staring at David, mouth agape in surprise. "I...I'm sorry, David," he said quickly. "I don't know what came over me. Quatre Bras was certainly not my first action, yet since that day I've felt lost, like I'm standing on the abyss. If I take another life, I fear I will fall off the edge, lost forever."

"Everyone has their breaking point," David reasoned. "I'm surprised it took this long to find yours."

"Lieutenant Shanahan meant well, mentioning me in despatches," the private continued. "But I think it made things worse for me. If a dozen frogs aren't dead at my feet when this is done, I will somehow have failed him, and all of you."

"You got seven of them at Quatre Bras," David noted. "And not just injured either. Five shot in the head and two more bayonetted through the heart, including a cuirassier! Most of the

252

lads have no way of reckoning whether they got a single frog, yet we've confirmed you got seven."

"I always know," Eric stated quietly. "Do you know how many I've killed since I first donned the uniform, including those at Quatre Bras? Thirty-five…thirty-five men have died by my hand. Most went the entire war without knowing whether or not they killed anyone, and for that they should think themselves fortunate. I was not simply bragging when I told you that my father taught me how to shoot at a very young age. Chest, throat, and head; those are the only places I've ever shot an enemy soldier. Not once have I hit a man in the arm or leg, it's always been a killing shot. I cannot see the face of my wife, as much as I try, yet I can see every one of their faces clear as day."

There was a lengthy pause as Eric tried to catch his breath, as if he'd just run a great distance. Along with Douglas Farrow, David considered Eric Adams to be one of his closest friends. Eric's wife looked at him like a younger brother, and their children found his accent amusing and called him 'their Irish uncle'. After Toulouse, and now Quatre Bras, David could rightly call himself a combat veteran, yet Eric had seen and experienced horrors beyond his comprehension. It made the corporal feel powerless to help his friend, as there were no words of encouragement or advice he could give him. On that cool June morning, as the sun started to rise in the east, all he could do was spare a few moments to allow his friend to unload his vexations on him.

"Besides being able to shoot," Eric continued, "about the only other skill me dad taught me was how to read and write. Mum spoke fluent French, so of course I picked that up, too. Well, after Toulouse, I found a diary on a young French soldier I'd killed. The mistake I made was reading it. I had only set eyes on him during the few moments it took to bring my weapon to bear and blast his life from his body. And yet, after reading that diary, I know Jean-Paul Javert like he was me own brother. It was then that I came to see every man I slew, not as an enemy, but as one who could have been my friend and brother. They were men, just like you and me, though many were so young they were little more than boys. After that, I swore not to kill ever again. I stayed with the army, not knowing what else to do. It was the only way to provide for the family. My wife has told me that in my sleep she'll sometimes hear

253

me say, *how can we kill one another?* Over and over again, I'll say it; *how can we?* Seven more now lay dead by my hand, and still I ask, how can we?"

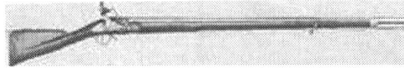

French Cavalry

Marshal Ney sat atop his horse and watched as two dozen men tried to wrench an artillery piece that had sank into the mud. All around men struggled to even walk as they sank up to their ankles in the thick sludge. He said nothing, but simply turned his horse and rode the short distance to the house, known as La Belle Alliance, where the emperor had attempted to gain a few hours' sleep. A groomsman took his horse as he dismounted; a grenadier of the Imperial Guard opening the door to the house, which led directly into the dining room where Napoleon and at least a dozen officers sat. Servants were already serving up breakfast and pouring glasses of water and other drinks for the men.

"Ah, Michel!" Napoleon said excited. "Glad you could join us."

"You are looking much better this morning, sire," Ney observed as he walked in and removed his bicorn hat.

"Yes, well I cannot let a little stomach bother keep me from my destiny with Wellington today," Napoleon said as he took a long drink of water, which a servant immediately refilled. "What time is it?"

"Just past 7:00, sire," Soult replied, checking his watch.

"Good," the emperor nodded. "We attack in two hours." This order led to a stir amongst the assembled leaders of his army.

"Sire," his chief of artillery spoke up, "our cannon are not in position yet. The ground is too soft, and we can hardly move."

"We've fought in the mud before," Napoleon rebuked. "You are charged with having my artillery ready to smash the English into oblivion, and I do not want to hear excuses. The longer we wait for the ground to dry allows Wellington time to bring up his errant corps. And I want this Englishman brought to his knees before the Prussians can even have thoughts about continuing the fight. Entire wars are won or lost within a matter of minutes. The English are feverishly trying to bring their wayward troops to bear, and the longer I wait, the more of our men will die as they arrive and reinforce Wellington."

"Sire, about Marshal Grouchy," Soult spoke up.

"What of him?" Napoleon asked, taking a bite of sausage. "He was late engaging his pursuit, granted, but he should be on the heels of the Prussians; provided they haven't fled all the way back to Berlin."

"Well, sire, it's just that we've heard rumours," the emperor's brother, Jerome, added. "A waiter from the *King of Spain Inn* in Genappe overheard talk between some English officers that the Prussians intend to reform at Wavre and advance on our flank. We've yet to hear which road Grouchy took in his pursuit. He may not even be chasing the Prussians at all."

"A waiter?" Napoleon scoffed. "You want me to change my entire battle plan on the word of a waiter? Your pessimism is unbecoming, brother, as it is to you, Soult."

"All the same, sire," Soult persisted, "we must recall Grouchy immediately. He has 30,000 men, which we can use to envelope Wellington..." Napoleon slammed his fist on the table.

"Don't you dare tell me what I must do!" he barked. "Know this; while I appreciate candour and honesty, what I will not suffer is a direct challenge to my orders! Let the Prussians come. I've dealt with them enough times already. It will take them two days to assemble and march on us, and by then the English will be destroyed and Wellington on the run back to London with his tail between his legs. Besides," his voice calmed considerably, "Grouchy will deal with what's left of the Prussians. He has his orders, now you'd best follow yours."

"Of course, sire," Soult bowed slightly.

"You embarrass me, all of you," the emperor scolded the assembled generals. "You are all terrified of Wellington, why? He bested all of you, so you think he's a great general. Well I tell you this, he is a lousy general, his army a bunch of inexperienced schoolboys, and this entire affair will be less difficult for me to decide than my breakfast. Whatever he did to you in Spain, I will *not* be defeated by this upstart and his army of shopkeepers!"

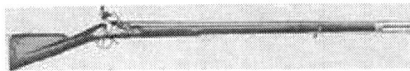

Wellington lay with his head against the bulging roots of a tree, fast asleep. While Uxbridge was baffled by this, neither DeLancey nor Somerset appeared concerned. They issued the orders to division and brigade commanders that the Duke had spent half the night writing. All were explicit in detail, making certain every unit knew its place on the battlefield and what was expected of them.

"England expects every man to do his duty," Somerset said, echoing the words of Horatio Nelson, spoken just before the immortal Battle of Trafalgar.

He handed a sheaf of orders to Sir Thomas Picton, who though pale in the face, looked markedly better than when DeLancey had seen him the night before. Usually one for biting remarks, especially towards Somerset, Picton was strangely quiet this morning. Most of the staff officers surmised it was due to fatigue from lack of sleep, in addition to the strain from the pending cataclysmic battle. Only DeLancey knew the real reasons for the old general's lack of rapport. The two made eye contact briefly; just long enough for each to subtly nod to the other in understanding. The sound of the Duke's snoring caused a chuckle from some of the men.

"Is it really advisable for his grace to be napping at a time like this?" Uxbridge asked Somerset.

"He was up late, writing these," the major replied, holding up the stack of orders yet to be distributed. "This is going to be a long day. I think the Duke is obliged to take a moment to rest up before the coming storm. Besides, he knows that with the ground being but an impassable bog in so many places, Boney won't be able to move for several hours. Trust me, sir, his grace will join us long before then."

There was a snort from by the tree, and the Duke opened his eyes before yawning and stretching his arms over his head. He then looked over at his second. "Ah, Uxbridge," he said. "Good of you to join us."

"Arthur, I must know," Uxbridge said hesitantly. "It is imperative that I know your plans. I have no indication as to how you intend to deal with Bonaparte, and as I am your second-in-command…"

"First off," Wellington interrupted, "my intent is to beat the French and put an end to this war. Second, the orders are all there with Somerset, including those for your cavalry corps. They will suffice should the worst happen to me. And thirdly, you know how much I detest the idea of seconds-in-command. It is a useless position that means absolutely nothing. Your sole purpose is commanding my cavalry, nothing more. Should I fall, and believe me, I will be giving Boney's men plenty of opportunities to blast me off my horse, only then will you assume overall command. All this talk of being second-in-command is utterly pointless."

"Understood," Uxbridge replied. He then gave a twisted grin. "And don't worry, Arthur, I don't intend to try to expedite your death so as to gain control of the army."

"Well, why not?" Wellington shrugged as he sat upright. "The bloody frogs have been trying to kill me for years; might as well have someone with a bit of competence take a shot at it."

"Thank you…I think," the earl said with his brow furrowed in puzzlement. "You know, our history has not always been pleasant."

257

"That was a long time ago, Henry," the Duke noted as he stood and yawned once more. It was perhaps the only time he'd ever called Uxbridge by his given name. He then quickly shook his head and looked fresher and more alert than any man on the field that morning. "Five years ago you married my brother Henry's ex-wife, and you were having a liaison with her long before then. What is still between you and my brother is your own business. What I do know is you're one of the best cavalry officers in the entire world. You covered our withdrawal from Quatre Bras with much skill and cunning and without needlessly losing lives. I don't need you to be my friend, I need you for your skill and valour. And you, sir, possess much of both."

"I'm obliged to you, Arthur," Uxbridge replied. "I will take my orders and brief my brigade commanders."

"Don't go far," Wellington directed. "I feel I will have much need of your skills before the day is done."

Henry William Paget, Earl of Uxbridge

Chapter XVIII: Prelude to the Storm
Field of Waterloo
18 June 1815
9:30 am

French cavalry advancing

A short time later, Napoleon was kneeling beneath a tree alongside the road, his hand over his mouth and elbow resting on his knee in contemplation as he watched men, horses, and artillery wagons struggle to move through the quagmire.

"Are you alright, sire?" Marshal Ney asked, walking up behind him.

"Why does everyone always ask me that?" the emperor replied with irritation. He let out a sigh. "You think I was too hard on them?"

"On Soult and your brother? Not even a little bit."

"My brothers have been a constant disappointment for me," Napoleon grumbled. "I made Joseph King of Spain, and he lost that for me. Well, today, at least Jerome has a chance at redeeming himself to me, so he'd best stop cowering in the face of this damned Sepoy General."

"The ground is still sodden," Ney noted.

Napoleon nodded and scowled. "I'll tell you this; I despise having my battle plans dictated to me, even by God. However, it seems the Lord has won out this time. Tell me, Michel, when will the army be in position to attack?"

"11:00 at the earliest sire," the marshal confessed. "Entire companies of infantry have been employed to drag every last one of our cannon into position through this awful muck."

"Then that is when we will attack," Napoleon asserted. "But as I do not like wasted time, we will give the English a proper showing of our might before we unleash on them." He then looked up at his marshal, who would lead the main attack. "You are the bravest man in my entire army, Michel. I know you are not afraid of Wellington."

"Wellington is but a man, sire," Ney replied with emphasis. "You just tell me where to strike, and I will break him."

"Soon, my friend," Napoleon said as his marshal helped pull him to his feet. He then pointed to the centre of his line, where his cannon were slowly being staged. "I will be there, astride my horse, and I want every last division in this army to conduct a pass-and-review before I send them into battle."

"Very good, sire," the marshal replied.

"I need this, Michel," the emperor explained. "Though I intend to destroy Wellington today, many of our finest will fall and never rise again. I need to see them one more time, *all* of them. From the generals, down to the lowest conscript privates who've only now been able to serve under the eagles, I need to have this last moment with my boys."

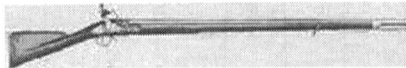

"Well there's something you don't see every day," Somerset observed as he sat on his horse beside Wellington. Far below, in the rise behind the enemy guns, tens-of-thousands of French soldiers stood in parade formation. Drums beat a continuous cadence as the regimental bands struck up with various pieces of French patriotic music. Column after column paraded just behind the cannon in a show of military might that would make even the most hardened veteran tremble in both admiration and fear.

"Seems Boney wants to try and terrify us first," DeLancey noted with revulsion. "We'll make corpses of them soon enough."

"And yet, it really is quite beautiful," the Duke said quietly. He could not help but be mesmerized by the sight of such disciplined power. He was distracted momentarily as an artillery captain named Mercer quickly rode up to him.

"Your grace!" the battery commander said quickly. "Over there, seated astride his horse, where the columns are passing in front of. It's him!"

Wellington calmly brought his telescope up to his eye and scanned where Mercer pointed. Despite the extreme distance, there certainly was no mistaking the great white horse. Though posterity would forever link their names together, this was the first and only time Wellington would ever see his arch nemesis. It was impossible to make out any details at all; just a man with a black hat and grey greatcoat who appeared to be waving to his men as they rode past him.

"So there is the great man himself," Wellington said.

"Sir, if I elevate my guns to maximum, I could chance a shot at him," Mercer said excitedly.

"That does not sound convincing at all," Wellington scolded. "Save your ammunition for his columns, rather than wasting shot trying to unseat one man on a horse."

The artillery officer looked disappointed, but he simply saluted and rode back to his battery.

In the distance, the bands continued to play, as seemingly endless columns of men passed before the emperor. The unmistakably French music coming from the numerous regimental bands echoed across the landscape, permeating the audio senses of the entire Anglo Army. As it appeared the display would last at least an hour or more, the Duke was concerned about the psychological affect it would have on his men, in particular his less-experienced allied militia. So it was with a certain sense of relief when British regiments spontaneously struck up with their own inspirational battle songs. Normally Wellington detested

261

cheering, as he felt it gave the impression of the men possessing an opinion. On this day, however, he was glad to hear the battalions behind him strike up with a cappella rendition of *The British Grenadiers*.

Some talk of Alexander, and some of Hercules,
Of Hector and Lysander, and some of Meltiades.
But of all the world's brave heros, there's none that can compare
With a tow row row row row
To the British grenadiers!
Now none of these ancient heros ever saw a cannon ball
Or knew the force of powder to slay their foes withal,
But our brave boys do now them and banish all their fears
With a tow row row row row
To the British grenadiers!

Still others joined in with a more familiar and even older song, *Over the Hills and Far Away*. Though it originated during the reign of Queen Anne, one hundred years before, a simple change to parts of the lyrics made it relevant for the soldiers who stood ready, for *King George commands and we obey*.

Hark! Now the drums beat up again,
For all true soldier gentlemen,
Then let us enlist and march I say,
Over the hills and far away.
Over the hills and over the main.
To Flanders, Portugal, and Spain,
King George commands and we obey.
Over the hills and far away.
All gentlemen that have a mind,
To serve the king that's good and kind,
Come enlist and enter into pay,
Then over the hills and far away.
Over the hills and over the main.
To Flanders, Portugal, and Spain,
King George commands and we obey.
Over the hills and far away.

Here's forty shillings on the drum,
For those that volunteers do come,
With shirts, and clothes, and present pay,
Then over the hills and far away.

Though the overwhelming music from the French bands would mean their enemies would be unable to hear the boisterous singing of the redcoats, at least it kept Wellington's men in better cheer before the coming battle. It was the Duke who was now growing impatient, as he drew his telescope once more and surveyed the field below.

"How long will Bonaparte play at this game before he decides to fight me?"

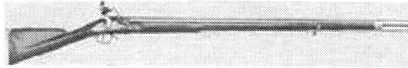

Napoleon knew that the time for posturing was nearly over. His marshals may have scoffed at his pompous show of force before attacking the Anglo Army, however, it was not just for them that he paraded his men. His face showed his deep sense of pride as he tried to take in the sight of every last soldier who marched before him. He noted especially his glorious eagles; personally given to each regiment by the emperor himself. That he had placed his hands on every last standard somehow made them sacred in the eyes of the men, as if he were sanctifying them. Though Napoleon certainly felt the surge of semi-divine essence when he presented his eagles to each regiment, he was still leery about taking the display too far. His speech often seemed to dismiss the presence of God during these harrowing days yet he still believed and hoped his displays would not bode ill with the Almighty.

Like Wellington, he felt that everything would be decided this day, and he needed it to start properly. The sun was out and warming the saturated earth. He knew it would not be sufficient to dry the mud, but it did not matter. He still had the most powerful and experienced army in the world. No amount of boggy ground was going to deny him his victory over the insufferable English upstart who he was finally facing.

"He's positioned himself well," Napoleon observed as he scanned the ridge through his spyglass. "We'll see how well he holds his ground once we start toying with him a bit." As he spoke, columns of his famed Imperial Guard marched past him, their bands striking up songs fit for announcing the presence of France's elite. The emperor knew this would be a difficult day, despite the superior quality of his troops compared to Wellington's. The English still had a distinct terrain advantage, and though he never admitted it publicly, Napoleon had much respect for his adversary. He may have berated his subordinates for having been beaten by Wellington time and again, but the emperor was wise enough to recognize his foe's tactical savvy.

Because of this, he was holding his best troops in reserve. The Young Guard would act as a mobile reserve, ready to manoeuvre wherever needed should his army become hard-pressed. The Middle and Old Guard would be kept well back from the main line. Once he sensed that Wellington was ready to break, he would unleash them and finish this day. It was a simple strategy; grind Wellington down, finish him with the Imperial Guard, while waiting for word from Grouchy to see if the Prussians needed another beating to put them out of the war.

"Sire, the army awaits your command," Marshal Soult said. His demeanour was of a man finally getting his revenge against a long-hated enemy. He'd made it very plain that he wanted the English annihilated, but he also wanted Wellington alive, so that he may not use death as an escape from the humiliation of defeat.

"We'll begin there," Napoleon directed, pointing towards Hougomont. "Unleash Reille's corps against the farmhouse that the English now use as a stronghold and we'll tease him a bit. Whether Wellington shifts his right wing to reinforce, or trusts it to stand on its own will tell me the true calibre of my enemy. If he attempts to check me there, then I can dictate the entire course of the battle. And then I will know the true quality of this Englishman."

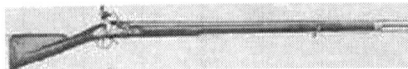

From atop his horse, James could see perfectly down into the valley. The sight of so many French soldiers assembled impressed him greatly. The sounds of fife and drum of their band echoing loudly, even at such a great distance. He then observed just how much their blue and white uniforms contrasted with the landscape. Many scoffed that the British army wore red, yet when James looked down the line of his men, most of their uniforms were faded to a degree and worn. In such a state they looked more of a reddish brown, rather than the deep scarlet of their dress uniforms. From a distance one would almost mistake the mass of redcoats for a large formation of clay. Whereas there were no colours in nature that matched the 'Prussian blue' worn by the French.

"I suppose this will be an historic day," Henry D'Oyley said as he calmly rode up next to his captain. "But I'll be damned if I can feel it."

"Sir, I've often wondered if those who turn the page of history feel anything at all at their moment of immortality," James conjectured.

"And do you feel anything, Captain Webster?" Henry asked.

James scanned the length of the valley floor, where tens-of-thousands of French soldiers still marched in their parade.

"To be perfectly candid, sir, when I look at that, I feel terror."

"Hmm," Henry replied. "Well you'd be a fool not to. But what's the worst that could happen? You die, and then it does not matter anyway."

"No, sir," James said, shaking his head. "The worst thing would be facing defeat at the hands of Bonaparte and not being spared with death."

"Then we'd best not lose," the major replied nonchalantly. "If our Guards Division cannot hold against Boney, then no one can. Even God will not be able to save Europe should we fail."

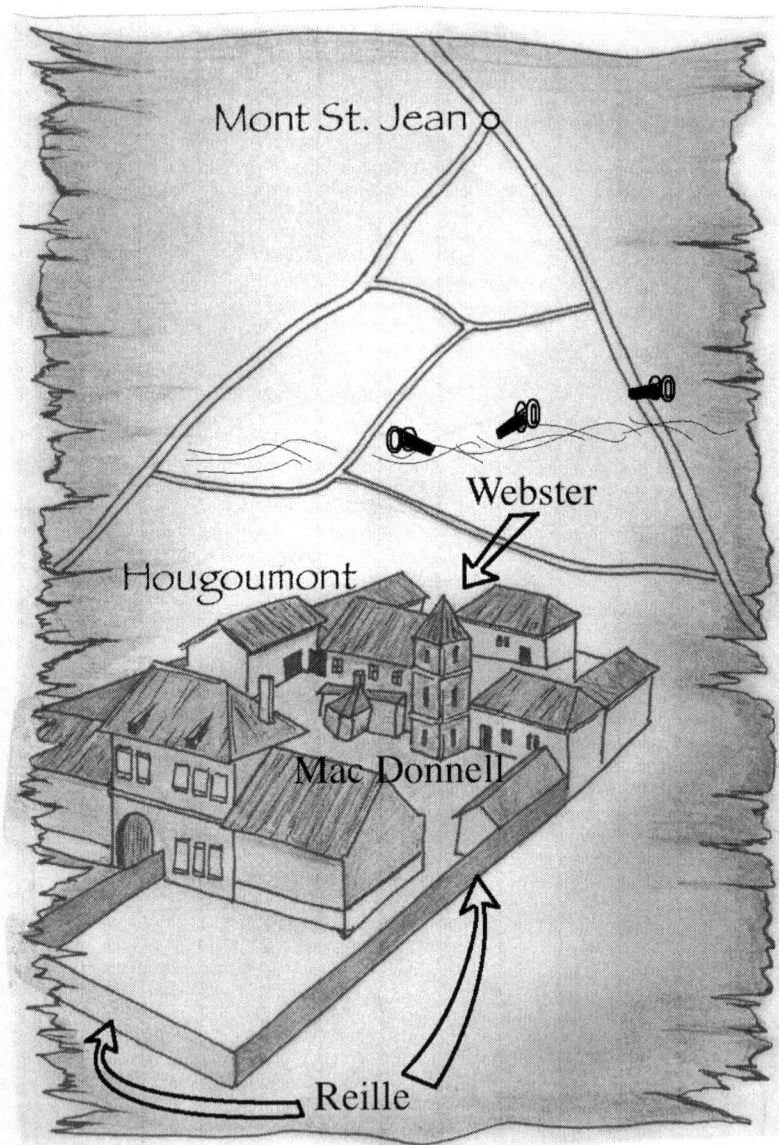

Reille's initial assault on Hougomont. Webster's reinforcements move to the east, to link up with the regiment's skirmishers.

Chapter XIX: Hougomont
Field of Waterloo
18 June 1815
10:30 am

French soldiers assaulting Hougomont

The burst of a single cannon from the French lines erupted, echoing throughout the landscape. The contrast of fear and relief enveloped both armies as the battle now commenced.

"About time we get this started," a soldier grunted.

Most of the Guards Division stood behind the reverse slope, and therefore could not see what was happening below. The regimental sergeant major walked the line with a large jug of gin, pouring each soldier half a cup.

"Drink up, lads," the RSM said. "No sense having frayed nerves before the frogs get to us."

Even the officers were imbibing in preparation for the coming storm. Many had personal flasks filled with a far better fare than the gutter-water gin the RSM gave to the enlisted men. The captain of the grenadier company walked over and handed Patrick

Shanahan his flask. More than just sharing a drink before battle, it also signified that the captain accepted the Irish lieutenant as a right and proper officer. Patrick took a long pull off the flask before handing it back with a nod of understanding.

The battalion's attached artillery, which was placed on the other side of the slope, to their left-front, now erupted in a volley of return fire. The French guns across the valley had them terribly outnumbered. However, it seemed most of their fire was being concentrated on Hougomont. In the absence of orders, British battery commanders directed their crews to open fire on the French guns. The thunder of friendly artillery shook the men of the Guards, shockwaves rocking them with each blast.

"Can't see a damn thing," a private on the line muttered. Between being behind the reverse slope, plus their frontage now socked in with a thick cloud of continuous smoke from the roaring cannon, and it was as if they were now made completely blind as to the rest of the battlefield.

"Well, they can't very well see us either," Corporal O'Connor pointed out. "I'll take a loss of situational awareness, if it means not having to stand in the path of Boney's cannon, thank you very much."

At the top of the ridge, Captain James Webster knelt alongside his company commanders. All had removed their hats and were trying to keep a fairly low profile. Captain Stables had the commanders of the left wing with him on the other end of the battalion line. The only one absent was Captain Daniel Roberts, who was hunkered down with his light company, well in front of the battalion, awaiting the enemy advance.

They watched intently as enemy cannon unleashed on Hougomont. The steel balls hammered into the walls with a fearful crash. However, the thick stone appeared to be holding.

"Over there, sir," Patrick Shanahan said, as he lowered his telescope. "They're advancing on the farmhouse."

"Hard to tell just how many," James replied as he scanned the area. Groves of trees masked the enemy movements, though he could still make out the tricolour flags and eagle standards of individual regiments. "Best I can guess is at least one, maybe two divisions conducting the assault."

"And how many more in reserve?" Patrick wondered aloud.

"Those walls are fairly high," the commander of 2nd Company stated. "And with men stationed on every rooftop, the frogs will be taking fire from above, as well as trying to dislodge the men on the walls."

"Are they on the move yet?" Major D'Oyley asked as he rode up on his horse.

"They are, sir," James confirmed. "And by the looks of it, they're sending an entire corps against Hougomont."

"So they are," Henry confirmed after making a quick count of enemy standards through his telescope. "I doubt they'll be able to get over the walls, not with the Coldstream Guards holding them. Still, you'd best take your two reinforcement companies down the slope. Link up with Captain Roberts and provide enfilade fire into the enemy flank. Reinforce the farmhouse if necessary, but be ready to pull back on order."

"Yes, sir," James said. He then stood, drew his sword, and shouted, *"1st and Grenadier Companies on me!"*

With subsequent shouted orders from their NCOs, the two companies formed into marching columns and quick-stepped to the captain. Lieutenant Shanahan and the Grenadier captain stood with their swords drawn. Their men forming up on them.

"You ready to do this?" James said to Patrick, who grinned.

"Sir, the lads and I will follow you anywhere; even into *that.*" He nodded towards the chaos below to emphasize his point.

British artillery that had been designated to support Hougomont were now firing over the building complex and into the massed columns of French Infantry that were emerging from the woods. Though the boggy ground negated much of the effect of solid shot, heavy cannon balls did land amongst the densely-packed ranks, smashing hapless enemy soldiers to pieces.

Even more effective were the explosive carcass shots fired by each battery's lone howitzer. The shells would burst in the air, raining down white-hot shards of metal and cinders, creating horrifyingly painful injuries to those who were not mercifully killed in the blast. James and his men were too far away to hear the screams of pain from the stricken, yet they could guess at the havoc being wrought upon the enemy columns that still advanced with rigid discipline.

269

"With me!" he shouted as he turned and bounded down the slope.

Smoke from their cannon was already gusting about and helping to mask their movement. Their numbers were so few when compared to the larger battle at hand that James reckoned the enemy would not even notice their advance. The tall grass had been beaten flat by the incessant rains of the past week, and it made the slope extremely slippery. Men tumbled and many slipped and fell onto their backsides, and they stumbled to the bottom. After many such falls, the ground evened out and their momentum carried them forward.

As it was still another half mile to the road where the light company lay in a ditch next to, James, along with his officers and NCOs quickly formed the men back up and started at the brisk, yet disciplined walk. They could just see the edge of the French columns advancing with ladders to assault the southern wall. The first crash of musket fire from the defending Coldstream Guards was unleashed in a disciplined volley, sending a number of attackers tumbling to the earth. After, they fired as quickly as individual soldiers could load their weapons, with the majority directed at the hapless ladder bearers who fell in heaps, crying in agony as their bodies were smashed and torn by the large calibre musket balls. The rooftops were also covered in British soldiers, who used the reverse slope to protect themselves as they lay prone and fired deep into the enemy formations.

"There's Captain Roberts' company," Sergeant Donaldson said as the two companies quickly approached a low ditch alongside the road that led directly to the east gate of Hougomont.

The men of the light company lay prone along the ditch, while Captain Roberts and his colour sergeant looked over the top.

"Captain Roberts!" James shouted as his men knelt at the near side of the ditch.

"Ah, James, good to see you," Daniel said as he crossed the ditch and shook hands with his friend. "Sorry there isn't more room for the rest of you."

"We'll make due for the moment," James replied.

"As you can see," Daniel said, looking over his shoulder, "the frogs have commenced their assault on the south wall."

"Just so you know, there is an entire corps coming at them," James added.

"Is there really?" Daniel asked, frowning in contemplation. "Hmm, we couldn't tell from our position. Well, that just means they will undoubtedly try and envelope the entire complex. We're in perfect position to catch them in the flanks and rear when they try and take the east wall. Still, if they realize it's just us and 2nd Battalion's light company, they can send an entire division to wipe us out. And no offence, old friend, but I don't think your two companies will make much of a difference at that point."

"Just keep harassing them," James said. "If they turn a substantial force against us, we'll withdraw up the slope, bounding by companies."

"That works for us," Daniel remark. "Whatever happens, glad you're with us."

"Here they come, sir!"

Daniel quickly jumped back into the ditch and crawled up the far side. His men crawled up to the edge to where, through the grass, they could just make out a battalion-sized column sweeping around the complex.

"Form two ranks, both companies kneel," James ordered.

His men quickly complied, anxious to not be spotted by the massed numbers of enemy soldiers who were double-timing around the small grove of trees that stood between them and the east wall. Shots echoed from the wall, as the Coldstream Guards defending fired through the gaps in the trees. The French soldiers moved quickly and with precision, seemingly oblivious to the cries of their wounded as they were struck down. Stray musket balls slapped into the earth not twenty yards from the ditch, kicking up spurts of mud. The danger of firing into your own men was always a risk when looking to envelope an enemy force.

"Bataillon, halte!" the French battalion commander shouted at the front as he turned to face his men, sword held high. *"Roue gauche...avancer!"*

The enemy soldiers turned to face the east wall, ladder bearers moving quickly to the front, even as more were struck down by well-placed shots from the defenders. They were either oblivious to the presence of British soldiers behind them or simply ignoring them.

271

"Bloody officers make it all-too-easy," a light infantry soldier sneered as he looked down his weapon at the French battalion commander.

As soon as the entire enemy force turned and started its advance towards the trees and the wall beyond, Captain Roberts gave his order. *"Fire!"*

The musket shots that came from the light infantry were not in a concentrated volley. Rather their commander's order gave them permission to fire once they had enemy soldier dead-to-rights. The infantryman who scoffed at the enemy officer was the first to fire, his shot slamming into the small of the battalion commander's back, causing him to arch up and then fall to his side, writhing in pain. Other shots from the light company were focused on ladder bearers, officers, and NCOs. With the glaring differences in uniforms and kit, it was little wonder that leaders on both sides suffered a disproportionately high percentage of casualties.

James stood, raised his sword, and brought it down in a hard slash, signalling his two companies to engage.

"Front rank...up!" Lieutenant Shanahan shouted. *"Fire!"*

Unlike the sporadic and deliberate fire of the light infantry, the 1st Company fired as one, adding a degree of savage shock as they unleashed.

"Second rank...up! Fire!"

Identical commands were echoed by the grenadier captain. Even if the Frenchmen at the front of the attack were aware of being caught between two British forces, they were left choice-less except to continue the assault. And despite the fearful losses from taking fire from two directions, the British numbers were so few that the majority of the attackers would still make it to the wall with their assault ladders.

James glanced to his left and right and watched as his men quickly reloaded their weapons. Not surprisingly, the men of the 1st Company finished about ten seconds before the grenadiers.

"Down!" James ordered as his men gratefully dropped to a knee.

Though they did not have the same level of protection the ditch offered to the light company, who continued to take the occasional shot at exposed enemy soldiers, they did not wish to so blatantly announce their presence to enemy units following. The cloud of smoke from their musket volleys did offer at least a little concealment.

The rough terrain the enemy corps had to pass through just to get to Hougomont broke up their larger formations. While an entire brigade should have attacked each wall simultaneously, the best they were able to keep together were individual battalions; another of which was advancing to the same position as the one that preceded them. Despite the large numbers of dead and dying men strewn about, it seemed none of the subsequent French leaders noticed that many of them had been shot in the back.

"*Roue gauche...avancer!*"

James grinned and shook his head, praying that the rest of the battle was going so smoothly. He knew that theirs was but one tiny piece of a gigantic struggle, and even though the Frenchmen attacking the eastern wall of Hougomont were receiving punishing fire from both in front and behind, there were no English troops outside either the south or western walls with which to envelope them.

The crack of well-placed shots from the light company echoed in his ears as he signalled for his two companies to unleash once more.

"*Front rank...up!*" The two company commanders shouted almost simultaneously. "*Fire!*"

A follow-on volley from their second rank, and another score of enemy soldiers fell to the ground, many in the throes of death, their bodies torn to pieces by multiple shots.

Both James and his men were starting to relax as training and instinct now took over. Weapons reloaded, the men fidgeted from down on a knee, waiting for either more Frenchmen to appear from the south or for the attack on the walls to be decided. The shouts of fighting men and constant crash of musket fire were continuous. The French cannon had ceased firing on Hougomont, a sign that substantial numbers of their men were now engaged upon its walls. Through the trees it was impossible to see what was happening on the walls, even though the sounds of battle rang clear as day. James could just see the roofs of the buildings on the eastern edge of Hougomont, where redcoats would appear from to fire upon their advancing foe. The French were returning fire, as James saw several men struck down by enemy musket balls. One poor fellow took a shot to the face and fell screaming from the rooftop.

"Retraite! Retraite!" The frantically shouted order, which was being echoed all along the enemy lines of attack, perked James up. He spoke enough French to know the order to retreat. That it was being shouted with a trace of panic told that the attack on Hougomont's walls had completely failed. Though they readied to engage the massed numbers of retreating men, they could see through the trees that the French were instead rushing due south instead of back through the woods. They were simply trying to get away from the hated stronghold as fast as they could. Assault ladders were left where they fell, as were the now hundreds of dead and wounded.

"We need to see how the Coldstream Guards are managing," James said after calling together all the company commanders.

"I'll leave the grenadiers here to support you," he told Daniel. "1st Company will come with me. We'll assess the situation, and see if they need us to provide additional support."

"James, if we get pushed back, you'll be trapped inside the compound," Daniel stated.

"In which case, you will have to step up and command the right wing," James replied. He then signalled to the 1st Company with his sword. *"With me!"*

So as not to be somehow mistaken for another enemy assault, James led his men in a long arc around to the north side, which given the lack of any bodies strewn about, told him had not been attacked yet.

"Friendlies approaching!" he shouted at the top of his lungs as they approached the walls.

A few heads from defenders looked over the wall.

"Sir, the gates are all barricaded!" a sergeant shouted back, waving to them. "There's some frog ladders just up against the northeast corner of the wall. You can come in that way."

James and his men skirted along the north wall, through the sparse trees until they reached the corner of the wall. Several ladders lay strewn about, one still against the wall. A French soldier was sprawled upside down, his legs caught in the rungs towards the top. He was covered in blood from wounds that could not be seen, and he groaned in pain.

"Lower him down," James directed.

"Sir, we don't have much time…" a soldier started to protest.

"Double up damn you!" the captain snapped.

A dozen men quickly moving to follow his orders. Soldiers placed other ladders against the wall and started to ascend into the compound. James helped the other men lower the ladder with the stricken enemy soldier, placing it gently against the ground. There was little else they could do. Dozens of other wounded soldiers were thrashing about or trying to crawl away.

"Vive l'empereur," the badly wounded soldier said weakly as James and the other redcoats set him beneath a tree. The captain simply shook his head and patted the man on the shoulder.

"Hate not your enemy," Private Eric Adams said quietly.

"Move out," James directed his men, leading them up the nearest ladder. The last time he'd climbed an assault ladder was during the attack on Badajoz. Just placing his hands and feet on the wooden rungs brought back a slew of bad memories.

As he got to the top, a cheer came from the defenders along the wall, some of whom were tossing the bodies of French dead over the side. The enemy wounded were being carried away towards the casualty collection point somewhere in the centre of the compound. Details were also carting away the British wounded. Their dead were laid out in a long row, near the wall of the closest building. One badly mangled corpse had its head smashed in, with the right arm contorted grotesquely; the soldier who James had seen shot off the rooftop.

The distant sound of French cannon preceded the resounding impact of cannonballs into the walls. Though most were concentrated on the south wall, as well as the largest building, the occasional shot slammed into the eastern wall as well.

"Better get down, sir," the sergeant who'd spoken to James earlier said. The captain complied and jumped down to the courtyard.

"Who's in command?" he asked.

"That'd be Lieutenant Colonel MacDonnell, sir," a nearby corporal replied. "I'm to bring a detail to cover the north gate, where we should find him."

As the corporal led James and his men to the gate, there was an overwhelming sense of tension amongst the defenders. They had

275

held against the first assault, but knew that once they regrouped, the French would return in even greater force. There was a distinct whistling of artillery shot that sailed over their heads from the British guns on the ridge and hammered the woods to the south.

At the north gate, which had thus far not been assaulted, the commander of 2/Coldstream Guards directed the emplacement of men on the wall, as wells as those who would hold in reserve should the gate be breached.

"Who the devil are you?" he asked as James walked up and saluted.

"Captain James Webster, 1st Foot Guards," he replied.

"Lieutenant Colonel James MacDonnell," the colonel replied. "You're a bit lost, aren't you? Your lot are supposed to be up on the ridge."

"Yes, sir," James replied. "Our light company is helping cover the woods to the east. General Maitland detached a small group of us to assist temporarily. I've brought two companies. One is still outside the walls, supporting the light troops. The other I brought with me, if you think we can be of some use."

"Of course," MacDonnell said. "Glad to have you here. Place some of your men on the northwest corner. That is where I believe they'll come from next, as the terrain gives the frogs the best possible avenue of approach. The rest of your men will assist us in holding the gate."

"Very good, sir," James nodded and then turned to Patrick, who saluted and turned to his NCOs.

"You said this is a temporary assist?" the colonel asked.

"Yes, sir," James answered. "General Maitland wants to ensure we repel the enemy and keep them from taking Hougomont. However, should Bonaparte advance on the western sector of the ridge, we'll be compelled to return up the slope. And unfortunately, sir, we'll have to withdraw our light company as well."

"I wasn't counting on any kind of support," MacDonnell noted, "so I will be sure to make good use of your men while I can."

"Here's as good a spot as any," David O'Connor observed as he sat on the very corner of the wall and scanned over the barrel of his musket. "There's trees and a pretty good defilade the frogs can make use of. However, they'll still have to cross about a hundred yards of open ground in order to hit us."

"I like having a couple feet of stone between me and those bastards," Private Farrow added as he positioned himself to the right of his corporal.

David had approximately a dozen men with him, half on each side. Lieutenant Shanahan had the rest in two battle lines, ready to repel any breach of the gate.

"They're really not expecting the gate to hold, are they?" a soldier to his left asked.

"It's a bloody farmhouse gate, not a portcullis of a fortress," David stated. "It might slow the frogs down a bit, but at least they'll be channelled into the rest of our lads."

"Nothing to do but wait now," Farrow said as he rested his chin across his forearm along the top of the wall.

"Still with us, Eric?" David asked as Private Adams positioned himself on the wall next to Farrow. The corporal had watched him out of the corner of his eye during the engagement outside the walls.

While Eric appeared to function just fine, his load and firing speed still as fast as ever, his face bore a pained expression like he was about to break at any moment.

"I'm still here," Eric managed to say, his voice distant, eyes fixed on the far wood line.

"I want to see you pop one's head off as soon as they show their faces," Douglas Farrow said with a chuckle as he sighted down his own weapon, searching for any trace of enemy soldiers. He glanced to his left as he saw David's ears perk up. "What is it?"

"You hear that?" the corporal asked.

In the distance they heard the tell-tale thunder of their cannon, still firing from up on the ridge.

"Just the sound of our guns," Farrow observed.

"They're firing, yes," David remarked. "But what aren't you hearing? There's no sound of the shells going over our heads. Damn it!" He climbed up and stood on the wall, his hand shielding the sun from his eyes as he scanned the ridge before climbing back down. "Damn it all!"

"What is it?" another soldier asked, concerned.

277

"I could see bursts of enemy rounds landing amongst our guns," the corporal answered. "Our artillery's been drawn into a duel with theirs, which means we've lost our goddamn covering fire!"

In the courtyard below, James and the other officers overheard the corporal's rant. They pricked up their ears and listened for the sounds of friendly artillery shells screaming overhead, yet heard nothing.

"If your man is correct," Colonel MacDonnell said, "that means Boney's troops are able to manoeuvre freely and form up without fear of taking a beating from our guns while they organize themselves."

"Which means he can mass his numbers against us as he pleases," James added.

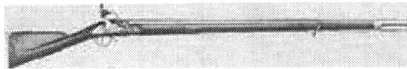

General of Division, Prince Jerome Bonaparte had noted the shifting of the English artillery as well. During the confusion of the first assault on Hougomont, his division had been mercilessly assailed by cannon and howitzer fire from the ridge, along with murderous fire from the farmhouse itself and the light troops in the woods.

The prince had rallied the remnants of his 1st Brigade, which had taken the brunt of the enemy artillery fire. He had stumbled upon the smouldering and shattered corpse of the brigade commander, General Bauduin. A howitzer carcass shot had exploded directly above him, blowing his and his horse's bodies apart, along with every staff officers who'd ridden too closely. The stench of still-burning flesh made Jerome wretch and almost lose his breakfast. He shook his head and regained his composure. Now was not the time for weakness, and if his brother had seen him lose his bearing, he would have been promptly relieved on the spot.

"Colonel Maigrot!" he shouted to the nearest officer who was not lying in burning pieces on the ground.

"Sir?" the dazed colonel replied. He had been just beyond the blast of the carcass shot when it exploded, though his once-

278

immaculate uniform was now peppered with burn holes and his face blackened and cut in numerous places.

"Reform your men behind General Soye and the 2nd Brigade," Jerome ordered. "You will swing around to the left, using the terrain to cover your move. At the woods, you will split off and continue north, around the outer wall. Both brigades will then launch simultaneous assaults upon the north and south gates. There cannot be more than a single battalion holding this stronghold, and with four times their strength attacking in each wave, I will hand Hougomont as a prize to my brother within the hour!"

"Sir!" Maigrot acknowledged with a salute.

What neither Jerome, his corps commander, Reille, nor even Marshal Ney had comprehended was that Hougomont was to be a simple diversionary attack, nothing more. Napoleon had only intended to see what Wellington's reaction would be. Would he pin himself to his ridge, or would he divert mass reinforcements to protect the farmhouse from falling? The emperor knew that if he could dictate where the British sent their troops, he could in turn dictate when and where each phase of the battle took place, depriving the English of any sense of initiative.

Instead, the battle around Hougomont was having the exact opposite effect. The total number of British troops in and around the farmhouse complex was less than 1,500 men. Count Reille, having received no countermanding orders from Ney, was committed to unleashing the vast majority of his corps in the taking of Hougomont. At least 14,000 French soldiers were converging for another assault on a position that the night before had been viewed as having minimal strategic importance by both sides. Now, it was becoming one of the pivotal points of the larger battle.

Hougoumont
June 1815

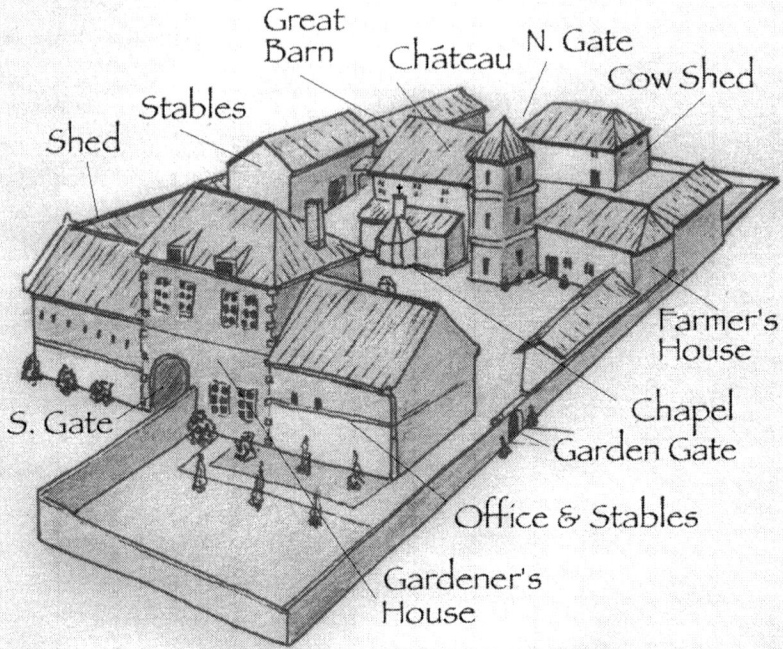

Great
Barn

Château   N. Gate

Cow Shed

Stables

Shed

Farmer's
House

S. Gate

Chapel

Garden Gate

Office & Stables

Gardener's
House

View from south corner.

Chapter XX: Hold the Gate!
Hougomont
18 June 1815
Noon

British Guards defending the North Gate

Sweat formed on the brow of Colonel Maigrot as he led the 1st Brigade of Prince Jerome's division around the western flank of Hougomont. His men kept low as they raced through the trees, their breath coming in short gasps, their uniforms soaked in nervous sweat. Despite the terrible losses they'd suffered, his oversized brigade still had over 3,000 men with which to take the north gate. He was also thankful that the British cannon on the ridge were still engaged with the near-hundred guns of their division artillery.

The carnage was horrific, with bodies laying in piles the entire length of the south and eastern walls. The concentrated fire of British cannon had left scores of broken bodies strewn throughout the woods. The colonel was unaware of the horrific mauling the battalions who assaulted the eastern wall had taken, as they'd been attacked from behind by English soldiers hiding in the low ditch along the road. All he knew was that a comparatively small number of enemy troops had held against the first assault by Reille's corps, and that if they did not breach the north gate, then those who had fallen already would have done so in vain.

Poised to lead the attack was a lieutenant named Legros who, instead of his sword, carried a large axe. His captain having been terribly wounded during the first assault, the young officer was determined to make good his loss and that of the others in his company who'd fallen already this terrible day. He directed his men to form into columns, still keeping back well within the woods. He could just make out the north wall of Hougomont through the undergrowth. Numerous redcoats lined the walls and rooftops. The lieutenant swallowed hard as he tried to get the best of his frayed nerves.

"Avenge General Bauduin and I'll see to it the emperor rewards you personally," Colonel Maigrot said as he leaned down from his horse.

Legros nodded in reply, his eyes cold and determined as his gaze was fixated upon the gate. The colonel then nodded to his bugler who sounded repeatedly the call to charge. The sounds of the bugle were cut short by the single crack of a British musket, followed by the young man's head snapping back as brain and bone exploded out the back. His eyes were wide and lifeless as streaming blood ran into them from the fearful entrance hole in the crown of his skull.

"Bâtards infâmes!" a soldier shouted as the bugler's lifeless body fell into the tall grass next to a pair of trees.

"With me!" Lieutenant Legros shouted, giving a subsequent shout of rage as he sprinted towards the gate.

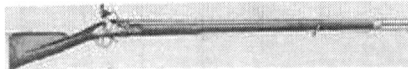

"Make ready, lads," Corporal O'Connor said as he placed the butt of his musket into his shoulder. "Looks like the frogs are ready to dance."

Eric Adams was reloading his musket, having felled the enemy bugler while his companions leaned into their weapons and sighted in on their charging assailants.

The men in the courtyard had heard the sound of the French bugles and were making ready to repel the attack, should it breach the gate.

"Easy lads," Patrick Shanahan said calmly. "Let them burn themselves out getting through the gate."

"Must be a lot of them," a private said quietly before kissing the rosary he kept around his neck.

"O'Connor!" Sergeant Donaldson shouted. "How many do you reckon there are?"

"How the piss should I know?" the exacerbated corporal shouted back. He then paused and did a quick count as best he could of the wall of men rushing towards them, screaming at the top of their lungs. "I'd say a brigade, at least."

"Shit," another private on the ground grumbled. "How are we supposed to hold against that?"

This brought a reproving smack across the head from Corporal Harvey.

"Enough of that!" he snapped. "You hold them off with your sodden weapon!" He shook his own musket to emphasize his point.

The loud snap of gunfire from the wall caused them all to take a deep breath and brace themselves. Even the bravest could not help but let nerves get to them, especially in light of Corporal O'Connor's assessment of the enemy's strength.

"We'll hold the gate itself," Colonel MacDonnell told James. "Your men will provide covering fire while we push those bastards back."

"Yes, sir," the captain replied, drawing his pistol.

As it was Shanahan's company, he was allowing him to coordinate the fire of the unit. MacDonnell and a Guards captain named Wyndham were positioned on either side of the gate, their men bunched up against each other behind them.

A gargled scream on the wall startled them as a soldier fell to the cobbled courtyard with a loud clatter. He thrashed violently, clutching at his throat, which was spurting torrents of dark crimson. The few seconds it took for the poor man to expire seemed like an eternity to those who could not avert their gaze. A cry from another stricken soldier came from the corner, where a man fell from the rampart, clutching his shoulder, his forehead covered in blood from where a second shot had grazed his hairline.

"Steady, lads!" James said as he knelt in the centre of the front rank.

"Front rank, kneel!" Patrick ordered. He stood directly behind James, his sword draped over his shoulder. As he had not acquired a pistol, he could only direct the fire of the company.

Another man cried out as he fell from the wall, clutching his face.

"Bugger it all!" David swore as the man just to the right of Private Adams tumbled back into the courtyard. *"Keep firing, lads! They're taking it worse than we are, by God!"* To underscore this, he looked down his weapon right at the chest of an advancing enemy soldier and fired. The man, who looked to be only in his late teens, threw his arms out to his sides, his musket flying from his hand, eyes shut and mouth open in a cry of agony as he fell face-first to the ground. The corporal then ducked back behind the wall to reload as musket balls from French return fire chipped and gouged the stone wall.

It was a challenge in the confined space, especially since he had to reach higher than the protection of the wall in order to pour the powder and place the ball down the barrel. He half expected to get his hand shot off at any time, especially as the hissing of enemy shots snapped past him. As he replaced the ramrod he took a deep breath and closed his eyes for a moment. Without thinking, he stood, aimed his weapon towards his enemy once more, and fired. Instinct and training had taken over as he knelt back down and began to reload once more. All along the rampart, men were going through the exact same sequence. The rate of enemy fire was increasing as their numbers massed outside the wall, and it was taking its toll on the defenders. Over the screams and musket fire, he could just make out the sounds of an axe slamming into the gate.

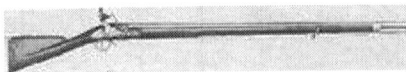

284

Lieutenant Legros' jaw ached as he clenched his teeth hard while leading his men in the attack. At any moment he expected to be felled by a British musket shot. Their only saving grace was that the English had yet to shift their artillery fire back towards the defence of the farmhouse. The young man's heart pounded in his chest as he ran as fast as he could, eyes fixed on the gate. All around him men were struck down by the fire from the wall. A younger drummer boy ran alongside him, beating his cadence as fast as he could, while soldiers fell to the earth, writhing in agony as large calibre musket shot smashed limbs and tore through their guts and other organs. The fortunate ones were those shot directly in the head or through the heart, as death came mercifully quick. These were the minority, as most of the fallen would either die slowly as they bled to death or even the less fortunate who were fatally struck, but would only succumb days later when gross infection set in.

A soldier just behind the drummer boy, who was unfortunate to be more than a head taller, was shot through the lungs just as Lieutenant Legros came within striking distance of the gate. As the soldier's arms flew out to his sides and he fell to the ground in mortal agony, the young officer gave a loud battle cry and raised the axe high, sprinting the last few dozen feet and letting his momentum carry the weight of the axe as it slammed hard into the wooden gate with a crash.

Legros was surprised when the gate did not simply fly open, but rather just buckled beneath the blow of his tool. He took a step back and started to swing the axe hard against the tall planks of the gate. As many men as were able clustered on either side of him and either pushed against it or started kicking it hard. Soldiers behind them were returning fire against the ramparts, whose defenders were now directly above them. The hated redcoats had the wall to protect them and would only expose themselves just long enough to fire. Still, what the French lacked in protection, they made up for in sheer volume of musket fire, which was taking its toll on the British.

Men continued to fall as the attackers managed to wedge open the gate just far enough to expose the cross brace, which Legros attacked with every ounce of his strength. He swung the axe as hard and as fast as he could, the wood splintering as the brace began to crack. All around him, his men were still being shot down by the relentless defenders on top of the wall. At last, the cross brace snapped!

The French breaching the North Gate

"They've broken the gate!" Farrow shouted firing off one last shot before jumping down from the wall. "Come on, David, we have to fall back!"

"You lads go ahead," the corporal said calmly as he sat against the wall and reloaded his musket. "I can die here just as easily enough."

"What the hell, man?" Farrow protested as the shouts of men trying in vain to hold the gate back started to turn to panic. The men who'd once manned the wall were now fleeing for the perceived sanctuary of the inner compound.

"Look," David explained, his face surprisingly calm, "I promised Old Nosey that if Hougomont fell, I would not be found again amongst the living. And since the frogs are about to take the gate with a few thousand men swarming behind them, we're pretty well fucked, wouldn't you say?"

"Dear God, you've gone mad!" Farrow lamented.

"Ha!" David scoffed as he finished loading and replaced his ramrod. "I went mad when I went hunting for our supper in the bleeding rain last night! Now go on, leave me to make an honourable end." Without another word, he very calmly, almost serenely, stood back up and fired into the horde of enemy soldiers that were ready to burst through the ruptured gate.

"The gate's breached," James stated as he palmed his pistol. He raised an eyebrow when he noted that the only man left manning the rampart was Corporal O'Connor, who calmly engaged the enemy outside the wall as if he were conducting target practice.

A final surge from the French and the soldiers holding the gate suddenly let go and rushed to get behind their officers who manned either side. As the north gate of Hougomont flew open, all James could see was an ocean of blue jackets.

"Front rank...fire!" Patrick shouted.

The wall of muskets unleashed a storm of death into the concentrated opening where the French were rushing through as fast as they could. The first dozen or so were immediately felled by the company's first volley.

"Second rank...fire!"

As the line of weapons exploded in a fearsome barrage, James raised his pistol and fired at a lone soldier, who'd somehow escaped the initial flurry of death. The shot went low and struck the man in the thigh. Though he was in enormous pain, the man would not comprehend just how fortunate he was to have fallen outside of the gate opening. Sporadic shots came from outside the gate and two men from the company were struck down. One fell, shot to the face, and he thrashed about on the ground as blood spurted between his fingers. The other was shot in the guts and he tumbled forward, clutching his stomach as vomit and bile spewed from his lips.

Before the men could load their weapons, dozens of enemy soldiers spilled into the compound and a fierce melee ensued. James drew his sword as his men in the front rank stood and all

287

lowered their bayonets towards the French. With much discipline and control, they marched straight into the frenzy, where inexplicably, the corporal who'd led James to the gate somehow managed to drive the remaining attackers back with his musket held level across his chest. He then smashed one last enemy soldier across the face with the butt of his weapon as Colonel MacDonnell and Captain Wyndham, along with a dozen other men, managed to force the gates shut. The corporal then grabbed the splintered cross brace and shoved it back into place before picking up his musket and joining in the frenzy of hand-to-hand fighting, where a young French officer and approximately thirty men were now in a fight for their lives.

James ran at the enemy officer, who was wielding an axe which he held up to block the perceived strike from the captain's sword. Instead, James kicked him hard in the groin, sending him to his knees before slicing his sword across the side of the man's neck. The artery burst in a spray of blood, some of which caught James on the face and chest. The French officer fell to his side in shock for the minute it took for his life to bleed away through the slice in his neck.

Screams of men being bayonetted filled the courtyard as the handful of enemy soldiers were surrounded and overwhelmed. There had been no attempt by any of them to surrender, and so all were mercilessly stabbed by maddened redcoats. At last only the drummer boy remained. He stood in utter shock, his face, uniform, and drum kit splattered in blood and gore. A soldier had his bayonet pointed at the lad, who looked to be maybe twelve. The Guardsman then shook his head and extended his hand to the boy.

"Allez, mon gars…come on lad."

The drummer boy, who was in a complete stupor by what he'd just been through, stood open-mouthed, his eyes vacant. He still extended his hand, which the British soldier took, and then guided him away from the scene of death at the gate.

Not one enemy soldier who'd made it through was now alive. All had fought to the very last, and James could not help but admire their bravery.

"Imagine the stories that lad will have to tell his grandchildren," Patrick Shanahan mused as he nodded towards the terribly shaken drummer boy, "To be the only French soldier to get inside Hougomont and live!"

Though no older than twelve or thirteen, it was impossible to think of the youth as a boy after what he'd been through. He stood pale-faced, entire body trembling, eyes fixed on the corpses of his mates who lay in a long heap in front of the gate. British soldiers were dragging the bodies over and using them to brace against the gate.

"Poor boy," James said, still watching the drummer as a Guard soldier offered him a drink from his canteen. "He's become an old man before he's even old enough to shave."

Though dozens of French soldiers were still massed on the other side of the gate, with hundreds more still forming in the wood line, it seemed that their attack had lost all momentum. Amazingly, Corporal O'Connor still stood on the rampart, firing random shots at his foe, which from the commotion that they could hear, was now withdrawing as soldiers re-manned the wall.

As British cannon fired in the distance, the familiar whistle of incoming shells and the impact of solid shot outside the walls told of the return of their covering fire. A cheer erupted from the men in the courtyard just as a stray shot slammed into the wall, sending David O'Connor flying face-first from the wall in a spray of smashed stone.

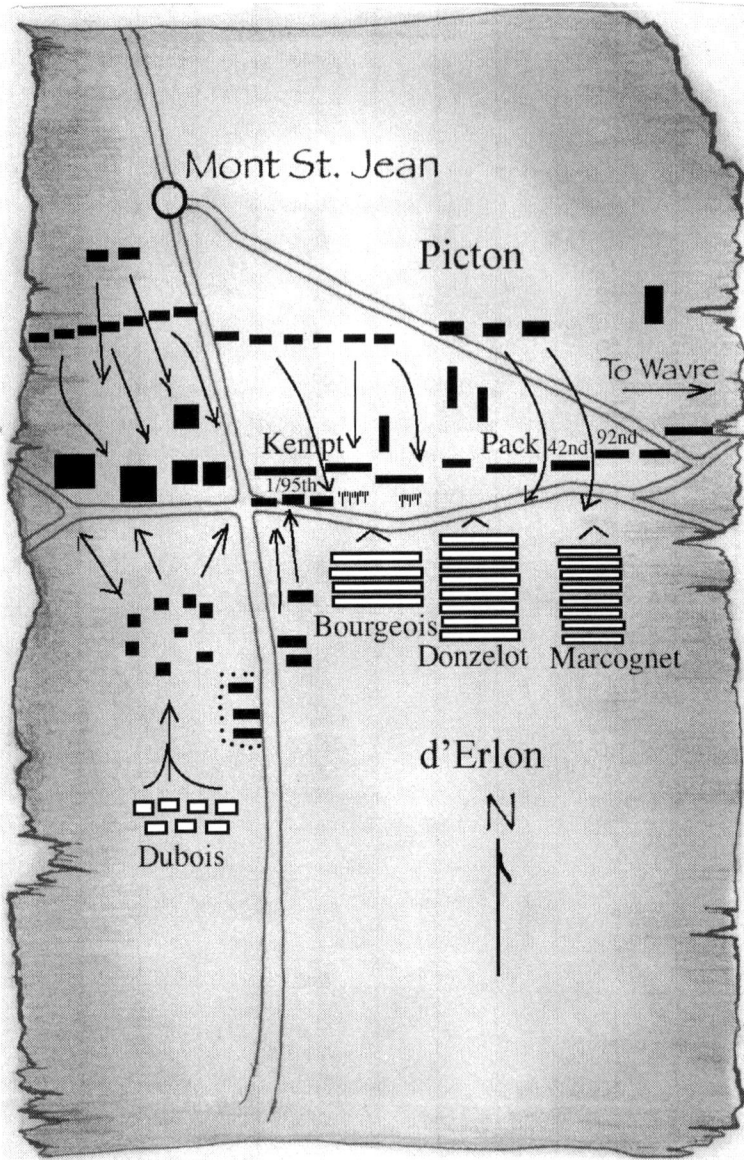

Mont St. Jean

Picton

To Wavre

Kempt

1/95th

Pack 42nd 92nd

Bourgeois

Donzelot Marcognet

d'Erlon

N

Dubois

D'Erlon's assault and Picton's counterattack

290

Chapter XXI: Picton's Fall
Field of Waterloo
18 June 1815
1:30 pm

Lieutenant General, Sir Thomas Picton

Though Napoleon's attack on Hougomont had thus far failed, Wellington knew that the struggle was far from over. He still had the entire battle to coordinate. Nevertheless, word of thousands of enemy casualties in utterly fruitless attacks on the farmhouse gave him at least some confidence. On his left wing, a much greater action was unfolding, as the entire right wing of the French army was advancing just east of the road that led up to La Haye Sainte. A handful of Dutch troops were the only ones visible to the enemy, the rest holding behind the reverse slope. Thus was Napoleon denied the knowledge of Wellington's exact disposition. Unlike the

brave but reckless Marshal Blucher at Ligny, who'd allowed the
French to clearly see the placement of his entire army.

"Hougomont is holding," DeLancey said as he looked through
a series of despatches. "La Haye Sainte is being hard pressed but
has not fallen yet."

"Is there any way to get more ammunition to those men?"
Wellington asked. "They will not be able to hold once their
muskets run empty."

"We tried," DeLancey said, shaking his head. "Neither side is
able to maintain a decisive hold on the ridge. Cuirassiers are now
roaming the area, waiting to ambush any units that try and relieve
or resupply the defenders. Dear God..." his voice trailed off as he
read yet another despatch.

"What is it, man?" the Duke asked impatiently.

"Somerset is down," DeLancey explained. "He was leading an
effort to assist the left wing when he was hit by a burst of musket
fire and shot from his horse."

"Is he alive?" Wellington persisted. He was particularly fond of
his secretary, who never hesitated to take the lead during a
hazardous mission whenever the need arose.

"It just says he's badly wounded," his chief-of-staff answered.

"Your grace!" another staff officer said as he rode up. "We've
spotted movement off to our left, several columns of infantry. They
are still too far away to identify who they are, but we can tell that
it's at least two brigades."

"But whose?" DeLancey asked. "Could it be the Prussians?"

"If General Muffling was correct in his report, then that is
exactly who it is," the Duke noted as he rode quickly down the
ridgeline to a small rise topped with a solitary oak tree. He drew
his telescope and scanned the horizon. "Those are definitely
infantry columns, perhaps five to six miles away. There is no way
of knowing who they are and how many there may be."

"The roads are still terribly bogged down," DeLancey noted,
"and moving cross-country is even more arduous. So whoever they
are, they are at least two hours' march from here, if not more."

"This battle could be decided well before then," the Duke said
darkly. "Even if it is Blucher, he'll be able to do very little unless
he's managed to rally his entire army."

"And if it's Grouchy?" DeLancey asked.

"Then they will come at us in the same old style," Wellington remarked dryly, "And we will knock them down in the same old style."

"Sire, look!" an aide said to Napoleon excitedly. In the far distance, about five miles from their right wing, they could just see the first signs of advancing infantry columns.

"It cannot be Grouchy," Soult said as he squinted through his telescope.

The emperor did not even bother to check for himself.

"The Prussians?" the aide asked. "How in God's name did they get here?"

"God had nothing to do with it," Napoleon asserted. "It would seem Blucher has some fight left in him. It does not matter; they are too late. D'Erlon will crush Wellington's left wing readily enough. Dispatch Lobau's corps and the Young Guard to check them. Soult, send word to Grouchy. He will envelope the Prussians and annihilate what's left of them."

"Right away, sire."

"I've made one mistake in my life," Napoleon repeated to himself, "I should have burned Berlin to the ground."

Though he could not see Wellington's exact placement of his corps, Napoleon was intuitive enough to surmise that the Anglo Army's weakness was its left wing. If d'Erlon could take the farmhouse of La Haye Sainte, as well as roll up Wellington's left, the battle would essentially be over. The English would be caught in both the front and flank, at which time it would only be a matter of counting their dead. It would still be at least a couple hours before the Prussians even reached the field, and they would be held in place by Lobau and the Young Guard. Once it became clear that Wellington was beaten, even the relentless Marshal Blucher would be forced to cede the battle.

"I don't think the emperor understands the concept of time and distance on this field," the aide whispered to Soult as the marshal handed him the hastily-scribbled despatch to Marshal Grouchy.

293

"It's nearly a dozen miles from here to Wavre. No horse can move at a full gallop in these conditions. I'll be lucky if I can get there in an hour. And even if Marshal Grouchy is not tied down by a sizeable Prussian force, what then? If we had paved roads to march on, then we could have them here in a couple hours. As it is, I'll be lucky if I can have a single company from Grouchy's corps here before the sun goes down."

"You think I don't know that?" Soult retorted with exasperation. "This battle has been a much harder issue to decide than the emperor first envisioned. He thought we would have Wellington and the English broken by now, but they still hold the ridge and all the building complexes. If Grouchy were here, then perhaps we could have finished this battle already. As it is, it will be a close-run affair. Now go, the longer you delay, the longer it will take Marshal Grouchy to arrive!"

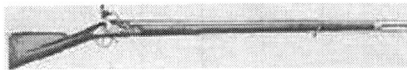

Eccentric as always, Sir Thomas Picton sat atop his horse in a shabby overcoat and top hat. He even carried an umbrella, which he now used to shield himself from the sun. His division had taken a severe pounding at Quatre Bras and was well below its optimal fighting strength. His three brigades, two Anglo, one Hanoverian were some of the most battle-hardened and disciplined troops in the entire army. However, they were terribly outnumbered by the advancing French corps under d'Erlon.

The pain in his side caused him to wince, and it was emphasized as he saw the badly injured Somerset being carried away by stretcher bearers. He turned his horse towards the men and slowly rode over to the man whose his relationship with had been an unusual combination of contempt and mutual respect. Despite his own injuries, which Sir Thomas knew he would never recover from, he pitied the major, whose right arm looked to have been shot a dozen times and was little more than a mass of splintered bone and torn muscle.

"A bad turn for you," Picton said as Somerset opened his eyes and looked up at the old general.

"A bad turn, indeed," the younger man said through gritted teeth. "At the very least I'll be losing my right arm."

"I suppose you'll just have to learn how to write left-handed," Picton reasoned, drawing a pained laugh from Somerset.

The intense trauma of his grievous wounds made further speech for Somerset impossible.

As the medics carried him away, Picton made a dark prediction. "If you don't survive, at least I will be joining you soon enough."

His thoughts were interrupted by Major General Sir James Kempt, who commanded Picton's 8th Brigade, as the general rode quickly over to him. "Sir, the enemy has launched another assault on La Haye Sainte," he said. "If it falls, our centre will collapse."

"There is little we can do about that," Picton noted. "We have an entire corps to face, which outnumbers us at least two-to-one. The 95th Rifles are providing support fire for the farmhouse. We can only hope that the defenders can hold until reinforced." He then winced and instinctively clutched his injured side.

"Something you ate, Sir Thomas?" Kempt asked, not knowing that his division commander had been gravely wounded two days before at Quatre Bras.

"You could say that," Picton replied with dark humour. Just over the crest of the slope he could hear the sporadic fire from the single Dutch brigade that screened their front. He turned his horse about and looked to his division.

Aside from the mounted battalion commanders, the vast majority of the men either knelt or lay prone in the grass in order to provide protection against incoming artillery fire, as well as to mask their numbers.

His two Anglo brigades were disproportionately Scottish, and though a proud Welshman, Picton was glad to have such a large number of clansmen. The Royals Scots, 92nd Gordon Highlanders, 79th Cameron Highlanders, and the venerable 42nd Black Watch would not run. They would leave the field victorious or not at all.

"Vallen terug! Vallen terug!" The panicked call to retreat from the advance Dutch brigade baffled Picton. The best he could reckon, they'd scarcely engaged the enemy at all. Most likely each man firing a single shot and then retreating. And far from a well-

disciplined withdrawal, the Dutch were fleeing en masse, each man running as fast as he could to save himself.

"What the hell is this?" the RSM of the 42nd shouted as he rose to his feet. He then turned to his men. "Make ready, Black Watch! We'll show these damned cowards how to fight!"

As fleeing Dutchmen ran between the files of English, Scottish, and Hanoverian regiments, Picton calmly turned to his bugler and nodded. As the bugle sounded, the entire division rose to its feet, the musicians of the Highland regiments striking up their bagpipes and drums. The brawl they'd engaged in at Quatre Bras had decided nothing, and they were determined that it should end on this day at Waterloo.

A cheer erupted from the advancing French corps as their enemies in the Dutch brigade suddenly turned about and fled over the ridge.

"Steady lads!" d'Erlon shouted. "Remember, our enemy is on the other side of that slope!"

The Comte d'Erlon had extensive experience fighting against Wellington and was quite familiar with the English Duke's favourite tactics. He knew that the Dutch troops his corps advanced upon were but a fraction of the enemy force; their main body waiting behind the rise. Even without seeing his enemy, he knew they would be arrayed in long, thin lines, in order to employ all of their muskets at the same time. He had therefore ordered his battalions to form into lines and advance in close order behind each other. He knew this would not allow his men to alter formation, and that lateral movement would be difficult. However, he also knew that bringing as many guns to bear at once was the only real way to defeat superior British firepower.

The Comte's breathing increased as he watched his first battalions reach the top of the ridge. A concentrated volley from the other side tore into the front ranks, the men behind them sprayed with blood and gore as their companions were torn apart. D'Erlon closed his eyes for a moment but then noted that his men's discipline held, and they continued over the crest with shouts of *"Vive l'empereur"* and *"Vive la France!"*

"That's my boys!" Picton shouted in wake of the terrible volley his entire division unleashed. Bugles and bagpipes then sounded the advance, drummers beating the familiar cadence. The old general's face twitched, and he placed a hand on his badly injured side once more.

"It is time," he said quietly before spurring his horse and giving a loud shout. *"On, on 5th Division! On, you brigands! On, my brave bastards...on!"* He rode just in front of and between the Gordon Highlanders and Black Watch regiments, who now had their bayonets protruding forward and were advancing at the quick step.

It must have been surreal to the advancing French to see the gentleman in tattered tails and a top hat, carrying an umbrella, riding between two regiments of battle-mad highlanders. However peculiar the sight was, the men of d'Erlon's corps knew the man had to be someone of importance, and a number started to fire at him.

Still he came on, shouting to his men, who increased their step in order to keep pace with him. The soldiers of the Scottish regiments were renowned for their valour, and yet even they were awestruck by the utter contempt Sir Thomas Picton held for their enemy. Indeed, he was now shouting profane insults in English, French, and even Welsh at the advancing French battalions.

"I'm already a dead man," Picton scoffed. "My task in this world is done." He was now laughing at his enemy, who seemed to be concentrating every musket they had on him. He found it a source of profane amusement that they would waste their shots on him, rather than the men with bayonets protruding who were the actual threats. As he broke into another fit of laugher, the shot of a French infantryman found its mark. The shot went through the front of his top hat and smashed into his skull and brain. His umbrella fell from his hand, his mind clouding over, and in his final thoughts, Sir Thomas Picton implored the Lord to send his soul to wherever he saw fit.

Though their commanding general had fallen, the men of the 5th Division were rallied by his example and utter loathing of their enemy. Bayonets forward, every regiment met the French with a murderous crashing of steel and howls of rage. Bayonet fighting was a particularly nasty and terrifying business. It was one thing to take a shot at a man from across a short space; another entirely to look him in the eye as you attempted to stab him like one would a wild boar. And if one did manage to kill his foe, but was careless enough to stab him in the chest, the bayonet would often become stuck in the ribs and it was but a matter of a couple seconds before the hapless assailant was brutally stabbed to death by the slain man's companions. The terrible wounds wrought by the bayonet were horrifyingly painful, and neither the brave nor cowardly were spared. Even the most fanatically fearless highlander was helpless once the long spike punctured his stomach or throat.

General Kempt, now in command of the entire division, rode down the line, quickly ordering men in the subsequent ranks to reload their weapons. As fierce as the fighting was, he knew that d'Erlon's numbers would soon prove too much, and that the only way to hold was to keep a steady volume of fire in their enemies' faces. Behind them, he saw the Dutch troops reforming, having been berated and shamed by their officers into returning to the fray. As the Anglo and Hanoverian regiments engaged the French with both bayonet and musket fire, Kempt rode back towards La Haye Sainte to see about the 95th Rifles. The green-jacked sharpshooters were ideally suited for skirmishing and haranguing the enemy with well-placed rifle fire. However, if hard pressed they had little chance in close combat with line infantry and were completely helpless against cavalry. The general came upon a skirmishing band of approximately twenty riflemen commanded by a single NCO.

"What is your name, soldier?" Kempt asked the man.

"Corporal Martin Shepard, 1/95th Rifles!" the rifleman answered proudly. "Our battalion is spread all over, sir. We've got men inside La Haye Sainte, the rest of us are attempting to harass any bands of French Cavalry and keep them from flanking the main line. It's been a rough go, sir, no doubt about that. We've been pinned down to these woods by the constant attacks of cuirassiers."

"Any chance of creating an avenue of approach for resupply?" the general asked.

"No, sir," the corporal replied, dejected. "We tried, and all that happened was a murdering squadron of those armoured giants fell upon us. It was only the cover of the tress that saved us all from being chopped to pieces. As it was, we lost a dozen men just in our withdrawal. If you move further to our right, Colonel Barnard is coordinating the rest of the battalion."

"Hold this position, but be ready to move," Kempt ordered. "You may get your retribution against the cuirassiers before this day is done."

"Sir!"

Soldiers of the 95th Rifles defending La Haye Sainte

Chapter XXII: Charge of the Heavy Cavalry
Field of Waterloo
18 June 1815
2:00 pm

Sergeant Charles Ewart of the Scots Greys capturing a French eagle

Wellington watched the battle on his left wing disintegrate into a chaotic brawl. The havoc caused by the French cuirassiers had completely isolated La Haye Sainte. And while Hougomont and the right wing still held, the Duke knew that if the left wing collapsed, La Haye Sainte would fall, and then his entire army would be undone. He was further vexed by the sight of the advancing columns of infantry off to the extreme left, not knowing whether they were Prussians from Wavre, or if it was Grouchy returning to aid his emperor. And like Napoleon, Wellington reckoned that even if they were Prussian, their arrival would be too late if his left wing could not hold.

"General Picton has fallen, sir," DeLancey said as he rode up on his horse. Wellington closed his eyes for a moment but said nothing. DeLancey continued, "His division is holding, but not for long. The French have them too badly outnumbered."

"And with La Haye Sainte now cut off, I think it is time to commit the heavy cavalry," the Duke said. He then turned to Uxbridge, who'd been waiting with rapt anticipation for this moment. "Drive d'Erlon from the field, and see if you can create some breathing space for La Haye Sainte."

"Right away, your grace!" Uxbridge replied excitedly as he wheeled his horse about to where his cavalry corps was waiting in reserve, well behind the ridge. His two most distinguished units were the Household Brigade under Major General Lord Edward Somerset, who was the elder brother of Fitzroy Somerset, and the Union Brigade under Major General Sir William Ponsonby.

As decades of warfare had deprived most of continental Europe of its best horses, the comparatively fresh British Cavalry were the best-mounted on the battlefield. Their swordsmanship training was also superior to any contemporary force, however, they were lacking in actual combat experience. Still, they were eager to prove their worth. The opportunity arising as the left wing was starting to fold under the weight of d'Erlon's relentless assault.

"Household and Union Brigades, with me!" Uxbridge shouted with his sword raised high.

Sabres were drawn en masse, and a wall of horsemen started to move as one towards the crest of the ridge, where the 5th Division was now in a fight for its life. Bugles sounded the advance over and over, and Uxbridge felt his heart pounding in his ears. There were still bands of cuirassiers threatening Kempt's flank, though their numbers were too few in face of the coming onslaught of British horsemen and flashing steel.

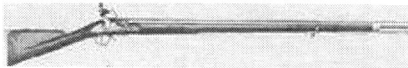

Major General Kempt rode hard towards the right flank of his division, where the remainder of the 95th Rifles were still attempting to provide fire support for the hard-pressed defenders of La Haye Sainte. Dozens of men were scattered throughout the woods on either side of the complex, harrying the attacking French Infantry with well-placed rifle fire. Kempt's greatest concern was the roving squadrons of cuirassiers that were covering d'Erlon's flank, especially after the report he'd received from Corporal Shepard. Though groups of the armoured horsemen had attempted to harry the men of the Rifles who were in a far more defensible position, they had attacked in too few numbers and were constantly driven back with terrible losses.

As Kempt rode up to the northern edge of the grove of trees, he was waved down by a major of the 95th.

"General, sir," the major said. "I regret to say that Colonel Barnard's been badly hurt."

"I understand," Kempt replied. "How are your men holding?"

"We've taken a beating, sir, especially amongst the officers," the major replied candidly. "Those damned cuirassiers are a bastard to deal with. If they are ever able to mass their numbers against us, we're all dead, even with the cover of trees."

The sound of bugles playing the call to charge repeatedly and rapidly interrupted them.

Kempt looked over his shoulder and saw the two brigades of cavalry cresting the ridge. "I think your cuirassier problem has been resolved. Deploy your men forward; our cavalry will channel them into a natural defilade below. They'll be bunched up and unable to manoeuvre."

"Yes, sir!" the major said enthusiastically. He then shouted to his men, "The 95th will advance by sections! Come on, lads, let's get some payback on these bastards!"

Orders were relayed and General Kempt saw Corporal Shepard and his men at the lead of the battalion. As swarms of green jackets rushed through the trees to covered positions that would allow them to engage the French Cavalry with enfilade fire, Kempt turned back to see the Household and Union brigades swarming past the 5th Division in a flurry of men, horses, and flashing blades.

"There he is! He's still with us."

302

The voices sounded muffled to David O'Connor as his eyes struggled to focus. The last thing he remembered was a loud blast and flying from the rampart. He'd been knocked senseless before he even landed on the cobblestones below, though his cheek was now swollen and this inside of his mouth bleeding.

"Bugger all, my head hurts," he grumbled as he fought to sit up.

"There you are, lad," the voice of Lieutenant Shanahan said as he helped him up. "You shouldn't be feeling any pain! You should be dead, by God!"

"That was quite the nasty fall you took," Corporal Harvey said, handing David his weapon. "Can you walk alright?"

"I think so," David said, shaking his head as his vision cleared.

"Well, come on, we're pulling back," Harvey explained. "The Coldstream lads have this covered. We've been recalled back up the hill. Captain Webster thinks the frogs must be planning a massed attack on the right wing."

The Scots Greys were among the finest mounted and best swordsmen in all of Europe. They fell upon the French *45e Régiment de Ligne* (45th Regiment of the Line) with a flurry of steel. The regiment had been making to form a defensive line when the British Cavalry unexpectedly crashed into their ranks. Though the lines had broken, a number of horsemen also found themselves cut off. One man, Sergeant Charles Ewart, was in the fight of his life as French Infantry supported by a few mounted lancers attempted to hold against the onslaught.

The sergeant brought his sabre down in a hard smash, the heavy and sharp blade cleaving through the skull of a French infantryman whose body convulsed as his brain was sliced open. Ewart wrenched his weapon free as a lancer bore down on him. His superior swordsmanship training coming into play, he somehow managed to parry the lance and spurred his horse forward as he brought his sabre up in a hard slash, cutting through the lancer's neck and jaw in a spray of blood, flesh, and bone. A musket burst in a loud spray of flash and smoke, yet remarkably the shot

303

intended for the sergeant missed. Ewart once again managed to parry the following bayonet thrust and brought his sabre down in a hard chop behind the man's ear.

It was then he saw the mounted ensign carrying the regimental eagle. Sergeant Ewart made straight for the man, who was oblivious to him in the fray. Releasing the reins of his horse, he grabbed the eagle and ran the ensign through the throat with his sabre. As he wrenched his weapon free, blood from the man's neck sprayed forth, he fell twitching violently from his mount. Ewart could not believe his good fortune, and he quickly spurred his horse away from the fray. Capturing an imperial eagle was no small feat, and it was crucial that it not be allowed to fall back into enemy hands.

General Ponsonby had spotted the eagle as well, and he galloped his horse through the chaotic mass over to the sergeant.

"By God, sir, you've captured an imperial eagle!" he shouted excitedly.

"Yes, sir!" Ewart acknowledged. "It will make quite the prize when we return to Brussels."

"Well, off with you then," Ponsonby directed. "No sense hanging about and risking losing our prize! Return to Brussels at once!"

"To Brussels, sir?" the sergeant was baffled but then quickly saluted with his sabre and galloped towards the rear of their lines. All around him, men of the two brigades were brawling with French Infantry and Cavalry. The British forces were still concentrated, whereas the shock of their attack had scattered their enemy, leaving small pockets of men vulnerable and cut off. Flashes of sabres, the crack of sporadic musket fire, and the unending cries of stricken men and horses assailed his senses. Though he felt like he was running from the battle, his companions cheered him as they saw the eagle standard with its tricolour flag carried over his shoulder. The eagles had all been touched by the emperor himself, and to lose one was a terrible disgrace to its regiment.

Charge of the Scots Greys

As Sergeant Ewart galloped away with their prize, General Ponsonby saw that the French Infantry formations had collapsed completely, and they were now on the run.

"To the guns!" he shouted, pointing his sabre towards the French artillery that was but a couple hundred yards from them.

Though their horses were nearly spent from the charge through boggy terrain and the ferocious melee that followed, the men of the two cavalry brigades gave a renewed shout and spurred their mounts towards the enemy cannon. The Scots Greys, who were tasked with forming a reserve, instead sprinted their horses towards the fearsome weapons. A crash of canister shot from a pair of guns tore into their ranks, but they quickly overwhelmed the crews, sabres viciously cutting down those who had mauled their friends.

Far from being beaten, however, the French on the extreme left had formed into infantry squares and were throwing back assaults from the Scots Greys, inflicting fearful losses. Both Wellington and Napoleon saw the recklessness of the British Cavalry around the same time. Though they'd scattered the cuirassiers around La Haye Sainte, smashed an infantry regiment, and overrun several batteries of French artillery, their horses were now blown. Their attack was completely spent, and with the Scots Greys initiating their own attack, there was no reserve force to help the two brigades extract themselves.

Wellington cringed as he watched fresh squadrons of cuirassiers and lancers envelope the British Cavalry. A bugler was frantically sounding the order to recall, but given the distance and the din of battle in the valley below, no one could hear him or if they did, they simply chose to ignore it.

"Damned cavalry!" the Duke snapped. "They go galloping at everything, with no thought to situational awareness. They simply feel the need to rush every which way, like a dog chasing squirrels!"

"Only these squirrels bite back," DeLanccy noted with the same grim tone as Wellington. "Ponsonby will be hard-pressed to pull himself out of this one."

What neither DeLancey nor Wellington knew was that for Major General Sir William Ponsonby, it was already too late. His elation at his men capturing a French eagle and overrunning a number of guns quickly turned to panic as fresh waves of cuirassiers and lancers charged both of his flanks. As they attempted to beat a hasty retreat, the general himself was caught from behind by a lancer and skewered off his horse. As he fell face-down into a puddle with a splash, two more lancers rode up and stabbed his twitching body repeatedly. Many of his men suffered similar fates as they attempted to escape from what had turned into a complete disaster. Their only saving grace was that Marshal Ney had ordered cavalry not to pursue them further, as he had another more pressing mission for them.

The Fall of General Ponsonby

"Well, that settles the troubles from the English Cavalry," Napoleon noted. His face was pale, and he leaned against his carriage. He did his best to hide his affliction, but then he suddenly doubled over in pain, clutching his stomach.

"Sire!" Soult cried out as he rushed to the emperor's side. A pair of grenadiers from Napoleon's bodyguard helped steady him.

"I'm okay!" Napoleon said unconvincingly through clenched teeth.

"You must rest for a little while," Soult insisted.

"And what good am I if a little stomach problem keeps me from the battle?" the emperor grunted. He then braced himself against the carriage wheel and removed his hat. His eyes then grew wide as he watched Marshal Ney leading the bulk of his cavalry in a large mass up the gentle slope.

"What is Ney doing?" he shouted.

"Sire?" Soult asked.

Napoleon then furiously waved his hand towards the ridgeline. "Damn him!" the emperor swore. "D'Erlon has been pushed back. Ney is sending our cavalry in without any infantry support!" Soult and the other staff officers scanned the slope and saw that d'Erlon had been forced to withdraw by the British Cavalry, along with the counterattack from their 5ᵗʰ Division. He was reforming his men, but was still in no position to assist the cavalry.

"He's making the same error the English just did," Soult noted with disdain.

"Does he think this is the time for the pursuit?" Napoleon stammered. "La Haye Sainte hasn't even fallen yet! Damn him, how many times has he faced Wellington? By now he should know that Englishman's favourite tactic, yet he is recklessly falling right into it. Curse him to hell if he loses my cavalry!"

Not wishing to watch what he knew to be a pending catastrophe, the emperor shoved the guards away and staggered back towards his headquarters, taking Soult's advice to rest for a few minutes. His chief of staff helped him along till Napoleon decided he'd found as good a spot as any next to the outer wall of the farmhouse of La Belle Alliance.

"My body is dying, Nicolas," he confessed. "But my mind is as strong as ever. Do you know what I would give anything to see right now? My son; I love him more than my life, and I would gladly sacrifice all that I own just to hold him again. You have children, you understand."

"Yes, sire," Soult agreed. "Two sons; the oldest, Napoleon, is thirteen."

"Ah," the emperor smiled. "I apologize, old friend, I had forgotten the honour you bestowed upon me by naming your son after me. Tell me, what is the word from Plancenoit on our right flank?"

"Lobau is holding but has committed his entire corps," Soult replied. "The Prussians are still arriving a few companies at a time. With Lobau having to keep them at bay, that leaves us without a reserve, except for the Imperial Guard."

"And the Guard I will save for Wellington," Napoleon noted. "Damn it all, where is Grouchy? He'd better be crawling up Blucher's backside! Well, there's nothing for it."

"Yes, sire," Soult acknowledged. "And as best as we can tell, despite the English Cavalry repulsing d'Erlon's corps, they have not been able to resupply or reinforce the farmhouse at La Haye Sainte. Unless they were stocked with enough ammunition for an entire division, I suspect they will run out within another hour or so."

"Then I'll rest here for a bit," Napoleon remarked, "and if Ney is still alive by then, he'll renew our assault on La Haye Sainte. Lobau can hold for that long, he is well fortified at Plancenoit. What about our left wing?"

"It would seem there was a breakdown in communication as to what your intent was," Soult explained. "Instead of using the attack on Hougomont as a diversion, Reille committed his entire corps against it. Every attack failed, and they've lost several thousand men as a result. We did, however, beat back any counterattacks from Wellington. His army has too many inexperienced militia to be used effectively as a cohesive unit."

"And so he pins himself to his ridge," Napoleon finished for him. "Whatever Ney's folly, he is the bravest man I've ever known. And who knows, perhaps Wellington is close enough to being beaten that Ney's attack with the cavalry will finish him. And if not, I will break him with the Guard once the farmhouse is ours."

Chapter XXIII: How can we?
Field of Waterloo
18 June 1815
4:00 pm

Allied soldiers forming a square to repel cavalry

Captain James Webster did, indeed, surmise that the French were planning something big for the right wing. Up till this point, the main attacks on the right of the line were focused on Hougomont. He had no situational awareness as to how things were faring on the left, where even as he led the survivors of his detachment up the slope, the Union and Household Cavalry were smashing hard into d'Erlon's corps and driving them back. Captain Roberts and his light company provided a rear guard for them as they withdrew. They were to then join Captain Stables, where they would anchor the extreme left of the battalion.

Though they moved at a walk, James found he was out of breath when they reached the top. He also noted the numbers of enemy dead that littered the slope leading to where the Guards Division was assembled on the far side. Men stopped at the top to catch their breath as James looked back over his shoulder to where the battle for Hougomont still raged.

"A damn waste of time," he said. "We've pinned down an entire enemy corps that is trying to take a position which is strategically meaningless."

"Sir, down there!" a soldier shouted, pointing off to the east, where the Household and Union Cavalry Brigades were withdrawing in disorder. Divisions of French Cavalry were forming for a massive charge.

"They think this is the weak point," James stated. "Damn it all, they're going to come right for us!"

Wellington had seen the same thing and was racing his horse down the line, ordering men to fall back behind the ridge and form into squares. James led his two companies past a battery of nine-pound cannon as the crews were removing a wheel from each gun. Knowing that an enemy cavalry attack was imminent, this prevented the cannon from being captured and wheeled away.

The battalion square was the most effective means for repelling cavalry, though it also held inherent risks. Because soldiers were so closely formed up, with impeded mobility, it was a prime target for artillery and was also far less effective against infantry assaults. Thankfully for the men of the Anglo-Allied army, their positioning on the reverse slope kept them out of sight of Napoleon's guns. Even more fortunate was that the massed wall of French Cavalry, while a fearsome sight to behold, was attacking without any infantry in support.

The 3/1st Foot Guards were formed into a square, four ranks deep. The first two were kneeling with bayonets protruding forward. The third and fourth ranks stood, and would primarily engage using musket fire. As officers paced behind their men,

311

Lieutenant Shanahan noted that his best shot, Private Adams, was kneeling in the second rank.

"Adams!" Patrick shouted. "Switch places with Private Collins in the third rank." The soldiers complied, though Adams had a look of dread upon his face. Corporal O'Connor noticed it, as Adams now stood next to him in the massed formation.

"What is it, man?" David asked. "You've held this long."

"How can we keep doing this?" Adams answered with his own question. His face was pale, eyes vacant. "I don't want to kill anymore, David. I just can't..."

"Well, if you don't, we're all dead men!" the corporal snapped as the thundering of thousands of horses grew louder.

A last minute burst of cannon fire and soon the crews were sprinting away from their guns.

"Take cover in the squares!" their officers shouted from atop their horses.

"Let them through!" James shouted as a dozen cannon crewmen raced towards his battalion's square. Though Major D'Oyley remained mounted, the captain had chosen to fight this engagement on foot. He drew his pistol and stood near Patrick; the Irishman's presence giving him a sense of strength as the first wave of French Cavalry crested the ridge.

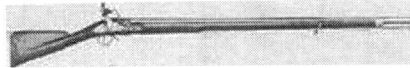

The saturated ground not only impeded the effects of cannon solid shot, it also hindered the movement of horses as Marshal Ney was discovering. Their mounts stumbled and struggled through the quagmire as they made their way up the slope. It was impossible for his men to move in formation at the full gallop, though Ney was not terribly concerned. As best he could reckon, the English had fallen back in disarray and abandoned their cannon crews to their fate. It was impatience that was getting the best of him, as his desire for vengeance upon Wellington increased his ardour.

As always, the Marshal of France rode towards the head of his men, inspiring them with his fearless example. A volley of canister shot from the British guns tore into his men and horses as the crews fired one last time before fleeing. Thousands of small lead balls burst from the cannon, ripping into man and horse alike. The sounds of bugles, men shouting, and the trampling of hooves drowned out the screams of pain from the stricken.

Ney crested the ridge, hoping to ride down and gut one of the gunners personally when he pulled the reigns of his horse in utter shock. The English had formed numerous squares of infantry that their cannon crews were now racing towards. The French Cavalry spilled over the ridge, surprised at the sight of the British readying to fight, but now it was too late to turn back. Columns of cavalry rode past the squares, unable to reach with their sabres past the wall of bristling bayonets; those who tried were skewered off their mounts. Lancers, whose long weapons had sufficient reach, were specifically targeted by marksmen in the third and fourth ranks of the squares.

Ney spurred his horse forward, only to have it shot out from under him, giving a horrifying scream as several musket balls smashed into its neck. The marshal flew from his mount and landed hard amongst the rocks. Despite the jarring pain in his shoulder and side from his fall, he still managed to retrieve his sword and stagger to his feet. Horsemen fanned out on either side as they made their way into the fray. There was much confusion, as no one knew quite what to do. With the English squares out of cannon range, and no infantry to assist, the French horsemen could do little except try and keep moving, so as not to make themselves easy targets to the designated shooters within the squares. The marshal watched, horrified as a score of cuirassiers attempted to break one of the squares only to have their horses rear up at the last, refusing to gallop into the gleaming mass of bayonets. Over half threw their riders, who were immediately shot or stabbed in their vulnerable places by the redcoats.

While most of the artillery crews fled for the safety of the squares, a steadfast and brave officer, Captain Alexander Mercer, kept his six-gun battery of nine-pounders manned. He was flanked by battalions of Brunswick Infantry, and he questioned their steadiness underneath the oncoming assault of French horse.

313

"Sir, should we not withdraw to the squares?" a sergeant in charge of one of the gun crews asked.

"No," the captain said, shaking his head. "Load the guns up with double canister. We'll saturate the ground with enemy dead so that they cannot even get up the slope to reach us." Mercer grinned sinisterly as he watched a mass of cuirassier columns riding up the slope, directly for his battery.

"Double canister loaded!" his subaltern shouted from down the gun line.

"Wait for it!" Mercer ordered. "We'll let these bastards get a little closer before we send them to the Almighty."

It was a maddening wait for his men as they stood behind their guns. With only some Brunswick Infantry to support them, they knew that if they did not break the oncoming assault, they would all be cut down by the armoured enemy horse. The French moved slower than expected, hindered by the deep mud which had been churned up in previous assaults. As the enemy force grew closer, he could hear the sounds of their bugles and battle cries. Mercer raised his sword high and when the cuirassiers were within fifty yards gave his order.

"Fire!"

The entire front rank of French Cavalry was blown to pieces in a spray of blood and body parts. The entire advance column simply ceased to exist; not one man or horse stood after the horrific blast of double-canister from Mercer's guns.

"Reload! Fire round shot into their successive columns," the captain ordered.

His men were extremely well trained, and the heightened rush brought on by the imminent assault of French Cavalry led them to reload their cannon remarkably fast. Much to the battery commander's relief, the Brunswick Infantry held firm and were firing relentless volleys into the subsequent waves of cavalry.

"Fire!"

Though round shot would not ricochet sufficiently in the boggy earth, the tightly-packed ranks of cuirassiers made them still a viable target, with nine-pound steel balls smashing into man and horse alike. Mercer had been correct in his prediction, as the ground within a hundred yards of his battery was so completely saturated with dead and wounded cavalry, it was now completely impassable. The gun crews became more brazen, elevating and firing solid shot into the deep columns of floundering French Cavalry, smashing men and horses to pieces in a horrific display of shattered bones and bloody flesh.

The stand of Mercer's battery

While the cuirassiers were giant men, who relied on fear and intimidation as much as their military prowess, they were impotent against the close-knit squares of British Infantry. And while their armour was effective against sword and bayonet, it was useless against a musket ball at close range. Ney, now in a half daze due to his fall and the growing clouds of black powder smoke in the ensuing chaos, watched one hapless cuirassier shot a dozen times in quick succession before finally falling lifeless from his mount. The terrified beast did not know which way to run and was only just caught by the bridal by Ney, who despite his bruising fall, managed to mount. He gritted his teeth as he watched his glorious cavalry being torn apart in the relentless barrage of British firepower. Through the smoke, he saw the most curious sight. It appeared that a redcoat had left the relative safety of his battalion's square and was now walking lost amongst the frenzied mass of French horsemen.

"Comment pouvons-nous? Pourquoi?" he thought he heard the man cry out; *"How can we? Why?"*

It was no illusion. What Marshal Ney had seen was the mental and emotional breaking of Private Eric Adams. As the battalion fought back against an assault by French lancers, tears rolled down his face. The scream of a horse echoed in his ear as the poor creature fell over backwards, while being stabbed by several men in the first two ranks. Its rider, a Polish lancer, had been thrown and was now trying to get to his feet. As the man, who looked to be more of a young boy, turned his head their way, Corporal O'Connor fired his weapon into his face. The lad's neck snapped back as the musket ball burst through his eye socket and exploded out the back of his head.

Everyone has their breaking point, and despite the numerous battles he'd fought in during the Peninsula, Eric Adams never got used to the horror of men killing each other. Every time they'd gone into battle, he'd buckled down and done his duty. His thoughts were always focused on his wife and children, as well as protecting his mates. Yet in the fury of watching the hapless French Cavalry being helplessly mauled, with the occasional cry from his fellow Englishmen as cuirassier and lancer occasionally managed to breach the bayonet wall and inflict death upon them, Eric's soul completely shattered.

He fired one last shot from his musket, lamenting that he scored a precise hit to the side of a cuirassier's helmet. The man's sword arm fell limply to his side, his eyes crossing, mouth open, and tongue protruding as he twitched in involuntary convulsions as he fell from his horse, which was subsequently shot several times by errant musket fire.

"Stay with it!" Corporal O'Connor shouted to his men, who were all in a near state of panic.

Only their iron discipline and the instinct of relentless training and combat experience carried them. The confused French and their horses knew not what they should do and many were finding themselves lost in the confusion and endless billowing smoke. The taste of traces of black power and the smoke parched David's mouth, and he quietly wondered if he would ever be rid of the taste and smell as he fired yet another shot into the hapless cavalry column that raced past them.

"How can we do this?" Adams said, quietly at first. He then tore his shako from his head and threw it to the ground. "How can we keep killing one another?"

"Damn it, Eric, reload your weapon!" David shouted, but to no avail.

The private had completely broken, and he was now trying to force his way out of the square, as if struck by a bout of claustrophobia.

"How can we kill one another?" he shouted. "How can we? Why? *Why?"* He was sobbing openly, as he forced himself past the men in the first two ranks.

"Damn it, what the hell is he doing?" Sergeant Donaldson shouted from further down the line. "Somebody stop him!"

"Hold formation!" Lieutenant Shanahan ordered before men could break out of the square and try to retrieve their errant comrade. "Staying together is the only thing keeping us alive!"

"Eric!" O'Connor pleaded as he tried to reload his musket while watching his friend's display of madness.

He was now stumbling about in a daze, pleading loudly. The despairing soldier threw down his musket and held his hands out to his sides, now crying out to their enemies. *"How can we? How can we kill one another?"* He started shouting the same words, only now in French. *"Comment peut-on tuer un autre? Comment pouvons-nous? Pourquoi? Pourquoi?"* His pleas were cut short by a passing cuirassier who swung his sword in a wide arc, slicing through the soldier's throat. His arms fell, and his head tilted back as blood from the severed artery spurted forth. As his life left him, he fell face-first to the ground, his body trampled in a wave of French Cavalry.

317

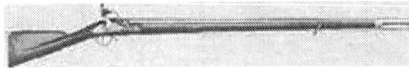

"Cease fire!" Captain Mercer had to order a halt to the constant hammering of his guns, as the Duke of Wellington himself was passing by on the road in front of his guns.

"Well done, Mercer! Well done!" the Duke said as he rode past. "Infantry will be advancing past you; concentrate your fire on Boney's infantry formations bellow!"

"Yes, sir!" Mercer saluted before issuing subsequent orders to his battery.

Though they had savaged the enemy cavalry, they were still subject to harassment fire from French skirmishers, as well as enemy artillery. Though casualties amongst his cannon crewmen had been sustainable, French cannon fire had wreaked havoc upon his limbered horses. Though there was little time to think about it at this moment, he did wonder if he'd even be able to move his battery at all, once the battle was decided for good or ill.

"How are we sitting for ammunition?" the captain asked his colour sergeant.

"We've enough to smash those columns below us," the NCO asserted as the nearest gun hissed while one of the crewmen swabbed out the barrel. "I daresay both sides will have shot their last round before this day is done."

"A hard pounding," Wellington asserted as he rode up next to the men. "Let's see who pounds the longest."

There had been no order to retreat. Within thirty minutes of coming upon the waiting British squares, the survivors of Marshal Ney's heroic, albeit futile, cavalry charge fled back down the slope. Lack of proper coordination between the cavalry, artillery, and infantry had led 9,000 of Napoleon's finest horsemen to conduct at least a dozen assaults, where they were completely savaged and achieved nothing. The regiment, *Empress' Dragoons*, had been especially bloodied, losing over half their men during the fruitless assault.

"What the hell was Ney doing?" Napoleon shouted to his staff, once more on his feet, the pain in his stomach gone. "You never send cavalry forward without infantry or artillery support!"

"Sire, Reille's II Corps is advancing to support Ney," Soult noted, looking through his telescope.

The emperor looked through his own spyglass and could see the ever-reliable Reille advancing his men to repel a counterattack by the British Cavalry. Satisfied that his centre still held, he turned to his chief-of-staff. "Soult, any change in the Prussian attack on our flank?"

"Lobau and the Young Guard are being pressed hard, but they are holding," the marshal replied, reading the latest despatch from the corps commander. "I must tell you, sire, that if the Prussians are able to bring up their entire army, not even the Young Guard will be able to hold onto Plancenoit."

"Have Ney renew his assault on La Haye Sainte," Napoleon ordered. "It has been largely unsupported, and I doubt they've been able to resupply on ammunition. One more attack, combined with artillery support, and the farmhouse will be ours. Once it falls, then Wellington will be beaten and the Prussians of no matter."

French Chasseurs

319

Chapter XXIV: Hammer and the Anvil
Field of Waterloo
18 June 1815
6:30 pm

French soldiers storming La Haye Sainte

"General Cooke is down!" Maitland shouted as he rode over to Major D'Oyley. "Damn cannon shot took his arm."

"That's a bad spot of luck," Henry said, shaking his head. He noted the battered state of his battalion. "Sir, we repelled the enemy cavalry, but we've been in a bloody grind with their infantry, and I dare say we are at less than half strength."

"This slugfest is getting us nowhere," the general concurred as he watched the melee below. His Guards were in a brawl with the advancing columns from Reille's French corps, with both sides exposed along the slope.

"Sir, La Haye Sainte has fallen!" an aide from Wellington's staff said in a panic as he rode up to the men. "The Duke wants what's left of the Guards Division to fall back behind the ridge and await instructions from him personally."

"Understood," Maitland acknowledged. "My compliments to his grace. We'll be waiting for him." He then turned back to Henry. "Pull your men back. Get them out of this damned mess!"

"Yes, sir!" Henry replied, then calling for his immediate subordinates, *"Captain Stables, Captain Webster!"*

"A right bloody mess down there," Stables observed as he and James joined the major.

The sounds of musket fire were relentless, coupled with the maddened shouts of men as each side gave everything they had to break the other.

"We're to pull back behind the ridge," Henry directed. "Wellington himself has something planned for us."

"Whatever it is, I hope it's brilliant," Stables remarked as he nodded towards the La Haye Sainte farmhouse, where through the clouds of billowing smoke they could see the unmistakable French tricolour.

"If the enemy has La Haye Sainte, then our centre has fallen," James added quietly.

Before another word could be spoken, a French mortar shell exploded nearby, sending all three men flying from their mounts. The fuse had been set too long, and so it had not burst in the air as intended. Though James was furthest from the blast, with Henry and Captain Stables shielding him, the concussion still sent him sprawling over backwards, his vision clouded for a moment as he landed hard on his back, the wind knocked out of him. He took a moment to catch his breath and rolled to his side. As best he could tell, he had not been hit by enemy shrapnel, and it seemed all of his injuries came from the fall. He saw Henry D'Oyley sitting upright, trying to cut a piece of burning metal from his leg. The stench of burned flesh made James want to vomit.

As he stumbled over to his battalion commander, he saw that Henry was wounded in numerous places. His jacket was shredded and his silk undershirt splotched with blood.

"Damn it all," Henry grunted as he tried to fight off the pain. He was breathing hard, sweat dripping down his face. "Where is Stables? I need him to take the battalion."

James quickly looked around to try and find his fellow captain, who'd been sitting on his horse right next to them just a moment before. Not ten feet away he saw him. The poor man was lying on his stomach, head turned to the side towards them, eyes wide and lifeless as the flat rock his head rested on was slowly starting to overflow with dark crimson.

"He's gone, sir," James lamented.

"Then the battalion is yours," Henry said. "Get our men out of here, reform and wait for Wellington."

"Yes, sir," James replied. He signalled for the bugler. "Sound recall; drummers, beat a slow cadence. We are withdrawing, not running!"

As the bugle sounded and a handful of drums started to beat, James and several men started to pick up their fallen battalion commander.

"Leave me be, damn it!" Henry shouted. "I'll not have you risk more lives on my account! If the frogs don't bayonet me, you'll know where to find me when this is over."

As much as it pained James to do so, he obeyed. Captain Stables' horse lay dead, and their other two mounts had run off. The battalion, along with Lieutenant Colonel Askew's 2nd Battalion, fought its way back up the slope, regrettably leaving behind scores of dead and wounded. With the entire battle balancing on the edge, neither side seemed inclined to waste time handling prisoners. And so the slowly advancing French Infantry simply walked over their fallen enemy. The persistent hammering of British artillery prevented them from pursuing and so, as the Guards retreated up the ridge, the French reformed at the base of the slope.

"Who is going to break first?" Patrick Shanahan wondered aloud as his company reformed behind the ridge.

Their numbers were alarmingly few, as were those of the rest of 3/1st Foot Guards.

"I'm battalion commander," James said in disbelief, as much for his own benefit as Patrick's. He then surmised his unit and reckoned there were fewer men still standing in the entire battalion than he'd had just in the right wing two days before. He nodded to his bugler, who sounded the officers' call. James was shocked to see that Daniel Roberts and the commanders of the Grenadier and 5th Company were the only other captains still in the fight. The remaining company commanders were all lieutenants or ensigns.

"The battalion is now yours," Daniel acknowledged. Though he was three years James' senior in rank, he appeared relieved rather than disappointed that his friend had been given the posting over him.

"So it would seem," James said, his shaking voice betraying his complete exhaustion. "I need a count of how many men we still have in the fight, as well as how much ammunition is left. We've been in another bloody grind this day, and the hour grows late. Wellington is leading our next action personally. Both sides are close to breaking, and it is time we show the Duke, and the French, why we are the best damned infantry regiment in the entire world!"

"Our line is too thin, your grace," an aide said with unusual candour. "We cannot possibly hold."

"There was no way to get ammunition to the defenders of La Haye Sainte," DeLancey added. "When their cartridges ran out, the French simply rolled right over them."

"It would seem," Wellington said quietly to Uxbridge, "that we're losing the battle." He then looked down the line and off to his right saw something that no one else did.

"There!" he stated. "That is where he will strike!"

"What are you saying, sir?" Uxbridge asked, clearly not catching the Duke's intent.

Wellington ignored him for the moment. "DeLancey," he said, "you will come with me. Uxbridge, send word to the Guards Division. I'm planning a little surprise for our Corsican friend."

"Right away, sir," Uxbridge emphasized before relaying the orders to a messenger.

DeLancey rode as fast as he could to keep up with Wellington as they neared the spot the Duke was looking for.

"He's been holding his Imperial Guard in reserve this whole time," the Duke explained. "Right here is where he sees our line being weakest. It's close to La Haye Sainte and is an easy enough rise that it gives the illusion of being flat. By God, Boney won't know what hit him!"

He then spurred his horse on to where soldiers of the 52nd Oxfordshire were in a minor skirmish with the last gasp of French divisions sent forward to try and wrest the position from them. The fire was still coming in pretty heavy, and several soldiers shouted over their shoulders that the Duke should either get back up the slope or find cover. He appeared to not hear them, or was ignoring them, as he calmly pulled out his telescope and scanned the enemy positions in the valley below.

"Can't see a damned thing if I pull back," he said calmly, more to himself than anyone else. He looked back to DeLancey. "If I call this one right, we can end the war on this ridge. But damn it all if this hasn't been a close-run thing already!"

DeLancey grinned and started to turn his horse about when an enemy cannon round shot somehow managed to find purchase in a dry enough patch of ground that it ricocheted perfectly and smashed into the colonel's back, sending him flying forward off his horse and landing some yards away. The poor man hit the ground so hard that his body literally bounced up to its feet, right in front of a fresh company that was moving forward to join the Oxfordshire. DeLancey's expression was vacant, and he fell face first onto a flat rock. Men quickly gathered around to help the stricken colonel. The staff officers all dismounted and went to aid their friend. As Wellington rode up, DeLancey looked up at him, his face twisted in pain and eyes pleading.

"Please tell them to leave me," he said through gasps of pain. "Let me die in peace." He then collapsed onto his face. The back of his jacket was torn, though remarkably enough the skin wasn't broken. Yet just by a quick feel, one could tell the cannon ball had done terrible damage to his insides.

"Evacuate him to the rear," Wellington ordered. As his staff officers complied and carried the stricken man away, the Duke sighed and shook his head in sorrow. More than just his chief-of-staff, William Howe DeLancey was a personal friend. Though Wellington was nine years the elder, he'd known DeLancey since he was a young lad, and he'd always been like an older brother to him.

"How many of my friends will fall this day?" Wellington asked, looking up to the heavens. Another close friend, Alexander Gordon, had fallen, and there was no word on if Somerset would survive his fearful injuries. "And will you still leave me here, unscathed, while they die?"

As he watched DeLancey being carried away towards a waiting hospital wagon that was already piled with wounded, he nodded sadly before turning his attention back to the battle. The enemy force that had been battling with the Oxfordshire was withdrawing, their will to fight taken from them. It helped Wellington's confidence, knowing that Bonaparte's men were as equally battered and exhausted as his. He was further thankful for the Prussian forces that had arrived and were bringing more troops to bear on Plancenoit. Still, the Duke was fully aware that even if the Prussians did breach Napoleon's flank, it would be for naught if he could not hold against the pending final assault that the turning in his guts told him was coming.

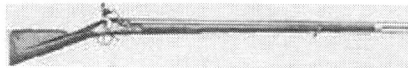

It was now 7:00 in the evening. With La Haye Sainte now in French hands, the Prussian attack checked for the time being, and the appearance of Wellington's entire army withdrawing, the decisive end to the battle sought by Napoleon needed but one final stroke to complete his victory.

"Message from Ney," Soult said, reading a despatch. "He asks that you commit the final stroke of the hammer, and Wellington's army will shatter like glass. Sire, it does appear that Wellington is beaten. If we end this now, then France will be saved and we can send word to Paris that we not only won the battle, but also the war!"

Napoleon nodded solemnly and took a deep breath through his nose. He'd been waiting for this moment for some time. His army had been savaged far more than he thought possible given the calibre of his army compared to Wellington's. Secretly, he knew the credit lay with the Duke for having held for so long while inflicting such terrible losses on the French.

"He nearly had me," Napoleon confessed, drawing a confused stare from Soult and the other staff officers. "It reminds me of the Battle of Marengo. You remember, I had lost the battle at 5:00, yet by 7:00 I had won it back."

"That you did, sire," Soult acknowledged.

An indescribable feeling overwhelmed the emperor. He felt as if the page of history would be turned within the next thirty minutes. Lobau was in a murderous fight against the relentless Prussian assaults, but it was no matter. Napoleon would send a message to Blucher, calling for an immediate ceasefire once Wellington was broken. Finally, it was time to bring the unbeaten English Sepoy General to his knees!

"Make ready the Imperial Guard!"

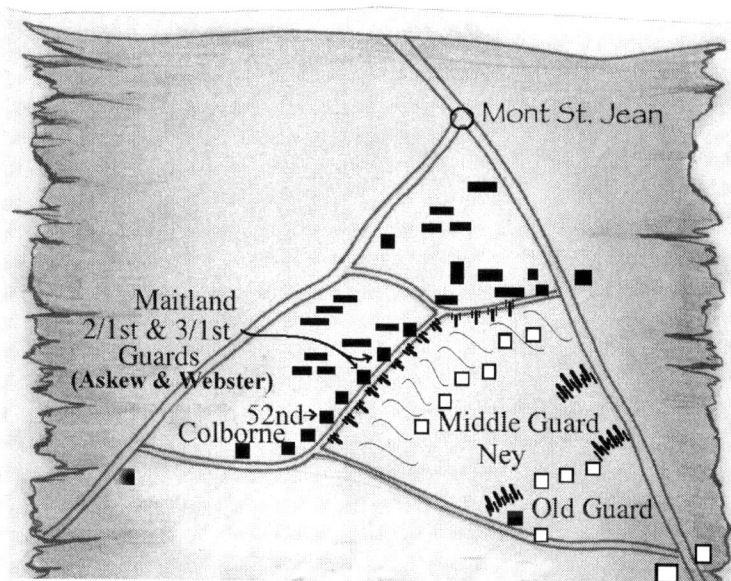

Advance of the Imperial Guard. While the Young Guard holds the Prussians off at Plancenoit, Ney leads the Middle Guard in its assault, with the Old Guard in reserve. They are unaware that Maitland's brigade is hidden behind the reverse slope.

Chapter XXV: Now, Maitland! Now's your time!
Field of Waterloo
18 June 1815
7:30 pm

British soldiers from the 1st Regiment of Foot Guards

There was a feeling of utter exhaustion amongst the few still able to stand. It was hard for James to fathom that whereas just two days before he led a single company, he was now in command of the entire battalion or what was left of it. Officers and NCOs were assessing their numbers, as well as getting a count of ammunition. With as much as they'd expended throughout the day, James was surprised they had any cartridges left at all.

"Sir, we have the numbers of our fighting strength," Patrick Shanahan said. "We've taken what ammunition we could off the dead and wounded of both sides, but it still is not good."

James looked at the hastily scribbled list and shook his head. "We cannot possibly hold another attack like that." As best he could tell, the battle had been raging for close to eight hours. The defence and the holding of the gate at Hougomont felt like eight lifetimes ago. Most of his men had various injuries of one sort or another.

As he looked into the tired faces of his soldiers, it seemed every man's tunic was torn in numerous places and spotted with blood from where they'd been peppered with hot shrapnel. Others had various cuts and gouges to their face, hands, and legs from enemy bayonets. And still there were those who'd been shot, yet managed to extract the musket balls and bandage themselves sufficiently so as to remain in the fight. Expressions varied from determination to resignation at their fate, and all were completely exhausted. They could only hope their enemy was as spent as they.

"Captain Webster!" It was General Maitland, now in command of the entire division. "Wellington is forming up the Guards to make a final stand. As you know, he's taking personal command of this action. You're to follow me."

"Yes, sir," James nodded. He then turned to his company commanders. "You heard him, get the battalion ready to move. Wellington is personally leading this action, and we will *not* fail him. If we are to die, then we die standing with him, like true soldier gentlemen. Now move out!"

Completely spent, yet still determined to make a last show of strength for 'Old Nosey', the men of the Guards shouldered their weapons and marched at the quick step behind General Maitland to where Wellington sat on his horse by a large oak tree. Where there was usually an entourage of staff officers, the Duke was now alone. DeLancey and Gordon lay dying from their horrifying injuries, and Somerset was likely to lose his right arm. Despite the extreme strain, combined with lack of sleep, and the emotional trauma of watching so many of his friends and soldiers fall, the Duke's countenance was one of defiance and contempt for his enemy. That he was personally overseeing what many believed would be the final decisive action of this brutally long day heartened the men in the ranks. James and Colonel Askew of 2nd Battalion joined the Duke and General Maitland.

"Captain Webster," Wellington noted. "You're commanding the battalion now?"

"Yes, your grace," James replied. "Major D'Oyley was badly wounded, and Captain Stables was killed. I should let you know, sir, that we are well under half strength."

"We're right there with you, James," Colonel Askew spoke up. "I've lost both my battalion majors and over half my company officers. How the fuck I'm still standing is beyond me." His expression was of complete exacerbation and exhaustion, combined with the agitation of his wound from Quatre Bras, his snap of profanity understandable.

"Form your brigade into three company lines," Wellington ordered. "And have them get down on the ground. Boney thinks we're beaten, and that this area is undefended. Your men will be a little surprise for him when he unleashes his final weapon against us."

"Final weapon, sir?" James asked.

Wellington did not answer. Instead he addressed General Maitland. "Peregrine, I will give the order for you to unleash," he said. "Wait for my command. I do not want to see a single redcoat rise out of the grass until I give the word."

"Of course, your grace," Maitland replied. He dismounted his horse and signalled for his battalion commanders to execute their orders.

With shouts from the officers and NCOs, the two battalions formed what remained of their companies into two ranks each. James placed his first three companies in a long line, with the next three behind them, and the remaining three in the rear. The light company was dispersed in a skirmish line on their right flank.

With a few minutes to spare, James walked over to where Captain Daniel Roberts had dispersed his men in a long line. Daniel had unbuckled his sword and scabbard, shoving it into the ground so it all stood upright. He then removed his shako and placed it on top of the pommel before slinging a cartridge pouch over his shoulder and picking up a French musket.

"The sod who carried this won't be needing it," he reasoned. "Besides, he had almost a half complement of ammunition; might as well put it to some good use." He then knelt down with his men and shook his head, gazing at the ground in front of him.

James removed his own shako and joined him. "I need you to hold on just a little longer, Daniel," he said quietly. "I daresay it will all be over soon enough."

"I'm glad they made you acting battalion commander," his friend replied, still staring at the ground. "My seniority be damned. I would have broken long before now."

"To be honest, old friend, I'm surprised I haven't," James replied.

"You know I was just thinking," Daniel began, "should I not get through this, I'd like you to look after Carolyn and my son. I thought perhaps maybe when he and your daughter are older they could…damn silly for me to be having such thoughts at a time like this."

"Not silly at all," James disagreed. "After what we've been through, and with oblivion bearing down on us, it is natural for our thoughts to turn to those that mean the most to us."

"Well, I know your thoughts must be on Amy," his fellow captain observed. "But tell me this, do you also think about Emma right now?" He finally looked James in the eye, and his expression was one of extreme fatigue, coupled with sorrow.

"I confess, I do," James replied.

"That is good," Daniel nodded. He then fumbled with the musket. "Haven't had the chance to fire this yet. I hope the bloody frog it belonged to knew how to load it properly."

James grabbed his friend by the shoulder reassuringly as he stood and re-donned his shako, before taking his place at the centre of the battalion. He soon joined Colonel Askew and General Maitland, who knelt at the edge of the ridge, eyes wide as they watched the last blow of Napoleon's army forming for the attack. "Sir, I think you're the only senior officer in the entire corps who has not been hit yet," James said to Maitland with a trace of dark humour.

The general snorted in reply. "You're more right than you know. The Prince of Orange was shot down; our division's commander, General Cooke has lost an arm; General Alten of the 3rd Division was badly wounded; and General Halkett was hit four times throughout the day! Colonel Ompteda of the King's German Legion was killed just before the Prince of Orange was hit."

"This is a dark day, even if we should be the victors," Colonel Askew said coldly. He appeared to have fresh wounds to his face and body; his arm still in a sling from the injuries he'd sustained at Quatre Bras.

"Sir, my men are down to five rounds apiece," James explained.

"That's exactly where we're at," Askew added. "Five rounds, then the bayonet."

"It will be enough," Maitland asserted. "Though God help us if it's not."

Below, the bands of the French Imperial Guard struck up as they were finally committed to battle. Though the Young Guard was holding down the Prussians, the core of Napoleon's elite troops had yet to engage. The emperor held them in reserve, ready to smash like a great hammer.

"Lobau is being hard-pressed by the Prussians," an aide reported. "If they take Plancenoit, our flank will be exposed."

"I'm well aware of the situation," Napoleon said with agitation. "Blucher may press us hard, but he cannot win this battle if Wellington should break. Ney has taken La Haye Sainte, and the English centre is now completely exposed. His army is spent. They have nothing left. I, on the other hand, have my best troops advancing to decide this matter once and for all."

Secretly, the emperor was indeed worried about the situation on his right flank. He'd underestimated Blucher and the Prussian's resolve. With Grouchy nowhere to be found, he could only assume that his marshal was either completely lost or engaged with the Prussian rear guard at Wavre, in which case, Blucher was not attacking with his entire army at Waterloo. As he watched the battalions of the Middle Guard start their advance up the slope to the left of La Haye Sainte, Napoleon felt like his heart was about to explode from his chest.

"It should be too easy, Soult," he said quietly to his chief-of-staff. "D'Erlon has turned to also face the Prussian threat from the right in support of Lobau, and he has not been further pressed by Wellington. That alone tells me the English are beaten. And with La Haye Sainte in our hands, it is only a matter of the Guard cresting that ridge and falling on what's left of Wellington and his army of shopkeepers."

"I daresay, sire," Soult added, "The fate of France will be decided within the next few minutes."

"Not just France," Napoleon corrected. "The fate of the *world* will be decided on that ridge."

The bands played loudly and with more passion than the emperor had ever heard as the Imperial Guard made its advance. What remained of Wellington's cannon was in a duel with Napoleon's, and the sheer number of French guns proved overwhelming. This left the advancing Guard mostly unmolested as they reached the base of the gentle slope and started up. Their columns were perfect, their discipline and march-step exact. Napoleon tried to sear the image into his memory, for his instincts told him that regardless of how the next few minutes played out, this would be the last action of the Imperial Guard.

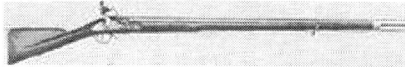

James never thought he could feel a greater sense of tension than when he led the Forlorn Hope at Badajoz, yet somehow as he knelt between two of his companies, that terrible siege seemed like a lifetime ago. The battle had ground to a halt, with the French holding against the Prussians, and now the Imperial Guard advancing as the final stroke.

"Follow the Duke's command," Maitland directed as he rode up behind where James knelt. "He's but a few yards behind you. Do not wait for subsequent orders from me. I daresay that by the time he gives the word, you'll be able to smell the garlic on the breath of the Imperial Guard."

"They won't stand, sir," James assured him. "They may be the Imperial Guard, but they are just men. They die just as easily as any other."

James looked around him. Aside from Wellington on his horse by the lone oak tree, one could scarcely tell that there were any British soldiers behind the ridge. He and Lieutenant Colonel Askew knelt at the centre of their battalions. All other officers and men lay prone on the ground, the tall grass hiding them from the advancing French soldiers.

"By God," a soldier said, fumbling with his musket as the sounds of the French drummers grew louder. "It's really the Guard…the fucking Imperial Guard!"

"So what if it is?" Corporal O'Connor chastised. "True, they've never been bested in battle, but then neither have we!"

At the end of the company line, Private Farrow rolled to his side and opened the front of his trousers.

"Farrow, what the blasted hell are you doing?" Corporal Harvey asked.

"I have to piss," Farrow explained. "If I don't go now, I'll surely wet myself once the frogs are in our faces, and it would not do for a proper soldier gentleman to die with pissed on trousers!"

"Any gets on me, and you'll have me bayonet in your arse," the soldier lying behind him said with a nervous chuckle.

"Vive la France! Vive la France!" The battle chant of the Imperial Guard sounded as a cadence in time with their drums and the heavy falls of their footsteps.

"Five volleys," James said quietly as he looked down and fumbled with the pommel of his sword. "I hope it's enough."

"Five volleys and then the bayonet, sir," Patrick said as he knelt down next to him. "Beg your pardon, but since this may be the end, I just wanted to let you know, sir, that it's been an honour." The Irish lieutenant extended his hand, which James readily took.

"Thank you, Mister Shanahan," the captain replied. "You bring honour to both the Guards and to Ireland."

Patrick clasped his hand hard, his face in a hard grimace. He then nodded and, hunkering low, returned to his place at the centre of his company.

James let out a deep breath, the anticipation becoming maddening.

"Vive la France! Vive la France!"

Marshal Ney sat atop his horse, his expression one of complete triumph. It would all be over soon; the destruction of the English army and final victory for France. Whatever troubles they may still face from the Prussians, without Wellington and the English to support them, they would quickly capitulate.

334

Ney noted with approval that General Morvan marched at the head of the Imperial Guard. The brave general had led his men with distinction at Ligny, and now he would lead by his own example, on foot at the head of the finest troops in all of Europe.

"Baïonnettes !" Morvan shouted, raising his sword high.

The men in the front ranks lowered their muskets so their bayonets were protruding forward. They marched in a standard deep column, which had been used repeatedly to shatter every army the coalitions had sent against them. That the British tended to rely on firepower to break the column did not matter now; they were already beaten and would put up little resistance in the face of the Guards!

"Vive la France! Vive la France!"

The battle cries of their enemy grew louder, the drum cadence increasing slightly. James could just see the bayonet points of shouldered muskets. He lay flat in the grass, lest he draw fire from the enemy's front ranks. He knew Wellington would wait until the French were almost on top of them. As the chants of the enemy grew almost deafening, he knew it was almost time.

"Hold steady, lads," he said. "Wait for the Duke's command!"

"Bugger all, there they are," a soldier said through gritted teeth. He had to crane his head back from where he lay, but he could just make out the silhouettes of their advancing foe; their cadence and battle chants growing louder.

"If we cannot hold," Corporal O'Connor said, "at least Old Nosey is here to die with us."

"Vive la France! Vive la France!"

From atop his horse, Wellington had perhaps the best view of anyone on the field. He could see clearly both the advancing French columns, as well as his own troops, who lay prone in the grass. Like Napoleon, he knew that the fate of all would be decided in the next few minutes. The Imperial Guard advanced steadily and with purpose; the Duke could not help but admire their discipline. One of their columns was marching directly for him, and Wellington reckoned they had to see him and know who he was. He was the prize. They would bring him before their emperor in triumph! The columns were all on line with each other as they crested the gradual slope, their front ranks now within thirty feet of his still-prone troops. He raised his hand and gave the rarest of full smiles of triumph.

"Now Maitland! Now's your time!"

James heard the call, blood rushing through his veins as he stood. It was only now that he could fully see the French Imperial Guard, whose distance from him could be more easily measured in feet than yards.

"Front line...up!" he shouted at the top of his lungs. The enemy were so close that he could clearly see the look of panic in their faces as a wall of redcoats rose up in front of them.

"Fire!" shouted Lieutenant Shanahan and the other company commanders.

There were no controlled volleys; it was simply a matter of firing as fast as each company line could. As a concentrated mass of muskets erupted into a hellish storm, James watched the entire first ranks of the advancing French columns disintegrate as they were blown apart by point-blank fire. The once pristine uniforms of the men in the subsequent ranks were now sprayed with blood and gore. James could clearly see the horrified expression on one man's face as his companion in front of him was shot through the forehead; the back exploding in a horrifying burst of blood, bone, and brain matter. The captain then looked to his left and right and saw his front companies kneeling and reloading as the French bore down on them.

"Second line...up!"

The enemy soldiers in subsequent ranks were now subjected to the same fate as their hapless fellows in the front had been, as the British Guards second company line rose up and unleashed a fury of musket fire. Though it took but a couple seconds for each volley to fire, to James it felt as if time moved at a crawl. As French soldiers fell to the ground, faces contorted in agony, it seemed as if there were an endless number of men following behind them. The captain knew there was nothing he could do except to continue in his commands until either the enemy broke or he fell in their onslaught.

"Third line...up!" The last company line rose, and another storm of shot unleashed.

336

Marshal Ney's eyes and mouth grew wide. He had spotted a man on a horse by a large tree in the distance, and recognized him to be Wellington. Whereas a few seconds before he had sneered at the Duke in triumph, he now watched in horror as walls of British soldiers rose from the tall grass and fired close-range volleys into the advancing Imperial Guard. The English were spacing the volleys enough so that when the third line of companies fired, those in front were finishing reloading and rising up to fire again. In the half minute it took for the French to realize what they'd run into, the first several ranks of the columns had been shot to pieces. Individual soldiers were starting to return fire, but in a column it was impossible for the French to mass their fire against the British lines. Each time a wall of redcoats rose from the grass to unleash again, a few were felled by shots from the advancing French; yet the English volleys were so concentrated, with so many guns firing at once, that entire ranks of the Imperial Guard were cut down each time.

Ney's horse then cried out as it collapsed, hit several times in the latest British volley. Somehow the Marshal himself was not shot, and he struggled to his feet. He was still in a state of shock as he tried to regain his bearings. The Guard continued to advance, yet they were now buckling under the merciless onslaught of the British volleys. As Ney clawed his way up the slope, which was already covered in bodies of slain and terribly wounded men, he found General Morvan trying to pull himself from a pile of the badly maimed who had fallen on him.

"By God, Marshal!" the general cried as Ney pulled him from the heap. "Where did they come from?"

Morvan, who was among the most fearless men Ney had ever known, looked like a man broken. His bicorn hat was gone, his sword shattered. The general's face and uniform were covered in blood, though one could not tell if it was his or that of his men. Another eruption of British fire smashed into their ranks, men all around the marshal and his general screaming as they fell stricken.

"Come, Paul-Jean!" Ney shouted, addressing the general by his given name. "The English cannot sustain this type of fire for long. We must rise up for our men to follow us!"

The Guards general nodded, though his expression was vacant, etched with horror. Even Marshal Ney, who had survived the horrific Russian campaign, could not have been prepared for the sight of the Imperial Guard's destruction; yet the volleys from the British lines were unrelenting, and with each burst it looked as if an entire rank of French columns were blown apart. No matter how bad a battle went, it was unheard of for units to suffer 100% casualties. Yet he was certain that in this close and brutal savaging, entire companies were lost in each musket storm.

"Maintain the advance!" Ney shouted as he struggled past wavering ranks of men. "We almost have them! Fall upon their lines and they will break!" He then climbed upon a rock, willing himself to be shot down if it should allow him to rally the Guard for a final thrust into what he knew to be Wellington's last stand. *"You know me! I am Ney, Marshal of France!"*

His selfless act led to a renewed battle cry from the Guard, and they pressed forward. It was not to be. For as the encouraged men reformed and advanced past the marshal, the British volleys smashed into them once more, and the bravest men who led from the front fell screaming in terrible pain as musket shot ripped into their bodies.

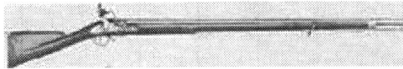

To the right of the Guards regiments, Sergeant William Lawrence and the 52nd Oxfordshire held their position impatiently as they listened to the storm of gun fire coming from where the elite Guards of both nations clashed.

"Sir," the sergeant said to his company commander, "The Guards are giving Boney hell, but they won't be able to hold if their ammunition runs out."

"I concur," the captain replied. "But let us see what the colonel wishes."

As the two men spoke, Colonel Colborne rode up on his horse. "Damn it all," he spat. "There is nothing for us to fight! Not one frog company is so much as making a step towards us."

"Sir, we can get into the fight if we wish," Sergeant Lawrence spoke up. "What's say we advance down the slope and hit the Old Guard in the flank?"

"I like the way you think, sergeant," Colborne grinned. He then addressed the battalion, *"The 52nd Oxfordshire will advance!"*

"Third line...up!" James shouted as yet another merciless volley slammed home into the hapless ranks of Napoleon's Imperial Guard.

"That's five, sir!" the regimental sergeant major said from his position with the colours, just behind his battalion commander.

James nodded and held his sword high. Wellington was now riding up behind him.

"Up!" the Duke shouted. *"Up Guards, and at them!"* Wellington then rode over to where General Maitland had remounted his horse, behind what remained of his brigade.

"The Imperial Guard has fallen back!" the Duke said. "Advance on them, they won't stand!"

"Colonel Askew, Captain Webster!" Maitland shouted. "Advance by battalions and break them!"

"3rd Battalion...bayonets ready!" James ordered, a similar ordered echoed by Colonel Askew to 2nd Battalion.

Drummers beat the cadence and bugles sounded the advance. James marched a few paces in front of his battalion, the regimental King's Colour just behind him. Just a few feet from where they had held their ground was littered with bodies of the French Imperial Guard; companies that had formed their front ranks had been completely annihilated. The far more numerous wounded cried in pain, their bodies torn asunder; men with smashed arms and legs, splintered bones protruding through the skin. Others had their guts splayed open, intestines strewn across the ground that were now being trampled by the advancing redcoats. In the red glow of the slowly-setting sun it was the ultimate paradox; the glorious advance of the British Regiments of Foot Guards, with the colours waving proudly in the breeze, and at their feet hundreds of French soldiers who could not have been more badly maimed if they'd been put through a slaughterhouse.

Chapter XXVI: Disintegration
Field of Waterloo
18 June 1815
8:00 pm

Sir Rowland Hill implores the Imperial Guard to surrender

James could see to his left the other regiments of the Guards Division advancing as well. His heart soared, despite the stomach-turning carnage at his feet. The drum cadence was steady, his battalion keeping its discipline as they advanced down the slope. Then to his dismay, the Imperial Guard halted its retreat and was reforming.

"Damn it all," he said quietly. Despite seeing the Imperial Guard reorganizing for another assault, with numbers far greater than theirs, Captain James Webster and his men continued their advance. All were at the brink of falling over from utter exhaustion, and in that moment, few cared anymore if they fell and never rose again.

"Stand, men of the Imperial Guard!" Marshal Ney shouted as he walked amongst their ranks. "The Guard dies, but it does not retreat nor does it surrender!"

341

Having time to regain their composure, soldiers began to reform the columns. Ney, deprived of a horse and not even bothering to draw his sword, sprinted from one battalion to the next, attempting to rally the survivors to assault once more. He could now see the advancing British lines, and he was heartened when he noted how few their numbers were.

"Look!" he shouted. "The English advance on us with less than half our strength! Their bayonets are forward, their ammunition spent! Stand your ground, Middle Guard! One more push and we'll have them beaten!"

"Vive la France!" General Morvan shouted, which was echoed by the men of the Imperial Guard. Anxious now to avenge their slain and shattered friends, many of whom had served together for nearly twenty years, they gave a loud battle cry and brandished their bayonets once more.

The Imperial Guard were now reforming, with men in the front dropping to a knee and firing up at the advancing British lines. As men started to fall, the entire brigade faltered. With no ammunition left, and with the enemy outnumbering still at least two-to-one, James knew that even a bayonet charge rushing downhill would not be enough.

"God damn it!" he shouted before turning to his bugler. "Sound the recall! Drummers, beat a reverse cadence up the slope."

It was maddening to see their final victory suddenly snatched away. James could not believe that they had broken the Imperial Guard, only to have their numbers prove too few when attempting to finish them. Still, he was not one for throwing away lives needlessly, and in that moment of overwhelming defeat his only thought was trying to save as many of his men as he could.

"Sir, down there!" a soldier shouted, pointing off to their right. "By God, it's the Oxfordshire!"

"By God, so it is," James said quietly with a sigh of relief. He then shouted, *"Battalion...halt! Everyone down!"* They may have been few in number with no ammunition left, but there would be no retreat. The 52nd Oxfordshire was by far the largest battalion in the entire army; their numbers as many as both battalions of the 1st Guards Brigade combined. They were also relatively fresh, having only faced light opposition most of the day. The reforming French columns were oblivious to them until the very last, when a long line of muskets fired into their flank.

Ney's relief turned to dismay and defeat as the crash of musket fire tore into the left flank of the reformed Imperial Guard. Men cried out in surprise and pain as they were cut down. Men on the flank attempted to form up and return fire on the flanking English, but it was proving to be in vain.

"Merde!" an officer shouted. "We've been flanked!"

The Oxfordshire had suffered relatively light casualties when compared to the savagery the British Guards had taken and so were fresh with a full complement of ammunition. Their volleys were measured and deliberate, each slamming home into the now-exhausted and demoralized files of the French. There was now nothing that Ney or Morvan could do. Their men saw nothing but death around them, and even the bravest could no longer stand.

"Lost!" another officer shouted. "All is lost!"

As if in penance for his cowardly speech, the officer was torn apart in the subsequent volley of musket fire from the Oxfordshire, his face and torso torn apart as he fell twitching violently.

"What can we do, marshal?" Morvan asked, all hope lost in his eyes.

"Die," Ney replied calmly.

Bitterness creased Napoleon's face as he scanned the ridge through his telescope. Whereas the Middle Guard should have pressed past La Haye Sainte, with the battalions of the Old Guard ready to follow in reserve, they were now inexplicably fleeing back down the slope, advancing ranks of redcoats in pursuit. He grimaced as he watched an English regiment fire into the flank of his retreating force.

"It isn't possible," Soult lamented, watching through his own telescope. "By God, sire, the Imperial Guard has broken!"

Though he wished to lash out at his chief-of-staff for making such a blasphemous remark, the emperor could see with his own eyes that it was true. As if to add insult to injury, a rider rushed over from Lobau's corps.

"Sire, the Prussians have taken Plancenoit!" the man said in a panic. "Their numbers were too many, and our right flank is collapsing."

Napoleon stood with his telescope clutched in his hands, which were now clasped behind his back. His head was bowed slightly, eyes fixed on the scene of retreating French soldiers and the hated lines of redcoats with their flags flying in defiance. He knew Lobau would not be able to hold the Prussians indefinitely, yet he had gambled that it would not matter once Wellington was beaten. Yet far from beaten, Wellington seemed to mock him. In a final blow, the emperor could see, even without his telescope, a lone redcoat climbing to the top of La Haye Sainte. The man threw down the French tricolour with utter contempt, replacing it with the British Union Jack.

"Have the Old Guard form a rear holding action!" Soult said to an aide. "They must delay the English long enough for us to evacuate the emperor."

"I'm not leaving, Soult," Napoleon said, his gaze still fixed on the chaos in the distance. "If France falls, then I will die with her today."

Soult swallowed hard and shook his head. "Forgive me, sire." He then snapped his fingers and a dozen grenadiers of the Old Guard surrounded the emperor, several of whom grabbed him under the arms and started to drag him away.

"No!" Napoleon screamed. *"Not like this! Not like this! God damn you, Soult!"*

"Sire, we cannot let the English or the Prussians take you!" Soult implored, tears streaming down his face. He whispered, "Please, forgive me…"

Despite his curses and protestations, the men of the Old Guard carried their beloved emperor to a waiting coach. Fearless men, hardened by years of war and devoted to the bitter end, yet now they wept openly. They could not save both Napoleon's dignity and his life, and yet they would not allow him to fall to their enemy.

Exhausted and resigned to his fate, Napoleon gave one last cry as he was carried into a waiting carriage. *"Vive la France!"*

Prussian soldiers capturing Plancenoit

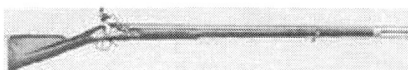

"Sir, the entire French Army has collapsed!" Uxbridge said with glee as he rode over to Wellington.

The Duke was doing his best to stifle a fit of laughter, brought on by frayed nerves and overwhelming relief. All along the ridge he could see regiments advancing of their own accord. It was as if the army had one mind, and that was to drive Bonaparte completely from the field.

"I'll be damned, Uxbridge," Wellington chuckled, "if I ever saw 30,000 men run a race!"

"Shall we give the order for the entire line to advance?" Sir Rowland Hill asked, having joined the Duke after watching his 52nd Oxfordshire Regiment finish breaking the French Imperial Guard.

345

"But of course," Wellington replied. "The whole line will advance as far as La Belle Alliance. We'll let Blucher and his Prussian Cavalry conduct the pursuit after."

"Very good, sir!" Hill replied with a salute. He started to ride away, but turned back for a moment. "Well done, Arthur. You turned the page of history today."

Wellington nodded and grinned broadly at Hill's assessment. He and Uxbridge continued to watch as their entire army advanced in a mass of red jackets, as well as those of their allied troops. The Dutch-Belgians, Hanoverians, and Brunswickers were as much a part of the victory as the British. And for all his differences with his Germanic allies, the Duke would be eternally grateful to Marshal Blucher and the Prussians, who under their black flags were driving in the French right wing and ending Napoleon's hopes of reforming his now disintegrating army.

The occasional bark of cannon was the only thing to interrupt the scene of glory that played out below. The survivors of Wellington's staff lined the ridge, their faces full of relief and joy and the defeat of Bonaparte. The whistling of an incoming shell alerted the Duke, who looked about to try and guess where it came from in the brief moment before it shattered against a rock near where he and Uxbridge sat on their horses. Wellington's horse, Copenhagen, whinnied and reared up, having been scraped by a shard of metal. The Duke quickly patted himself down and made certain he had not been hit; the shell having burst unnervingly close. He then glanced over at Uxbridge, whose expression was one of shock as it turned white.

"By God, sir," his second said, "I seem to have lost my leg."

Wellington looked down and could see that the earl's right leg was a shattered mass of blood and protruding bone fragments. "By God, sir," he replied. "So you have." Staff officers quickly gathered around and helped the stricken Uxbridge from his mount. Despite the horrifying maiming of his leg, he made not a sound. Wellington marvelled at how he had been but a few feet away, his horse had been grazed, and yet he himself was once again unscathed.

He glanced up to the heavens. "The hand of God was on me once more," he said quietly. "I hope it will be for the last time." He took a breath and looked through his telescope at the chaos unfolding where his advancing army was now overrunning the French positions. So many of their enemy were refusing to surrender and were being bayoneted as a result. Whatever joy the Duke felt in his moment of triumph was quickly turning to sorrow.

"This is no longer a battle," an aide lamented, his face full of sadness and pity. "We're committing murder, your grace."

"I pray," Wellington said quietly as he spurred Copenhagen forward, "that I've fought my last battle."

"Allez-vous donner?" James implored a French officer, asking him to yield as he pointed his sword at the man.

The Frenchman, who James guessed was at least a major, leaned against a cannon. His uniform was bloodied, and his face covered in burns and soot. The man was completely exhausted, yet he still held onto his sword.

James raised his up and asked once more in French, "Allez-vous donner? *Will you yield?"*

"Je pisse sur vous, l'Anglais!" the French officer retorted. "I piss on you, Englishman!" He then spat at the captain, though he did not raise his sword to defend himself.

While James respected valour and extreme courage, he was contemptuous of officers who would needlessly throw away their own lives, as well as those of their men. His rage boiling over, he drew his pistol and fired it into the French officers face, which exploded in a spray of blood and bone as the twitching corpse fell back against the cannon. All around him, similar scenes played out. Lieutenant Shanahan stood over an enemy soldier who was on his knees. The Irish officer's eyes were wet with tears as he held his sword high and begged the man to surrender. When the contemptuous enemy soldier gave Patrick a similar response to that James had gotten, he gave a shout of both anger and grief as he slashed the man across the throat.

"What the fuck is wrong with these goddamn frogs?" Corporal O'Connor shouted as he stabbed an enemy soldier on the ground. "They've lost! Why will they not surrender?" The young soldier's

eyes were filled with tears. Like Wellington's aide, he felt they were no longer fighting a battle.

The slaughter of these men was nothing short of murder, yet it was murder they brought upon themselves in their refusal to yield.

"These men are of the Old Guard," James said with a mixture of both admiration and contempt. "The Guard dies, but it does not surrender."

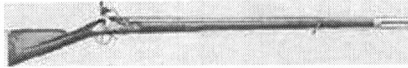

"La Garde meurt mais ne se rend pas!" an Imperial Guard officer echoed in French.

Sir Rowland Hill, at Wellington's urging, had approached under a flag of truce the remnants of the Imperial Guard, who were holding in place until Napoleon could escape. The rebuking officer, later identified as General Claude-Etienne Michel, was gravely wounded and being propped up by a pair of fellow Guardsmen. Blood and spittle ran out of the corner of his mouth, and his eyes soon rolled into the back of his head. His act of defiance taking the last of his strength, he collapsed into the arms of his soldiers.

"I say to you one last time," Sir Rowland said, "His Grace, the Duke of Wellington, admires your valour and devotion to your emperor and to France. The battle is done. You have done all that honour and valour can ever ask. His grace implores you not to throw away your lives needlessly. *Will you yield?"*

The sun was starting to go down in the west, adding an ethereal feel to the scene of death. The ground was strewn with corpses and badly wounded men. Their pitiful sight moved Sir Rowland, and the soldiers of his corps who now surrounded the remnants of the Imperial Guard. In his eyes, any further deaths would be utterly pointless and an affront to human decency; that is, if any could still be found amongst the thousands of broken souls and mutilated bodies. Just as he felt he was going to have to order his men to slaughter what remained of the once proud French Imperial Guard, a lone soldier, utterly dejected and spent, threw down his musket. The man then fell to his knees, his hands over his face as he wept uncontrollably. Within moments, other weapons clattered to the ground, followed by cries of defeat and sorrow. But for Sir Rowland Hill, the sobs of the Imperial Guard came as an immense relief. He said a silent prayer of thanks that he would not have to order another death this day.

Chapter XXVII: Next to a battle lost…
Field of Waterloo
18 June 1815
9:00 pm

French dead near a cannon

The sun had set by the time Wellington found Marshal Blucher. The two men found each other at Napoleon's headquarters, near La Belle Alliance. Accompanying the Marshal was General Gneisenau, who despite his lack of trust or confidence in Wellington and the English, was in that moment almost in a sense of admiration for the Duke. Wellington was accompanied by Sir Rowland Hill, General Muffling, and the handful of men from his staff that were not dead or gravely injured.

"Battle is won!" Blucher said in his heavy accent, fist raised high in triumph.

Wellington nodded and then turned to Muffling. "Tell the Marshal that I am grateful for his assistance. Tell him we would like to give him the honour of conducting the pursuit against Bonaparte."

Gneisenau gave a grin of what one may think of as contempt, given that Wellington, in essence, admitted that his army was completely spent and unable to pursue the French. The general's loyalty to Blucher made him keep his silence.

Blucher furrowed his brow as Muffling translated Wellington's words for him. His face then brightened. "Yes, yes, pursuit!" he said excitedly, raising his fist once more.

He spoke quickly to Gneisenau who nodded and wheeled his horse about, shouting orders to the Prussian Cavalry officers who'd assembled a short ways from La Belle Alliance. The old Cossack extended his hand to Wellington, which the Duke graciously accepted. With nothing left to say, Wellington turned his horse about and rode back towards his shattered, yet triumphant army.

There was a general sense of listlessness as the Duke rode past the men; no cheers or shouts of exultation. Details of men lethargically searched through the piles of bodies in an attempt to find any survivors amongst the carnage. An occasional musket or pistol shot echoed across the field, driving off the roving bands of scavengers and looters that fell upon every battlefield since the beginning of warfare. Though historians and scholars would speak of the glories won at Waterloo, at the end of the battle all Wellington could see were the exhausted and vacant expressions worn by those who would spend the rest of their lives trying to make some sense of it all.

James had never felt so utterly spent in his life. Many of his men, what few remained, were sporting French greatcoats taken from the enemy dead and wounded.

"No sense freezing to death in the rain again," Sergeant Donaldson explained as James walked in silence. "It's not like the frogs will be needing these anymore."

Even with the battle now over and night coming on, James knew that for his men, at least those who could still stand, their day was not done. Soldiers were disarming and leading enemy prisoners away, while others were starting the arduous process of trying to find wounded friends amongst the thousands of bodies that littered the landscape. James saw the adjutant talking with the regimental sergeant major. The RSM was reading off a number of lists. James already knew what they contained.

"Casualty tallies as best we can manage, sir," the RSM said as James joined them.

It was still overwhelming for him, having to now command the entire battalion; whereas just two days prior he'd had but one of its

351

ten companies. He took the parchment from the adjutant who was quick to explain.

"This is our total strength and losses from both Quatre Bras and Waterloo," he said. "We left Braine-le-Comte with 40 officers and 982 other ranks, 1,022 total. Combined losses for both battles are 106 dead, 491 wounded."

James was silent as he looked through the names compiled by the company commanders. He particularly lamented the losses of men from his former company, as they had been closest to him over the previous year. He failed to fight back the tear that ran down his cheek when Patrick handed him the list of those lost from the 1st Company:

Lieutenant Edward Grose – killed
Ensign William Barton – wounded (serious)
Sergeant Thomas Billings – killed
Corporal David O'Connor – wounded
Private Douglas Freemantle – wounded
Private John Wallace – wounded
Private Eric Adams – killed
Private James Collins – wounded (serious)
Private John Collins – wounded
Private Arthur Davis – wounded
Private Peter Davis – wounded
Private John Williams – wounded (serious)
Private John Smith – wounded
Private Richard Vaughn – killed
Private Mitchell Lewis – wounded
Private Miles Harper – wounded

There were others, but James could not bring himself to read further. Of the near-five hundred wounded in the battalion, he wondered how many would succumb to their injuries, and how many of those will be so badly maimed that they would lose arms, legs, and otherwise be disabled. Such images had haunted him after the Peninsula battles, in particular Badajoz. The only solace he took was in the knowledge that Napoleon's army had taken it far worse than they had. Having to advance over open ground against a foe who had a decisive terrain advantage, combined with repeated assaults against several fortified strongholds, and it was reasonable to surmise that whatever losses Wellington's army had suffered, Napoleon's were substantially larger; at least double, if not more. And with the Prussian Cavalry now in pursuit, still more would be cut down before this hateful affair was over.

As he walked through the area around the French cannon, where the 3/1st Foot Guards was making ready to bivouac for the night, James came upon the light company, which were forming the skirmish line and pickets near La Belle Alliance. He was glad to see his old friend, Daniel Roberts, had managed to escape death once more. The commander of the Light Company still carried the French musket he had taken before the final attack.

"Still alive, old friend?" James asked with a smile, taking his fellow captain's hand.

"A good thing Boney and the frogs are broken," Daniel said. "I talked with the quartermaster, and he said we went through the entire regiment's supply of ammunition. Half my lads have maybe a couple cartridges, the rest nothing at all."

"It's that way everywhere," James replied. "I've spoken with Colonel Askew, and his men are in the same predicament as us. We don't anticipate an enemy counterattack, but then again, I doubt that we'll just sit here either. We've won a decisive victory, and Boney is on the run. However, that does not mean the French are completely beaten."

"I hope Blucher drives the frogs all the way back to Paris," Daniel grumbled. "I won't lie, James, I'm tired. I thought I'd seen my share of death in the Peninsula, yet even Badajoz could not have prepared me for this day. By God, did you see the Imperial Guard as we shot them to pieces?"

"Yes, Daniel, I was there," James said with a trace of sarcasm.

Daniel did not seem to notice. "On and on they came," he continued, staring past his friend. "The strangest thing happened towards the end, just before they broke. They'd gotten so close to us that I was down to having to use my pistol. I remember looking one poor fellow in the eye, just before I raised my weapon and shot him in the forehead. He was that close. I said to him, *'S'il vous plaît pardonnez-moi'*, please forgive me. And I will swear before the Almighty Himself that the man nodded, as if he acknowledged that he was about to die, and I had his forgiveness. Never did he miss a step, on he came! I hope I can one day face death with even half the dignity that brave man demonstrated."

For the Emperor of the French, there was no dignity in his defeat. Though he had wept briefly after the grenadiers of the Imperial Guard forced him into the carriage, exhaustion and the recurring pain in his stomach prevented more tears from coming. He then desperately wished for sleep, hoping that perhaps this would all have been a nightmare. Until the end of his days, Napoleon would never fully comprehend how he had lost the Battle of Waterloo.

"Wellington was not a better general than me," he said quietly as he watched the rain starting to beat down on the carriage window while it raced through the night. "I have faced far better opponents and still been triumphant. My army was far superior to his. He had nothing but Dutch militia and English shopkeepers. How could this have happened?"

It was incomprehensible for Napoleon that he would be denied what he foresaw as his destiny. If he was not meant to die on the Isle of Elba, yet he had just suffered a terrible defeat at the hands of Wellington, what could it all mean? With no one except the handful of grenadiers who'd spirited him away, he had no way of knowing the disposition of his army. Certainly their casualties had been fearful, yet Napoleon had yet to realize that compounding the volume of dead and wounded was that so many of the survivors had thrown down their arms and fled, leading to his entire army's near disintegration.

"This is not over," he said to himself as he stared out the window into the blackness.

A change in the sound of the wheels going over a bridge told the emperor that he was crossing the River Sambre. It seemed that Soult had directed the carriage to take him all the way back to Paris.

A smattering of rain was starting to fall as Wellington rode in silence. Though victorious, his army looked anything but. Exhaustion and devastating casualties had rendered them completely spent. Details were already forming to dispose of the Anglo-Allied dead, which numbered in the thousands. The bodies of the French dead and wounded were being plundered for anything of value. Perhaps the most significant find was that most of the French had their greatcoats, and the British took them with eagerness. It was a distinct contrast to see French greatcoats over British red tunics, but Wellington could hardly fault the men. After all, it looked like the weather was about to turn sour once more, and at least now his men would have some reprieve from the incessant rain. As he rode to where the infantry squares had held against Marshal Ney and the French Cavalry attack, he was appalled by the sheer numbers of dead and maimed. Among the fallen the Duke came across was Private Eric Adams, who had been slain pleading for both sides to cease killing each other. His skull was crushed, numerous bones shattered from where his corpse had been trampled by dozens of armoured cuirassiers.

For the first time in eighteen hours, Wellington dismounted his horse and knelt alongside a number of the bodies. He removed his hat, and for one of the only times in his life, he placed a hand over his eyes and openly wept; sorrow and complete exhaustion overwhelming him. In that moment he briefly ceased to think of his men as the infamous 'scum of the earth', and instead saw them for what they were. They were simply men, soldiers doing their duty. The Duke had taken cover in one of the squares during Ney's cavalry attack, and he had seen Private Adams' piteous display before he was brutally slain. Now Wellington understood the soldier's plight, and he, in a way, viewed the dead as the fortunate ones.

After several minutes, he managed to regain his composure and stood. He put his hat back on and looked to see Sir Rowland Hill standing behind him, guiding his own horse.

"I'll tell you something, Rowland," the Duke said. "Next to a battle lost, the saddest thing is a battle won."

Chapter XXVIII: Aftermath of Battle
Paris, France
22 June 1815

French cannon, captured at Waterloo
Displayed at the Tower of London

Despite the emperor forever damning him for not achieving the impossible task of coming to his aid at Waterloo, Emmanuel Grouchy had done a superb job of rallying the remnants of the Armee du Nord in and around Paris. Their numbers were few, as so many of the survivors had thrown down their weapons and were never seen again. Still, from a purely military standpoint, all was not lost. Both Wellington and the Prussians had suffered fearful losses in achieving their victory, and with so much of their ammunition and logistics stores exhausted, they were hardly in any condition to lay siege to Paris.

On this particular day, Napoleon was set to meet with the chambers and decide on how to proceed with the expulsion of the foreign troops from French soil. As he entered the great hall, he was first greeted by Louis-Nicolas Davout, the Minister of War. The emperor had, at first, sought to meet his younger brother Lucien, but Davout made certain he saw him first. The minister's grey hair was badly receding, which almost made him look comical, yet his manner was grim and serious.

"The chambers will not allow the war to proceed any further," he stated matter-of-factly.

"Nonsense!" Napoleon protested. "We've suffered a setback, yes, but we are far from beaten. The people will follow me, and if they do, so must the chambers."

"By God, sire, have you not seen the demeanour of our people?" Davout said. "They love you, but they are tired of war and all the inherent sufferings. Even now, those wounded souls not taken prisoner by the English have started to pour into Paris. The people weep for them."

"Would they rather weep for our wounded or allow the English and the Prussians to become masters of France?" Lucien Bonaparte interrupted, walking in from the back room. "Forgive me for being late, brother."

"I am glad you are here," Napoleon replied. "At least *someone* still believes in us, and in France." He glared sternly at Davout as he spoke.

Most of his generals, at least those not killed or captured, were still with the army, trying to bring some semblance of confidence and order to the survivors. The news from the east, that the Russian and Austrian forces had been checked, gave a much needed boost in morale. And for his own campaign in Belgium, he had won decisively at Charleroi, Ligny, and Wavre. Quatre Bras was, at worst, a tactical draw, and his only defeat had been Waterloo itself.

"I still believe in France," Davout retorted, "and so do the chambers. And the people would have followed you to hell itself, had you given them victory. But whether you will ever fully appreciate it or not, the truth is you lost. The nation rose to your banner one last time, and now tens-of-thousands lie dead or maimed, with no victory. I do not want to see the English destroy Paris!"

Napoleon stood with his hands clasped behind his back and stared at Davout until the minister became very uncomfortable.

"Leave us," the emperor said calmly, much to Davout's relief. "Tell the chambers that I will address them shortly."

The two brothers waited until they were certain Davout was out of earshot before they spoke once more.

"To hell with him and with the chambers!" Lucien spat. "I say we dissolve the chambers and appoint you dictator. At least then

there will be no squabbling old women interfering in our affairs."
He looked back at his brother.

Napoleon was still silent. His hands remained clasped behind his back, and he now stared at the floor. "Would Wellington destroy Paris?" His voice was much quieter, and it unnerved Lucien.

"We won't allow that English bastard within fifty miles of Paris!" Lucien stated firmly. "The army…"

"The army is but a shell of what it was just two weeks ago," Napoleon interrupted. "I may be able to rally enough of our people to defend Paris, but what then? If I do not have the support of the chambers, then the people will fracture rather than unite. I fear, dear brother, that France died when the Imperial Guard was broken at Waterloo. We may have stopped the Austrians and Russians, but as long as there is an influx of English coin, they will continue to send more troops against us. And despite how close the issue was at Waterloo, with thousands of English and Prussian soldiers lost, Wellington will be able to paint a fantastic piece of propaganda to make the people in England think he's won some sort of great victory over me. He will puff out his chest and claim to still be unbeaten in battle. Whatever the truth may be, the English will believe their beloved Duke to be the only man to defeat me in head-to-head battle on even terms. Far from being war weary, they will dive into the conflict like jackals on a stricken ox. The entire campaign hinged on destroying Wellington, and he still stands."

"What will you do then?" Lucien asked.

"Try and save our dynasty."

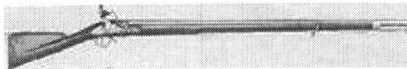

Though they had put a number of miles between themselves and the fields of Waterloo, Captain James Webster knew it would be with them for the rest of their lives. All told, his battalion had suffered more than 60% casualties during the actions at Quatre Bras and Waterloo; two engagements fought with such ferocity that his, and indeed many regiments, were largely combat ineffective. He'd received word that both Lieutenant Colonel Steward and Major D'Oyley would eventually recover from their injuries, so his assumption of command was to be temporary. Henry D'Oyley would be convalescing for about a month, Colonel Stewart twice as long. And even if they had perished, it would have been just a matter of time before a major with funds or another lieutenant colonel seeking a battalion command assumed the vacancy. For the time, though, Captain James Henry Webster led the 3rd Battalion of the 1st Regiment of Foot Guards, whose actions were already becoming the word of legend.

The weather in Belgium and northern France had finally started to cooperate, giving some reprieve to the men who were tired of the never-ending rain. It was late afternoon, and the army was bivouacked somewhere between Waterloo and Paris. James was not entirely certain if they were still in Belgium or had crossed into France. He pondered this as he walked towards the tent that was acting as the officers' mess when he was approached by General Maitland.

"General, sir," James said, saluting sharply. "A fine afternoon this is."

The general returned the courtesy. "We finally have ammunition. The quartermasters get little credit when they do well and are usually only mentioned when the men are complaining about cold rations or not enough socks, but by God they came through for us! The Duke of Richmond organized the escort and brought it down personally; there's only enough for a half-issue of ammunition per man, but it is still far better than marching into France with our muskets empty."

"I am grateful for the news, sir," James replied, matching the general's sense of relief. "Would you honour me by joining us in the battalion's mess this evening? There are plenty of empty chairs, I'm sad to say."

"I would, indeed, be honoured, sir," the general replied. He looked past James' shoulder. "It would seem the Duke of Richmond did not come alone."

James turned around and saw Richmond riding his horse towards them, on his way to see Wellington. His wife, Lady Charlotte, rode next to him. There was an entourage of soldiers and local government officials with them, as well as two of Richmond's daughters, Sarah and Georgiana, who had handed their horses to groomsmen and were walking through the camp. It was then that James noticed another woman with them.

"Apologies, sir," he said, turning to face the general. "But I fear an unexpected commitment will keep me from the officers' mess this evening."

"Of course," Maitland acknowledged. He nodded towards Lady Sarah. "There is a matter I must attend to as well."

James' heart soared as he saw the radiant smile on Emma's face as she walked slowly towards him. He removed his shako as he increased his step, unable to control his feelings of euphoria. He stopped just short of her, regaining his composure. He swallowed hard, unsure what to say, so he took her hand and kissed it. He breathed in her scent deeply, relishing the sweet fragrance that contrasted with the smells of filth and death he'd dealt with the past two weeks. Still unsure what to say, he kissed her gently on the lips, at first afraid she might pull away. It was a foolish thing to fear; indeed she seemed disappointed when after a moment he pulled his lips away from hers.

"I was so afraid I would not find you here," Emma said at last, laying her head on his shoulder for a moment and letting out a sigh. As she looked him in the eye, James saw hers were wet with tears. "We passed through Waterloo and La Belle Alliance. By God, what did they do to you? So many dead had not even been given a proper burial."

"There was no time," James said, shaking his head sadly. "We did what we could for the living, but then had to move on. We buried as many of our own fallen as we were able. Bonaparte's army took it far worse than us, and there was little we could do except separate out any of the wounded we could find."

"As long as I live, I will never forget the horrid sights and smells around Hougomont," Emma continued, with her eyes now downcast. "Charles had thought to perhaps use the house for the night, as it was late when we arrived."

"Dear God," James thought aloud, suddenly feeling for Emma. He would never forget the horrendous fighting that had gone on at Hougomont, but at least he did not have to deal with the mutilated bodies of the slain a week after they'd fallen. "I'm glad you've come, but I would rather you had not and spared you the horrors of what we've done."

"That men can do this to each other so willingly, I will never understand." Emma was having a hard time speaking at this point.

James could only guess at how decayed and rotten the more exposed bodies had become, particularly those left out in the sun. He'd seen corpses a week after a battle, and they not only stank, but were oftentimes blackened and bloated if left exposed in the sun and elements. "But for all that," James reasoned, "at least it was the French who yielded the field and not us. Even now it terrifies me to think what would have happened had we lost at Waterloo."

"We heard at least a dozen rumours before an official messenger arrived," Emma stated, taking James by the arm as they walked through the camp. "Most of the news was terrible, though thankfully exaggerated. Farmers, merchants, anyone wishing to draw attention to himself, or herself as it turned out a few times, came to Brussels with wild tales of what they had seen ever since all of you left the Duchess' ball."

"I daresay that will be the most famous ball ever," James conjectured. "As we left, I remembered wondering to myself how many of us would return."

"I was with Sarah when we received word about the Duke of Brunswick and poor Lord Hay," Emma added.

"How did she take it?" James asked. "I seem to remember her and Hay being rather fond of each other."

"Oh, she appreciated his military dashing," Emma replied. "And he was quite the attractive young man. Had he lived, well, one never knows. Her mother took it harder, I think, although that may have been because we received word at the same time that the Duke of Brunswick was killed. Charlotte and Charles were very close to him."

"How is Amy?" James asked suddenly.

Emma stopped and faced him, her face flush with embarrassment.

"I cannot believe I failed to even mention her," she stammered. Then, answering quickly, "She is fine, though the nanny says she cries for her papa a lot."

"I swore I would never leave her again," James remarked as he took Emma by the arm and started walking once more. "I feel for those suddenly widowed and orphaned...on both sides."

361

"You do not hate the French, do you?" Emma noted, laying her head on his shoulder as they passed rows of tents where men sat cleaning their weapons and kit.

"Hate not your enemy," James replied, echoing the words spoken by Private Eric Adams at Hougomont. "I respect them, especially the way they stood against us, both at Hougomont and then when the Imperial Guard made its final assault against us. Such discipline and valour!"

"And what did it get them, except an early grave," Emma retorted.

There was much anger now in her voice, and James sensed it had been building for a while.

"I'm sorry, my dear," Emma said after a moment. She then took and squeezed his hand in reassurance. "It just saddens me to no end to see what you and all those poor boys went through. When he was exiled, Bonaparte was lauded for his valour and personal virtue. Even your soldiers admired him."

"They still do," James concurred. "I overheard the Duchess of Richmond confess to Wellington that she was a bit of a Bonapartist."

"But if you admired each other, how could you all kill one another?" Emma asked.

James stopped abruptly, startling the young woman.

"I am sorry if I sound naïve, and if I have offended you."

"Not at all," James replied. "It's just that one of my men asked the same question. I will never forget as we fought back the cuirassiers from our squares, how one of my elite Guards soldiers completely lost it. This man was a hardened veteran, one of the best soldiers I've ever seen. Yet, at that moment, it became too much for him. He threw down his weapons and left the square, asking all of us how we could kill one another. He even made his plea to a cuirassier in French before the bastard split him open with his sabre."

"What was his name?" Emma asked. "I never see the names or stories behind those who fall."

"Private Eric Adams," James answered. "He was twenty-eight years old, married for six years, and had two little children. He was one of our bravest soldiers and best shots. According to Sergeant Donaldson, he shot five enemy soldiers at Quatre Bras and bayoneted two more, including a cuirassier. At Patrick Shanahan's request, Major D'Oyley made certain he was *mentioned in despatches*. I had hoped to get him a personal commendation from Wellington himself once this was over."

"Thank you for sharing that with me," Emma said quietly. "I never knew him, but my heart breaks for him and his family. Having Anne Shanahan's constant company reminded me that the ranks may come from the poorest classes of society, but they are still people. All we ever see are the numbers, unless of course a nobleman or someone of social importance like Lord Hay, falls in battle. The rest just don't matter to society."

"They never have," James added. "The soldiers in the ranks are a disposable asset, nothing more. It has always been that way, and as long as it remains in men's nature to murder one another, it always will be. I think the even greater tragedy is what happens to those who do survive their terrible injuries but are left disabled. They far outnumber the dead. When I was wounded at Badajoz and had to be evacuated back to England, I finally saw first-hand the terrible price we pay for military glory."

"And yet you came back," Emma observed. "You understood the terrible tragedy that is war, you faced an enemy you admired rather than hated, and you could have sold or resigned your commission at any time. And yet for all that, you still returned to the line."

"King George commands, and we obey," James replied. It was a non-answer, but the only one he had. It was really the only way he could justify it all to himself.

Emma kissed him on the cheek, her next words bringing both comfort and closure to the issue. "Over the hills and far away."

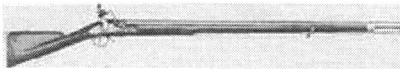

"I have abdicated in favour of my son," Napoleon stated. "What more do they want from me?" The now-former emperor was utterly defeated. His escape from Elba, advance through France, ousting of the hated Bourbons once more, and his battles at Charleroi, Wavre, Ligny, Quatre Bras, and Waterloo had all been in vain. His destiny, and that of France, had been stolen from him, like a thief in the night. By abdicating in favour of his young son, who was now Emperor Napoleon II, he had hoped to save both the Empire as well as his life.

"The Prussians will want your head," his aid, Count Bertrand said. "If they reach Paris before the English, then you are a dead man. There's nothing for it, sire, you must escape."

"And go where?" Napoleon asked, shaking his head. "Doubtless there will be a sizeable bounty on my head no matter where I go. I would seek asylum with the English, but the Prince Regent is so erratic that I know not if he would receive me, hand me over to the Prussians, or lock me in the Tower for his own amusement. There is nowhere in the world where I can be safe."

"America," Bertrand answered. "The wounds are still fresh between them and the English. Surely the Americans will welcome the Emperor of France with open arms! James Madison is not only their president, but also the man who wrote their constitution. I expect him to be a great admirer of yours, both militarily and for your revolutionary ideals."

"America," Napoleon echoed, allowing a trace of a smile for the first time since before Waterloo. He shrugged. "In the very least, President Madison will treat me more kindly than the Prince Regent of England or King Frederick of Prussia."

"We must away before long," Bertrand emphasized. "I will make the arrangements for our transport and find a suitable embarkation point. Once we clear the English blockades, there will be no stopping us."

Napoleon was rather fascinated by the thought of traveling to America. His health being as poor as it was, he finally had to accept that he would never rule France or any part of Europe ever again. He lamented the thought of leaving Europe altogether. However, he knew Bertrand was right. In the very least, the English would have him exiled to some remote hellhole worse than Elba. And if he were caught by the Prussians, he'd be lucky enough to avoid being guillotined before being brought to trial and subsequently shot. At least in America he could live out his days in peace. He suspected Bertrand's notions about President Madison to be genuine. Napoleon only lamented that George Washington, the very man who'd wrested the colonies away from King George, had died more than fifteen years prior.

"If I cannot live out my years in France, then let it be in America," he said to himself.

Chapter XXIX: The Pursuit
HMS Bellerophon
Off the coast of Rochefort, France
28 June 1815

Naval Captain Frederick Lewis Maitland

Despite the furore that had engulfed mainland Europe since the return of Napoleon, it was quiet around the Bay of Biscay. The HMS *Bellerophon*, a 74-gun, third-rate ship of the line, patrolled the gently rolling waters. Ever since Trafalgar, which the Bellerophon had taken part, the seas had unquestionably belonged to Britain. It may have cost Admiral Horatio Nelson his life, but it ensured his immortality and established British supremacy on the high seas, once and for all. *Rule Britannia* was more than just a patriotic anthem. It now signified the start of a new era, for indeed Britannia ruled the waves.

At the prow of the ship stood its captain, the thirty-seven year old Frederick Lewis Maitland. Though bearing the same uncommon last name as the British general who commanded the 1st Guards Brigade, the two were not related. A veteran of numerous actions and a variety of commands, he'd been given the Bellerophon soon after Napoleon's return. His orders had been simple; to prevent French corvettes from escaping the English blockade, and to garner the number and disposition of enemy warships in the area. Nothing was to get in or out of France.

Ten days before, whilst Napoleon and Wellington were locked in their death struggle at Waterloo, Maitland had detained a French supply vessel with ship's timber bound for the Rochefort garrison. His only other action had been three days later capturing, without incident, a transport ship carrying two companies from the French 9th Light Infantry. Such had been the extent of Bellerophon's actions during this period of renewed strife, and the captain had yet to receive any word at all from the continent. So it was with much interest when, on the early morning of the 28th, a lookout reported a corvette making its way from Rochefort.

"She's not making a run for it," Maitland noted as he watched the vessel through his telescope. Indeed, the small ship appeared to be moving directly for Bellerophon.

"I can see the tricolour on its flag," his first lieutenant said. "It's definitely a Bonapartist ship."

"Run out the guns and have a boarding party make ready," Maitland ordered as he collapsed his telescope. "Let's see what news the frogs bring us."

An hour later, the commander of the French ship, a very young midshipman, stood in Maitland's cabin where the captain sat behind his desk. The corvette had put up no resistance and had, in fact, seemed anxious to surrender to the British.

"Quelles sont les nouvelles du continent?" Maitland said, asking the French officer for news from the mainland.

"Bonaparte has been defeated by your Wellington," the young officer said in English, with only a slight accent. He eyes were downcast, and he had a sad air about him. He took a deep breath before looking Maitland in the eye. "France has fallen."

"When?" Maitland asked matter-of-factly, doing his best to conceal his excitement at the news.

"Ten days ago," the French officer replied. "At a place called Waterloo."

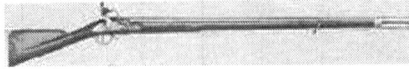

The city of Reims was a little over halfway between Charleroi and Paris. It had been captured and recaptured by the allies during the previous war so many times that the people were uncertain as to where their loyalties should lie. As it was, the last foreign occupiers had been Austrian and Russian, so to see the British redcoats in their city was a bit of a novelty to the populace.

One luxury the men had been deprived of, but now took full advantage, was the means for washing their clothes as well as themselves. Captain James Webster lay in a steaming hot bath tub while waiting for his uniforms to be dried after being thoroughly washed. The heated water did much to sooth his aching muscles and joints. As the Duke of Richmond and his entourage had elected to accompany Wellington's army, James had spent a lot more time with Emma, who surprisingly showed up in James' room, carrying some towels that she'd taken from the maidservant.

"Not disturbing you, I hope," she said with a playful laugh, startling James out of his half stupor. His face turned red, and unsure what else to do, he attempted to lower himself deeper into the tub.

"N…no," he stammered. "You're not disturbing me; just startled me a bit is all. Are you certain it is *proper*, us being together like this?"

"A friend of yours said something to me once," Emma said. "It was Edward Grose, God rest him. He said to me that if there was anything between you and I, that one could never call it improper."

"I remember that," James replied with a sad smile, "for he said the same to me. I miss him, you know. Mind you, I miss all of my boys who we lost during those terrible days, but there was something special about Edward. In retrospect, he was like a younger brother to me. I guess I took him for granted, because only now that he's gone do I realize how much he meant to me."

"I hear William Barton lost a leg," Emma said.

"It's true," James confirmed. "He was the first to fall as we advanced on the Bossu Wood at Quatre Bras. What makes it even more tragic is that it was our own cannon that struck him down."

"He was a pompous fool, but still I would not wish that upon anyone," Emma added.

"What's even more significant was that he gave Patrick Shanahan his sword after the battle," James remarked. "It was his way of making amends, as well as acknowledging Patrick as a proper officer. His body may be broken, but perhaps William Barton will make a fine gentleman after all."

"James, I took the liberty of picking up your uniforms with mine," Daniel Roberts said from the outer room as he stepped in, carrying James' tunic. He was startled by the sight of Emma. "Oh, beg your pardon, Miss Capel."

"Not at all, Daniel," she laughed with a curtsey. She then turned back to James. "Will you dine with us tonight?"

"Delighted!" James said, his head barely visible over the side of the tub as Emma left the two officers. James peered over the side.

Daniel was stifling a fit of laughter. He cleared his throat and held up his friend's tunic. It was battered and worn, but at least it was clean. "There's no place to hang this, so shall I just leave it on the bed?"

"Perfect," James replied. "And Daniel, nothing improper was going on here."

"James," his friend said, shaking his head, "even if there was something happening between you two, it could never be deemed improper."

"By God," James said as he abruptly sat upright in the tub with a splash. "Did Edward say that to everyone we know?"

"He did," Daniel confessed, his previously boisterous demeanour replaced with a trace of sadness, which James matched.

"Damn, I will miss him."

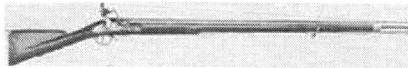

Two days later, the Bellerophon's crew captured a second corvette, this one bearing a letter that was unaddressed and without any names or subscription. Captain Maitland furrowed his brow in contemplation as he read its contents. It was in English, though from the grammar he could hazard that it was not written by an Englishman.

With great degree of certainty, being informed that Bonaparte might have come last night through this city from Paris, with the new Mayor of Bordeaux, with a view to flight, by the mouth of this river, or La Teste, the author of the last note sent by Mr (illegible) hastily drops these few lines, to give the British Admiral advice of such intention, that he may instantly take the necessary steps, in order to seize the man. His ideas will certainly have brought him to think it natural, that the British stations will be less upon their guard in this quarter than anywhere else.

It is supposed the British Admiral is already informed of the Grand Army being totally defeated and destroyed, the abdication of Bonaparte, &c. and the arrival of the allies near the Capital. An attempt should be made on this Coast, with no less than 8,000 men altogether. Immediate steps are wanted to put a stop to the supposed flight.

Should the attempt be made on the Coast from La Teste to Bordeaux, an immediate diversion should be made on this side; the success is beyond any doubt.

A sharp eye must be kept on all American vessels, and particularly on the Susquehannah, of Philadelphia, Captain Caleb Cushing; General Bertand and another goes with him. The two entrances of Bordeaux and La Teste must be kept close; a line or two is expected, on the return of the bearer from the Admiral, or Chief Officer on the Station. As this is writing, the news is spread generally, that the Duc de Berri and Lord Wellington are in Paris.

"What do you think, sir?" his first lieutenant asked. "The writing is clearly from a Frenchman, but with not so much as a name attached to it, we have no way of knowing who it is from."

"And conveniently, the name from the previous letter is illegible," Maitland added. "This could be actionable intelligence or it could all be a ruse."

"What are your orders then, sir?"

"Signal the Myrmidon and Cephalus," the captain ordered his boatswain. "Have their captains meet me here for dinner."

"Yes, sir."

Frederick spent the remainder of the afternoon contemplating the contents of the letter. It was clearly meant for Admiral Hotham, however, the French had no way of knowing where he may be, so all they could do was hand the message on to the nearest British vessel. Communications at sea were more arduous than on land, where all one needed was a single man with a fast horse to pass messages on. With the Royal Navy scattered all along the French coasts, communication was haphazard at best. Maitland wasn't sure if Admiral Hotham had even received word yet regarding Napoleon's defeat at Waterloo, and if he did, what else had he heard that Maitland had not?

It was night when the captains of the two other vessels boarded the Bellerophon. Maitland met them in the ornate main cabin, where a servant offered them a glass of cabernet. They were joined by the senior officers of all three ships, who gathered around the large table.

"To the fall of Napoleon," Maitland said, raising his glass, which the other captains did in return.

"To the fall of Napoleon," the men echoed in unison.

Aside from the decanter and a few delicacies, the only other thing on the long table was an oversized map of the region. The position of British warships was noted all along the coastline, as well as those of enemy vessels that still remained at anchor in various ports.

"Bonaparte has been defeated and is now on the run," Maitland stated. "He cannot remain in France any longer; that much is certain. The question now is where will he run to?"

"America," one of the captains spoke up. "It is the only place that makes any sense."

"I agree," the other added. "Nowhere in Europe will Napoleon feel safe. Doubtless he will be quite the novelty amongst our former colonists."

Maitland's face twitched at the remark. "I have had similar thoughts. That is why we must keep a vigilant eye on any American vessels operating around France. We cannot simply board every one of their ships conducting business with the French, but we must make it absolutely clear to them that any attempts to smuggle out the deposed French emperor will be treated as an act of war."

"We just finished a war with them," the first captain said. "I don't think they have the stomach for another."

"Agreed," Maitland concurred. "They may have beaten Ned Pakenham at New Orleans, but they suffered just as ignominious of a defeat when they attempted to take Canada from us. Besides, whether they admit it openly or not, they are still smarting from the fact that the bottom dregs of the British army burned their precious Washington to the ground. They will not risk His Majesty unleashing the very man who defeated Bonaparte on them. However, should the emperor escape on his own and ask for asylum in America, then they are perfectly within their rights to grant it to him."

"Where then, sir, do you surmise Napoleon will attempt to leave from?" the second captain asked. "Whatever his intended destination, he must still escape from France."

"Bordeaux," the first captain answered, pointing to the map. "It is the only port that makes any sense, and this letter you have even states as much. Smaller embarkation points have too little sea traffic to provide any sort of cover from our blockades. We must take what vessels you need to Bordeaux immediately and bring the Monster to His Majesty as a prize."

"Yes," Maitland replied. "We will send the *Myrmidon* to Bordeaux and *Cephalus* to Aracasson. However, I will remain off Rochefort with the Bellerophon."

"You really believe Bonaparte intends to depart from there?" one of the men asked, raising an eyebrow. "You risk handing the glory off to one of us should you be proven wrong."

"It is a risk I accept," Maitland replied. "And yes, I do believe that Napoleon will try and escape via Rochefort. This letter alludes to a previous one that reached Admiral Hotham, yet we have not heard from him personally, so this cannot be verified. This could also be an attempt to have our ships concentrate around Bordeaux while Napoleon escapes via another embarkation point. The name on this damn letter looks like it's been deliberately smudged out, so we have no idea who it's from."

"Napoleon will fear the Prussians," another officer spoke up. "Perhaps if he senses they are closing in on him, he may decide to more readily accept surrendering to us."

"Whatever move he makes, it will come sooner rather than later," Maitland added.

Chapter XXX: Imperial Amnesty
HMS Bellerophon
Off the coast of Rochefort, France
10 July 1815

Napoleon aboard the HMS Bellerophon

The Lords Commissioners of the Admiralty having every reason to believe that Napoleon Bonaparte meditates his escape, with his family, from France to America, you are hereby required and directed, in pursuance of orders from their Lordships, signified to me by Admiral the Right Honourable Viscount Keith, to keep the most vigilant look-out for the purpose of intercepting him; and to make the strictest search of any vessel you may fall in with; and if you should be so fortunate as to intercept him, you are to transfer him and his family to the ship you command, and there keeping him in careful custody, return to the nearest port in England with all possible expedition; and on your arrival you are not to permit any communication whatever with the shore, except as herein after

*directed; and you will be held responsible for keeping the whole
transaction a profound secret, until you receive their Lordships'
further orders.*

Rear Admiral Sir Henry Hotham, K.C.B.

For Captain Frederick Maitland of His Majesty's Royal Navy,
the order from his superior verified that he'd been right to dispatch
his ships as he had. This despatch had reached him three days
before, just after another message denoting that Bonaparte's
intended debarkation point was still unknown. This told Frederick
that the situation was quite fluid, and clearly Sir Henry Hotham
had received updated intelligence after sending the first message.
Per the instructions from the admiral, the ship carrying the
message, the *HMS Slaney*, was now patrolling the waters around
Rochefort along with the Bellerophon. A previous despatch had
also recorded intelligence that Bonaparte had two frigates under his
disposal with which to make good his escape. There were two such
vessels clearly in the captain's view as he eyed the port through his
telescope.

"There they are," he said to his first lieutenant.

"If those are indeed the frigates Admiral Hotham spoke of then,
that means the deposed Emperor of France is within our grasp," his
subordinate stated with a grin of triumph. The noose was
tightening around Bonaparte, and with British warships blockading
every possible avenue of escape, Maitland reasoned he had to
know that it was futile to run any further.

"Schooner approaching, sir!" the voice of a lookout shouted.

Again, this vessel was not attempting to flee past the English
blockade, but rather came bearing a message from the emperor
himself.

Sir,

*The Emperor Napoleon having abdicated the throne of France,
and chosen the United States of America as a retreat, is, with his
suite, at present embarked on board the two frigates which are in
this port, for the purpose of proceeding to his destination. He
expects a passport from the British Government, which has been
promised to him, and which induces me to send the present flag of*

truce, to demand of you, Sir, if you have any knowledge of the above-mentioned passport, or if you think it is the intention of the British Government to throw any impediment in the way of our voyage to the United States. I shall feel much obliged by your giving me any information you may possess on the subject.

I have directed the bearers of this letter to present to you my thanks, and to apologise for the trouble it may cause.

I have the honour to be,
Your Excellency's most obedient, etc. etc.
Grand Marshal Count Bertrand

"I have no knowledge of any promise of passport from His Majesty's government," Maitland said when he finished reading.

"I understand you must be on strict orders from your government to try and intercept the emperor," one of the men spoke up in heavily accented English. "But answer me this; supposing the emperor were to depart in another vessel, a *neutral* one? Will the English risk violating the sovereignty of another nation?"

"There will be no need for that," Maitland replied as he scanned the letter once more. "You must understand, sir, that this letter is specifically addressed to the commanding admiral of this fleet. I am not him. He is Sir Henry Hotham, and he is currently in Quiberon Bay. You are correct in that as our nations are still in a state of war, I cannot allow any French warship to pass out of these waters. And unless Admiral Hotham is aware of said passport for the emperor, and without his authorization, I cannot allow *any* vessel with such a personage of consequence to pass, regardless of what flag she flies. Not to worry, I will forward your despatch with all due haste. I will give this reply in writing as well, and I do ask for the emperor's patience as we await Admiral Hotham's reply."

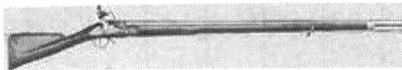

There was a sense of relief, yet also uncertainty in the air. Napoleon had fled from Paris but had yet to be found. Rumours

376

abounded, though word had yet to reach them from the Bellerophon. As the victorious Anglo-Allied Army marched through France, what James sensed most was a sense of weariness from the French people.

"Clearly Boney's return was not as universally hailed as he would have had us believe," Daniel Roberts said as he rode up next to his acting battalion commander.

The faces of the peasant farmers and traveling merchants they passed showed the strain that years of war had taken on the populace of France. It contrasted sharply to the people of England, who, despite their own troubles, had been spared having their lands and homes invaded by a foreign army. And for the French, no ideals, however just and revolutionary they were, could withstand decades of brutal war. They scarcely noticed the marching columns of redcoats and appeared almost indifferent to the British flags that were paraded along their roads to the tune of English bands and Scottish regimental pipe and drums.

"I'm glad to have you with me, Daniel," James said with a tired smile. "I would hate to have to try and lead this battalion, what's left of it, by myself. I am surprised that you have not assumed command."

The other captain could only shrug nonchalantly. "Henry chose you to take control of one of the wings, and Maitland gave you the battalion when he fell. Honestly, I would not have traded places with you out there."

Though Daniel had three years seniority over his friend, the bad fortune that he'd been deployed forward with the light company had made him unavailable to assume command when Major D'Oyley fell. James had placed him and the grenadier captain temporarily in charge of the company wings, and as such they'd acquired a pair of horses whose former owners had no more use of.

"We scarcely have enough men to form a single wing, let alone two," Daniel stated as the two officers rode on. "What's our fighting strength down to?"

"Four hundred and thirty," James answered. "Some of the less severely wounded will return to us, though many others will not be so fortunate."

377

"I've never gotten used to it," Daniel confessed. "All the battles we fought in the Peninsula, all the dead and maimed who were left broken shells that were once men; none of that could have ever prepared me for what we faced at Waterloo. And how long did that even last, eight, maybe nine hours?"

"Nine hours that changed the world," James conjectured. "You know the lasting effects of our victory are not yet known, but given the reception of the French people, as well as the complete lack of resistance we have faced since then, I will be so bold as to say that those were nine hours that will echo for eternity. Most of Napoleon's army disintegrated during the Prussian pursuit; the survivors throwing down their arms and running for the hills."

"It ended with the Imperial Guard," Daniel thought aloud. "When they shattered under our volleys, we broke not just the Guard, we broke all of France."

"It was not just our volleys, old friend," James corrected. "I daresay history will give us the credit for their defeat, but you and I both know we owe a debt to the Oxfordshire lads."

Daniel thought for a moment and then nodded. "Didn't help that we were completely out of ammunition and they had scarcely been engaged all day," he observed. "But yes, I will give them their due for smashing the frogs in the flank, even if Old Nosey failed to mention it in his despatch."

"I did find it odd that he failed to mention Colborne and the 52nd at all," James concurred. "I hear he listed many senior officers by name for their contributions, so perhaps the omission of Colborne was a simple mistake."

"Nosey doesn't make mistakes," Daniel said with a slight hint of sarcasm. "If he failed to mention the Oxfordshire then it was deliberate, not malicious, perhaps, but still a conscious decision on his part."

Behind their two senior officers marched the 3/1st Foot Guards, where the 1st Company marched directly behind the grenadiers. Lieutenant Patrick Shanahan marched at their head, while Sergeant James Donaldson walked at the very back. Corporals Christopher Harvey and David O'Connor had dispersed themselves throughout. David's head was heavily bandaged, and he found he had to be supported by a couple of his mates as he was still prone to bouts of nausea, and his hearing had only just started to return.

"You know you could have gone back with the other wounded," Private Farrow noted. "You'd be resting in a comfy bed in Brussels right about now, with some lovey showing her appreciation for one of His Majesty's finest."

"Piss on that," David spat, though his head throbbed, and his friend had to help keep him upright. "You lot are not going to Paris without me! At least the bloody ground isn't spinning anymore. The real bugger is I've had to completely abstain from drink since me injury, as it made things utterly intolerable."

The young Irish corporal was hardly alone; the ranks of the army were filled with men with bandages around their heads, arms in slings, and other various injuries, yet who refused to be evacuated. To a man, if a soldier was still able to walk, then he resolutely marched with his mates. To what extent they had smashed Napoleon's army they could only guess, yet all were determined to see the matter to the very end. In his idealism, Captain James Webster always tried to see the best in his men. Battered, beaten, and filthy they may have been. Yet to the man who now led them, they looked magnificent.

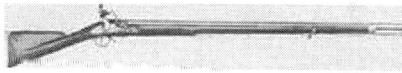

By waiting for Admiral Hotham's reply, Napoleon had sealed his own fate. The English blockade made any attempts at escaping to America now impossible. The twice-deposed Emperor of the French knew his only hope now lay in the mercy of his most hated enemies. A despatch had been sent to the Bellerophon on 13 July, addressed to the Prince Regent, stating the emperor's intent to hand himself over to them.

Altesse Royale,

En butte aux factions qui divisent mon pays et à l'inimitié des plus grandes puissances de l'Europe, j'ai terminé ma carrière politique, et je viens comme Thémistocle m'asseoir sur le foyer du peuple Britannique. Je me mets sous la protection de ses loix, que je réclame de votre Altesse Royale, comme au plus puissant, au plus constant, et au plus généreux de mes Ennemis.

Signé, NAPOLEON

Translated into English, the note read:

Your Royal Highness,

A victim to the factions which distract my country, and to the enmity of the greatest powers of Europe, I have terminated my political career, and I come, like Themistocles, to throw myself upon the hospitality of the British people. I put myself under the protection of their laws; which I claim from your Royal Highness, as the most powerful, the most constant, and the most generous of my enemies.

Signed, Napoleon

For Captain Frederick Maitland, he was making his name in history as Napoleon was brought aboard the Bellerophon. Bonaparte's aides had made a great showing of making it seem like Napoleon was still in control and coming of his own free will, rather than a desperate man on the run. It had been to no avail, though Maitland was magnanimous in dealing with the French rather than the gloating victor they'd envisioned.

"Vous êtes les bienvenus, sire," Maitland said, letting Napoleon know he was most welcome. As his French was not very strong, he asked if the emperor spoke any English.

"Non," Napoleon replied, shaking his head. "Je ne parle pas un mot de votre langue maternelle."

It puzzled Maitland that Napoleon would state that he did not speak a word of the Englishman's tongue. As he could not verify for certain one way or the other, he simply had to take the man at his word.

The crewmen aboard Bellerophon stood in awe of the man who had conquered most of Europe, and whose very name was now immortal. As he'd been more legend than real over the past twenty-some years, it was difficult to comprehend Napoleon as a man like them. Bonaparte seemed just as fascinated by the English sailors as they were by him. What baffled the British crews the most was just how mortal and frail Napoleon now appeared. The Waterloo campaign had weakened him even further, and his once full round face now appeared starkly gaunt and pale.

During the journey to England, Napoleon was given free rein to roam the ship as he pleased, provided he first checked with Captain Maitland, who would ensure that any areas visited by the French Emperor were satisfactorily cleaned. Napoleon was full of questions and genuinely fascinated by the inner workings of a British ship of the line. His grasp of the English language was proven to be practically non-existent, as he would constantly ask the meaning of even the simplest words in papers and pamphlets he attempted to read. And like Neil Campbell on Elba, Frederick Maitland found that he rather enjoyed Bonaparte's company and treated him more like a distinguished guest rather than the most sought after prisoner of war.

Napoleon appeared giddy once the ship finally docked eleven days later at Plymouth. Crowds of curious onlookers engulfed the docks. Numerous police and militiamen were posted to keep people back, as well as ensure Bonaparte did not leave the ship suddenly. Maitland surmised that it did much for the deposed emperor's ego to see the adoring crowds of the nation that had proven to be his most powerful nemesis.

"Je suis impatient de rencontrer votre Prince Regent," Napoleon said, stating that he looked forward to meeting the Prince Regent, as Maitland joined him at the prow of the ship.

The ship's captain said nothing. He suspected that Prince George would not even allow Bonaparte to leave the ship, let alone concede to a personal meeting. Still, he did not wish to dash the emperor's hopes. Whatever the British government decided, it was still preferable to what would have happened had the Prussian pursuit forces captured him. As it was, their cavalry had reached Paris just days after Napoleon fled. Were he taken by them, it would not be adoring crowds the emperor would be looking upon, but most likely a firing squad or the hangman's noose.

Chapter XXXI: End of an Era
British Army Camp, outside of Paris, France
27 July 1815

The Prince Regent (later King George IV)

A sense of calm had come over the Anglo-Allied Army. Despite skirmishes continuing between the French and Prussians as late as the 1st of July, there was a general feeling that perhaps peace had finally come after decades of incessant war. For Captain James Webster, there was the joy that came from seeing Emma whenever she accompanied the Duke and Duchess of Richmond. He was further grateful for being both alive and relatively unscathed.

There was also an immense feeling of pride amongst the soldiers of the 1st Regiment of Foot Guards, as no sooner had word of their decisive role in the victory at Waterloo reached London that a Royal Proclamation was immediately sent back.

"To the Grenadier Guards!" several voices said as James walked into the tent that was serving as the officers' mess. Daniel Roberts, Patrick Shanahan, and a score of other officers from both battalions stood along the outside of the long table, their glasses raised high.

James took a glass of claret from a servant and returned the gesture. "To the Grenadier Guards!" he echoed, referring to the regiment by its new name.

Whether the Prince Regent had come up with the name himself, or if it was recommended by senior officers at Horse Guards, or even perhaps came from Wellington himself, no one could say for certain. What they did know is that the name was derived from the regiment shattering Napoleon's feared Grenadier Division of the Imperial Guard. As a further symbol of honour, the regiment would be fitted with the same bearskin hats worn by their famed opponents.

"The seat at the head of the table is still yours," Captain Roberts said, motioning towards the seat normally held by the lieutenant colonel.

"For the time being," James replied as a servant held the chair out for him, and all the assembled officers were seated.

"Well, enjoy it while you can," Daniel asserted. "I think we'd rather the chair was occupied by the one who led us to the final victory over Boney and his damned Imperial Guard."

"I had command of the battalion for maybe the last thirty minutes of the actual battle," James chuckled. "That hardly counts as leading the regiment to victory."

"Your command time during the battle may have been short, sir," Patrick spoke up, "but it was you who led us in that moment when we earned our name, the Grenadier Guards."

"Here, here!" a number of officers echoed together.

"Captain Webster!" a voice called.

James turned to see it was General Maitland hailing him as he stepped into the tent.

"General, sir," he said, all of the men standing while Captain Webster saluted.

"Wellington has called for both of us," he said.

"Yes, sir," James replied. "Any word what this is about?"

"It wasn't said," Maitland replied, "though I can guess. He also wants Lieutenant Shanahan to come with us."

"General Maitland, Captain Webster, and Lieutenant Shanahan to see you, your grace," an aide said as the three men entered and saluted.

"Wait outside, Lieutenant Shanahan," Wellington ordered. Once Patrick had stepped out, he addressed the other two men. "Now that we have a moment's respite, we have a few matters to address amongst your officer corps."

"Yes, sir," Maitland replied.

The Duke looked at James, though it was always impossible to tell if his expression was one of approbation or rebuke. "Captain Webster," the Duke said slowly. "Looking at the official reports, you assumed command of the 3/1st Foot Guards, despite there being at least two captains senior to yourself."

"Yes, sir," James replied.

"Any reason as to why one of them did not assume command?"

"I cannot speak for them, your grace," James replied.

"Sir, I ordered Captain Webster to assume command," Maitland explained. "Captain Roberts was unavailable, as he was deployed forward with the light company. Captain Stables was the only other officer I knew of that was senior to Webster, and he was dead. I had but a moment to make a decision, and Captain Webster performed admirably, given the circumstances."

"In battle we often have but a moment to make a decision," Wellington noted. "I will concede that you made the correct one here." His expression still unchanged, the Duke laid a parchment on his desk. "As I am certain you will both be relieved to hear, Colonel Stewart is recovering well and will be assuming command of the battalion once more."

"I am relieved, sir," James replied earnestly. "He is a gentleman and a fine officer. It will be good to have him back."

"Major D'Oyley is on the mend as well," Wellington added. "He was fortunate in that none of Boney's troops used him for bayonet practice when you withdrew behind the ridge. Even so, there is still a major's vacancy within the battalion. I have here your orders, appointing you acting major." He then slid the paper across the table, which James took.

384

"Thank you, your grace!"

"Note I said *acting* major," Wellington continued. "I can temporarily appoint one to a higher rank, but even I am superseded by His Grace, the Duke of York, our commander-in-chief. This promotion can only be made permanent upon purchase."

"Understood, sir," James nodded. "I have the funds necessary."

"Very good," the Duke replied. "The matter can be finalized once we finish our business in France. Now, for the other matter. Peregrine, I understand you took it upon yourself to battlefield commission a man from the ranks."

There was no mistaking Wellington's disapproval, but James was glad to see Maitland remain firm in his conviction.

"Yes, your grace," he replied. "When Captain...or as I should say, *Major* Webster was placed in control of the right wing, there were no officers left to take command of his company."

"Your grace, I recommended Colour Sergeant Shanahan to General Maitland," James explained. "He is a leader of much experience, and is as well educated with the conduct and decorum of any who was born a gentleman."

"I'll not argue the semantics with you," Wellington stated. "You both know how much I deplore the commissioning of officers from the ranks, as necessary of an evil as it has been from time-to-time. I find no fault in this temporary commissioning, just as I did not in your elevation to acting battalion commander. However, just as your promotion to major cannot be made permanent without proper funds, Lieutenant Shanahan's commission cannot be held without proper purchase. I take it he has the means necessary for this?"

"No, sir," James replied, his expression crestfallen. "He told me as much."

"Then there's nothing for it," the Duke replied. "Once peace is settled and we can start replenishing our officers with men of the necessary means, Lieutenant Shanahan will have to revert back to colour sergeant. That is all." Maitland saluted and made ready to leave but stopped when he noticed that James had not moved.

"Your grace," the newly-promoted major said, "I will purchase Lieutenant Shanahan's commission for him."

Wellington looked up at him and raised an eyebrow. "Tell me this," he said, "can you afford both your promotion to major and

Lieutenant Shanahan's commission." "No, sir," James replied, his expression one of determination.

Wellington sighed, set his quill down, and leaned back in his chair. "You make a noble gesture, Major Webster. I know this man saved your life once, and you probably feel indebted to him for it. I am not one to tell an officer what to do with his money, however, I want to make certain you understand what you are giving up, should you decide to go through with this. A Forlorn Hope survivor and hero who shattered Bonaparte's Imperial Guard, you may be. However, that matters little when it comes to promotions of our officers. Even if I were inclined to allow you to retain your promotion and acquire Lieutenant Shanahan's commission without sufficient funds, which I am not, neither the Duke of York nor Horse Guards will allow it to stand. Once the issue of Bonaparte is finalized and the bureaucracy allowed to take back control of the army, you will be reduced to captain; another officer of means acquiring your promotion. Do you understand what I'm telling you?"

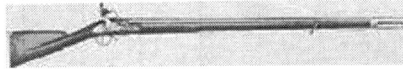

A mass deputation of allied diplomats and government officials gathered in the audience chamber of the Prince Regent. Representatives from Prussia, Austria, Russia, and the Netherlands gathered around the ornate chair on the raised dais where the prince sat. Standing to his right was his Prime Minister, Lord Liverpool.

King George III had ruled Great Britain and its domains for a staggering fifty-five years, yet in recent decades had been maligned with bouts of madness and other mental disorders. The king had lapsed five years before, brought on by extreme depression following the death of his daughter, Princess Amelia. As such, his son had been the de facto head-of-state. Prince George was hardly an inspiring figure. Fat, prone to gluttony, a blatant womanizer, with further rumours of various addictions did little to give him the aura of a man who would one day become king. And as he was just a few weeks from his fifty-third birthday, he was not exactly a young man either. His personal life was a disaster. He and his wife,

Caroline of Brunswick, despised each other. And while he did love his daughter, the nineteen-year old Princess Charlotte, there was constant strain between the two. George had hoped to wed Charlotte to Prince William of Orange, but his daughter had inexplicably called the wedding off.

Yet for all his personal failings, the Prince Regent was wise enough to defer the actual running of the British government to the Prime Minister and his cabinet. The forty-five year old Liverpool had been a constant source of level-headed reason and pragmatism for the Prince Regent. He had overseen the Treaty of Ghent, which ended the war in America, and along with Castlereagh had been one of Wellington's most prolific political allies during the Peninsular War. Despite occasional professional differences, Liverpool understood the Duke's talents and did his best to allow Wellington a free hand to prosecute the war as he saw fit. He had also been prudent enough to grant Castlereagh the necessary leeway in dealing with the Congress of Vienna, which still progressed while Napoleon made his second claim to the throne of France before his defeat at Waterloo.

"Bonaparte has come to England at last," the Prince Regent mused. He then gave an exaggerated chuckle. "The question now is what to do with our regal guest."

"The French Emperor is well-guarded and still aboard ship," Liverpool explained.

"Yes," George noted, "but what to actually do with him, now that he is finally in our grasp."

"Kill him!" a Prussian dignitary spat in a heavy accent. "Let his corpse hang from the gallows in retribution to all the lives he's cost!"

"I say, my dear sir," the prince remarked, "There will be no talk of hanging Bonaparte. And do maintain decorum when addressing me, there's a good fellow."

"Since the time of Charles Stuart, and with the ghastly executions of the royal family members during the French Revolution, our people have become averse to regicide," Liverpool explained.

The Prussian dignitary scowled but kept any further remarks to himself.

"Exile then," an Austrian diplomat surmised.

387

"Well, yes, of course," the Prince Regent agreed. "But certainly not here. Dear God, the common people are infatuated with him enough as it is! I daresay they would hail him as the return of William the Conqueror. Hence, I have not let him set foot on English soil."

"He cannot be sent back to Elba," the Russian dignitary stated.

"Your highness," Liverpool began, "there was talk while Bonaparte was on Elba of transferring him to Saint Helena."

"Saint Helena," George thought aloud. "Beastly place that. Tell me, Liverpool, what does our friend, the Duke of Wellington, have to say? It was he who defeated Bonaparte, and I think his opinion would hold great weight in this matter." He then glanced at the Prussian delegation, who all appeared to be seething at the remark.

There had already been much debate between the British and Prussians as to who actually won the Battle of Waterloo. Though Wellington and Marshal Blucher were courteous and openly appreciative of the other's contributions to Napoleon's downfall, there was still much resentment between the Duke and several senior Prussian officers.

"Interestingly enough," Liverpool answered, "Bonaparte appears to be under the impression that his greatest hopes for clemency lay in the Duke. After all, Wellington does view him as the worthiest adversary he's ever faced, and his respect for Napoleon is immense. However, we received a despatch from his grace just yesterday morning regarding this affair. He was adamant about two things. First, that Napoleon's life should be spared. And second, that he be exiled to Saint Helena without being allowed to set foot on English soil."

"Well, there you have it, gentlemen," the Prince Regent said, addressing the assembly once more. "Bonaparte will be sent at once to Saint Helena. He will be allowed a small retinue of servants and personal attendants, but that is all. No one from his Imperial Guard is to ever set eyes on him again."

"Your highness," the Austrian diplomat said, "What of his wife, the Empress Marie Louise?"

"What of her?" George shrugged. "She is an Austrian princess, and therefore your charge. Let her and their son remain in Austria."

"It is not the hangman's noose," Liverpool said to the Prussian representatives as the delegation broke up, "but it will more than suffice."

"Saint Helena," one of the men replied with an approving nod. "Let Bonaparte be tormented daily for the remainder of his existence."

"Believe me," Liverpool continued, "he will wish he had never returned to France. Saint Helena is but a fraction of the size of Elba. It is truly a place where one can be completely forgotten and alone."

British Prime Minister, Lord Liverpool

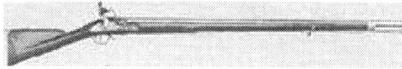

Thoughts of escaping to America were dashed like the waves upon the rocks. Napoleon stood on the bow of the ship that was taking him to the small island of Saint Helena. A tiny island, barely five miles by ten, it sat in the middle of the Atlantic Ocean, between Africa and South America. Like Liverpool had said, it was as desolate and isolated a location as one could comprehend. When he was on Elba, Napoleon had heard rumours that the allies were looking to transfer him to Saint Helena anyway, so it seemed his return to France only delayed the inevitable. This time there would be no entourage, no soldiers of his Old Guard to accompany him. Instead, he had but a small handful of personal attendants and was accompanied by a British admiral named Cockburn, who Napoleon had a very uneasy rapport with. At least Colonel Campbell had been amicable enough, and Napoleon had actually been fond of him. He sometimes wondered whatever happened to Campbell, whose name would now be tied to infamy as the man who'd allowed Bonaparte to escape from Elba. There were times during his return to France that Napoleon felt remorse for having deceived the Scottish colonel, who he had genuinely viewed as a friend. Those, along with every other feeling he'd ever known, were crushed as his ignominious fate bore down on him.

"I should have died at Waterloo," he lamented, as he leaned against the rail while the ship rose and fell in the waves and the island of Saint Helena approached in the distance. Death would have been preferable, and Napoleon felt that the supposed mercy shown by his enemies was anything but.

He was helped into a small rowboat once the ship dropped anchor, and as he stared into the water, Napoleon quietly wished there were sharks swimming about that he could throw himself to. For in his mind, their tearing his body to pieces would be a more dignified end than rotting away his last years on this desolate rock. Despite there being nearly a dozen persons in the boat, including the oarsmen and Admiral Cockburn, not a word was said by anyone. It was only when the boat was pulled onto the sand and Napoleon stepped off that he took a glance around and finally spoke.

"Dieu n'a pas besoin de m'envoyer en enfer quand je mourrai, car je suis déjà là." – *"God need not send me to hell when I die, for I am already here."*

Napoleon on Saint Helena

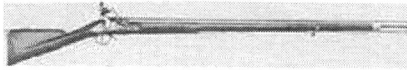

General Maitland left without a word as soon as they stepped out of Wellington's tent. James was full of mixed feelings, yet he could not help but feel he'd chosen correctly.

"What happened in there?" Patrick asked.

"You're keeping your commission," James answered as the two men walked towards the setting sun.

"But your promotion to major," Patrick protested. He took the major by the arm and for the first time ever, addressed him by his given name. "James, please tell me, what have you done?"

His friend and fellow officer smiled and shrugged. "The right thing."

Epilogue: Twenty-One Years Later
London, England
18 June 1836

The Waterloo Banquet, 1836

"Everything to your liking, Sir James?" the butler asked.

It was a rather posh suite off Park Lane, just a few blocks from Apsley House. A number of other senior officers were staying there as well, and the hotel staff member were doing everything possible to cater to their needs.

"Yes, thank you, Martin," James replied.

Martin Shepard was the grandson of his family's previous butler, Miles, who James had been close to growing up. His current butler was just a few years younger than he and was also a veteran of Wellington's army. He'd served with 1/95th Rifles as part of Sir Thomas Picton's division at Waterloo, rising to corporal before taking his discharge after staying on an additional two years with the army of occupation. James had known that Martin was with them, but it was not until his return to England that he heard full details of the brave corporal and his riflemen who stood resolutely against the cuirassiers.

James had arranged a temporary position for Martin, to assist the Duke of Wellington's household staff in preparation for the annual Waterloo Banquet. At least sixty distinguished guests were expected, and so the additional help was much appreciated.

"I cannot thank you enough for getting me this posting with the Duke's staff this evening," Martin stated. "It is an honour."

"It is an honour for me to have you there," James asserted. "Tell me, I know you will be in your butler's uniform, but will you be wearing your medal this evening?"

"I had hoped to, sir," Martin replied. "Provided you don't think his grace would object."

"I think he would object if one who earned such an esteemed honour did *not* wear it," James conjectured.

The decoration they spoke of was the *Waterloo Medal*. Most military medals were only available to senior officers, yet at Wellington's insistence, this one would be different. In what was the first of its kind, it was issued to every British soldier who'd fought in the campaign, from the lowest private all the way up to the Duke himself. In setting another precedent, the medal was also issued to the next of kin of all those killed or who died of their injuries. The front bore the image of the Prince Regent, in whose name it was issued, and the back bore the image of Victory, with Wellington's name above, and the words 'Waterloo, 18 June 1815' below. Each recipient's name was engraved around the edge of his medal. As it was specifically a British award, it was only awarded to British soldiers; those of the allied armies subject to whatever honours their governments chose to bestow upon them. In all, 39,000 Waterloo Medals had been awarded, either to the veterans themselves or to their surviving relatives.

A pair of servants entered the room, one carrying James' formal uniform for the evening's banquet. Despite still serving in His Britannic Majesty's Army, and being a senior officer, James still preferred to wear civilian clothes, especially when travelling. He wore his uniform strictly when he was on duty or during formal functions such as the evening's pending banquet.

The other servant carried a pair of small oak boxes; one bore James' *Waterloo Medal*, the other an honour that had come from the king himself. Following the defeat of Napoleon, the then-Prince Regent had decreed to expand the Noble Order of the Bath to, *"Those Officers who have had the opportunities of signalising themselves by eminent services during the late war."*

It would be a number of years later, after James had achieved sufficient rank that he would be made a *Knight Commander of the Most Honourable Order of the Bath (K.C.B.)*. For James, the honour had been unexpected, and perhaps not-so coincidentally came during Wellington's term as Prime Minister in 1830. It was also one of the last knighthoods bestowed by King George IV. Though he had effectively ruled Great Britain as the Prince Regent, George's kingship would only last ten years, following his father's death in 1820. By 1830 he had declined into severe mental and physical illness, though Wellington was able to secure honours to some of his former officers. King George died that June and was succeeded by his brother, who had since ruled as King William IV.

The Waterloo Medal

"Does it ever surprise you that Wellington secured that honour for you?" Emma asked as she walked into the room.

James opened the box and looked upon the ornate decoration that would be displayed on his uniform that evening, next to his Waterloo Medal.

"Every day," he replied. He then nodded to Martin, who gave a short bow and left. James smiled at his wife, who kissed him gently.

Whether Emma had grown more beautiful over the years, or it was simply his love for her that made her seem so, he could not say. What was certain was that Emma did not look like a woman in her late forties.

"Arthur always did have a funny way of showing gratitude," Emma noted. Born into the same social class, Emma had always privately referred to Wellington by his given name, though she refrained from this in public. She had come to respect the Duke in her own way, even though she still resented his extreme arrogance and abhorred how he'd treated his poor wife.

"Perhaps his recommendation to the king regarding my knighthood was his way of saying 'thank you' for what happened that night in Paris all those years ago," James remarked. "I honestly cannot think of any other reason he would do so. It's not as if we're friends who correspond regularly. In fact, I can only recall maybe a couple dozen words his grace and I have said to each other since the wars ended. And the only personal written correspondence I have received was the invitation to this evening's banquet. I suppose I finally have sufficient rank to warrant a place at his table."

"That and perhaps he's finally starting to understand people a little more," Emma observed. "I personally found his blatant womanizing reprehensible all these years. The word is that that house he built in Bath was not simply a weekend retreat, but rather was for one of his mistresses."

James could only shake his head and sigh. Whatever his status as a national hero, Wellington's character flaws were the worst-kept secret in Britain. It seemed some days that his reputation for conquering the ladies rivalled that of his conquering Napoleon.

"I know as a soldier, your feelings for him are different," Emma reasoned. "He did win in the Peninsula, and he did bring final victory over Napoleon. Those of you who fought beside him surely loved him in your own way."

"Oh, I would never say that," James chuckled. "He was belligerent to his officers, and he flogged the men while cursing them to no end. The men loved Sir John Moore and 'Daddy' Hill, but Wellington, not so much. However, he won victories when no one else could, and his claim to be the only unbeaten general in the entire Napoleonic Wars is not without merit. Besides, while he may have cursed and flogged the men, he always made certain they were well-equipped, had sufficient ammunition, and a hot meal waiting for them at the end of the day. You know, when we stood with him on that ridge during our final stand against the Imperial Guard, all of us knew that he was there to die with us. We never loved him, but we respected him."

"I think it was the same with his wife," Emma thought aloud. "She practically hero-worshipped him, despite his gross infidelities. Yet even he expressed at least some regrets about poor Catherine. I thought it strange that when she fell ill five years ago, she asked to have her bed moved into the room with all of her husband's war trophies; and that is where she wished to die. And when she was breathing her last, Arthur lamented that after all their years together, it was only at the end of her life that they finally understood each other. But enough of that, my love. I did not come here to discuss the personal life of the Duke of Wellington. Here, I've brought you something." She handed him an old leather-bound journal. It was faded, the pages crinkled from where it had gotten wet and stepped on more than once. There was a time when it had been one of James' most prized possessions, yet until this moment it had been all but forgotten.

"Ah," he sighed. "I have not seen this for many years. Where did you find it?"

"Martin found it," Emma replied. "He was going through one of your old campaign trunks to see if there was anything you might want for this evening's banquet, and he found it. I hope you don't mind, love, but I did thumb through it a bit. You were diligent about keeping it up to date all through the Peninsula, your time in Brussels, Paris, and Vienna. I see the last entry was on the night before Waterloo."

"I don't know why," James began, "but I never picked it up again after that. I don't even remember putting it in my chest."

"Martin added an inscription to the beginning," Emma added. "Think of it as a title page. I told him you would find it appropriate."

396

"*I Stood with Wellington*," James read aloud. "That is something he and I can both rightfully say. Perhaps it is time I finished it."

Emma kissed him once more and left the room. His daughter, Amy, was expected to join them later that afternoon, so James had time to sit and write. He took a deep breath as he thumbed through the old journal. A flood of forgotten memories washed over him as he scanned the weathered pages. Much detail had been given to the days prior to the assault on Badajoz, when James learned of the death of his first wife. There was a noticeable gap in the level of detail between the time he was invalided back to England, assigned as a recruiting officer, and then finally transferred back to Wellington's army two years later, just prior to Napoleon's return.

There was a small writing desk in the corner of the suite. As there were several hours to spare before he had to make ready for the Duke's banquet, he sat down and re-read the pages he'd scrawled just prior to Waterloo. He marvelled that he'd even been able to write anything that hateful night prior to the battle. Had it not been for David O'Connor's meagre fire that he somehow managed to keep alight in the pouring rain, James would not have been able to scrawl anything at all. As it was, the pages were barely legible, and he reckoned he should re-write them, lest they be lost. He shuddered at the memory and closed his eyes, taking a deep breath. When he opened them, he exhaled audibly, sat down and began to write:

By God, has it been twenty-one years, or twenty-one lifetimes? Today, I join the host of His Grace's officers for the annual Waterloo Banquet at Apsley House. I hear a famous painter named William Salter is to do a portrait of the event; including in it dear friends who have since passed on to the next life. How blessed my life has been since those hellish days! It is for my fallen friends that I attempt to make the most of and truly live every day. It has not always been easy, and I have endured the same trials that any man does; however, I thank God for my good fortune. I returned home in a far better place in life than any of the men in the ranks who fought beside me. That society is so unbalanced and unfair is something I will never understand, but then, maybe we are not meant to...

"Father!" a voice said excitedly, interrupting James' writing. He smiled as his daughter, Amy, walked into the study. Now twenty-four, she was nearly as tall as her father, with sandy blonde hair, pulled up this day, and a radiant complexion. She wore a yellow summer dress, which reminded James of the one he'd dressed her in when they first arrived in Brussels all those years ago. She also wore the locket with her mother's image that James had given to her around the time she was ten. She resembled her mother just enough to serve as a happy reminder, yet not so much that it would ever make James uncomfortable. His fears about how his daughter would appear as she grew older were completely unfounded. "I hope I'm not interrupting."

"My dearest," he replied, "you are never an interruption. Your early arrival is a joy to me." He set his quill down and saw Amy carried a pair of letters. "What have you there?"

"I hope you don't mind, but I just had to read them first," Amy said with a giggle. "One is from Neddy…"

"You know your brother hates being called that," James interrupted. "He prefers his given name, Edward."

"That's all well and good for his friends and army chums," his daughter shrugged, "but he'll always be 'little Neddy' to me." Amy was very proud of her brother who, although they were but half-siblings, had always been very close.

James had called in a few favours and managed to secure his son an ensign's posting with Horse Guards. Young Edward, now eighteen, did not know his father was to be in London for the Waterloo banquet, and so Amy had brought his letter with her when she arrived from Southend-on-Sea that morning. He would be among the mounted escorts that would accompany the honoured guests, and so James hoped to surprise him.

"Here," Amy said, handing James the other letter. "This one's from dear Uncle Patty."

Patrick Shanahan had maintained close ties with James and his family over the years, even if only by correspondence. Amy always referred to him as her 'Irish Uncle'. At his request, Patrick had left the Guards and taken a posting in Ireland. Knowing of the plight James and Patrick were in regarding the funds necessary to maintain their promotions, Emma had made a very generous gift to

Ann Shanahan, thanking her for her loyalty and service. A few eyebrows were raised when it was noticed that the amount was exactly that needed to purchase Patrick's commission, though no words were said. It was still more proper than James purchasing his friend's commission for him, and it also allowed him to make his own promotion permanent.

Officer promotions during the decades of peace following Waterloo still proved painfully slow, especially for one of marginal means who'd come up from the ranks. Indeed, Patrick had been most fortunate in that he did not end up languishing on half-pay with no chance of promotion, like so many officers once their regiments were stood down. As an officer within the Grenadier Guards, James was fortunate enough to be in one of the few regiments where officer career advancement still moved at a reasonable pace.

It was also a source of constant frustration that in a peacetime army, the only real way to advance was through the acquirement of funds and patronage of the right noblemen. Still, Patrick had been persistent; his status as a Forlorn Hope survivor, as well as one who had broken Napoleon's Imperial Guard during its last gasp at Waterloo proving useful, and he was now Major Patrick Shanahan of the Connaught Rangers. David O'Connor, the teenage Irish soldier who Wellington could have executed for looting a pig but instead elevated to corporal just prior to Waterloo, had stayed with the army as well. Patrick still referred to him as 'young David', even though the now thirty-nine year old Regimental Sergeant Major was showing more than a little grey in his hair. David had also eventually returned to Ireland, and was reunited with Patrick when he became the RSM of the Connaught Rangers.

James set the letters aside, and his gaze fell upon the locket around Amy's neck.

"A pity your mother can't be here to see you when I give you away," he said sadly.

Amy had recently been betrothed to the son of Daniel Roberts, who was also named Daniel. Though Amy was a few years older, and the two had grown up together, they'd later found their feelings to be more than that of childhood friends. The elder Roberts was now a colonel within the Grenadier Guards, where his son served as a lieutenant. They stood out from their

399

contemporaries, wearing the exploding bomb insignia on their facings. The ceremonial bearskin hats would come to symbolize the Grenadier Guards more than their French adversaries, whose defeat had led to its awarding in the first place.

"I go and visit Mother on occasion," Amy replied; her mother being laid to rest in the rose garden at the family estate, rather than in a cemetery. "Though I never knew her, it's almost as if I can feel her presence with me. Silly, I know."

"Not at all," James replied, shaking his head. "Perhaps she's never really left you. And if there is a Heaven, she'll be watching with love when Daniel takes you as his bride."

Amy smiled and wiped a tear away quickly. "I know she would approve of Emma, too," she said reassuringly, leaning down and embracing her father close. Amy then kissed him on top the head. "I'll leave you to your memoirs. I know you have much to write before the Duke's banquet this evening." James smiled as his daughter left the room. He then picked up his quill and continued:

I cannot change the way things are, I can only try and make the world a better place in my own ways. My daughter and my son have done this for me. How fearful I was when I found Emma was with child, for I did not wish her to share Amy's fate. God be praised, her confinement was without complication, and she gave me my beloved Edward.

I have passed the years as best I can, and I look forward to tonight's banquet at the Duke's London residence, Apsley House. Wellington has aged as gracefully as one can expect. His hair is mostly grey, but then, he did recently turn sixty-seven. I have a few grey hairs of my own, and they are all that gives away my forty-eight years. We are but the few who remain from that era. Bonaparte is long gone; a mock-up of his death bed and an exact replica of his body were placed at Madame Tussauds wax studio. I hear that the Duke visits it quite frequently, to spend time remembering and in his own way, honouring his defeated foe. So strange that they only faced each other once and never actually met in person, for their names are forever bound together in history.

Tonight we will remember those who have been absent these years; who have not been here to grow old beside us. Brave men

*like Sir William Howe DeLancey, who would have been fifty-eight
this year, will remain thirty-seven for all eternity. I remember
especially William Grose, who was but twenty-one when he fell at
Quatre Bras. What a fine officer and gentleman he was, despite his
lack of years! On this day, we raise our glasses to their memory,
and hoping by the grace of God that perhaps in the next life they
can raise theirs to us. As time passes, we will eventually be
together. I do not look to join them for many years to come, but I
know they will wait for me.*

*And whether my name is remembered or forgotten by history,
there is one thing that can never be taken from me or from any of
us; for*

I stood with Wellington!

*Major General Sir James Henry Webster, K.C.B.
18 June 1836*

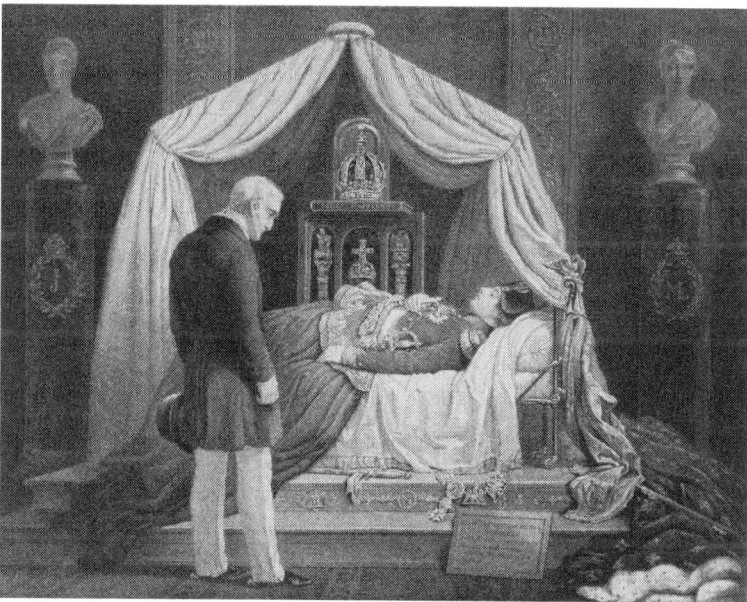

Wellington in later life, visiting the relics of Napoleon

Appendix A: Historical Afterward

The French

Michel Ney returned to Paris soon after the second abdication of Napoleon, where he was arrested, put on trial, and executed on 7 December 1815. He was granted his last wish, that he not be blindfolded, and that he would give the order for the soldiers to fire. He was often regarded paradoxically as both the greatest turncoat and bravest soldier France had ever seen.

Of interesting note, theories have risen that Michel Ney may not have been executed at all, but instead was able to fake his death, and with the aid of the Duke of Wellington, escaped to America, where he lived out his days as a schoolteacher under the name Peter Stuart Ney. While this has been dismissed in many circles as purely a legend, a number of factors have kept it from being dismissed altogether. Witnesses of the time noted a substantial similarity in appearance between Peter Ney and Michel Ney, and an analysis of their handwriting found it to be almost identical. Peter Stuart Ney died in North Carolina in 1846, at the age of 77. Whether or not he was the famous Marshal of France has never been resolved with certainty.

Nicolas Soult was spared the firing squad, as were many of the Bonapartist officers. Following his return to the throne, King Louis disbanded the French army, thereby freeing all officers of their oaths of allegiance. Soult was exiled for four years, yet in 1820 once again made a Marshal of France. He led a distinguished political career, as Minister of War, multiple terms as Prime Minister; and was honoured to serve as ambassador to the coronation of Queen Victoria in 1838. He died in 1851, at the age of 82. His oldest son, Napoleon, survived him by only six years. As he died without male issue, the title of *Duc de Dalmatie* (Duke of Dalmatia) became extinct.

Jerome Bonaparte was regarded as immaterial after Waterloo, despite being Napoleon's brother and was largely left alone. After the rise of the second French Empire, under his nephew, Napoleon III, he was made a Marshal of France. He died in 1860, at the age of 70.

Charles Reille, under whose command Jerome Bonaparte served, also remained largely unscathed following the return of the Bourbon Monarchy. He was even named a Peer in 1819, and later a Marshal of France in 1847. He died just three months before Jerome Bonaparte, in 1860 at the age of 84.

Jean-Baptiste Drouet, Comte d'Erlon would be haunted by having been needlessly diverted between Quatre Bras and Ligny, knowing that had his corps been involved at one or the other, the entire Waterloo Campaign could have ended very differently. He spent the next ten years in exile in Munich, before being granted amnesty in 1825 by King Charles X, who was the younger brother of Louis XVIII. He later supported the July Revolution in 1830, which deposed the Bourbons once more and led to the constitutional monarchy under Louise-Philippe. He died at the age of 78 in January 1844.

Emmanuel de Grouchy defeated the Prussian forces at Wavre, the day after Waterloo. He was unaware of Napoleon's defeat, by which time it was already too late to save the Empire. At his court martial he was, surprisingly, spared the death sentence, despite the fate of men like Michel Ney. He was still forced into exile and lived in America until 1821. Those looking for a scapegoat found him an easy target and gossips would portray him as one who had deliberately betrayed Napoleon, despite the fact that he'd followed the emperor's orders to the last, won the victory at Wavre, and managed to rally the remnants of Napoleon's army around Paris before the emperor abdicated. In 1830, following the July Revolution, King Louis-Philippe restored him as a Marshal of France and returned him to the Chamber of Peers. He died in 1847 at the age of 80.

Napoleon Bonaparte, former Emperor of the French and master of Europe, would spend his few remaining years in exile on the remote island of Saint Helena. Unlike his stay on Elba, where he'd been allowed to retain his title of emperor, here there was no mistaking he was a prisoner. It was during this time that he dictated his memoirs, which have endured as a source of propaganda by Bonapartists to this day, though many historians view them as bitter rants of a man seeking to explain why he should have won the Battle of Waterloo and not lost his empire. An interesting hobby he picked up was his attempt to finally learn English; his reasoning being because it was the language of Shakespeare. Some of the letters to his tutor, which were a type of homework assignment, still survive.

Perhaps the greatest personal tragedy for the man who an entire era was named for was that he never saw his young son again. As his health deteriorated, he became increasingly bitter that one whose name would encompass an entire age would meet such an ignominious end. He died at the age of 51 on 5 May 1821, less than five years after Waterloo. While rumours of assassination still persist, the fact that numerous tumours were found in his stomach during an autopsy lead many to deduce that he died from stomach cancer. His son, Napoleon II, died of tuberculosis in 1832 at the age of 21.

The Bonapartes would not be done with Europe, though, and Napoleon's nephew, Charles Louis-Napoleon Bonaparte, would revive the French Empire and rule as Napoleon III from 1852 to 1870. His son, and therefore Napoleon's great-nephew, Louis Napoleon, the Prince Imperial, was killed in June 1879, during the Anglo-Zulu War. The irony has not been lost that almost exactly sixty-four years after Waterloo, the man noted as the last of the Bonapartes was killed fighting for the British.

The Prussians

Gebhard von Blucher remained in Paris for some time, though his age and years of hard living finally took a toll on his health. He retired to his native Silesia, a region that covers parts of modern Poland, Germany, and the Czech Republic. He died just four years after Waterloo on 12 September 1819, at the age of 76.

August von Gneisenau was appointed to command the Prussian VIII Corps, but retired for a time, due to health issues. He later served as Governor of Berlin, and then during the Polish Insurrection in 1830 was assigned as a field marshal in command of the Army of Observation. The world-famous general and military theorist, General Carl von Clausewitz, who had also fought at Ligny and Wavre, served as his chief-of-staff. Gneisenau died the next year of cholera at the age of 70, with Clausewitz also succumbing shortly after.

Karl von Muffling served with the Army of Occupation in France, following the fall of Napoleon. An expert in topography, he helped modernize military maps to better show terrain features and elevation; his methods of which are still used today. He later served as Governor of Berlin for nine years, from 1838 to 1847. Ill health forced his retirement, and he died in January 1851 at the age of 75 at his estate outside of Berlin.

The British

Sir William Howe DeLancey was taken to a small cottage outside Waterloo, where he was tended to by his young wife, Magdalene. The trauma of his injuries was so severe that he never recovered, and he died a week later on 26 June 1815, at the age of 37. Magdalene DeLancey remarried two years later; dying in childbirth in 1822. She kept a journal of her time spent tending to her mortally wounded husband. In 1906 it was published under the title, *A Week at Waterloo in June 1815*.

Fitzroy James Henry Somerset would remain in the British army, despite having his right arm amputated. He taught himself to write left-handed and returned to his duties as embassy secretary in Paris. His marriage to Wellington's niece, Emily, produced two sons; the eldest, Arthur, was killed during the First Anglo-Sikh War in 1845. Somerset would later serve with Wellington again, this time as master general of ordnance, and as Military Secretary when the Duke was made Commander-in-Chief of all British armed forces. In 1852 he was appointed to the Privy Counsel of Queen Victoria, as well as named Baron Raglan. He was further promoted through the ranks to field marshal, serving in the Crimean War, where he died of dysentery in June 1855, at the age of 66.

Prince William of Orange recovered from his wounds at Waterloo. Though much-maligned for his tactical follies, he should also be given credit for his strategic situational awareness that made him keep his men at Quatre Bras, thereby possibly saving the entire battle. Even the prince's most ardent detractors were also quick to credit him for his extreme personal bravery. His father had a massive earthen mound erected upon the spot where the young prince was wounded. A great lion statue sits atop, and while it is a magnificent monument, it drastically altered the layout of the field. The Duke of Wellington hated the mound and later remarked, "They ruined my battlefield". In 1816, Prince William married Grand Duchess Anna Pavlovna, the younger sister of Tsar Alexander of Russia. Upon his father's abdication in 1840, he ascended to the throne as King William II of the Netherlands. He ruled for just nine years, overseeing constitutional reforms to the Netherlands monarchy and government, many of which are still in effect today. He died suddenly in 1849, at the age of 56.

Alexander Cavalié Mercer stayed with the wounded after Waterloo. His battery, which had heroically stood its ground, was unable to move due to losses amongst their horses. His six cannon expended an astonishing 700 rounds of ammunition during the battle, inflicting terrifying losses amongst the advancing French columns. He served twice in British North America, and despite his exemplary service at Waterloo, promotion came slowly. He eventually retired from active service as a lieutenant general in 1854 after a lifelong 54 years in uniform. He died in 1868 at the age of 85. His *Journal of the Waterloo Campaign kept throughout the campaign of 1815,* was published by his son, two years later. As it was written contemporaneously with extreme detail, it is viewed as one of the most important first-hand historical accounts of the time.

Peregrine Maitland was made a Knight Commander of the Order of the Bath immediately following Waterloo. In October 1815, at the Duke of Wellington's headquarters in Paris, he married the Duke of Richmond's daughter, Lady Sarah Lennox, by whom he had seven children. In 1818 he was appointed lieutenant-governor to Upper Canada, which he held for ten years before being assigned as lieutenant-governor of Nova Scotia. In 1832 he returned to England, citing his health. In 1852 he was made Knight Grand Cross of the Order of the Bath, just two years before his death in 1854, at the age of 76. The village of Maitland, in Hants County, Nova Scotia, is named in his honour.

Sir Rowland Hill was thought to have been slain during the charge against the Imperial Guard towards the end of the Battle of Waterloo. He actually escaped unharmed and continued to have a long and distinguished military career, eventually succeeding the Duke of Wellington as Commander-in-Chief from 1828 to 1839. He also served as Governor of Plymouth in Devon from 1830 until his death in 1842, at the age of 70. As he had no male issue, his barony became extinct, though his Viscountcy passed on through the line of his nephew, which is still in existence.

Henry William Paget, Earl of Uxbridge recovered from losing his leg at Waterloo. His amputated limb was maintained at a special shrine at a local museum, where it served as a tourist attraction. Lost limbs seemed to be a curse of his family, as his brother had lost his right arm at the Battle of Porto in 1809, and even his daughter lost a hand tending to her badly injured husband on a battlefield in Spain. Uxbridge was fitted with an artificial leg, and his career continued unabated. Two weeks after Waterloo, the Prince Regent made him Marquess of Anglesey. When the Prince Regent ascended to the throne as King George IV, Anglesey was named Lord High Steward of England. He was twice Lord Lieutenant of Ireland; his first tenure came during Wellington's term as Prime Minister. He achieved the military rank of field marshal, and despite being a year older is one of the few to outlive Wellington. Anglesey died a year after the Duke, on 29 April 1854, just three weeks before his 86th birthday.

Sir Arthur Wellesley, Duke of Wellington returned to England a national hero, after overseeing the Treaty of Paris in November 1815. Despite universal admiration for his triumphs, his return to politics was far more contentious than had been his career as a soldier. Though he served two years as Prime Minister from 1828 to 1830, and very briefly again from November to December 1834 he did so with much reluctance.

Whatever his political difficulties, Wellington was, until the end of his life, regarded as the 'The Greatest Living Briton'. In his private dining room at Apsley House hung giant-sized portraits of all the monarchs of Europe from the Napoleonic Era, with the Duke always seating himself across from that of Louis XVIII. His reason for this is left to speculation, though given his vanity, which he cannot be faulted for, perhaps he viewed it as his way of dining with the monarchs who all owed their existence to him. The portraits still hang in the same dining room to this day.

The Duke lived a long life, substantially outliving both Napoleon and Blucher by decades. In 1850 he was named godfather to Queen Victoria's son, Prince Arthur, who was named after the Duke.

Upon his death on 14 September 1852, at the age of 83, he was given an elaborate State Funeral. Only a small handful of non-royals have ever been granted this honour; other examples include Admiral Horatio Nelson and Sir Winston Churchill.

It is of interesting note that Wellington's most famous nickname, *The Iron Duke*, actually had nothing to do with his military prowess. Instead, it was said to have originated when he installed metal shutters on the windows of his London residence, Apsley House, during a series of riots in 1832. Posterity has been more kind, and today when one mentions *The Iron Duke*, it conjures up images of the iron-disciplined hero who defeated Napoleon and brought about the ending of an age.

In 1947, Gerald Wellesley, 7th Duke of Wellington, gave Apsley House to the British Government, for the first time opening it to the public. Today, the house is preserved almost exactly as it was during the original Duke's lifetime. The magnificent collection of approximately 200 paintings is alone worth the admission. Almost half of these were captured after the Battle of Vitoria in 1813 from Joseph Bonaparte's baggage train.

And though, as of 2012, there have been eight Dukes of Wellington, Sir Arthur Wellesley is still regarded *The* Duke. Doubtless he would approve.

Appendix B: Titles and Honours of the Duke of Wellington

Arthur, Duke and Marquess of Wellington,
Marquess Douro, Earl of Wellington,
Viscount Wellington and Baron Douro,
Knight of the Most Noble Order of the Garter,
Knight Grand Cross of The Most Honourable Order of the Bath,
One of Her Majesty's Most Honourable Privy Council, and Field Marshal and Commander-in-Chief of Her Majesty's Forces
Field Marshal of the Austrian Army,
Field Marshal of the Hanoverian Army,
Field Marshal of the Army of the Netherlands,
Marshal-General of the Portuguese Army,
Field Marshal of the Prussian Army,
Field Marshal of the Russian Army,
Captain-General of the Spanish Army
Prince of Waterloo, of the Kingdom of the Netherlands
Duke of Ciudad Rodrigo
Grandee of Spain of the First Class
Duke of Victoria, Marquess of Torres Vedras, and Count of Vimiera in Portugal
Knight of the Most Illustrious Order of the Golden Fleece, and of the Military Orders of St. Ferdinand and of St. Hermenigilde of Spain
Knight Grand Cross of the Orders of the Black Eagle and of the Red Eagle of Prussia
Knight Grand Cross of the Imperial Military Order of Maria Teresa of Austria
Knight of the Imperial Orders of St. Andrew, St. Alexander Newski, and St. George of Russia
Knight Grand Cross of the Royal Portuguese Military Order of the Tower and Sword
Knight Grand Cross of the Royal and Military Order of the Sword of Sweden.

Knight of the Order of St. Esprit of France
Knight of the Order of the Elephant of Denmark
Knight Grand Cross of the Royal Hanoverian Guelphic
Order
Knight of the Order of St. Januarius and of the Military
Order of St. Ferdinand and of Merit of the Two Sicilies
Knight Grand Cross of the Supreme Order of the
Annunciation of Sardinia
Knight Grand Cross of the Royal Military Order of
Maximilian Joseph of Bavaria
Knight of the Royal Order of the Rue Crown of Saxony,
Knight Grand Cross of the Order of Military Merit of
Wurtemberg
Knight Grand Cross of the Military Order of William of the
Netherlands
Knight of the Order of the Golden Lion of Hesse Cassel,
Knight Grand Cross of the Orders of Fidelity and of the
Lion of Baden

Appendix C: British Military Ranks (company-level)

Other Ranks

Private – The rank held by the vast majority of soldiers, privates outnumber all other combined ranks approximately ten-to-one. Most line companies have between 85 to 100 privates, though Guards units are traditionally larger, with up to 120 per company. **Chosen Man** – Not actually a rank, but rather an honorary title given to privates with special abilities, such as designated marksmen. It was later superseded by the actual rank of *lance corporal*. An arm band or single chevron denotes their status.

Non-Commissioned Officers

Corporal – The first rank of leadership, line companies normally have three corporals, though Guards companies could have more. **Sergeant** – Prior to 1813, sergeant was the highest NCO rank at the company-level. Senior to the corporals, there are two per company. **Colour Sergeant** – First raised in 1813, colour sergeant was awarded to senior NCOs who distinguished themselves, placing them senior to other sergeants. One is authorized per company.

Officers

Ensign – Lowest subaltern rank. **Lieutenant** – Also a subaltern, the senior lieutenant acts as second-in-command of the company. **Captain** – Company commander.

Commander – Captain (1)
Subaltern – Ensign or Lieutenant (2)
Colour Sergeant (1)
Sergeant (2)
Corporal (3 to 5)
Other Ranks – Privates with a few chosen men (up to 120)

Note: During the Waterloo Campaign, most companies were understrength. Example: the average strength for companies within 3/1st Foot Guards was about 98 men.

Ranks and organization above company-level

Battalion – Consisted of ten companies; one grenadier, one light, and eight line companies. The following ranks were specific to the battalion.

Regimental Sergeant Major – The senior non-commissioned officer within the battalion, it was also the highest rank an enlisted soldier could attain.

Major – In charge of coordinating a 'wing' of companies, also acted as next in command, based on seniority. Each major was in charge of four line companies, along with either the light or grenadiers.

Lieutenant Colonel – Battalion Commander.

Brigade – Consisted of two or more battalions and was most often commanded by either a **Colonel** or **Major General**.

Division – Made up of two or more brigades, with attached artillery and sometimes its own cavalry. It was commanded by a **Major General** or **Lieutenant General**.

Corps –Consisted of two or more divisions, with attached artillery and cavalry squadrons. Corps were very large entities, often in excess of 20,000 men. It was commanded by a **Lieutenant General** or **General**.

Army – An enormous force of multiple corps, usually the overall military force in a given theatre. Commanded by a **Field Marshal**

Appendix D: Order of Battle, the Anglo-Allied Army

Army Commander – Field Marshal Sir Arthur Wellesley, the Duke of Wellington

I Corps – HRH Prince Willem of Orange
  1st (Guards) Division – General George Cooke
    1st Brigade – Major General Peregrine Maitland
      2/1st Regiment of Foot Guards – Lieutenant Colonel Henry Askew
      3/1st Regiment of Foot Guards – Lieutenant Colonel the Honourable William Stewart *(Captain Webster's battalion)*
    2nd Brigade – Major General Sir John Byng
      2/Coldstream Guards – Lieutenant Colonel James MacDonnell
      2/3rd Regiment of Foot Guards – Lieutenant Colonel Francis Hepburn
    Artillery
      Sandham's Battery, Royal Field Artillery – Captain Frederik Sandham
      Kuhlmann's Battery, King's German Legion – Captain Heinrich Kuhlmann
  3rd Division – Lieutenant General Sir Charles Alten
    5th Brigade – Major General Sir Colin Halkett
      2/30th Cambridgeshire Regiment – Lieutenant Colonel Alexander Hamilton
      33rd Regiment – Lieutenant Colonel William Elphinstone
      69th South Lincolnshire Regiment – Lieutenant Colonel Charles Morice
      2/73rd Regiment – Lieutenant Colonel William Harris
    2nd Brigade, King's German Legion – Colonel Baron Christian von Ompteda
      1st Light Battalion – Lieutenant Colonel Louis von dem Bussche
      2nd Light Battalion – Major Georg Freiherr von Baring

5th Line Battalion – Lieutenant Colonel Baron Wilhelm von Linsingen

8th Line Battalion – Lieutenant Colonel Johann van Schroeder

1st Hanoverian Brigade – Major General Friedrich Graf von Kielmansegge

Field Battalion Bremen – Lieutenant Colonel Wilhelm von Langrehre

Field Battalion, 1st Duke of York's Osnabruck – Major Carl von Bulow

Light Battalion Grubenhagen – Lieutenant Colonel Baron Friedrich von Wurmb

Light Battalion Luneburg – Lieutenant Colonel August von Klencke

Field Battalion Verden – Major Julius von Schkopp

Jaeger Battalion – Captain de Reden

Artillery

Lloyd's Battery, Royal Field Artillery – Major William Lloyd

Cleeves' Battery, King's German Legion – Captain Andreas Cleeves

II Corps – Lieutenant General Sir Rowland Hill

2nd Division – Lieutenant General Sir Henry Clinton

3rd Brigade – Major General Frederick Adam

52nd Oxfordshire Regiment – Lieutenant Colonel Sir John Colborne

71st Glasgow Highland Regiment – Colonel Thomas Reynell

2/95th Rifles – Lieutenant Colonel Amos Godsell Norcott

3/95th Rifles – Lieutenant Colonel John Ross

1st Brigade, King's German Legion – Lieutenant Colonel George Du Plat

1st Line Battalion – Major Frederich von Robertson

2nd Line Battalion – Major Georg Muller

3rd Line Battalion – Lieutenant Colonel Frederich von Wissell

4th Line Battalion – Major Frederich Reh

3rd Hanoverian Brigade – Lieutenant Colonel Hugh Baron Halkett

Landwehr Battalion Bremervörde – Lieutenant Colonel Frederich von Schulenberg

Landwehr Battalion 2nd Duke of York's – Major Baron Louis von Munster

Landwehr Battalion 3rd Duke of York's – Major Baron Clamor Bussche-Hunefeld

Landwehr Battalion Salzgitter– Major Frederich von Hammerstein

Artillery

Bolton's Battery, Royal Field Artillery – Captain Samuel Bolton

Sympher's Battery, King's German Legion – Captain Augustus Sympher

4th Division – Major General the Honourable Sir Charles Colville

4th Brigade – Colonel Sir Hugh Henry Mitchell

3/14th Buckinghamshire Regiment – Major Francis Tidy

1/23rd Royal Welch Fusiliers – Lieutenant Colonel Sir Henry Walton-Ellis

51st Regiment – Lieutenant Colonel Hugh Henry Mitchell

1st Netherlands Division – Lieutenant General John Stedman

1st Brigade – Major General Ferdinand d'Hauw

16th Light Battalion – Lieutenant Colonel Stefan Rudolf van Hulstein

4th Line Battalion – Lieutenant Colonel Ernst de Man

6th Line Battalion – Lieutenant Colonel Pieter Arnold Twent

9th National Militia – Lieutenant Colonel Johann Simons

14th National Militia – Lieutenant Colonel Willem Poolman

15th National Militia – Lieutenant Colonel Pieter Colthoff

2nd Brigade – Major General Dominique Johann de Eerens

18th Light Battalion – Lieutenant Colonel HSH Prince August van Arenberg

1st Line Battalion – Lieutenant Colonel Willem Kuijck

1st National Militia – Lieutenant Colonel Frederik Augustus Guicherit

2nd National Militia – Lieutenant Colonel Albert van Bazel

18th National Militia – Lieutenant Colonel Frederik van Ommeren

Foot Artillery Battery – Captain Pieter Wijnands

Cavalry Corps – Lieutenant General Henry Paget, Earl of Uxbridge

Household Brigade – Major General Lord Edward Somerset

1st Regiment of Life Guards – Lieutenant Colonel Samuel Ferrior

2nd Regiment of Life Guards – Lieutenant Colonel Richard Fitzgerald

Royal Regiment of Horse Guards – Lieutenant Colonel Sir Robert Chambre Hill

1st King's Dragoon Guards – Lieutenant Colonel William Fuller

Union Brigade – Major General Sir William Ponsonby

1st Royal Dragoons – Lieutenant Colonel Arthur Benjamin Clifton

2nd Dragoons, Scots Greys – Lieutenant Colonel James Hamilton

6th Inniskilling Dragoons – Lieutenant Colonel Joseph Muter

3rd British Brigade – Major General Sir Wilhelm von Dornberg

1st Light Dragoons, King's German Legion – Lieutenant Colonel Johann Bulow

2nd Light Dragoons, King's German Legion – Lieutenant Colonel Karl von Jonquieries

23rd Light Dragoons – Lieutenant Colonel John Dawson

4th British Brigade – Major General Sir John Ormsby Vandeleur

11th Light Dragoons – Lieutenant Colonel James Wallace Sleigh

12th Prince of Wales' Light Dragoons – Lieutenant Colonel the Honourable Frederick Ponsonby

16th Queen's Light Dragoons – Lieutenant Colonel James Hay

5th British Brigade – Major General Sir John Colquhoun Grant

7th Queen's Own Light Dragoons – Lieutenant Colonel Edward Kernison

15th King's Light Dragoons – Lieutenant Colonel Leighton Carthcart Dalrymple

2nd Hussars, King's German Legion – Lieutenant Colonel August von Linsingen

Appendix E: The Regiments Today

The King's German Legion, despite its fame from the Napoleonic Wars, had a relatively short history. Their valour and staunch discipline earned them a reputation as one of the finest regiments in the entire British army. After the war, the Legion was absorbed the newly created Kingdom of Hanover in 1816.

42nd Regiment of Foot, The Black Watch, was formed in 1667, disbanded, and then reformed by King George II in 1725. Though it is uncertain exactly how they came about their name, it has remained with the regiment through numerous amalgamations. From 1882 to 1885 they served in numerous expeditionary forces in Egypt. All through the 20th Century, the Black Watch served with distinction through World War I, World War II, Korea, as well as Northern Ireland. Most recently, the regiment saw service in Iraq. As of 2006, they are known as *The Black Watch, 3rd Battalion of the Royal Regiment of Scotland.*

1/52nd Oxfordshire Regiment of Foot, first formed in 1755, it remained in Paris following Waterloo; returning to England in 1818. Over the next two hundred years, the regiment would see a variety of postings around the British Empire to include Ireland, India, Canada, Malta, and Gibraltar. In 1881 they merged with the 43rd Monmouthshire to form *The Oxfordshire Light Infantry.*

95th Rifles are perhaps the most famous regiment of the Napoleonic Era, due in no small part to Bernard Cornwell's 'Sharpe' series of novels and subsequent film adaptations, starring Sean Bean. Historically, they were first formed in 1802, and were the first to wear green jackets instead of red; the 5/60th Regiment of Foot later following suit. From 1816 to 1966 they were known as *The Rifle Brigade (The Prince Consort's Own).* In 1966, the old 95th and 60th Regiments were at last merged into *The Royal Green Jackets.* A series of amalgamations have led to them being reorganized once again, along with a number of other regiments that included the former 52nd Oxfordshire, into *The Rifles* in 2007. Today they are the largest infantry regiment of the British Army.

1st Regiment of Foot Guards have remained on continuous active service since 1656. It was by Royal Proclamation that in 1815 they were renamed *The Grenadier Guards*; a name they have held ever since. *Her Majesty's Coldstream Regiment of Foot Guards* is the only regiment slightly older, having been formed in 1650. Despite this difference in age, the Grenadiers are still ranked as the most senior regiment of the British Army. In addition to the Grenadier and Coldstream, three other regiments make up the rest of the Guards Division; the *Scots Guards*, active since 1661; the *Irish Guards*, since 1900; and the *Welsh Guards*, since 1915. Though still active as combat infantry units, the Guards are most famous for their public duties, namely guarding the royal palaces and the Tower of London.

Author's Final Thoughts

When I first decided to write this story, what surprised me the most was the complete lack of other novels based around the Waterloo Campaign. History text books were plentiful enough, yet the only novels I could readily find were the *Sharpe* series by Bernard Cornwell. Several readers of my previous novella, *Forlorn Hope: The Storming of Badajoz*, have noted the subtle tribute I make to Cornwell and Sharpe. I have done the same again in this story, as I have much respect for Cornwell and am a fan of his work.

Another challenge I found was that I was writing about such a well-known subject. A number of my previous works, to include *Forlorn Hope*, as well as the campaigns set during my Roman series, *Soldier of Rome: The Artorian Chronicles* are based around actual events, yet ones that most readers were initially unfamiliar with. Since the Battle of Waterloo is such a well-covered subject, the challenge was writing it in the format of a novel that would not only entice readers, especially those who may not wish to read a dry history book, while also maintaining as much historical integrity as possible.

Something else I tried to ensure was that ambiguity as to whether or not there was a 'good guy' or 'bad guy' to this story. My personal bias had always been decidedly in favour of the British; however, during my research for this project I became far more sympathetic towards Napoleon than I had anticipated. Given the level of respect his many enemies had for him, this can hardly be surprising. Though the predominant perspective in this story is from the British, my intent is to tell the story in all its graphic brutality without needlessly attempting to vilify one side or the other. Many readers may also note the lack of detail given to the Prussian perspective. This is not done to minimize or disrespect their contributions, but rather is simply about time and space for a story. The Battle of Waterloo was a gigantic event, involving as many as 200,000 total combatants. When writing a novel, one has only so many characters and individual storylines that can be effectively developed before the reader either becomes completely lost or the main characters' story arcs drastically diminished. As such, I elected to focus predominantly on Captain Webster and the 1st Foot Guards, as well as following Wellington and Napoleon's story arcs.

Readers may also note the rather blunt manner with which I wrote about Wellington himself. The 'Iron Duke' has long been one of my heroes, and I felt it would do him a great disservice if I only focused on his military prowess while glossing over or neglecting his personal traits, to include his numerous character flaws. Personally, I don't think the Duke would have had it any other way.

James Mace – November 2012

Further Reading / Bibliography

Adkin, Mark. *Waterloo Companion, The: The Complete Guide to History's Most Famous Land Battle.* London: Stackpole Books, 2002.

Campbell, Sir Neil. *Napoleon on Elba: An Eyewitness to Exile.* London: Ravenhall Books, 2004.

DeLancey, Magdalene. *A Week at Waterloo.* London: Reportage Press Despatches , 2009.

Hofschroer, Peter. *Waterloo 1815: Quatre Bras and Ligny.* London: Pen & Sword Books, 2005.

Holmes, Richard. *Wellington, The Iron Duke.* London: Harper Collins, U.K., 2003.

James, Lawrence. *The Iron Duke.* London: Vintage Digital, 2011.

Maitland, Sir Frederick Lewis. *The Surrender of Napoleon.* London and Edinburgh: William Blackwood and Sons, 1906.

Snow, Peter. *To War with Wellington: From the Peninsula to Waterloo.* London: John Murray, 2010.

Illustration Credits

Cover: *Arthur Wellesley, Duke of Wellington*, by Sir Thomas Lawrence, copyright English Heritage

Back Cover: *The British Defence*, by Chris Collingwood, copyright Steve Stanton and the Waterloo Collection

Chapter I: *Nicolas Jean-de-Dieu Soult, Duke of Dalmatia*, artist unknown

Chapter II: *Field Marshal Sir Arthur Wellesley, Duke of Wellington*, by Thomas Phillips

Chapter III: *Napoleon's Farewell to the Imperial Guard*, by Antoine Alphonse Montfort

Chapter IV: *Field Marshal Lord James Somerset*, by Jan Willem Pieneman, copyright English Heritage

Chapter V: *Colonel Sir William Howe DeLancey*, artist unknown (possibly Magdalene DeLancey)

Chapter VI: *Napoleonic Imperial Eagle,* author's private collection

Chapter VII: *Portrait of Louis XVIII of France in Coronation Robes*, by François Pascal Simon, Baron Gérard

Chapter VIII: *Napoleon's Return from Elba*, by Charles Steuben

Chapter IX: *Napoleon Bonaparte*, by Robert Lefevre, copyright English Heritage

Chapter X: *The Duchess of Richmond's Ball*, by Robert Alexander Hillingford

Chapter XI: *The French Assault*, by Chris Collingwood, copyright Steve Stanton and the Waterloo Collection

Chapter XII: *Marshal Michel Ney, duc d'Elchingen*, by François Pascal Simon, Baron Gérard

Chapter XIII: *Ride Them Down*, by Pamela Patrick White, copyright Steve Stanton and the Waterloo Collection

Chapter XIV: *Ompteda*, by Pamela Patrick White, copyright Steve Stanton and the Waterloo Collection

Chasseur a Cheval Captain, by Jose Ferre Clauzel, copyright Steve Stanton and the Waterloo Collection

Chapter XV: *Prince William of Orange*, by unknown Dutch artist, circa 1815

Chapter XVI: *Karl von Muffling*, by Julius Ludwig Sebbers

Chapter XVII: *Wellington at Waterloo*, by Robert Alexander Hillingford

Closing for the Kill, by Mariusz Kozik, copyright Steve Stanton and the Waterloo Collection

Chapter XVIII: *To the Guns*, by Karl Kopinski, copyright Steve Stanton and the Waterloo Collection

Chapter XIX: *The French Assault*, by Chris Collingwood, copyright Steve Stanton and the Waterloo Collection

Chapter XX: *Hold 'Em, Lads!* by Chris Collingwood, copyright Steve Stanton and the Waterloo Collection

Chapter XXI: *Lieutenant General Sir Thomas Picton*, by Sir Thomas Lawrence, copyright English Heritage

Pick Your Targets! by Pamela Patrick White, copyright Steve Stanton and the Waterloo Collection

Chapter XXII: *The Fight for the Standard*, by Richard Ansdell

Reignolds and Ponsonby, by Mariusz Kozik, copyright Steve Stanton and the Waterloo Collection

Chapter XXIII: *Steady the Brunswickers*, by Jose Ferre Clauzel, copyright Steve Stanton and the Waterloo Collection

No Retreat, by Karl Kopinski, copyright Steve Stanton and the Waterloo Collection

Chapter XXIV: *54th to the Gates*, by Chris Collingwood, copyright Steve Stanton and the Waterloo Collection

Chapter XXV: *The British Defence*, by Chris Collingwood, copyright Steve Stanton and the Waterloo Collection

Chapter XXVI: *General Hill invites the last remnants of French Imperial Guard to surrender*, by Robert Alexander Hillingford

Chapter XXVII: *Attack on Plancenoit by Prussian Divisions*, by Adolf Northern

Chapter XXVIII: *French Cannon, Tower of London*, author's private collection

Chapter XXIX: *Royal Navy Captain Frederick Lewis Maitland*, by Henry Meyer

Chapter XXX: *Napoleon on the Bellerophon*, artist unknown

Chapter XXXI: *King George IV*, by Sir Thomas Lawrence

Robert Banks Jenkinson, 2nd Earl of Liverpool, K.G., by Thomas Lawrence

Epilogue: *The Waterloo Banquet*, by William Salter

Wellington Visiting the Relics of Napoleon, copyright English Heritage

All maps by Brian Baker, copyright Brian Baker and Legionary Books

For more information, please visit
http://www.englishheritageimages.com
http://waterloo-collection.com/index.html

Read the earlier exploits of Lieutenant James Henry
Webster in the prelude novella:

Forlorn Hope: The Storming of Badajoz

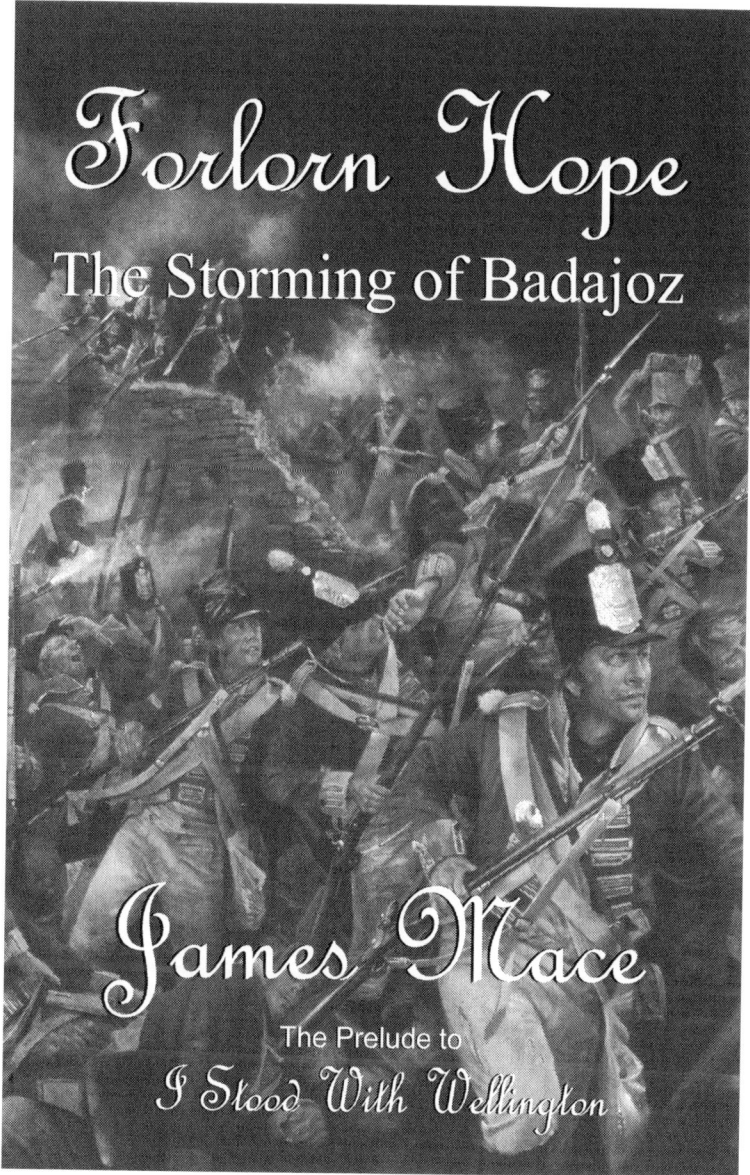

Forlorn Hope
The Storming of Badajoz

James Mace

The Prelude to
I Stood With Wellington

Printed in Great Britain
by Amazon